W9-BQY-524

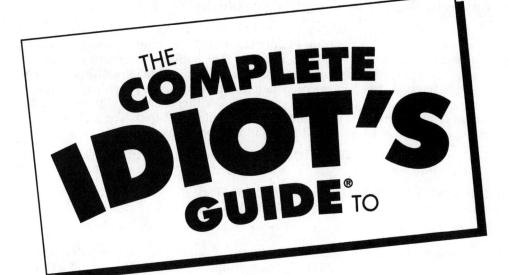

THE COMPLETE IDIOT'S GUIDE® TO

A Healthy Relationship

Second Edition

by Dr. Judy Kuriansky

ALPHA

A Pearson Education Company

Copyright © 2002 by Dr. Judy Kuriansky

All rights reserved. No part of this book shall be reproduced, stored in a retrieval system, or transmitted by any means, electronic, mechanical, photocopying, recording, or otherwise, without written permission from the publisher. No patent liability is assumed with respect to the use of the information contained herein. Although every precaution has been taken in the preparation of this book, the publisher and author assume no responsibility for errors or omissions. Neither is any liability assumed for damages resulting from the use of information contained herein. For information, address Alpha Books, 201 West 103rd Street, Indianapolis, IN 46290.

THE COMPLETE IDIOT'S GUIDE TO and Design are registered trademarks of Pearson Education, Inc.

International Standard Book Number: 0-02-864206-6
Library of Congress Catalog Card Number: 2001091097

04   03   02   8   7   6   5   4   3   2   1

Interpretation of the printing code: The rightmost number of the first series of numbers is the year of the book's printing; the rightmost number of the second series of numbers is the number of the book's printing. For example, a printing code of 02-1 shows that the first printing occurred in 2002.

Printed in the United States of America

Note: This publication contains the opinions and ideas of its author. It is intended to provide helpful and informative material on the subject matter covered. It is sold with the understanding that the author and publisher are not engaged in rendering professional services in the book. If the reader requires personal assistance or advice, a competent professional should be consulted.

The author and publisher specifically disclaim any responsibility for any liability, loss, or risk, personal or otherwise, which is incurred as a consequence, directly or indirectly, of the use and application of any of the contents of this book.

OVERTON MEMORIAL LIBRARY
HERITAGE CHRISTIAN UNIVERSITY
P.O. Box HCU
Florence, Alabama 35630

Publisher
Marie Butler-Knight

Product Manager
Phil Kitchel

Managing Editor
Jennifer Chisholm

Acquisitions Editor
Mike Sanders

Development Editor
Lynn Northrup

Senior Production Editor
Christy Wagner

Illustrator
Jody Schaeffer

Cover Designers
Mike Freeland
Kevin Spear

Book Designers
Scott Cook and Amy Adams of DesignLab

Indexer
Lisa Wilson

Layout/Proofreading
Mary Hunt
Ayanna Lacey

Contents at a Glance

**Part 1: The Signs of a Healthy Relationship
in the New Millenium**   **1**

1 What Makes a Relationship Healthy?   3
*Discover the keys of sounds, sights, and feelings to a
healthy or unhealthy relationship. Quiz yourself. Learn
the eight dimensions of a healthy love in the new millennium.*

2 The Seventh Dimension of a Healthy Relationship:
Spiritual Love   19
*Reach higher states of bliss by connecting on a higher
plane. Test yourself and learn new and exciting ways to
get more spiritual.*

3 The Eighth Dimension of a Healthy Relationship:
Digital Duos in Cyberlove   31
*Are computers crashing your relationship or catapulting
you into love cyberspace? How to make the digital age and
new technology work for you.*

4 Is It True Love?   45
*"How do I know I really love her?" "How can I be sure
he's the one?" Find out if it's the "real thing." See if you
pass the test.*

5 So, You're a Couple—but Are You Friends?   61
*Find out how being friends can contribute to a loving and
long-lasting relationship.*

6 The Importance of Matching Your Love Styles   71
*Creative, Emotional, Conservative, or Intellectual? Find
out what kind of lover you and your mate are, and learn
how to resolve love style conflicts.*

**Part 2: The Secrets of a Healthy and Lasting
Relationship**   **81**

7 A Healthy Self First   83
*Learn how to be a healthy individual first in order to have
a healthy relationship.*

8 Are We Compatible?   91
*Take the compatibility quiz. Find out how much you and
your mate really have in common and how to get on the
same wavelength.*

9 Cooperation—Whose Team Are You On?   115
*Consider your relationship a team—here's how to make
both sides win.*

10 Communication—Can We Talk? 131
*Test your communication skills and learn how to speak
clearly, listen actively, and provide helpful feedback to
each other.*

11 Commitment—Warming Up Cold Feet 145
*Are you ready for the big "C"? Test your readiness for
commitment and fidelity.*

Part 3: How to Keep the Passion Alive 163

12 Making the Honeymoon Last 165
*To keep your love alive, you have to keep dating each other
with enthusiasm and passion—just like when you first
met.*

13 Resurrecting Romance 179
*Planned acts of romance as well as spontaneous surprises
are key to maintaining a rich and fulfilling love. Keep a
romance calendar.*

14 The Art of Seduction 187
*How to set the stage for hotter lovemaking that brings you
to deeper levels of intimacy and excitement.*

15 How Important Is Sex? 197
*Unresolved sexual problems drain your energy for ecstasy.
Learn how to maintain good sexual chemistry that keeps
your passion alive.*

16 What's Healthy Sex for Couples? 207
*Everyone wants to know what's "normal" or "right" in
bed. Take the "Is It Healthy?" Sex Quiz with your partner
and find out what you both think works to heat up your
passion.*

17 Keeping the Sex Fires Burning 213
*How often is often enough? What new things can you do?
Discover exciting ways to add spice to your love life.*

Part 4: Obstacles to a Lasting Relationship 223

18 Preventing Love Burnout 225
*Too tired for sex? Too busy for candlelit dinners or long
walks together? Find out the top 10 turn-offs and learn
how to overcome boredom and keep your relationship
fresh.*

19 Ghost-Busting Your Relationship 233
*Patterns of your past affect your present choices in love.
Confront past decisions, resolve "unfinished" business
with past lovers, and get the ghosts out of your love life.*

20 Dollars and Sense: A Healthy Couple's Guide to
Handling Money Issues   239
*Money is one of the leading sources of tension between
couples. Learn how to handle money so it doesn't come
between you.*

21 Working Nine to ... with Time Off for Love   253
*How to achieve a healthy balance of work and love. Tips
about what works in the bedroom and the boardroom.*

22 Offering Constructive Criticism   265
*Criticism bites—but it can be constructive. Here's how to
deliver—and take it—well.*

23 Time Out on Fighting   275
*Yes, you can be peaceful, if you know how to prevent ar-
guments and blow-ups. And if you squabble, find out the
rules of fair fighting.*

24 Affairs: How to Stay After One of You Strays   285
*Betrayal is painful. Understand why lovers are unfaithful
and find out how to forgive and forget—and rebuild trust.*

25 Dealing with Crises as a Couple   297
*Every relationship goes through its share of crises. Learn
how to weather major ones.*

26 It's Not Just the Two of Us   309
*How to have a healthy relationship with parents, siblings,
kids, friends, exes, and even pets so your primary relationship with your mate stays intact.*

Part 5: Where Do We Go from Here?   **323**

27 S/He's the One for Me!   325
*So, you recognize the signs of a healthy relationship and
have decided that your mate is the one for you. Now
what?*

28 Keeping Your Love Exciting with New-Millennium
Body and Mind Techniques   337
*Fun, unique, and exciting exercises you and your mate
can do together to enhance your relationship.*

29 Helping Each Other Toward a Healthier Relationship   357
*Stress and problems can chip away at the solid founda-
tion your love is built on. Here's how you can get back on
track together, including advice on when to go for professional help.*

Appendixes

A Answers to the "Is It Healthy?" Quiz in Chapter 1   377

B Answers to the "Is It Healthy?" Sex Quiz in Chapter 16   381

C Resources   387

Index   391

Contents

Part 1: The Signs of a Healthy Relationship in the New Millinnium   1

1 What Makes a Relationship Healthy?   3

A New Buzzword for the New Millennium 4
When It's Not Healthy 4
    Priorities 5
    Who Is Number One? 6
When It's Healthy 6
    That's Healthy with a Capital "H"! 7
    Spelling a Healthy Relationship 8
    What Else Is Important? 10
The Importance of Agreements 11
Being a Team Player 12
The "Is It Healthy?" Quiz 13
The Ten Commandments of a Healthy Relationship 15
A Concept Whose Time Has Come Regarding a
    Healthy Relationship in the New Millennium 15
    The Eight Dimensions of New Millennium Health 16

2 The Seventh Dimension of a Healthy Relationship: Spiritual Love   19

What Is "Spirit" to You? 20
The Time Is Right 20
The Alternative Has Become Mainstream 20
You Gotta Have Heart 21
A Test of Spirit 21
The Secret of Breathing Your Way to a Healthy
    Relationship 23
    Breathing on Your Own 23
    Breathing Together to Get Closer to a Spiritually
      Healthy Love 24
Connecting to Your Own Soul First 25
The Third Eye 25
Getting the Energetics to Flow Between You 26
The Ritual of Love 27

Letting Go in Love: A Spiritual View of Loss 27
Putting It All Together 28

3 The Eighth Dimension of a Healthy Relationship: Digital Duos in Cyberlove   31

Keeping in Technological Touch 32
The Upside of Technology on Love 32
The Downside of Technology on Love 34
How Much Is Too Much? 34
Loveonline Netiquette 36
Do's and Don'ts of Digital Love 37
When Only One of You Is a Techie 38
Cybersex 40
Cybercheating 41

4 Is It True Love?   45

What Is This Thing Called Love? 46
Seven Love Truths You Can Count On 47
Love Myths 47
What's Wrong with Love Myths? 49
Is This the Real Thing? The Five Requirements 49
"True Love" Tests 50
"Love at First Sight" 51
A Good First—and Lasting—Impression 52
Love but Not "in Love" 52
It's Time for a Love Inventory 53
Too Good to Be True? 54
Turn-Offs 56
Intimacy Junkies, Love Junkies, Sex Junkies 56
Learning How to Love 57
Heart and Soul 58

5 So, You're a Couple—but Are You Friends?   61

Can Lovers Really Be Friends? 61
Can Friends Really Become Lovers? 62
How Good a Friend Is Your Lover? 64
The Ten True Tests of Friendship 64
How Friendship Changes as Love Grows 65
When It's Either/Or 67
The Madonna-Prostitute Syndrome 67
The Daddy–Don Juan Syndrome 67

6 The Importance of Matching Your Love Styles   71

"How Do I Love Thee? Let Me Count the Ways ..." 72
What's Your Love Style? 72
The Four Love Styles 75
Resolving Love Style Conflicts 77
Are You a Giver or a Taker? 78
If You Give Too Much 79
If You Take Too Much 79

Part 2: The Secrets of a Healthy and Lasting Relationshp   81

7 A Healthy Self First   83

Building Up Your Confidence 83
Are You Fit for Love? 84
Time for an Attitude Adjustment 84
Your Love Script 85
Are You Scared?—Face Your Fears 86
Fear of Intimacy 87
Fear of Missing Out 87
Setting Yourself Up for Failure: Fear of Success 88

8 Are We Compatible?   91

What Is Compatibility? 92
The Twelve Major Areas of Compatibility 92
How Compatible Are You? 94
What Are the Big Compatibility Roadblocks? 101
Sex Drive 101
When to Have Sex 102
How Often It Happens 102
Not Tonight, Dear, I Have a Headache 104
Cultural Clash 104
Religious Rights 104
Family Matters 105
Age Gaps 105
Expressions of Affection 106
Five Ways to Handle Compatibility Roadblocks 108
Other Trouble Spots 108
Shared Chores 108
Politics 109

Bad Habits 109
When They Make You Crazy *110*
Dealing with Your Mate's Bad Habits *111*
Kicking Your Own Bad Habits *112*

9 Cooperation—Whose Team Are You On?　　**115**

What Is Cooperation? 116
Compatibility Does Not Equal Cooperation................*116*
The Seven Main Areas of Cooperation 117
How Well Do You and Your Mate Cooperate with
　Each Other? 118
Cooperation Problems and Solutions 120
A Major Cooperation Impediment: Gender-Based
　Stereotypes 121
The Chore Wars: Ten Gender-Based Questions *121*
Are You an Old-Fashioned Couple?........................*122*
Call a Chore War Truce 123
The Friend/Roommate Test....................................*124*
The Teflon Test *125*
Save Competition for the Ring 125
Five Tips to Team-Building....................................*127*

10 Communication— Can We Talk?　　**131**

The Importance of Communication 132
Test Your Communication Skills *132*
What Do Your Scores Mean? *134*
Communication Techniques 134
Direct Communication *134*
Active Listening *135*
Giving Feedback..*136*
Show Appreciation *137*
Eight Communication Don'ts 137
What Should You Tell—and When..................................*138*
When a Mate Won't Talk...139
What to Do If Your Mate Is the Silent Type *139*
What to Do If You're the One Who Doesn't Talk *140*
Talking About Sex 141
When Silence Is Not Golden in Sex.........................*141*
Asking for What You Want *143*
Saying What You Don't Like *143*
Can't Say No *143*

11 Commitment—Warming Up Cold Feet   145

The Nature of Commitment 146
  What Makes You Want It? *147*
Are You and Your Partner Ready to Commit? 147
Terms of Commitment 150
  Until Death Do Us Part? *150*
  What About Monogamy? *151*
  Can You Be True to Each Other? *151*
Talking About Commitment 152
  Agreement Plan *153*
When Commitment Becomes a One-Way Street 154
  Cold Feet: His and Hers *154*
  Can Those Cold Feet Be Warmed Up? *156*
  Their Feet Are Frozen *158*
Timing Is Key 158
  Eleven Considerations Along the Commitment
    Timeline *158*
  On Different Wavelengths *160*
Making the Dreaded Ultimatum 160
Four Major Commitment Mistakes 161
Long-Distance Love: When Separations
  Threaten Commitment 162

Part 3: How to Keep the Passion Alive   163

12 Making the Honeymoon Last   165

Keep Dating! 166
  Rule One: Do Something You Both Enjoy *166*
  Rule Two: Do Something Your Partner Enjoys *167*
Rule Three: Make Time 168
  Reality Bites: Do You Ever See Each Other? *169*
  How Often Would You Like to See Each Other? *169*
What to Do Together 170
Staying In 170
  Just Kick Back *171*
  Or Get Busy *171*
Having Fun Right in Your Own Backyard 171
  Musical Affairs *172*
  A Volunteering Heart *173*
  Shop for Love *173*
  Work It *174*

On the Go 175
Going Back to School 176
Business and Pleasure 176
Improving Yourselves and Each Other 177

13 Resurrecting Romance   179

The Importance of Keeping Romance Alive 179
The Real Meaning of Romance 180
The Four "F" Words of Romance.........................182
Your Very Own Romance Surprise Calendar 182
Are Time and Distance Romance-Ruiners? 183
Keeping Romance Alive with Kids Around.........185

14 The Art of Seduction   187

Seduction in Healthy, Lasting Relationships 188
Heightening Your Senses 189
Wink, Wink, Nudge, Nudge: How to Flirt with
  Your Partner 190
Basic Flirting Techniques 191
Sensuous Suppers and Other Seductive Feasts ...191
How to Pillow Talk 193
What Is Your Mate's Pillow Talk Style? 193
What to Say—and Not Say 194
The Seductive Power of Being in Shape 194

15 How Important Is Sex?   197

The Waiting Game: When's the Right Time? 197
Why Sex Is Good for You 199
Why Sex Is Good for Your Relationship 200
Sexual Chemistry...201
Six Signs of a Bad Chemical Reaction................201
Chemistry and Self-Confidence.........................202
What Men and Women Really Want 203

16 What's Healthy Sex for Couples?   207

Making Decisions About Sex................................208
The Wrong Reasons to Have Sex........................210
Four Different Approaches to Sex 210
The Ultimate Decision: Safe Sex and Contraception 211

17 Keeping the Sex Fires Burning   213

A Question of Timing 213
Variety Is the Spice of Good Sex 215
Sex Fantasies 217
   Five Common Fantasies and What They Really Mean 218
   Five Guidelines for Sharing and Acting Out Fantasies 219
How to Negotiate for Better Sex 220
Getting over Inhibitions 220

Part 4: Obstacles to a Lasting Relationship   223

18 Preventing Love Burnout   225

What Is Love Burnout? 226
   The Top Ten Love Turn-Offs 226
   The Love Burnout Quiz for Couples 228
Overcoming Boredom 228
Make More Time for Love 229

19 Ghost-Busting Your Relationship   233

Uncovering Your Love Ghosts..234
Family Love Ghost Scripts..235
You and Your Shadows: Ghost-Busting Your Love Life ..236
   Completing "Unfinished Business" 237
   Staying Together by Moving On 237

**20 Dollars and Sense: A Healthy Couple's
       Guide to Handling Money Issues   239**

Sex, Love, and Calculator Tape 240
   Ruled by Rubles 240
Tracing the Roots of Money Matters..242
   A Money Quiz 242
For Love or Money?..244
   Twelve Routes to Derailing on the Money Track 245
What to Say When Money Talks..247
   A Wise Investment in Your Future 250

21 Working Nine to ... with Time Off for Love 253

Do What You Love 253
What If You Hate Your Job?..............................*254*
Appreciate Each Other's Work *255*
Married to the Job 255
All Play and No Work 257
Mixing Business and Love...................................258
Working Around Your Ball and Chain *259*
Love on the Job *260*
Bringing a Bad Day Home..................................261
What Works in the Boardroom May or May Not
Work in the Bedroom 262
Five Steps to Better Business (but Not Better Sex) *262*
Five Steps to Better Business AND Better Sex......................*263*

22 Offering Constructive Criticism 265

"I'm Saying This for Your Own Good ..."........................266
Giving Criticism 267
How to Receive Criticism 268
Sexual Criticism..270
Toxic Criticism..272
Criticizing Yourself 272

23 Time Out on Fighting 275

Preventing Blow-Ups 276
Lessons in Love from Fighting 277
Fair Fighting Rules..*277*
Fightis Interruptis...*278*
"I Gotcha!": Using Smokescreens to Win Control
Battles...279
Preventing Mountains from Growing Out of
Molehills 280
Using Truth as a Weapon 281
Can Fights Fuel Sex? 282
Twelve Ways to Stop Fights Before They Start 283

24 Affairs: How to Stay After One of You Strays 285

Perceived Betrayals: Is Flirting Harmless? 286
Testing Your Suspicions *286*
Collaring a Flirt..*288*

Signs of Cheating...288
Cybercheating 290
Rules for Confronting an Affair 290
Why We Cheat...291
  My Three Affair-Proofing Questions 292
Relationship Recovery 292
  Will I Ever Forget? 293
  Can Trust Be Rebuilt? 293
  Can a Leopard Change Its Spots? 294
The Affair Survival Checklist................................294

25 Dealing with Crises as a Couple   297

Five Expected Reactions.......................................297
When Sickness Strikes 298
The Four F's to Deal with Health Crises 301
Ups and Downs: Handling Emotional Problems
  Together 302
Family Illnesses 304
Crises with Children 305
The Mid-Life Crisis 305
  Male Menopause 306
  Growing Old Gracefully and Together....................306
  Posing the "Hypothetical Test of Devotion"...........307

26 It's Not Just the Two of Us   309

The Importance of Family.....................................310
  Who Comes First? 310
When Parents Love or Hate Your Love 311
  The Do's and Don'ts of Dealing with Disapproving
    Parents..311
The Enmeshed Family 312
  Intrusive Parents 314
  Dependent Parents 314
  An Eight-Step Plan to Avoid Parental Interference
    in Your Relationship..315
How Kids and Other Family Members Figure
  Into Your Love Life 316
  The Hansel and Gretel Syndrome 317
Figuring Friends Into Your Relationship.................318
How Past Loves Figure Into Your Present Love.........319
How Pet Love Affects Your Love Life 321

Part 5: Where Do We Go from Here? 323

27 S/He's the One for Me! 325

Moving in Together 326
  Setting Up House Together 326
  Five Important Adjustments to Living Together 327
Getting Engaged 327
  How to Pop the Question 327
Saying "I Do" 328
  Where People Marry and Divorce 330
  When People Marry 331
  When Should You Get Married? 331
  Jitters 332
Going Ahead with the Wedding Bells........................333
  Wedding Vows 334
The Honeymoon 335
Starting a Family 335
Remarrying an Ex 336

28 Keeping Your Love Exciting with New-Millennium Body and Mind Techniques 337

Starting with the Basics—the Joy of Exercise 337
  Choose a Workout Routine 338
  Simple Stretching Exercises 338
  Eight Ways to Make Workouts Also Work in Sex 340
Inner Guidance on Sex 341
Magnetic Love 341
Laying on of Love Hands 342
Mutual Meditation..343
Massage 344
Acupressure for Lovers..346
Reflexology..347
Aromatherapy 349
Making Beautiful Music Together 350
Toning 350
Love Molding...351
Feng Shui 351
Past Lives 354

**29 Helping Each Other Toward a Healthier
   Relationship   357**

Self-Help..358
  Keep Dating...*358*
  Modeling...*360*
  Self-Disclosure..*360*
  Taking Time Out..*360*
  "As If"...*360*
  "Back in Time"...*360*
  Couples' Journal..*361*
  Picturing It Makes It So..*361*
Communication Workshops...361
  I-Power...*361*
  A Love Ritual...*363*
  Bare, Dare to Share...*364*
When to Go for Therapy...365
Couples Counseling..365
Couples Therapy...366
  Finding the Right Therapist...*367*
Does Couples Counseling Work?...368
Couples Sex Therapy...369
  Finding a Sex Therapist...*369*
  When to Go for Help With a Sexual Problem...........................*370*
  Common Sexual Problems..*370*
  What Does Sex Therapy Cost?...*371*
  Prognosis for a Cure..*371*
Newer Alternative and Nontraditional Sources
  of Therapy..372
  Advice on the Radio...*372*
  Television Talk Shows...*373*
  Online Advice...*374*

Appendixes

**A Answers to the "Is It Healthy?" Quiz
in Chapter 1**   **377**

**B Answers to the "Is It Healthy?" Sex Quiz
in Chapter 16**   **381**

C Resources   **387**

Index   **391**

Introduction

After the pleasure of writing my last book, *The Complete Idiot's Guide to Dating*, and its success, the next step quite naturally surfaced. Once you find that special someone in the dating game, what comes next? Making the relationship work, of course. Making it last.

But how do you do that? After much meditation and reflection, the answer rang clear: A lasting love can only emerge from a healthy relationship. The word "healthy" felt so right. After all, your health is a rightful goal for the new millennium. Indeed, a lasting love has to nurture your health on many levels.

In the three years since I first penned this book, and with all the changes in our fast-paced society, it has become clear to me that there are eight dimensions of a healthy relationship required for the new millennium. These eight dimensions form the substance of this new edition of *The Complete Idiot's Guide to a Healthy Relationship*, to which I have added much that I have learned and that has evolved in our new age. The eight dimensions are: physical, mental, emotional, familial, financial, sexual, spiritual, and technological.

As you go through these pages, you'll see that each dimension and quality of a healthy relationship is explored with advice, examples, and exercises on how to achieve it. The words just flowed, as your relationship and love should flow. I feel confident that if you integrate these qualities into your daily life and your relationship, you'll find the happiness you so desire and deserve.

From my years of counseling couples, I've learned that in order to find true health in life and love, you need to be open enough to share what is deepest on your mind and in your heart with someone who really cares. Then you should be known, appreciated, and loved for who you are—at your core! What does that lead to? Good health, of course! Research proves it—the more love you feel, the more emotionally healthy you are, the stronger your immune system, the more physically healthy you are, and the longer you'll live.

Reading *The Complete Idiot's Guide to a Healthy Relationship, Second Edition*, will certainly be valuable to those of you already in a relationship. But it can also be useful if you're just hoping for one—to offer you inspiration. Also, those of you who have just gotten out of a relationship will find this book helpful, because it will motivate you to seek a healthier union.

When it comes to making relationships work, I believe that active involvement and "doing" is as important as understanding. That's why you'll find lots of quizzes and exercises in this book. They make the information come alive, so you can experience what I mean, what you are going through, and what is possible for you. Do the exercises alone, and then do them with your partner. You'll be surprised at how writing things down can help you focus on both the problems and the solutions. Also, feel free to repeat the quizzes over time, because your attitudes and answers may change, and working at these changes can give you a measure of your growth.

Keep in mind that achieving a long-lasting, loving, and healthy relationship is a process, not an end goal—it keeps growing, changing, and evolving. The lesson is one that reverberates in my head from the title of a song by my brilliantly talented musician friend, Jaiia Earthschild: We're all just "Learning How to Love." It's an ongoing—and beautiful—process, even with all the bumps along the way.

How This Book Is Organized

The chapters in this book are divided into five sections that take you through the process of developing a healthy relationship.

Part 1, "The Signs of a Healthy Relationship in the New Millenium," presents an overview of the qualities of a healthy love and the eight dimensions of love relevant for the new century we are in. There are many useful quizzes and exercises you can take to see if you have a relationship that can last and bring you fulfillment. These quizzes are based on surveys and research done by myself as well as other experts, distilled into simpler forms so you can analyze and apply them easily.

You know the phrase, "You have to love yourself first before you can love anyone." Similarly, you have to be healthy yourself before you can have a healthy relationship. So I begin **Part 2, "The Secrets of a Healthy and Lasting Relationship,"** with how you can make yourself healthy first! Then you're ready to explore the four C's of a healthy partnership: compatibility, cooperation, communication, and commitment.

Far too many couples suffer from the seven-year itch (that has been reduced these days to the two-year and even six-month itch), when they no longer feel as excited about each other. But in a healthy relationship, you are always interested and excited about each other, even as time goes on. In **Part 3, "How to Keep the Passion Alive,"** I give you valuable tips to help you keep that romance and sexual attraction going. After years of being a sex therapist, I sure do know plenty of those tips—and now you will, too!

The journey of love is rarely smooth. Don't be discouraged if you hit rough spots and rocky roads. The key to getting through them is supporting and caring for each other and yourself. In **Part 4, "Obstacles to a Lasting Relationship,"** I'll go over problems like love burnout, criticism, fighting, affairs, work, money, family stresses, and other crises—and how you can prevent these from derailing you from having the love you want.

There comes a point in your relationship when you have to decide whether this is "It." In **Part 5, "Where Do We Go from Here?"** there's help for making that decision and lots of information about assistance that is available. I've included many wonderful techniques for you to do on your own, or with professional help, to enhance your relationship on these eight crucial dimensions or to fix simple as well as more serious problems. And most exciting of all, I've included some interesting new millenium techniques that you will undoubtedly be as fascinated about as I am.

Extras

I thoroughly enjoy not only the concise style of *The Complete Idiot Guide* series, but also the opportunity to put certain bits of information into clear categories. So, you'll find these extras bits of information throughout these chapters.

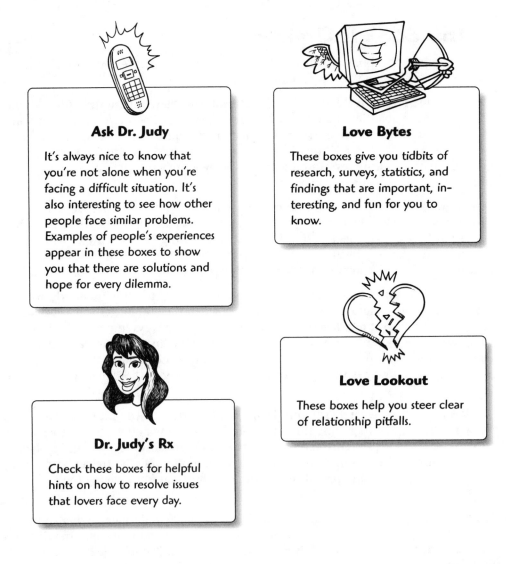

Ask Dr. Judy

It's always nice to know that you're not alone when you're facing a difficult situation. It's also interesting to see how other people face similar problems. Examples of people's experiences appear in these boxes to show you that there are solutions and hope for every dilemma.

Love Bytes

These boxes give you tidbits of research, surveys, statistics, and findings that are important, interesting, and fun for you to know.

Love Lookout

These boxes help you steer clear of relationship pitfalls.

Dr. Judy's Rx

Check these boxes for helpful hints on how to resolve issues that lovers face every day.

Healthy or Unhealthy?

Given the goal of establishing a healthy relationship, it seemed highly appropriate to highlight certain activities, attitudes, and behaviors that may make you wonder whether or not they are good for you and your love. The "Healthy or Unhealthy?" boxes that are sprinkled throughout this book address these issues.

Last but certainly not least—especially because they come first, in the front of this book—you'll find a host of love coupons. Tear them out and give them to your love partner for the gift described. Or write in your own request on the "wild card" coupon. Deliver one whenever you feel the urge. Have fun and watch your love grow!

Acknowledgments

What a gift you are—all the men and women of all ages who have joined me nightly on my radio shows, as well as on various television shows, on the Internet, in my private office, and thorough my newspaper and magazine columns—sharing what's in your heart and soul. I am eternally grateful to you and dedicate my heart and soul to your growth and happiness.

So, too, am I grateful—and blessed—for eternity with cherished family and friends who teach me daily about unconditional love, wisdom, and the gift of being "known" at your core, especially my beloveds, my mother Sylvia, my husband Edward, my assistant Alissa Pollack, and my guide Carol Maracle. I am also eternally grateful to my extended family, friends, and colleagues, especially my *LovePhones* family of Jagger and Badger and everyone who brought such love, joy, fulfillment, and fun to every day we were together. My heart fills with warmth, a smile spreads on my face, and sometimes even a tear comes to my eye when I am in the presence of these loved ones, think of them, or hear a loving word from them. I am blessed to have them in my life, as shining examples of what is healthy in life and love.

No man is an island; everyone needs a team—in all aspects of life. During the evolution of this book, my team has extended to wonderful people with whom I work, learn, laugh, and grow in my daily life, including the Remeron team at Organon and Spectrum Science, where we worked so hard and did so much good on Blues in the Bedroom, and the Advance White and PM team at BSMG and Church and Dwight, where we worked so hard and did so much good on the First Impressions Campaign, and my editors Peter Block and Deirdre Goldbeck at *Penthouse* and everyone at *Cosmogirl*, where we worked so hard and do so much good getting out responsible messages about sex.

My team extends, too, to book publishing, including all those included in the first edition of this book, who provided such a solid foundation, and now those included in this second edition. My special, heartfelt thanks go to Mike Sanders for his inspiration and support, Christy Wagner and Lynn Northrup, who meticulously went through all the additions, and publicist Gardi Wilks for her devotion and "always being there." As the world becomes smaller, I'd like to acknowledge the foreign publishers who have put their faith in this series as *The Complete Idiot's Guide to Dating* and *The Complete Idiot's Guide to a Healthy Relationship* have been printed in other languages like French and Chinese, languages of countries I feel a deep connection to. I am particularly moved by Liaoning Education Press in Shenyang, People's Republic of China, who have become my dear friends. Their gracious hosting of me through a five-star book tour of China touched my soul forever and imprinted an indelible feeling of the smallness of this world, the beauty of all souls, and our similarities and capacity for love despite any cultural differences. The language and look of love is the same no matter what our ancestry.

Get in Touch with Me

I'm always interested in what you experience and need. And I prefer a two-way street of communication. That's why I love the nightly back and forth on the radio and why I conduct my lectures with a lot of interaction and participation. As you read these pages, there may be things you want to ask or share with me. Maybe you have a personal story to share or need a session to share up your love. In this age of technology, you can contact me through the Internet at DoctorJudy411@aol.com.

Trademarks

All terms mentioned in this book that are known to be or are suspected of being trademarks or service marks have been appropriately capitalized. Alpha Books and Pearson Education cannot attest to the accuracy of this information. Use of a term in this book should not be regarded as affecting the validity of any trademark or service mark.

Part 1

The Signs of a Healthy Relationship in the New Millennium

Choosing a life partner is the most important decision most of us will ever make. That's why it matters that you keep wise criteria in mind when deciding if this person is "it." Surely you want to exercise good judgment.

Many of the questions people have asked me through all my advice radio shows and columns over the years are variations on the same theme: "Should I pursue this relationship or end it? If this is the way s/he acts, is this going to work?"

In this part of the book you'll learn the answers to these questions. Those answers show you what makes a relationship healthy or unhealthy. The answers are put into the context of this new age, as there is no denying that the new millennium demands a new understanding of healthy love. You'll understand why being friends with your mate is so important, and then assess if your feeling for him or her is the "real thing." There's no point to holding onto someone who's simply not right for you, but you also want to be able to recognize a gem!

Chapter 1

What Makes a Relationship Healthy?

In This Chapter

➤ What's a healthy relationship?

➤ Ways to assess if your relationship is healthy

➤ The 12 signs of an unhealthy relationship

➤ A "healthy relationship" quiz

➤ Preview of the eight dimensions of a healthy relationship

"We're captains of our ship: partnership, friendship, lovership."

That's a saying I once heard passed along that describes the very topic of this book—a healthy relationship.

Is it possible to be happy, in love, and have a relationship that lasts in today's electronic, e-mail, voice-mail culture? Absolutely, yes! But like everything else that is worthwhile to achieve, you have to work at it. Of course, every relationship goes through changes. Surviving the ups and downs becomes the glue that keeps you together. Even wife Camille forgave TV celebrity Bill Cosby for his affair when he went public about it, saying that they had been through so much together that she was not willing to give up their love and partnership.

I'm sure you're as tired as I am of hearing families or relationships referred to as "dysfunctional." A popular New York radio station even named their day-long music concert the "dysfunctional family picnic." Dysfunctional has become the buzzword of the 1990s. Fortunately, there are causes for dysfunctionality that we can point to: dissolution of the family, lack of corporate security or loyalty, disconnection from communities and religion, desire for instant gratification precipitated by flashing images of MTV, and the desire to escape into the anonymity of the Internet.

"Toxic" is another buzzword of the 1990s. Once the environment was recognized as toxic, everything else became subject to being labeled as bad for your health—employers, families, children, and even lovers were called toxic, especially when they were out of control or hurtful.

A New Buzzword for the New Millennium

Everywhere you look, there are dangers to our emotional and physical well-being. That's where this book comes in. Since our entrance into the new millennium, declare with me that the new buzzword is healthy. Commit to that new attitude toward life in general and relationships in particular. Let's face it, designing a health plan for all Americans was the major challenge of the previous political administration—fraught with major roadblocks. At least these efforts have reflected how much Americans today care about health. Let's strive for—and remove the roadblocks on—a successful and loving healthy relationship. This book is not about dwelling on dysfunctional relationships, but about how you can achieve a healthy love.

A healthy relationship can come naturally to some people—they fall in love and everything else seems to fall into place. They always seem to get along and rarely argue. But if this doesn't happen for you, don't despair. You can learn (and relearn, and relearn) to get past the rough spots. A healthy relationship takes time and work. However, it also takes trust—that is, trust in your own feelings, and trusting your partner with your feelings. This is critical—and my wish for you—since an unhealthy relationship can make you feel literally ill! This book will inspire you to not get caught up in dead-end, unhappy, and unhealthy relationships, but to aspire to a growing one—one that makes you feel strong, invigorated, and renewed. That's healthy.

When It's Not Healthy

Let's face it. You just don't wake up one morning in a bad relationship. The unhealthy symptoms have been there all along—you just weren't paying attention to them ... or you chose to ignore them.

For instance, you and your mate may have explosive sexual encounters, but how does he treat you outside the bedroom? Remember how you felt when she stared at and flirted with other guys in front of you, after you said how that made you feel? Remember when he didn't give you the support you needed when you had to make that important life decision?

Throughout the coming chapters, I'll address when a relationship is healthy and working, and when it's not healthy and needs to be reevaluated. For now, let's take a quick look at how an unhealthy relationship may make you feel.

Signs of an Unhealthy Relationship

❑ You feel insecure and weak around each other.

❑ You suffer from low self-esteem as a result of what happens between you.

❑ You are dishonest with each other.

❑ You spend more time feeling hurt than feeling good about how you treat each other.

❑ You find yourself complaining to others about your relationship.

❑ You are unable to talk about your feelings or problems with your mate, much less solve them.

❑ You are unable to resolve your differences together.

❑ You become unenthusiastic about life because of what goes on between you.

❑ Your trust is irrevocably broken.

❑ Seemingly small things erode your relationship, like trickling water that wears away at a rock over time.

❑ Priorities other than each other constantly present themselves.

❑ What goes on between you interferes with other aspects of your life.

Think about what you would never put up with over the long-term. What would make you end the relationship? For most men and women, dishonesty is intolerable—just as honesty is the most desirable quality. For Alex, "She has to be into personal growth all the time. And I couldn't stay if we couldn't be physically active together." George couldn't put up with his girlfriend's constant criticisms. Sherry had to break up with her boyfriend when he wouldn't stop flirting with her friends. Ladonna left when her boyfriend cheated on her, and Christine broke her engagement when her fiancé admitted, "I love you but I'm not in love with you." Kelly said, "I know this sounds silly, but smell is important to me. He has to smell good." Other irritants men and women have told me about over the years include complaining or nagging, forgetting important events, criticizing, and being ignored. What keeps bothering you?

Priorities

For your relationship to last, the two of you must have similar priorities. For example, if hot sex matters to one of you but not to the other, there will inevitably be arguments, strife, and disappointments in your love life.

Who Is Number One?

In a healthy relationship, there are three "people" involved—each of you, and the relationship itself. All three have to be number one at appropriate times. You and your mate each need to have enough self-esteem so you matter, so you respect yourself (so others will respect you) and so you are not desperate (meaning you wouldn't fall apart if you separated).

Healthy or Unhealthy?

Making the other person number one all the time—being too much of a giver or people pleaser—is unhealthy. People who do this subvert their own needs and often drive others away by being too suffocating. By the opposite token, those who always demand to be number one are narcissistic and feel that others are only extensions of themselves. This is equally unhealthy, as they can never truly love, because the only one they love is themselves.

When It's Healthy

So far, I've outlined what makes a relationship unhealthy and how you may feel if you're stuck in one. Now, what makes a relationship healthy? Good judgment about this requires a three-part analysis: using your mind, heart, and intuition. Use your mind, analyze the qualities of your relationship and determine whether it is healthy. (Take the quizzes in this book to help.) Use your heart and the emotions you have for your mate. And follow your intuition, that gut sense that tells you whether pairing the two of you is "right."

Signs of a Healthy Relationship

❏ You feel secure and happy when you're together and alone—not sad, suspicious, angry, or deprived.

❏ You are inspired by each other to fulfill your dreams and become the best you can be.

❏ You are generous and giving—you want to give all you can to your partner, and are so fulfilled that you also want to give to everyone else around you.

That's Healthy with a Capital "H"!

Since we are always learning about life and love, I enjoy referring to different concepts that are important in this book in terms of the alphabet, like in school. For example, in my book *Generation Sex* (Harper, 1995), I summarized the three R's of good sex: Respect, Responsibility, and the Right to say "yes" and "no" to sex. Here, let's look at the six H's to a healthy relationship:

1. **Honesty.** I have asked thousands of men and women in surveys over the years, "What is the most important quality of a lasting relationship?" The number one quality mentioned was honesty. Finances can be shaky, sex imperfect, stress overwhelming, but all those things can be overcome. Trust is essential. If trust is broken, your heart is broken. Everything else seems to tumble down, problems become less tolerable, and compromises less appealing.

2. **Harmony.** The sweetest sounds in music are created when two voices harmonize with one another—one hits a note that is not exactly the same as the other, but blends in perfectly. Better yet, it enriches the first note, filling out the sound. Two people in love similarly make beautiful music together. They don't need to be the same; in fact, they are more well-rounded when they have differences, like the harmonized musical notes. Their individual choices of notes fit. You make a harmonious duet together.

3. **Heart.** The heart is the major organ of the body. It pumps the blood supply throughout the body, bringing nourishment. Having "heart" for one another means nourishing each other. Opening your heart to one another exposes your deepest feelings. And connecting your hearts binds you deeply and inextricably.

Love Bytes

Opposites can be harmonious when they blend together to create a whole, as feminine and masculine, light and dark, positive and negative. For example, all colors blend together to create white. Men have feminine energy and women have masculine energy. The goal is to achieve a state of balance in which energies complement each other.

Dr. Judy's Rx

To get to the soul, close your eyes and sense the other person, feeling what's in his or her heart and inner being.

Dr. Judy's Rx

In intimate times, couples can ask each other, "How can I help you heal?" The answer may be, "Tell me you love me." "Never betray me." "Help me trust again."

4. **Honor.** It's a word used in marriage vows for a reason. Honoring each other means holding each other in high esteem, considering each other's needs, and respecting each other—and an even more revered consideration of each other, worshipping each other. This means knowing each other to the core, believing in each other's soul, and appreciating each other beyond the physical body.

5. **Healing.** In ancient India men came to a specially trained female, called a Dakini, to be healed after war. The Dakini helped him clear his mind from the traumas he had been through, so he could reopen his heart and love again.

You may have to similarly suffer through love wars before you find your one true love. The rejections and hurts along this path require healing in order to open up your heart again. I'm not suggesting that you become each other's therapists—it would be unhealthy to expect a partner to repair all your past hurts or to project onto your partner all the ghosts of your past. But there is some aspect of healing in every healthy relationship. A true love partner becomes a haven from the hurts of the past, while providing a new positive example of how nurturing love can be.

6. **Hot.** Satisfying, sensuous, and erotic sex can certainly be a part of the healthy relationship equation. Having such a healthy sexual connection can increase your intimacy and bind you closer together.

Spelling a Healthy Relationship

Consider these other crucial elements of a healthy relationship.

The Five E's:

➤ **Empathy.** Being able to feel what each other feels, walking a mile in the other person's shoes, being able to put yourself in his place. This goes beyond sympathy where you can feel for the other person (you're sad if something sad happens to them) to the point where you feel what it feels like to be in his skin (feeling sadness as he does).

➤ **Equality.** Respecting the fact that you both count.

➤ **Energetics.** The exchange of vibrations between you, experienced like an electrical force, drawing you to each other and allowing your interactions to feel like well-oiled and perfectly fitting gears.

➤ **Enthusiasm.** Excitement about being together.

➤ **Empowerment.** Supporting each other to feel effective.

The Five A's:

➤ **Acceptance.** Knowing that you approve of each other.

➤ **Accommodation.** Making adjustments for each other's needs.

➤ **Appreciation.** Being responsive to and grateful for each other.

➤ **Adaptability.** Being able to make changes when necessary.

➤ **Agreements.** Making and keeping agreements is essential for trust in a relationship. When agreements are broken, trust is shattered and must be carefully rebuilt with new agreements that are kept.

The Five L's:

➤ **Love.** Cherishing each other and holding one another dear. Love should be unconditional, meaning it does not waver depending on what you look like, earn, do, or say.

➤ **Loyalty.** Being devoted to each other unquestionably, knowing you would not betray each other.

➤ **Listening.** Paying attention to what each other says.

➤ **Laughter.** Humor is the most appealing characteristic that men and women find attractive. Laughter is both physically and psychologically healthy. Having fun is a great way to make you feel good about each other.

➤ **Lust.** Longing and desire draw you magnetically to someone. For a relationship to survive the stresses and grind of daily life, flashes of lust are necessary to spark the union and keep you together.

The Five T's:

➤ **Trust.** Feeling you can rely on one another without question, and that you will not hurt each other. Having confidence and faith in each other that you can depend and count on each other without reservation. Feeling safe with each other.

➤ **Talking.** Communication is key.

Love Bytes

More than three quarters of the 1,500 men and women surveyed in a recent Harlequin Romance Report found great security in being part of a couple. Ninety-eight percent of the men said their lover is their best friend. Half of the respondents said the best reason to marry is "because they love each other" and "want to share their lives together."

➤ **Time together.** Making time to be together without distractions.

➤ **Tenderness.** Treating each other with kindness.

➤ **Thoughtfulness.** Being understanding, showing consideration in thoughts and deeds.

And "Y" for "Yes":

Wipe the negative out of your life, mind, and love! Affirm, that "yes," you both care; "yes," you can make it work; and "yes," you will try to give each other what you need.

What Else Is Important?

Enjoy this exercise: Go over the following list of relationship traits. Circle the ones that are important to you. Then go back and rank your top 10, with number one being the most important. Have your partner do the same using a different-colored pen. Compare your answers. Discuss the importance of each quality to you individually and as a couple.

What's Important to Me in a Healthy Relationship

Acceptance ✔	Gentleness ✔	Responsibility ✔
Admiration	Gratitude ✔	Security ✔
Appreciation ✔	Honesty ✔	Sensitivity
Balance	Individuality	Sensuality
Caring ✔	Integrity ✔	Sex
Commitment ✔	Liveliness	Shared values
Common interests	Love ✔	Shared experiences
Communication ✔	Maturity ✔	Sincerity ✔
Compromise ✔	Nonpossessiveness	Stability ✔
Compatibility ✔	Openness	Supportiveness ✔
Fairness ✔	Passion ✔	Tact ✔
Family	Patience ✔	Tolerance ✔
Flexibility	Playfulness ✔	Trust ✔
Forgiveness ✔	Politeness	Virtue
Friendship ✔	Practicality	Warmth ✔
Fun	Reassurance ✔	Other: _____
Generosity	Respect ✔	

From all the surveys I have done over many years of thousands of men and women, here are the most often mentioned qualities: trust, honesty, communication, love, commitment, respect, good sex, and shared values. Other qualities often mentioned include: appreciation, friendship, forgiveness, compromise, passion, fun, not taking each other for granted, not letting stress interfere, learning new things together, and enjoying each other's company.

Sexual energy and compatibility often play a big role in the first phase of a relationship, but as time goes on, other factors become increasingly more important, such as honesty and mutual respect. Some qualities sneak up on you. For example, without being consciously aware of it, your mutual needs for closeness or separateness will affect how satisfied you are with the amount of time you spend together. While many factors affect your happiness together, studies show that the most important factor that determines a lasting relationship is a shared view of life that includes similar lifestyle preferences, career and family priorities, ideas about child-rearing, and shared values.

A recent Arizona State University study showed men are less selective than women when choosing a casual sex partner, while women select mates who better match their self-ratings of attractiveness and social status. When it comes to a longer-term, serious relationship, the gap narrows, whereby both sexes prefer partners close to their own emotional stability, agreeableness, attractiveness, and likelihood of having healthier, more attractive offspring. Additionally, women consider finances more than men.

The Importance of Agreements

"Cross your heart and hope to die!" It's an old-time pledge that kids used to say to each other when they made promises. We learn from childhood that making agreements and keeping them makes us feel secure. It's a sign of friendship.

Notice I said agreements, not agreeing. Each stage of a relationship requires making agreements. Keeping those agreements gives you a sense of integrity within yourself, is a sign of dedication to the relationship, and instills trust in you by your mate. On the other hand, breaking agreements destroys trust, breaks down communication, and erodes your intimacy. When agreements are broken, it is crucial to acknowledge that and make new ones.

Dr. Judy's Rx

Instead of panicking over disagreements, agree to disagree. Feeling you have reached some consensus, even on differing, gives you a feeling of working together.

Healthy or Unhealthy?

Disagreements are not automatically unhealthy in a relationship. They can be a way of considering your opinions, creating new options, expanding your individual and collective vision, and testing your ability to compromise. Healthy disagreements can lead to resolutions that make you more resolved about staying together.

Agreements are often implied instead of stated, with one person assuming the other will behave in a certain way, consistent with his own view. The perceived betrayal is then based on one person's expectations that are not met, and leads to disappointment and distrust. This is common in the case of one person having a so-called "affair" when you may not have made a fair and clear agreement to be sexually exclusive even though one of you assumed it.

I so often heard about that situation during my years of answering people's questions on the radio. One person calls upset about a mate having an affair, and I ask, "Did you agree that you would not see other people?" And the answer is, "We didn't talk about it, but we have been seeing each other for two months and neither of us has gone out with anyone else." I know it's nice to feel committed but you really have to spell out the terms so there are no misunderstandings and one-sided expectations.

Being a Team Player

Healthy love partners become more of who they are with the other person. They realize their potential. Notice I didn't say through the other person—that would be dependence or codependency. In a healthy relationship, you each preserve a separate sense of self, while still feeling and acting like a team.

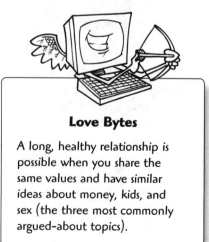

Love Bytes

A long, healthy relationship is possible when you share the same values and have similar ideas about money, kids, and sex (the three most commonly argued-about topics).

Relationships work when you both have the same goal: to be a happy, healthy family and be in love forever. Few celebrity couples make it. Superstar songstress Gloria Estefan is considered the most family minded singer in the music world. She has been married to her first and only boyfriend for 18 years and often brings her family on the road. Goldie Hawn insists her love of 14 years, Kurt Russell, check with her before taking roles, and even fly home if he's filming on location—to attend family dinners, Little League baseball games, and dance and piano recitals.

Dr. Judy's Rx

When you are in a healthy relationship, you feel connected. In Eastern terms, this connection happens on seven levels called "chakras," or energy centers in your body. These start from the base of your spine and work up your body, and each level is connected to an experience that describes qualities of a healthy relationship: security, sexuality, power, sensitivity, expression, mental connectedness, and spirituality.

Ever watch or play basketball, hockey, football, or any team sport? The team members know where the other members are on the field. They look out for each other. They cover for each other and rush in to pick up the slack if a teammate is out of action for some reason. Each depends on the other to do his job well for the good of all. They're even ready to beat up anyone on the other team who attacks one of their teammates. I'm not advocating violence, but I am recommending a fierce sense of loyalty toward your partner. My mother refers to it as the "mother lion" sense, that she would attack anyone who endangers her cubs. Devoted lovers have that sense toward each other.

Think of you and your partner as a team, working in tandem to reach a goal. Working toward a common goal facilitates closeness and helps you better appreciate each other's good qualities. The goal can be painting the living room, cleaning out the basement, budgeting, planning a trip, or buying a new car. Or the best goal of all—a happy and healthy life together.

The "Is It Healthy?" Quiz

Before you move on to other chapters in this book, let's examine what your current thinking is regarding relationships. Take the following quiz to see how good you are at recognizing the qualities of a healthy relationship. The answers are explained throughout the upcoming chapters, and in Appendix A at the end of this book.

Read each of the following statements and then circle in the appropriate column indicating whether you think it is healthy or unhealthy for your love life.

The "Is It Healthy?" Quiz

Statement	Circle One	
1. You say, "I love her/him to death."	Healthy	Unhealthy
2. You decide to marry because you're fed up with the dating scene.	Healthy	Unhealthy
3. You ask for all the details about a past love or affair.	Healthy	Unhealthy
4. You think that dreaming about an ex-love means you don't love your present mate.	Healthy	Unhealthy
5. You cannot bear to be separated.	Healthy	Unhealthy
6. Your mate's ex calls all the time.	Healthy	Unhealthy
7. You blindly agree with parents or friends about whether your relationship is good.	Healthy	Unhealthy
8. You disappear from your mate's children's lives if you break up (or you don't let your children see your ex).	Healthy	Unhealthy
9. Whatever worked to help you get ahead in your career, you should also do in your love life.	Healthy	Unhealthy
10. The more easy-going person should always be the one to go along with the other's plans if there's a conflict.	Healthy	Unhealthy
11. After you are together for a while, you can finally relax and not worry about impressing one another.	Healthy	Unhealthy
12. Pleasuring yourself or having more sex fantasies or dreams when you're with your partner than when you were single means that you aren't having enough sex (or satisfying sex) now.	Healthy	Unhealthy
13. Having lots of sex is essential for a good relationship.	Healthy	Unhealthy

The Ten Commandments of a Healthy Relationship

Before closing this chapter, I'd like you to remember the following commandments. Remember these rules during good and bad times in your relationship:

The Ten Commandments of a Healthy Relationship

1. I will do my best to be the happiest person I can be.
2. I will be honest in my dealings with my partner.
3. I will keep my agreements.
4. I will have integrity about my actions.
5. I will honor all others I am in a relationship with.
6. I will practice forgiveness for myself and others.
7. I will nurture my spiritual soul and that of others.
8. I will accept others for who they are without judging them or insisting they change to suit me.
9. I will be open to suggestions and change when it's in the best interests for both of us.
10. I will trust in the powers that be that what happens is for the best.

A Concept Whose Time Has Come Regarding a Healthy Relationship in the New Millennium

In re-reading this book now, three years from when I first took to tapping the computer keys to write the first edition, I realize that the messages about what it takes to create a healthy relationship are even more true now than ever before. I have always been accused of being "before my time," but now I see that time has come. The central theme of this book has come true more than ever before: that "health" is the key to a lasting relationship.

"If we have our health, and each other, we have everything," said one lovely woman to her partner. How well put. That word—"health"—has taken on deeper meaning in this new age. It is no longer just strength of physical being; in fact, a healthy relationship has eight dimensions.

The Eight Dimensions of New Millennium Health

So what exactly does health mean in this new age? Certainly it means a healthy body. You all know that when you are beset with the smallest touch of flu, you lose interest in nearly everything. You want to crawl into bed, pull the covers over your head, and wait for the illness to pass. But a sound body is only one dimension of what it takes for a healthy personal life and lasting relationship.

Certainly a healthy relationship requires the second dimension: a healthy mind. Distractions, obsessions, and confused thinking cloud your judgment about love and prevent you from recognizing true love or allowing it to blossom. Recent awareness about the interaction between body and mind has made it clear how integrally these two are tied. Negative thinking can cause ill health and vice versa. Either, or both of these, can harm your ability to open yourself to lasting love.

The third dimension of healthy love is emotional health. You know what happens when you are deeply hurt by something that goes awry in your life, work, family, or friendships, which can make you so discouraged or depressed that you feel like re-treating and giving up hope that anything—or anyone—can be trusted or meaning-ful. The foundation for emotional health is self-esteem, knowing that you are worthy and capable of loving and being loved. That's why I give you lots of encouragement in Chapter 7, "A Healthy Self First," so you can come together as two healthy and whole beings.

The fourth dimension of a healthy relationship for the new millennium is the ability to extend your love to your social environment—to an "extended" family. The mod-ern concept of "family" actually goes back to ancient days, going beyond blood rela-tives to include those with whom you develop such close bonds that you wish they had been part of your family tree. Think about the people in your intimate circle—these are the members of your "tribe." In this new millennium it is time to fix—or let go—of relationships that drain you and strain your love life and to embrace those into your tribe (extended family circle) who nurture you. I help you do that in Chapter 26, "It's Not Just the Two of Us."

The fifth dimension of a healthy relationship is having a satisfying daily life. This means handling the practical side of your life, including having your work and finan-cial life in order. Does your work truly satisfies you, or do you get up in the morning and dread your day? It's not just the privileged few who can enjoy what they do for a living; even if you feel trapped or strapped now, you can create more satisfaction in your job and finances. Chapters 20, "Dollars and Sense: A Healthy Couple's Guide to Handling Money Issues," and 21, "Working Nine to ... with Time Off for Love," show you how to do that, with many quizzes, and helpful tips about how to balance your work and love life as well as how to be compatible about money matters—so your in-vestment in each other pays off!

The sixth dimension of a healthy relationship is healthy sexuality. As a sex therapist, I know how a strong sexual connection can draw a couple to each other or how a "bad sex life" can tear you apart. That's why an entire part, Part 3, "How to Keep the Passion Alive," is devoted to keeping the love fires burning!

But there are two other dimensions of a healthy relationship that have emerged in this new century and that are crucial for love to thrive. These dimensions are part of the reason for this new edition of *The Complete Idiot's Guide to a Healthy Relationship*.

The seventh dimension of a healthy relationship is spiritual connection. That aspect of our lives is being revived in this new century, as evidenced by more books published about "soul," "spirit," and "visions" and popular TV shows based on belief of spirit, like *Touched by an Angel* and *Beyond Chance*. The success of these books and shows has surprised many media critics and even the writers and producers themselves. But they reflect the direction that people are turning to in this new age. Chapter 2, "The Seventh Dimension of a Healthy Relationship: Spiritual Love," shows you how to achieve more "spirit" in your relationship, to reach higher states of bliss.

The eighth dimension of a healthy relationship is the technological connection. The world of computer chips can seem, on the surface, antithetical to striving for spirituality, but technological advances are an undeniable progress in our world today, affecting every aspect of our life. More about how to prevent the information superhighway from derailing your love life and how to harness electronics for a fulfilling relationship are in Chapter 3, "The Eighth Dimension of a Healthy Relationship: Digital Duos in Cyberlove."

The dimensions of health—emotional, physical, mental, social, practical, sexual, spiritual, and technological—are inextricably tied. But how do you get the whole package together? By working on the individual parts. This book will help you in this journey.

The Least You Need to Know

➤ Honesty is mentioned most often by men and women as the most important aspect of a healthy relationship.

➤ Other aspects of a healthy relationship include good communication, compatibility, and teamwork.

➤ Always keep your agreements, but never assume your mate will conform to certain behaviors unless there has been a previously discussed agreement.

➤ The eight dimensions of a healthy relationship—physical, mental, emotional, social, practical, sexual, spiritual, and technological—are all possible to attain if you and your partner focus on overcoming any blocks in each area, make necessary changes, embrace your worthiness, and work together for mutual fulfillment.

➤ Being in the process of building a love built solidly on these eight dimensions is guaranteed to be fulfilling.

Chapter 2

The Seventh Dimension of a Healthy Relationship: Spiritual Love

In This Chapter

➤ An explanation of the seventh dimension of spiritual love

➤ The importance of breath to achieve bliss

➤ How to transmit energy between the two of you

➤ How can you tell if you have a spiritual love? A Test of Spirit

➤ Ways to develop spiritual love

In the previous chapter, I mentioned the eight dimensions of a healthy relationship for the new millennium. The seventh dimension includes bringing "spirituality" into your loving.

What is spirituality? What do you think of when you hear that word?

Spirituality is an inner sense of being that is beyond anything you can touch or express in words. It is beyond space and time, something you "sense" when you are quiet enough to "tune in" to your inner being. The goal of a healthy relationship is to sense this within yourself—and then to connect this spirit with that of another person.

Because it comes from another place other than the rational brain, striving for spirit in your relationship is a concept that may be difficult to grasp at first. But stay with me on this and read on, and I promise you that you will find inspiration and excitement in discovering this potential in yourself and in your relationship.

What Is "Spirit" to You?

The identification of spirit or soul may remind you, as it does me, of a college introductory philosophy class, where you are challenged to identify "Who is the 'I'?" and "Where is the soul?" I remember finding these questions fascinating. Ask yourself those questions. What is the right answer? From that philosophy class decades ago, through the many scholars, guides, and spiritual leaders I have encountered and studied with over three decades, a useful answer to those questions is whatever you come up with, in your own way.

How do you get to that answer? By being quiet and reflecting on the question until thoughts, words, images, feelings, or sensations come to you. What if you come up with "nothing"? Identify even the tiniest sensation—that is your clue to how you define spirit.

Love Bytes

Famous psychoanalyst Carl Jung greatly contributed to the respectability of "spirituality" and mysticism in psychology. Jung described the search for spirit as a universal life force and archetypal drive like sex, aggression, and the search for food.

The Time Is Right

My own evolution as a person and as a therapist has taken me through looking at the world through an emotional, and then a logical, and now a more spiritual lens. Like many of my colleagues, I have integrated more spiritual views and techniques into my therapeutic practice and given conferences on "Spirituality and Psychotherapy." My travels and studies in the East (notably China, Nepal, and Japan) have nurtured this spiritual growth.

Thanks in part to the efforts of ancient prophets like Rumi, early pioneers in our lifetime like Ram Dass, and more recent popular spiritualists like Deepok Chopra, men and women alike are listening to more soulful, spiritual voices. These voices outside reflect the voices of people like you who want more love in their lives and more peace in the world.

The Alternative Has Become Mainstream

A few years ago, certain health approaches were referred to as "complementary" or "alternative" medicine. The traditional medical world frowned upon any unusual healings that involved herbs, massage, imagery, or—heaven forbid—the laying on of hands. In the first edition of this book, I even put such techniques in the chapter called "Keeping Your Love Exciting with Alternative Techniques." But now such techniques have gained more acceptance as our minds open to new ideas, and thus I have changed the title of that chapter to reflect this evolution (see Chapter 28, "Keeping Your Love Exciting with New-Millennium Body and Mind Techniques"). New ideas are blocked when people are afraid of change; when fear melts, love can take its place.

You Gotta Have Heart

A fundamental step to connect with "spirit" is understanding the meaning of "heart." The American Heart Association has done a good job in promoting the importance of a healthy heart, but this message has still only referred to eating right and exercising to prevent clogged arteries and heart attacks.

The true healthy heart is also unclogged from negative emotions, including fear, anger, envy, revenge, and even hopelessness. The healthy heart is pure in intention and open to love and being loved even when it has suffered.

Once you have an open heart, you are ready for a connection in spirit. This journey is open to anyone, not just those who are religious or feel the ultimate Divine or the Source of all Being. The journey is important for all, to heal ourselves, and to achieve peace in the world.

A Test of Spirit

If spirit is ethereal, how do you know you have it? While no test can fully determine a quality that defies detailed description, here are some questions that will help you know whether you are on the right track.

For each of the following questions, check either "Yes, often" "Sometimes," or "Not really." Unlike other quizzes you will do in this book, I'd prefer that you not spend time calculating your answers. Read each sentence, then close your eyes and let the words sink in. Let the answer come to you without trying to figure it out. Even if the questions seem strange, ask yourself the question again and see what answer comes to you.

The Test of Spirit

1. Are you able to take a deep breath and truly feel the breath down in the pit of your stomach?

   ❑ Yes, often   ❑ Sometimes   ❑ Not really

2. When you breathe, do you ever have the feeling that you are lighter?

   ❑ Yes, often   ❑ Sometimes   ❑ Not really

3. Breathe out. Do you have a sensation that you are suspended without the need for another breath?

   ❑ Yes, often   ❑ Sometimes   ❑ Not really

---

4. Do you have the feeling that a part of you is watching yourself even when you are doing simple things like walking in the street or writing a report for work?

   ❏ Yes, often   ❏ Sometimes   ❏ Not really

5. Do you get so involved in doing something (driving, gardening, cooking) that hours have gone by and you didn't even notice that time passed?

   ❏ Yes, often   ❏ Sometimes   ❏ Not really

6. Is there ever a "little voice" in your head or sensations in your body that tell you what to do even when you are not totally sure where it comes from?

   ❏ Yes, often   ❏ Sometimes   ❏ Not really

7. Do you "sense" your loved one/an imagined loved one is beside you or in front of you even if he or she is not really there?

   ❏ Yes, often   ❏ Sometimes   ❏ Not really

8. Breathe out. Can you imagine sending this breath into your loved one?

   ❏ Yes, often   ❏ Sometimes   ❏ Not really

9. Do you merge with your lover—in talking or making love—so that you feel like one person?

   ❏ Yes, often   ❏ Sometimes   ❏ Not really

10. Do you sense that guides, spirits, or angels are helping you?

    ❏ Yes, often   ❏ Sometimes   ❏ Not really

Dr. Judy's Rx

A spiritual connection requires unconditional love—that means being seen, heard, accepted, and honored just as you are and offering the same to another person.

If you answered "Yes, often" to five or more questions, you already have the experience of a spiritually healthy love, perhaps without realizing or labeling it as such. If you answered "Yes, often" to at least three questions, you have the right stuff to be able to learn what a deep, spiritually healthy relationship can be. If you answered "Yes, often" to fewer than two questions, practice doing what the question suggests, as well as the trying the exercise later in this chapter.

In fact, all of these experiences can be developed, no matter what your score. Read each question, then close your eyes and imagine the experience suggested by the question as if it's really happening.

No matter how you fared on the test of spirit, read on for suggestions on developing this spiritual quality in your life.

The Secret of Breathing Your Way to a Healthy Relationship

One pathway to bring the spiritual dimension into your relationship lies in your breath. Proper breathing not only supplies necessary oxygen to your cells, it also frees emotions and sensuality. Deep breathing is certainly relaxing, but *full* and deep breaths bring you close to that experience called "spirit." Read on to find out how to do this on your own and with a partner.

Breathing on Your Own

"Of course, I'm breathing," you say, but maybe you're not breathing the best way you can. Take a deep breath now. Notice where the breath is coming from. Is it from your throat or deeper down, from your belly? The truth is, many of us breathe much too shallow. The fault lies partly with fashion, which demands a slim figure and entices us to suck in our stomachs and don tight belts or slim-fitting pants. The result: Our air intake is constricted. Despite efforts like recent parental protests of young pop star Britney Spears for inspiring pre-adolescents to expose their belly buttons to copy her sexiness, the age-old pressure to be slim and sexy persistently plagues females. And washboard-stomached male TV hunks beleaguer everyday guys from letting their own real waistlines expand in a normal breath.

Another fault lies in our own fear. The less focused we are on breathing deeply, the less we have to really feel. Yes, it's true. When people are forced to really concentrate on their breathing, emotions can come flooding out—many of which can be uncomfortable. Try it. Allow yourself to be in a safe place, perhaps your bedroom. Make sure no one else is around who might be frightened or unprepared for any loud or strange sounds you might make. Take several deep breaths. Let the breath fill your belly until it fills out, like a chubby-bellied Buddha. Watch what happens. Your eyes may flicker. A thumb may twitch. Your throat may close. Your chest might feel tight. Those reactions are signs that your body is fighting what it has not done before—felt deeply!

Your mind will also fight. It will begin to chatter, telling you to resist. Thoughts will tell you to stop ("This is foolish"), distract you ("I have to finish that report"), or trigger anger ("What a waste of time!"). Push on. Take another breath, making this one deeper than the one before.

In Kim's story lies proof of the value of breathing in getting to the healthy love you want and deserve. If you take a deep breath and get more in

Love Lookout

Any time you protest that you do not have the love you want in your relationship, consider how you create the blocks. Perhaps you are not really ready to receive the love you say you want.

touch with your quiet self, you will know that the love you have inside is yours, no matter who comes or goes in your outer world.

Ask Dr. Judy

You'd be surprised at the resistance people encounter when asked to breathe deeply. But I promise you this is key. Let me tell you the story of a dear patient of mine, Kim. Kim is 34 years old and deeply in love with Thomas, whom she brought to therapy because she wanted him to love her more. A deeper problem was that Kim did not *allow* herself to be loved enough. I asked Kim to breathe deeply to let his love in and guess what? She couldn't. She choked, coughed, and blew her nose. But she couldn't breathe deeply. Why? Because when she did it even just a little, emotions welled up inside. Tears in her eyes told the story of a little girl hurt from desperately wanting love and never getting it and then being afraid that if she did, she would lose it or not deserve it. So she kept her breath shallow, to keep her feelings down—and the love at a distance.

Breathing Together to Get Closer to a Spiritually Healthy Love

Breathing on your own gets you close to your inner sense of love; breathing together with your loved one will help you exchange the feeling of love between you. Breathing together opens you up to more love and intimacy. Think of the breath as the source of life, essential food, and the ultimate gift of your love.

Try this exercise. Lie side by side or sit face to face with the woman in her partner's lap. Inhale and exhale together to a count of five. Imagine drawing the breath up from the base of your spine to the top of your head, then back down again. Next, create a circle of breath as one of you inhales while the other exhales, establishing a comfortable rhythm together. While doing this, maintain eye contact and imagine sending out love and bringing in your partner's love with each breath.

Don't be discouraged if this does not come easy. Remember my patient Kim and her boyfriend Thomas? In one of their sessions, I suggested that they sit opposite each other, hold hands and look into each other's eyes, and breathe. Kim could not do it at first, protesting, laughing, or turning the conversation to something else to distract us from the exercise. At my insistence she finally tried it. As she looked into Thomas's eyes, tears flowed down her cheeks and her breath quickened. Kim came to the same realization that many people come to when they do this exercise: When you see the deep love you want, you can be frightened and push it away. The mixture of deep feelings—of joy at getting what you want, fear of not getting it, and pain from not having it in the past—can be overwhelming.

It takes courage to stick with this and truly see that what you want is really there for you to have. But persistence is the way to truly healthy love that adds the extra dimension of spirit to your love.

Connecting to Your Own Soul First

I'm sure you've heard the statement that you cannot love another until you love yourself. From a spiritual standpoint, this means that in order to connect deeply to another person's soul, you need to know your own soul first.

The most effective way of connecting to your soul is through meditation. (This will be described later in Chapter 28.) Meditation no longer has to be a solitary act in a lonely, remote cave. In fact, you can meditate together in the comfort of your own home. Being in each other's presence, as you go deeper into your selves, can heighten not only your own development, but also the spiritual connection between you.

The Third Eye

To achieve a spiritual connection, your "door" needs to be open! The door to the more spiritual realm of existence is through your third eye—the symbolic eye on your forehead above the bridge of your nose between your two eyes. Opening up your third eye helps you go deeper into your own being and connect on a higher level with your loved one. To get the sense of your third eye, put your middle finger on the space between your two eyes, over the bridge of your nose. Close your eyes and imagine breathing into that place your finger is touching.

Dr. Judy's Rx

Arguments, anger, and resentment fade from interfering with your love when you practice compassion, the deepest empathy for one another. New Jersey healer Marcus Daniels's "Cellular Memory Healing" involves stating—and experiencing—"In my human heart I am feeling and receiving my love," "In my human heart I am feeling and receiving your love," and "Your love and my love are the same."

Love Bytes

An exciting technique for the new millennium is creating "love magic." Decide on what you would both like to manifest for your love. Picture what that would feel and look like in real life. As you breathe together, maintain eye contact and imagine it coming true.

Once you've opened up your door, you're ready to connect with the spirit of your partner. The connection between you is called "energetics."

Getting the Energetics to Flow Between You

"Energetics," the energy field between the two of you, can be felt when you "sense" each other, or seem to think the same thoughts. It is at work when you say that you are "drawn" to one another.

Dr. Judy's Rx

Awaken the "goddess" or "god" within yourself and each other by treating yourself and each other with the reverence of such a being. Create your own image or use archetypes as a guide, like the Hindu god Vishnu, the compassionate Chinese goddess Quan Yin, or the Greek prototypes like Demeter the mother or Artemis the warrior.

Dr. Judy's Rx

Do premeditated practices and rituals take the spontaneity out of lovemaking? Quite the contrary. Tantric practices elevate lovemaking to a dance, an art form, and a spiritual connection.

Couples who want to increase the energetics between them—to sustain love and passion for a lifetime—and who are open to trying new things can find value in tantric practices. These include Hindu or Buddhist rituals, exercises, and meditations. Tantra teaches the relationship between masculine and feminine as a spiritual act of love. The goal is not sexual performance or orgasm but a union between the god or spiritual essence within each partner and a cosmic consciousness or higher power.

Here are some simple exercises to increase the flow of energy between you. You may think them strange at first, but I promise if you do them, you'll appreciate their value.

➤ **"The Eye Lock."** Simply sit facing each other and look into each other's eyes without looking away. Concentrate on opening up your gaze so you allow your partner to truly look not only "at" you, but deep into your eyes. This may seem strange at first, but with relaxation and practice, you can reach the more enlightened stage where you look into each other's eyes and see more deeply into each other's souls.

➤ **"The Heart Hold."** Standing or sitting, face each other. Put one hand in the middle of your partner's chest, by his heart. He does the same for you. Then cover each other's hands on your heart with the other hand. Concentrate on sending energy from your heart, out your hand, into your partner's heart. Imagine the energy going out from your partner's heart, down their arm, through their hand into your heart. Follow the circle of energy from heart to heart.

The Ritual of Love

Another technique to help create a more spiritual love is through the use of ritual. Such rites are common in all religions and cultures—even Monday Night Football can be called a ritual for some people! Performing specific acts together, whether preparing dinner or walking the dog or rituals for lovemaking such as bathing together, lighting candles, etc. (see the love ritual in Chapter 29, "Helping Each Other Toward a Healthier Relationship," for a good example), can bring you closer and express reverence for your partnership and respect for the act of loving. Such rituals derive from ancient times, when lovers would prepare themselves and their love chambers for a tryst.

Letting Go in Love: A Spiritual View of Loss

All too often in love, we are terrified of loss. Nearly everyone has experienced loss or rejection, knows how painful that feels, and will do anything to prevent it from happening again. But let me remind you of the truth in the saying, "to truly love is to be able to let go." If you really love someone, set them free. If they are really yours, they will always come back to you. There is no loss in love on the spiritual realm. The love you have is always inside you, even if the person is not physically in your presence.

When you love on a spiritual level, you do not "possess" another being. In workshops called "The Art of Being," Hawaiian spiritual teacher Alan Lowen guides groups through experiences of letting go, like writing a letter to important people you have lost in your life, and ceremoniously throwing it into a blazing bonfire. In another ritual, each person brings a treasured possession and surrenders it, feeling lightened and energized (you may retrieve it or give it away after the ritual). Such processes of letting go are basic principles in Tibetan Buddhism as explained in the classic book *The Tibetan Book of Living and Dying* (Harper, 1994).

Love Bytes

Practices include loosening up the body by moving to tribal music. Face your partner and rock your pelvises toward each other. Increase the energy by adding sounds as you thrust forward. In another exercise, couples awaken powerful energy by taking turns lying on their stomach while the other vigorously taps the back on either side of the spine and out toward the shoulders.

Putting It All Together

The deepest spiritual connection can happen when all other dimensions unite (physical, mental, emotional, practical, social, and sexual). Doing this is an exciting, though challenging, journey that is best accomplished by a conscious practice in the same way as practice and mental focus make you good at a particular sport, playing a musical instrument, or cooking.

In one of the best trainings to achieve self-love and sacred relationships, spiritual leader Bodhi Avinasha guides men and women in using body exercises, breathing techniques, and emotional clearing to allow for personal bliss and ecstatic connection to a partner through body, heart, and soul. In workshops run by Tantrika International and exercises described in her book *Jewel in the Lotus* (Sunstar, 1994), Avinasha outlines specific processes men and women can do on their own or with a loved one. Connecting to such practices brings bliss into your life not only in love relationships but in everyday activities and assures you of the peace and joy you seek and deserve.

Love Bytes

There is an increasing, albeit small, body of evidence to support the existence and effect of spiritual dimensions on reality. These efforts come from doctor's studies on patients' recovery from illness using visualizations and quantum physics research relating properties of water and light to emotions like joy and love.

The Least You Need to Know

➤ A truly healthy relationship requires connection on the spiritual dimension, as part of the eight dimensions: physical, mental, emotional, familial, practical, social, sexual, spiritual, and technological.

➤ Breathing deeply and properly is a crucial path to opening yourself up to deeper love and connecting with your partner.

➤ You don't have to be religious to be spiritual; anyone can achieve a spiritual love.

➤ Time, effort, and practice are necessary to develop the dimension of spirituality in love.

➤ Developing the spiritual side of love puts you on a pathway to higher states of bliss, individually and together, both in love and in everyday life.

Chapter 3

The Eighth Dimension of a Healthy Relationship: Digital Duos in Cyberlove

In This Chapter

➤ How to keep up with the information superhighway to prevent breakdowns in your love life

➤ The computer vs. cupid: pros and cons of electronic gadgets on your love life

➤ The importance of using Netiquette

➤ What to do when one partner is a techie and the other is not

➤ Using technology to boost, not bust, your sex life

There's no doubt about it—we have entered the new millennium of technology, forcing us to change the way we view ourselves, our relationships, and our planet. Just as with the Industrial Age, there is no turning back from "progress," as the rate of growth for new computer networks is estimated to be 25 percent every three months. Eventually all electronic communications gadgets—telephones, televisions, and desktops—will merge into one system, demanding that you keep up or be left behind. Even those who could never figure out how to program the VCR, or who prefer writing in a daily planner to programming a Palm Pilot, are being forced to face the increasing role that devices play in modern life.

Just as the telephone drastically changed communications and relationships, so its derivatives—everything from cell phones to digital pagers, CD writers, games, wristwatch computer chips, and other James Bond–like gadgetry—are inextricably affecting who, what, where, when, and why we are in touch. That's why I consider technology the eighth dimension of a healthy relationship. What kind of ride will you take on this information superhighway, and what impact will you let it have on your love life?

Granted, no technological transmission can equal the tender touch of a lover, and no text message can transmit as much as a lover's smell or smile. But since these advances are here to stay, it's up to you how you allow their technology to boost—or bust—your love life. In this chapter I'll explore what to watch out for if electronics are shorting out your love and sex life and how to harness cyberspace to make your relationship stronger.

Keeping in Technological Touch

Massachusetts software engineer Dan Cookson explains the future of personal technological communication, called the "personal area network," as a collection of accessories on or near your body, all able to interact with one another and with other people's devices. "Wearable technology"—devices embedded in clothing or wearable items—include computers sewn into a wallet or tucked into oversized jacket lapels (that debuted at a Museum of Modern Art exhibit on "The Work Sphere"). Furthermore, a variety of communication devices—personal computers, PDA (Palm Pilots), laptops, and your wristwatch—will all be connected wirelessly to one another and to other nearby devices to allow instantaneous intercommunication.

Love Bytes

Portraits of Internet users conflict: One study concluded that people who logged on for even a few hours a week connected to the Internet experienced higher levels of loneliness and depression, while another study concluded cyberspace users were sociable and communicative.

So what does this mean for your relationship? As an increasing number of communication gadgets burst onto the market, there will be fewer problems with being in touch and fewer excuses for not making contact. With increasingly easy and economical access, you will always be able to find the opportunity to let a loved one know you're thinking of him or that you'll be late for dinner. Read on for the advantages—and challenges—this new technology will bring to your relationship.

The Upside of Technology on Love

There's no doubt that technological advances in interpersonal communication can benefit your love life. Consider all the times and ways that you can be in touch through e-mail, instant messaging, cell phones, Palm Pilot reminders, beepers, pagers, and computer chips in your wristwatch. Here are some advantages of the new virtual voice:

➤ Having time for one another is one of the biggest problems busy couples face these days. More options for contact mean more time together: You can use new devices to "Web woo" your partner by being creative with messages about how you feel and what you want to do together.

➤ Giving you an opportunity to use previously "wasted" time, by using digital gadgets while waiting for gas or in long post office lines, to be in touch with your partner.

➤ Providing inexpensive contact, as newer methodologies are often cheaper than long-distance phone calls.

➤ Providing instant access for impulsive love messages as well as important communications.

➤ Allowing exploration of various aspects of yourselves by surfing different Web sites, free from constraints of social or gender roles.

➤ Providing experience in self-disclosure by sending messages through digital devices, which can feel safer than saying them in person. That self-disclosure is fundamental to intimacy.

➤ Allowing you to practice communicating as a couple to build your confidence about sharing secrets or revealing parts of yourselves that you were shy or embarrassed about.

➤ Offering an opportunity to spend time exploring and experimenting together, in a playful way, as if learning a new game, sport, dance, or skill. You can surf for new Web sites you think you would enjoy with your partner and log on together and explore your new discovery. Undertaking any such project together can bring couples closer by sharing a mutual interest. It further creates a natural opportunity to spend time together.

➤ Decreasing the locations off-limits to contact. For example, since cell phones can send text messages, it's possible to communicate even in noisy public places (like restaurants, parties, sporting events, lecture halls).

➤ Easing the pain of long-distance relationships imposed by work or other responsibilities.

Love Bytes

Some Internet services—and large-scale telephone service—offer free phone calls, accessible locally or even internationally. As with any service, research the rules and regulations carefully and watch for hidden costs. More such services will become available as technology develops and communications take place through computer chips in your watch!

The Downside of Technology on Love

The virtual love story is not a totally happy one. A recent survey of over 4,000 adults found that 55 percent have access to the Internet, over a third of whom are regular users, spending five hours or more a week online. Of those, 13 percent report spending *less* time with family and friends, and a quarter say they talk less on the phone.

This worries me. Love can falter when people become wed to their laptops, surfing the Web instead of diving into dates, manning joysticks instead of planning joy in their relationship, filling up with computer-chip-fed information instead of challenging their own imagination.

Fast-paced instant communication and access in the cyberworld can speed up relationships as well. This can lead to a false sense of closeness, often resulting in disappointment and depression later.

Time online takes away from time with real lovers. The question is, how much does it interfere? Surveys show that an estimated 5 to 10 percent of Internet users (about 200,000 people) can be classified as cyberspace addicts. A University of Pittsburgh study showed that heavy Internet habits of men and women spending 30 hours or more online per week led to severe marital strife or even divorce, ignoring family responsibilities, job loss, and failure in school. Another study of 220 computer-using husbands showed that those who spent over 11 hours online per week reported being less available and less communicative with their wives and spending less time performing household chores. While researchers note that a person's refuge into RAM can be a needed escape from daily stresses, I have to warn about the potential damage to a relationship, since what wives say they most want from their husbands is time talking and help with household chores.

Even if the computer is used to foster instead of falter a primary relationship, constant computer contact with lovers during daytime work hours can cause trouble on the job. Companies used to be wary of employees making personal telephone calls during work hours. Now with most people having desktops, it is increasingly easier to instant message or e-mail a paramour. On the surface, it appears you have more privacy e-mailing or instant messaging because someone sharing an office or in a contiguous cubicle won't even overhear your conversation or know that you are not sending a business message. But beware that many offices monitor employee e-mails, so what you're writing to your sweetie may be read by the tech guys—and maybe even your boss! While there are no exact statistics on how much time employees are spending of company money and time on personal e-mailing, experts estimate that the practice is on the rise. My advice: Be wary of overloading on downloading love when you're supposed to be on the job!

How Much Is Too Much?

"Hilly" and her boyfriend "Tyrone" are an example of a couple who got so carried away with their technological contact that it almost ruined their careers as well as their relationship. Hilly told me, "When my boyfriend and I were first dating, we were constantly e-mailing, forwarding jokes, and sending e-greeting cards. I'd come in the morning and find 10 messages from him that I'd get so excited and download them before I read the work-related ones."

The turn-on through technology intensified, as Tyrone insisted that Hilly get a beeper and then gave her a cell phone for her birthday—so she could be instantly accessible—even in the bathroom. Beepers and cell phones went off constantly, and e-mail flew, and soon the torrid technological twosome was in trouble, as Hilly's boss noticed her decreased productivity and put her on probation. Tyrone became intolerant of the cutback in their cyber communication, and (albeit irrationally) took it personally. Hilly couldn't do enough to reassure him of her love when she couldn't answer his beeps instantly or when she had to curtail their cellular chit-chat.

Fortunately, Hilly asked for my advice before she and Tyrone were in serious danger of sacrificing their jobs in the frenzy of their technological tornado. I insisted they learn to delay instant gratification of their desires to communicate—either fondness or frustration—in order to get their work done. But more important, a deeper issue surfaced. Both Hilly and Tyrone were actually frightened to say how they needed one another in person. "I get so worked up at work," Tyrone admitted, "that I feel calmer once I hear her voice." "I need constant reminders that he cares about me," Hilly admitted. Once these needs were stated openly, they could both be reassured of each other's love and support, without the constant reminders.

Alicia and Anthony are another couple who heated up the technological airwaves as their relationship heated up. But the pressure became too much for Alicia. "I can't take it anymore," she told me. "He gets too furious if I don't answer immediately." The barrage was so bad that Alicia relished any time that her computer would crash or that her cell phone battery would go dead.

With such accessibility through devices of all types, couples like Hilly and Tyrone and Alicia and Anthony need to discuss their expectations and agree on limits to their digital duet. How often do you want to be called? When do you expect a return response? Be reasonable and understanding of

Love Lookout

Because employers and even other unknown sources can have access to your business (and even a personal) computer, never send any e-mail that you would be uncomfortable having anyone else read.

Love Lookout

Given the availability of so many means of communication, recognize that *not* staying in touch can increase the probability of a partner feeling neglected. Empty e-mail or a beeper that never goes off can be just as upsetting as incessant sending.

each other's needs, constraints, and patience. You and your partner might design some shortcuts to identify how important your message is or the need for an immediate response. For example, one couple uses a scale that rates a casual message as "211" and a must-answer message as "811."

Digital contact demands attention to your behaviors, just as if you were facc-to-face. So think about how you should behave "properly," and also how to protect yourselves from problems.

Loveonline Netiquette

All too often partners end up taking each other for granted over time and treat each other with less respect and attention than they did when they first met or than they would extend to strangers. Taking each other for granted is even easier when communicating with technology or over the Net, when speed, immediate gratification, and the sense of safety that technology allows can make you relax into being too casual. Yet maintaining politeness (a wonderful, all-too-forgotten word) fosters positive feelings in a couple, especially over the long term.

Cyberetiquette (or "Netiquette") means remembering certain considerate behaviors when sending messages over the Net. These include:

➤ Address your partner with a greeting ("Dearest …" "Hello my sweet,"), instead of simply launching into the message.

➤ Sign off with a phrase ("Affectionately yours," "Lovingly,").

➤ Use your partner's name (surveys show what most men and women want to hear is their name!).

➤ Avoid one-liners; these might indicate you haven't taken the time to compose a special message to your loved one.

➤ Spell out phrases as much as possible instead of typing overused shortcuts (including "emoticons") that your partner may not recognize. If you insist on using them, make sure you both are familiar with their meaning. For example:

       LOL = laughing out loud

       '-) or ;-) = winking

       :-) = said with a smile

       0:-) = angel

       :-* = kiss

➤ Choose a typeface and color that is easily readable (avoid all capital letters, which is like screaming in someone's ear, or bright background colors).

➤ Don't barrage your partner with instant messages or e-mail when you know she is otherwise occupied. Think of these like a telephone call—would you call every two seconds (or want to be called every two seconds if you were busy)?

➤ Let your partner know he doesn't have to respond every time instantly or risk your upset; if it's important, say so.

➤ Agree on the types of messages you want. Do you want jokes or other "junk mail" forwarded?

➤ Etiquette regarding other modes of communication is just as important and should follow similar rules. For example, avoid repetitive paging if you do not get an immediate answer.

Do's and Don'ts of Digital Love

Besides paying attention to Netiquette, harnessing technology to serve your relationship requires knowing what behaviors help or hurt your lives individually and together. Here are some tips:

➤ **Don't** be in touch in situations that require concentration. For example, sexy talk or arguments over the cell phone when driving can cause distraction and lead to a serious accident.

➤ **Do** investigate the security of your system, since activities over the airwaves or Internet can be traced by others.

➤ **Do** keep tabs on the cost of being in electronic contact. For example, keep track of the number of minutes on your cell phone plan; it can be all too easy to forget how long you are talking when you have a certain number of minutes free (even though you've pre-paid for them), and end up paying more per extra minute than for a land-line phone call.

➤ **Don't** become frustrated and blame your partner or make assumptions when a message doesn't get through right away. Glitches *will* happen.

➤ **Do** know what your service for each machine is. For example, you may go out of town expecting to be able to beep or call your partner on your cell phone, but your service does not cover the area where you have traveled.

➤ **Do** develop some communications that are special to the two of you, just as you would if speaking in person.

➤ **Do** take advantage of special services of your machines. For example, if you are at a loss for words, check out sites that send cards (for free), such as Blue Mountain Electronic Greeting Cards (www.bluemountain.com).

➤ **Do** treat the Internet like an adventure you are sharing together. Surf the Net together to make plans for a vacation, research a new hobby, or read up on the latest news together.

➤ **Don't** contact your partner (or have him contact you) in certain situations. For example, it's inappropriate to use your cell phone in theaters, in restaurants, on buses, and in other public places where you would clearly be disturbing others.

➤ And remember, as I mentioned above, **don't** send overly personal or sexy messages to a partner's work computer. You never know who might be able to log on to your partner's machine either by mistake or design.

When Only One of You Is a Techie

Research has shown that problems arise between couples when one jogs and the other doesn't. The nonexercising partner becomes jealous and threatened that the more active one is looking better and therefore more attractive to others. Similarly, when couples are imbalanced in their technological tune-in, there can be problems. The less plugged-in or knowledgeable partner may feel behind the times and resentful of the other's more advanced knowledge. Hearing a partner talk of URLs and hyperlinks, losing him to adventures in a MUD (multi-user domain), or watching her click away wildly (when you can barely pick and peck) can be intimidating and alienating. The Web can be a wedge between you if he prides himself on being a Webhead but you feel like a deadhead.

In this age of technology, there's even more for couples to argue about. A common problem emerges when the techie spends too much time or money on machines and gadgets—a natural extension of the traditional complaint that women have had about their husband splurging on high-fi equipment, car accessories, or power tools he doesn't need or use. In modern-day technological incompatibility, it can be either the man or the woman who complains about the others' indulgences in new gizmos (the remote mouse, the professional photo scanner), since surveys show contrary to the past, an increasing number of females are becoming wired. Regardless of which one of you is the techno-titan, if the other is upset over your indulgences, treat this behavior in the same way as you would if she objected to his constant TV watching or if he complained she was a shopaholic. Avoid strife by appreciating the different interests you each have and by making agreements about the time and resources that will be spent by each of you in the virtual world versus the real world.

One partner's electronic savvy can also be a source of attraction to the other. A person who knows how to navigate the Information Superhighway may present a tantalizing catch for someone who is frightened by technology. In fact, as a psychologist I have noticed that "he knows computers" has started to show up on lists of desirable characteristics in a partner in an exercise I always ask men and women to do: Write out the characteristics that describe their perfect match.

This happened to Caitlin. While waiting for her plane connection at the airport, Caitlin was working on her laptop when her program crashed. The young man sitting next to her offered to help. Impressed with his chivalry and his knowledge, Caitlin changed her seat to sit next to him on the cross-country flight. By the end of the trip, they agreed to stay in touch. "I thought I was a modern-day young woman who could take care of herself in every situation," Caitlin told me, "but I have to admit that I felt like something out of a fairy tale where the Knight in Shining Armor rescues the Fair Maiden and they fall madly in love and live happily ever after. When it really comes down to it, Gregg helping me with my computer, taking me shopping for software I needed, and hooking up all my machines captured my heart. I thought 'Wow, I like the fact that a man is really taking care of me.'"

Ask Dr. Judy

"Lara" was constantly nagging her husband "Zack" about the time he was spending on the Net until she realized in her therapy sessions with me that she was feeling insecure in comparison to his cyberskills. "I'm an Internet idiot," she announced to me, "while he is the Internet-intelligentsia." On deeper analysis, Lara revealed how she always felt intellectually inferior. This understanding helped her refocus her energies on boosting her own self-esteem and educating herself so that she felt more computer-literate and secure about her own intelligence in general.

Such electronic rescue fantasies reflect the new "RAM romance." But beware of dangers in such cyberseduction. Make sure you are really attracted to the person and not just to his technological know-how, in the same way you should not be lulled into falling in love with someone simply because that person is a gourmet cook or drives a cool car. Alas, when the computer-challenged partner learns the ways of the Web independently, the digital dazzle fades and the romance can die. Real life requires getting along on many other dimensions—as I describe in Chapter 8, "Are We Compatible?"

Another problem can arise when the more learned partner tries to teach the ways of the Web world to the other. My advice: Be aware of each other's teaching and learning styles. The more technologically savvy partner should not lose patience with the other. Realize, for example, that having the novice sit at the keyboard and learn by trial and error with some guidance may be more effective

Love Lookout

Some women fall prey to feeling they owe sex to a man who helps them do something traditionally "masculine," like fixing the air conditioner, remodeling the kitchen, and now, setting up the computer. While sex with the serviceman can be a healthy fantasy, it should never be an obligation.

than the teacher taking control of the typing on the keys and merely demonstrating. The best way to learn about computers is by doing, figuring things out for yourself at times, and following links to see where they go. There are also many computer classes for beginners. Check your local high school, college, library, or community center.

Cybersex

Many estimates concur that "sex" is the number-one-searched word on the Internet and that the most-visited sites are those with sexual content. This is likely because there are no restrictions on the nature of the material posted because it is so easily accessed and because there are few other comparable outlets for such sexual viewing (consider how much easier is it for a man to log on to a sex site than to visit a strip club and how few places women can go for similar experiences). But is cybersex dangerous?

Dr. Judy's Rx

A wonderful birthday or holiday gift is to get an attachment, upgrade, case, or other related article for a partner's electronic equipment. Or offer your partner an hour of your uninterrupted time to teach some new tricks or find some great Web sites.

An MSNBC online survey of 9,000 users (64 percent of whom were married or in a committed relationship) who visit sexual sites showed that men outnumbered women in visiting sexual sites six to one. Consistent with stereotypes, women favored chat rooms that offer more opportunity for relationships, compared to men's preference for visual erotica. The majority went in search of entertainment rather than sexual release and denied arousal. While most spent fewer than 11 hours per week surfing online sex sites, 8 percent were deemed at risk to become addicted (higher than the 5 percent of people estimated to suffer sexual compulsive behavior).

The computer can crash your sex life if one partner gets so absorbed in sex on the screen that it takes time and attention away from real-life love. By the opposite token, technological toys can become the new sex toys, bringing a new spark or inspiration to your sex life or facilitating sexual interactions that might otherwise not arise.

"*I'd* rather be on his lap than that laptop," Deirdre told me as she sat in my office complaining that sex with William had gone up in smoke since he got his new portable computer and propped it on his lap whether he was sitting on the couch, at the kitchen table, or even in bed. "He's as inseparable from that machine as I want him to be from me!" she complained. I asked Deirdre a challenging question: "What could he be getting from that machine that he is not getting from you?" Deirdre barely hesitated before saying, "The machine doesn't talk back." "What else can you think of?" I asked her. "I suppose there's wilder things going on there than with me," she admitted. With these realizations, Deirdre cut back on her criticisms and ramped up her eroticism so that William would be as captivated by her as by cyberspace.

The case of "Philip" and "Janine" proves how the Internet can become a powerful sex therapy tool. After being married for four years, Philip had withdrawn from sex and was spending more time on the computer. Janine's suspicions that he was having too-personal contacts with strangers were confirmed one night when Philip left his screen up while going in to another room to answer a phone call, revealing an explicit message to a very suggestive screen name ("Hot Lips") in a chat room. Janine used an ingenious (although risky) plan that she had heard about—she set up a new screen name for herself that sounded similar to the one she had spied on Philip's screen, put his screen name into her buddy list, and lured Philip into "chatting" with her about sexy acts that they had never done but that she imagined he would like. One night over a quiet dinner Janine revealed her secret, and luckily, Philip was not angry but amazed that he could be so excited over the Net by the very same woman—Janine—that he was avoiding in real life. He agreed to commit to making their real relationship as compelling as the virtual one they had developed.

Dr. Judy's Rx

Virtual reality sex simulations on CD-ROMs, complete with visual stimuli and headphones for audio effects, are not just voyeuristic but interactive, requiring you to supply missing pieces. These challenge real life sex to be as engaging and erotic.

Years ago I did a TV show on the booming business of couples selling home videos of themselves having sex in their bedroom, bathroom, or backyard. In the new millennium, people already post images of themselves in sexual poses or streaming video of their sex acts filmed through tiny Internet-ready video cameras on their home pages. But rather than publicizing your private sex life, the new visual components can be used to eroticize sex between you, adding a visual element to your fantasy exploration together. The video tech-

Dr. Judy's Rx

Just as with reading a book about sex or watching an erotic video, logging on to a sex site can provide a safe basis for discussion and exploration about sexual thoughts and behaviors.

nology can be especially useful for long-distance relationships. One camera company says 25 percent of PCs will have digital video cameras within the next year, making personal videoconferencing a possible element of your everyday love life.

Cybercheating

It's healthy to enjoy interests with others over the Internet and have fun connecting with strangers all over the world, but such flirtations turn unhealthy for a relationship if they violate the security or covenants of the couple. Perhaps the biggest danger of cybersex to a relationship is the possibility of sharing it with someone else. The increased popularity of computers have spawned a new variety of infidelity—cybercheating. Online flirtations and affairs have become increasingly easy and, therefore, increasingly problematic for couples. All someone has to do is log on to a chat room and end up enjoying typed conversations with a stranger—that can grow into more intimate exchanges or even titillating temptations. All the benefits of the Internet for facilitating love between two partners apply equally to facilitating an extramarital affair: The exchanges online are instant, easy, safer, accessible, and inexpensive! As a result, while the numbers of spouses having affairs has hit astronomical dimensions (up to 80 percent of men and 50 percent of women), these numbers are climbing with the addition of Internet infidels.

But should cybercontact of a sexual nature really be considered cheating? When America Online asked members whether cybersex constitutes cheating, the responses split evenly among the three choices: "Cybersex is definitely cheating," "It depends," and "Cybersex is not cheating." In a *Cosmopolitan* magazine survey, half of the women and 61 percent of the men who responded said cybersex is not cheating. One of the most common rationalizations is that there is no physical contact. Certainly Internet infidelity is a different behavior from real body contact, but the causes, emotional experience, and outcome can be similar. If the intention is there, the interaction explicit, and the energy diverted from the partner, the experience is illicit. Typing sexual messages on the computer can lead to phone sex or whispering in someone's ear in real love talk. Just because it seems more impersonal or distant, doesn't mean it is less valid.

Healthy or Unhealthy?

While it is healthy for people to have friendships outside of their primary relationship, it becomes unhealthy when the online chat gets too hot and interferes with the offline love. It is all too easy to delve into an anonymous person's deepest fears, needs, desires, dreams, and sexual fantasies as an escape from a real-life relationship.

How easy is it to discover the Internet infidel? Compared to true-life trysts, online affairs are easier to hide, as there are no credit card receipts for restaurants that the partner never went to or no telephone call records to strange telephone numbers to raise suspicions. Partners can have locked online accounts that are hard to crack and passwords that make discoveries of private correspondence impossible to happen upon accidentally. But tracing the trail of an Internet infidel is not as difficult as you may think, since people often forget that e-mail is like a written letter, leaving hard evidence. And the techniques of professional hackers are becoming more known to common folk. There are "cookies" and electronic trackings that can tell exactly who's online, where, and with whom. Previous numbers called remain on beepers and cell phone logs. So suspecting lovers with ingenuity can get hard evidence they need to test their worries.

What happens when such cyberaffairs come to light? Just as with a real-life affair, a cuckolded partner's response to the discovery of such terminal titillations could send the relationship right into the recycle bin. If the relationship is going to survive, all the same explanations and rehabilitation as for real-life cheating need to be addressed. These include a redefinition of the relationship, new agreements about fidelity, and time and tests of loyalty in order to reestablish broken trust.

All is not lost, however. Like all affairs, the impact of a cyberaffair can lead to a better relationship with your partner. If you are motivated to share more openly with each other, confront your needs, and work at more intimacy and commitment, you can establish a stronger bond.

With the increase of cybercheating, a new type of separation has emerged, called "cyberdivorce," whereby infidelity over the Internet and through digital devices has led to couples splitting up. The best way to prevent this is to go ahead and have a cyberaffair—with your spouse! Contact your partner in the same way you would a stranger using your electronic devices. Type an e-mail to him that you're waiting at home with a surprise. Beep her and ask her to meet you at a secluded hideaway. Once together, deliberately agree to turn off all machines, signaling the sanctity of your time together.

Love Lookout

Be aware, though, that cyberspying on your partner is just as invasive of his or her privacy as reading a diary. It can have a big impact on the future trust in your relationship.

The Least You Need to Know

➤ Using electronic devices such as e-mail, beepers, and cell phones can increase the time and intimacy you share with your partner—as long as both partners agree on their use.

➤ Practice virtual good manners—Netiquette—as you would in real life, showing respect and not taking others for granted.

➤ If one partner is more technologically savvy than the other, it can either lead to tension or it can be used to create new possibilities for sharing and bonding.

➤ Cybercheating *is* cheating. Never rationalize that you can type out harmless sexual messages online without jeopardizing your real-life relationship.

Chapter 4

Is It True Love?

In This Chapter

➤ The differences between love and lust

➤ Seven truths about love

➤ Six myths about love

➤ Is this the real thing? Tests of true love

➤ Can "love at first sight" last? The Three Golden Rules

➤ The importance of a good first—and lasting—impression

➤ The Love Inventory

➤ Learning how to love

"How do I know I really love her?" "How can I be sure he's the one?" "How do I know love will last this time?" These are questions that I have been asked so often over the years.

I usually answer by asking another question, "What do YOU mean by the word 'love'?"

Love has different meanings for different people, depending on their personalities, needs, experiences, and even their age. You have to know what love is for you before you can begin to know if your partner is "the one." Then, for relationships to work, your concepts of love should coincide, even though they don't always have to be identical.

What Is This Thing Called Love?

Scientists have tried with limited success to define love and many lovers object to demystifying the experience anyway. A U.S. senator once gave out satirical "awards" to researchers who tried to identify love, protesting that people didn't want the mysteries unveiled.

Love Bytes

Not surprisingly, women have been found to manufacture one particular chemical, oxytocin, known as the "cuddle chemical," more than men. This chemical makes you want to attach more to your mate.

Some people mistake lust for love. Lust is really an emotion triggered by changing levels of hormones that become elevated when you feel an initial strong attraction. Whether or not that initial attraction sustains the lust depends on how strong it is, how much it is reciprocated, and many external circumstances. A person can be in lust and feel in love at the same time, but lust can, and does, exist without love.

As our biochemistry makes love possible, it also makes long-lasting love more difficult to achieve. The love high we crave all too often begins to fade over time. That helps explain why so many people start questioning their love at the point where they have worked out their compatibility differences and other issues. Nature seems to have put time limits on our initial lust, while in our hearts and souls we yearn for the thrill that will last forever.

Fortunately, all is not lost. By working at it, lust can be revived, releasing those brain chemicals once again. And it can be built on a strong foundation of love. Creating this powerful combination is the purpose of this book.

Dr. Judy's Rx

What do you say when your partner says "I love you," and you're not sure if you reciprocate the feeling? Say "I care about/am devoted to/value/cherish you, too." Don't be negative or defensive with statements like "I wish you wouldn't say that" or "I'm not sure if I love you back." Words like that stick in a person's mind, damaging their self-esteem, and sabotaging the trust between you from which love between you has any chance to grow.

Seven Love Truths You Can Count On

Whether or not it can be accurately defined, and whether or not people show it, it's safe to say everybody wants to love and be loved. Here are some "facts" about love:

√1. We all want someone who will care about us and about whom we care.

√2. We want to find and hold on to the one special someone who will stand by us, no matter what, and who will appreciate us for who we truly are.

√3. Knowing someone loves you, faults and all, is what allows you to dare to be yourself around that person and others as well.

√4. Knowing you are loved gives you confidence to conquer fears and to reach new heights out in the world.

√5. The desire for love motivates most of our behavior whether or not we are aware of it. In obvious ways, it makes us go out and seek a special partner or do special things for the one we've found.

√6. Most of the pains and problems we experience can be traced to a lack of love.

√7. The love that exists is the love you create; it is always inside you regardless of whether you have a mate.

Is it possible for you and your partner to pass the tests in the chapters ahead, including those that test your compatibility, communication, and commitment, and still not be sure if this is love? Yes, it's possible. Maybe you're waiting for bells to ring or doves to fly, like in the movies. Or maybe you jumped to conclusions too quickly because you're so anxious to be "in love." But by the end of this book, after going through all the qualities that make up a healthy relationship, I guarantee that you will know what love is and will either be enormously delighted that your present relationship fits the bill, fired up to fix your relationship so it conforms more to the ideal, or resolved to find a relationship that does.

Love Myths

Where did you learn about love? Who taught you what love is and what it feels like? How do you know whether you're in love with someone? You've probably heard the phrase, "If you have to ask if it's love, it probably isn't," or "You'll know it when you feel it." Did you get your ideas about what love is from romantic novels, movies, music, and television shows? Did your parents make passing statements, such as, "You'll do that when you fall in love"?

Formal love education is almost nonexistent. Even rudimentary classes in sex education have only recently been part of school curriculum. Most are minimal at best, and many are currently under controversy with the threat of being restricted. In graduate school, working on my Ph.D. in clinical psychology at New York University, I took a unique course in "Human Sexual Love" (and subsequently taught that class). But before that, I never had any formal training in "love" despite my extensive professional preparation as a psychologist.

Lack of knowledge leads to misinformation and myths. I am surprised at how many myths about love persist today. It's almost as if our culture supports myths about love, much like those about Santa Claus and the Easter Bunny.

Some of these love myths are as follows:

➤ **All you need is love.** Or, true love conquers all. According to this myth, the starry-eyed lovers can overcome every problem from different backgrounds and disapproving families to poverty and limited job options. Their love is like Superman's powers; it knocks over every obstacle. The Beatles sang this refrain, and a generation wanted to believe it. The truth is, many couples become discouraged, and overcoming obstacles requires great strength and lots of work.

➤ **Your one true love is the only person who was "meant" for you.** It's not true that no one else could possibly do. Actually, there are probably many partners who could suit you well. This is very helpful to know if you have ever lost a love you cherished.

➤ **If it's true love, you will know immediately and never have doubts.** In this myth, the lovers look across the proverbial crowded room into each other's eyes and move in slow motion toward each other. From that moment on, there is never any doubt of their love. In reality, love can grow even if it didn't overwhelm you at first sight.

➤ **If the sex is good, it must be love.** How could something this powerful be anything less? Actually, it is entirely possible to feel a strong sexual attraction without feeling love.

➤ **Find true love and you will live happily ever after.** The two of you will grow together in perfect harmony and meet each other's changing needs as effortlessly as you now hold hands. The truth is, even the best partnerships have inevitable bumps. I'll explore, and help you resolve, these in the following chapters.

While these myths might sound nice, none of them is true. It takes more than love to conquer problems in today's complicated world. Love helps, but you need to shore up your relationship with many more bonds to survive stresses. There is not only one person for you; you can have other true loves. Even the most excited lovers suffer doubts and rocky times. Love makes sex greater, but if you have great sex, it doesn't guarantee you'll love—or even see—each other again. Life changes demand that you constantly refresh your love and work at it rather than expect it to naturally blossom.

What's Wrong with Love Myths?

It would be cruel to tell toddlers there is no Little Mermaid. Why shouldn't adults have their myths, too?

Because often unconsciously, we base our decisions on love myths. We commit to a partner because the sex is great or the attraction is immediate. As a result, sometimes we ignore warning signals of trouble ahead—often serious trouble like dishonesty, infidelity, addictions, or abuse—because we believe that the strength of our love will make these problems disappear. Or we waste time and energy pining for our "one true love," who loves us far less than we do them because we want the ideal so badly. In other words, we waste our time in dead-end, unhealthy relationships.

Is This the Real Thing? The Five Requirements

So many men and women wonder whether their love is "it"—"the real thing." Consider this woman's question: "I think I'm in love with the man I have been seeing for a long time, but I'm not sure. We have both had bad relationships in the past and problems with drinking and overeating that haunt us. But we've been through lots of crises together, and always seem to manage to stick it out. How can I tell if I really love him and he really loves me?"

Remember the truth is that everyone wants to love and feel loved, although fears and past experiences (of rejection, intimacy, or insecurity) often interfere with expressing or accepting it. Recognizing and sharing those fears is an important step to conquering them. Deprived of love, people fall into many addictions (to food, alcohol, drugs, even exercise, work, and sex) to fill a gaping emotional hole. Once those problems are worked through and you develop more inner security, a solid sense of self and self-love, you can be more sure that your relationship is based on genuine love rather than personal need or dependence.

Since love has so many meanings depending on your experience, needs, and personal definitions, you have to clarify your own definition by describing what it feels like. Refer to the qualities of a healthy relationship in Chapter 1, "What Makes a Relationship Healthy?" Include qualities like caring, good communication, honesty, sacrifice, standing by each other no matter what, being yourself, feeling appreciated, preferring each other's company, and sharing secrets and dreams. Remember, for relationships to work, your concepts of love should coincide, although they don't always have to be identical.

When I counsel couples, I recommend these five requirements of real love:

√ 1. Real love develops from being with a person over time.

√ 2. Real love requires sharing and supporting one another through happy and sad times.

3. Real love requires a combination of using your right brain (emotional feelings about a person) and your left brain (your logic about whether you are right for each other), physical attraction, and an intuitive sense of being right for one another.

4. Real love requires quieting expectations and romantic images of how it will be (either falling hard and fast, or being swept off your feet).

5. Real love requires being tuned in to the person, not wanting to be in love desperately that you simply cast the best partner for the role.

"True Love" Tests

You and your partner should each take the following "tests" that cover the characteristics that I consider essential to a good and lasting love relationship:

➤ **The Thoughtfulness Test.** Do you do special things for each other that show you know and appreciate your mate's interests and characteristics? If she collects refrigerator magnets, he can bring them home from his business trips. If he loves baseball and she doesn't, she can get him tickets to a game or agree to accompany him to some games this season.

➤ **The Unconditional Love Test.** Unconditional love means that you care for each other despite conditions, changes, and events. This is tested by the age-old question, "Would you love me if … (I lost my money, job, looks, health)?" Don't be afraid to ask it.

➤ **The Security Test.** When you're apart, do you trust your partner's care and faithfulness, or do you live in fear and uncertainty? The latter is unhealthy.

➤ **The Mood Barometer Test.** Do you feel good around your mate (peaceful, alive, excited) or pained (worried, threatened, depressed, criticized)? Life has enough emotional stress without suffering from a mate.

➤ **The Honesty Test.** Can you speak openly, or do you have to conceal your thoughts and actions? Telling the truth is key to feeling good about yourself and safe, open, and trusting with each other.

➤ **The Consideration Test.** Does he respond when you make a request that is really important to you even if it seems unreasonable in his view? Sometimes lovers need proof of their devotion in order to maintain trust and to feel they are loved.

➤ **The Compatibility Test.** Do you have similar values about life and attitudes about your lifestyle, including the role and importance of family, friends, children, work, and sex? Couples can have independent interests and time, as long as the overlap is mutually agreeable and satisfying. Find out more about this in Chapter 8, "Are We Compatible?"

➤ **The Communication Test.** Can you share your deepest fears and dreams and feel heard, understood, and appreciated? Talking together is key to a good relationship. Find out more about this in Chapter 10, "Communication—Can We Talk?"

➤ **The Commitment Test.** Do you both have a strong desire to make the relationship last and work out your disagreements, despite the normal stresses and strains that life brings? More about this appears in Chapter 11, "Commitment—Warming Up Cold Feet."

Relationship expert Joseph Campbell has said, "When people get married because they think it's a long-time love affair, they will be divorced very soon because all love affairs end in disappointment. Marriage is the recognition of spiritual identity. By marrying the right person, we construct an image of the incarnate God, and that's what marriage is."

Dr. Judy's Rx

True love endures the inevitable ups and downs of both partners' individual lives and disagreements with each other. It survives the test of time. If you doubt your love, time will give you the answers to all the questions you're asking now.

"Love at First Sight"

Gretchen described it perfectly: "The first time I saw Glen, I just knew he was the one. Our eyes locked. My heart melted." Immediately, like in a fairy tale, Gretchen just "knew" she'd found "the one." It was love at first sight.

Love at first sight is the instant attraction lovers dream about and the American film industry has been promoting since the days of silent movies. Does that magic exist in real life? Can it possibly last?

Dr. Judy's Rx

Take time to let lust at first sight mature into love after sharing time together. Don't dismiss a relationship that doesn't yield instant thrills. Excitement can grow.

Many times this fast and furious attraction fizzles out over time. But for some, it can last. It's important to understand what happens in that "magic moment." What usually attracts men in the first glance is looks, "the appearance quotient." For women, it is more of a "sense" of who the person is, what his "personality" is. This is not to say that true love cannot grow from simple initial visual or intuitive appeal, just as it can between couples who don't have that instant attraction. But for it to last and be truly healthy, it needs to be built on more than a first or fleeting impression or superficial appeal.

Do you think you've fallen in love at first sight? My advice: Close your eyes and listen to the person's heart. Pay attention to what they *do,* not just how they look. Then give yourself time to decide if it's really love.

Also, follow these Three Golden Rules:

The "Love at First Sight" Three Golden Rules

1. Enjoy the initial thrill, but have at least six dates before seriously entertaining the idea that he might be the one.

2. Be cautious for the next three to six months. Use this as an observation period. Observe her character. How does she deal with others (family members, friends, children, co-workers, authority figures, underlings, even pets)? What characteristics does he display (power, control, kindness, thoughtfulness)?

3. Observe your partner in times of stress. Is he caring and responsible? Is she there for you in an emergency? Is he honest when telling the truth may be difficult?

A Good First—and Lasting—Impression

Making a good first impression affects whether someone will pay attention to you to even find out whether there is a possibility for romance. Be prepared, because research shows that we can make judgments about others quickly—in only 15 seconds! It's just as important to realize that these judgments tend to last. Think about your first thoughts about a lover. What do you recall about how you felt and what you thought about him or her? Do you still have similar thoughts?

All too often, when people get into a relationship, they "let themselves go," not getting dressed up or made up like they used to when they first wanted to impress the other person. Research supports that slacking off is not a good idea. A recent Arm and Hammer First Impression Study showed that 84 percent of the 1,023 men and women interviewed felt that it is important to make a good first impression count all of the time, even when doing mundane chores like food shopping or walking the dog. The study supports my advice: Always try to impress your lover, as you would when you first met. Read more about how to keep love alive in Part 3.

Love but Not "in Love"

I often hear the complaint, as Renée said, "I'm deeply in love with a man I've been seeing. Several times in the heat of the moment, he told me that he loved me, but afterward he said he is not 'in love' with me. Even though I was very hurt by this,

I stay with him. Does he really *not* love me? What does he mean? What should I do?"

When people make this distinction between loving and being in love, they usually mean they care about you but are not really committed. Since they imagine someone else would really capture their attention and make them feel "in love" as well as loving, you may be better off finding someone else who would be more devoted to you. Surely this man cares for you, so you don't have to negate the experience entirely, but neither should you embellish it or hold out much hope for a fully satisfying healthy relationship on all five dimensions.

Some men or women will say, or feel, that they are in love at the height of a sexual experience in order to placate the partner or because they are swept away by the passion of the moment. But if, in more rational moments, they protest they are not in love, believe it. Appreciate the honesty as an opportunity for you to make an informed choice about whether to continue in the relationship yourself. Resist having false hopes and resolve that you can have, and deserve, someone who loves you AND is in love with you.

Love Bytes

Can you ever be 100 percent sure you love someone? Some people enjoy a flush of feeling that they have found the "perfect" person. But most people have some doubts, and few partners are "perfect" all the time. Resolve to accept imperfections if you're over 85 percent happy with a relationship.

Healthy or Unhealthy?

Can you be in love and still be attracted to others? A healthy person enjoys life, experiences, and people. Attraction reveals and generates energy. What matters is what you do about the attraction. Enjoy attractions but set limits on how far you let an interest go, particularly regarding sex. Unhealthy attractions come from fears of true intimacy and commitment and lead to obsessive thoughts about others and uncontrollable urges.

It's Time for a Love Inventory

Empathy, trust, honesty, courage, and the ability to share are the key qualities that make love last. If lovers have these traits, their love will deepen into true intimacy.

Recognize these qualities in yourself and in your partner by taking a love inventory:

❑ **Empathy.** Can you say, "I feel what you feel"? Can your partner say this, too? More than understanding each other's deepest feelings, you can feel them. Empathy is a much deeper level of understanding.

❏ **Trust.** Can you say, "I know I can count on you; and you can tell me secrets that I will never betray"? Equally important, can your partner say the same thing about you?

❏ **Honesty.** Can you say, "I know you will tell me the truth about important matters, even if the truth is difficult"? Can your partner trust you to be equally truthful? Honesty also includes sexual fidelity for most of us.

❏ **Courage.** Can you strip defenses, break through stereotypes, confront fears, and explore emotional boundaries together until you really touch each other? That kind of vulnerability is a form of personal courage.

❏ **Sharing.** Are you fully engaged with your partner without losing your separate life? Can your partner say the same thing?

As Philadelphia-based psychic counselor Ruth Green says, think of the word "intimacy" as meaning in-to-me-you-see. In true intimacy, two people express themselves beyond their masks and roles, to share hopes and hurts, dreams and disappointments. They are like two mountain climbers involved simultaneously in a personal as well as a shared adventure.

But beware of "false intimacy"—for example, the man who says "I love you" to seduce a woman, or the female martyr who continually falls in love with the "wrong" man. Both intimacy avoiders and intimacy junkies, described later in this chapter, can look like the real thing in the beginning.

Too Good to Be True?

With so many reasons and experiences leaving you disillusioned with true love, you may be skeptical when it seems to finally be just what you dreamed of.

Allow yourself to trust the possibility of happiness this time around. But to prevent being an unrealistic optimist, follow my Golden Rules for Lasting Love similar to those mentioned earlier for love at first sight.

The Golden Rules of Lasting Healthy Love

1. Insist that your mate's enthusiasm stand the test of time by observing his behavior for at least six months before you come to any major conclusions.

2. Discuss some past patterns so you are alert to any repetitions.

3. Be patient, because rebound relationships require a healing period.

4. Provide a safe place for him to be with you without pressure, and you will maximize your chances of your present attraction and compatibility continuing.

Ask Dr. Judy

Tricia's question to me on my *LovePhones* radio show was a perfect example of question-ing something that seemed too good to be true. "I've been dating a man who just got di-vorced," she explained. "He impressed me when he said he wanted to take things slowly before we had sex. When we finally did, he was so tender and didn't get up to leave like most men, but instead we hugged and talked. The next day he called to say he enjoyed it. He says he thinks of me. It all seems so right, but I worry, will it last?"

Resist the impulse to overgeneralize that all men cannot sustain intimacy and eventually will hurt or disappoint women. Many of us get so conditioned to feeling love doesn't last that we expect the worst. This man's tenderness, thoughtfulness, and follow-through are all positive signs that portend a capacity for closeness and commitment. Be thankful for, and enjoy, a good thing that comes your way.

You likely bought this book because you have a relationship in mind. The relation-ship matters, but you're not totally sure it's right for you. Throughout these chapters, you'll be able to make that assessment. Even at this beginning point, remind yourself of the things you've always liked about your mate—what you were initially attracted to and enjoyed about that person. Write them in the following chart. Keep adding traits as you think of them later, over time.

What I Like About My Mate

(For example, common interests, support for each other, mutual respect)

_____

_____

_____

_____

Turn-Offs

Now, review the things that keep coming to mind as shortcomings. Everyone has them. What turns you off can be as important as what turns you on, because attraction is often a balance of the good versus the bad. List them and see if you can dismiss those things that are unimportant. If so, cross them out. If that characteristic really needs changing, write next to it how it can be changed.

Shortcomings (e.g., She Smokes, He Has to Drink to Loosen Up, Sexual Incompatibility)	How Can It Be Changed?
_____	_____
_____	_____
_____	_____
_____	_____
_____	_____

Review your lists of likes and shortcomings as if they were a balance sheet. Love cannot be reduced to pros and cons—there is always some indescribable feeling or "draw." But it can help to be specific about what works and what doesn't.

Notice how many factors are in each column (of likes and shortcomings), and how important each of those are to your overall happiness. Everybody has some quirks that can be irritating. No one's perfect. The question is, can you live with those quirks? Are there positive factors that outweigh these annoyances?

Intimacy Junkies, Love Junkies, Sex Junkies

As with any other behavior, you can go overboard with love. Actually, "loving too much" ceases being "love" and becomes obsession and possession. Becoming dependent on a relationship destroys the possibility of a healthy exchange. Needing to have someone in order to feel good prevents you from freely allowing each other to grow and be yourselves. In this way, love becomes just as much an addiction as a dependence on drugs or alcohol.

Healthy or Unhealthy?

Any time someone tells me "I love to death," I say "Hold on. Rephrase that." Since research proves that words influence reality, it is unhealthy to imply death within a declaration of love, and healthier to use the word "life" associated with love. To imply your love is long-lasting, say, "I will love him all of my life," or to imply depth, say, "I love her more than anything."

Grace came to see me for therapy because the guy she had been seeing suddenly stopped calling. "I can't sleep or eat, and if he doesn't call me I'm going to die!" she sobbed. Grace is typical of millions of women (and some men) in America who are now called "romance junkies" or "love addicts." Because they have to be in love to be happy, they fall in love too fast, get too absorbed in a mate, and panic if love ends.

I reviewed Grace's relationship history with her so she could clearly see the pattern that leads her to that love roller coaster and her relationships with noncommittal men. She had to learn to be patient with love, testing it over time. Most important, she had to learn to rely on and love herself first.

Love Bytes

Sometimes prescribed antidepressant medications can help lessen extreme emotional swings and decrease obsessive urges in love as in other behaviors.

Learning How to Love

You'd think love would come naturally. It would if we grew up with less dysfunctional and more encouraging, supportive experiences. Fortunately, you can learn to love. It requires being open to caring about another, without fear of rejection or hurt.

For inspiration, here are the words from one of my favorite songs, by my friend, Hawaiian musician Jaiia Earthschild. Called "Learning How to Love," it describes the process of opening your heart. I play this song at some of my speeches to various groups. The words reverberate through my head often, as I'm sure they will through yours. It goes:

"I'm just learning how to love.

I'm new to loving you—can you help me through my shyness and my pain?

If you open up your door I'll step in.

I'm sure there's only love to gain.

If you felt a lack perhaps I held some back
try to understand I'm just learning how to live
learning how to give, learning how to love my fellow man.

If you let me in, then we can begin—to start the miracle of love."

© Jaiia Earthschild
PO Box 292, Paia, Hawaii 96779
www.earthschild.com

Heart and Soul

Imagine finding your true love—that feeling that you are perfect and meant for each other.

Love Bytes

In *Hot Chocolate for the Mystical Lover* (Plume, 2001), writer Arielle Ford recounts 101 inspiring stories of people who found their lifestyle soulmates through divine intervention and real-life miracles. The touching accounts are convincing that voices, visions, and spirits, magic, prayers, and unseen presences can bring new love or revive a lost one.

Experts disagree on how rare soulmates are. My friend, Reverend Roberta Herzog, says there are only several thousand "primary" pairs in the world at any one time. Other experts estimate more are possible, claiming that about 80 percent of people have a statistical chance of finding someone (called a "secondary" soulmate) who may not totally knock you off your feet, or feel like a perfect match, but who can be an extremely satisfying mate for life.

The acknowledgments in my previous book, *The Complete Idiot's Guide to Dating*, include "my soulmate Edward," with whom I feel a connection that goes beyond this life. He loves me regardless of what I do. We know each other at our core. Soulmates sense a divine purpose in knowing each other. They know each other so well, they can trigger each other's hot buttons to get upset or to be happy. They care about each other despite problems, obstacles, or differences that would disturb other people.

Even if these qualities are not immediately evident in a relationship, couples can work toward achieving the unconditional love, understanding, and acceptance that soulmates enjoy. The road to do this lies in the following chapters, in establishing the four C's—cooperation, compatibility, communication, and commitment—for a solid foundation for those four dimensions of a healthy relationship in the new millennium.

The Least You Need to Know

➤ Love goes deeper than lust—lust is that intoxicating feeling of being in love engendered by chemicals produced in our bodies that happens, for example, in lovemaking.

➤ Love myths can make you fall too fast or not at all.

➤ Love at first sight is more likely lust or strong attraction, but it can lead to a lasting relationship. More often, though, lasting love takes time to grow and can develop from humbler beginnings.

➤ Qualities that make love last include empathy, trust, honesty, courage, and the ability to share.

➤ You can, and should, put your love to the test.

➤ Love addiction requires as much recovery as addiction to other substances and things.

➤ You can learn to love.

Chapter 5

So, You're a Couple—but Are You Friends?

In This Chapter

➤ The importance of friendship in lasting love

➤ Can friends become lovers and lovers really be friends?

➤ The Friendship Test

➤ The Madonna-Prostitute and Daddy–Don Juan syndromes

Do you have to be good friends to have a healthy, long-lasting love relationship?

I would say so. You've probably heard it a million times: "You have to be friends first." It might be easier said than done, but above all else, you really have to make an effort to keep up your friendship in order to have a successful love relationship. If your friendship starts to fade as your love relationship develops, you could be in for trouble. Prevent that from happening by continuing to be open with each other. If you were friends before you started dating, remember what your friendship used to be like. Remember how you could share secrets with each other that you couldn't tell other people—that's why you became such intimate friends in the first place. This kind of intimacy needs to continue in your love relationship for it to remain healthy.

Can Lovers Really Be Friends?

Not only can lovers be friends, but lovers *should* be friends. If not, they might share intense passion and physical attraction, but have no friendship to carry them through the rest of their relationship. Above and beyond a sexual partner, you need a friend. A true friend is a confidant, a person who will be there for you in an emergency, to share your experiences, and to play out all the roles that a healthy relationship requires, like being a sounding board, or support system, a workout partner, or travel companion, a buddy through thick and thin.

Sure, romantic love is a wonderful thing. And sexual chemistry is electric. But friendship is the solid foundation that keeps the relationship together, even when romantic love and sexual attraction aren't at their peaks (and they won't always be). Friendship is what will pull you through, not only when your sex drive is on hiatus, but also when your baby is bawling all night, when your in-laws come to visit for a month, or when your company is downsizing and you're afraid of losing your job. At these times, you realize the value of a friend. True friendship is crucial if love is going to last.

Can Friends Really Become Lovers?

Before I get into further explaining the role of friendship in love, let me address all of you who are in those hazy beginning stages—when you feel that you want more from a good friend but are hesitant to pursue it.

Dr. Judy's Rx

Put your friend in the mood for this discussion. Rent the movie *When Harry Met Sally*—about two friends who become lovers and eventually marry—and watch it together.

Can friends really become lovers? That's a question I've been asked often. And the answer is yes, you can, because friendship is the best basis for love. On the other hand, there's definitely some risk involved in trying to turn a friend into a lover; changing the (sexual) status quo will put the friendship in jeopardy. What if you have sex and end up regretting it? What if there's just no chemistry between you in bed? What if one of you enjoys it while the other wishes it never happened? Or what if one of you wants recreational sex to be part of the friendship, while the other wants the sex to be exclusive, romantic, and eventually lead to commitment?

If you're one of the many people who are thinking about taking that leap from friendship to a lover relationship, you're also probably facing a big dilemma: Will we just be signing the death certificate of a perfectly good friendship if we try turning it into a romance? A concern I hear all the time is, "We've been such good friends. I'm scared that if we become lovers, it'll ruin our friendship."

The solution: Change your thinking. Instead of worrying that your friendship might be ruined, think, "Our friendship has a chance to be deeper and richer."

But, no matter which way you look at it, admitting that you want something more leaves you open to rejection—your friend could decide not to reciprocate your feelings. Only **you** can decide if the potential rewards are worth the risk to your ego or even to the friendship (that is, if the love relationship doesn't work out). As a believer in the adage, "Nothing ventured, nothing gained," I recommend broaching the subject.

Here are some tips on ways to get a discussion going to turn friendship into love:

➤ **Test the waters.** Start off with the old "trick" beginning, "I have a friend who ..." and talk about someone you know who turned a good friendship into a love relationship. Ask your friend what he thinks of that, so you can clue into his attitudes about those types of relationships.

➤ **Use the media.** If you don't know anyone who has taken this leap, discuss something similar that you read, heard about, or saw on TV.

➤ **Be direct.** This is the way to go when you've tried the above without success and you're still really unsure about your friend's feelings, and the uncertainty is wasting time and driving you crazy. Start by being subtle. Say something like, "I really love spending time with you," or "We should hang out more often," and see what the reaction is. Then, you can get even more direct and say something in a light-hearted way, like, "I'm always complaining to you about others, when you're really the perfect one for me!" or, "Have you ever thought of us like that?" Finally, get more direct. After all, you are friends and, presumably, friends can speak openly with each other.

Do these suggestions sound scary to you? If so, let me remind you that you've got to face your fears. What's the worst that can happen? You get rejected. Decide that you can deal with that rejection. Or, if you know that you wouldn't be able to handle the pangs of unrequited love, and aren't willing to take that risk, don't waste your energy wishing or hoping. Move on. Keep the friendship close, but not intimate.

Hopefully, if all goes well, your friend will be as open to the idea of a love relationship as you are. Once you've got that much figured out, you can discuss your thoughts on adding a sexual component to your relationship:

➤ **Share your mutual expectations of sex.** Be sure you both understand what each person wants from a sexual relationship. If one of you is thinking "love" and the other just "sex," there will be trouble ahead.

➤ **Explore the ramifications of lovemaking.** How will your friendship be affected by becoming lovers? Will one of you become more attached than the other? Will hurt feelings and unrealized expectations make returning to a platonic friendship more difficult for one of you?

In other words, it's not enough just to say, "Let's do it!" and rush blindly into bed. You should really have a frank discussion about what you both feel about and expect from a friendly-turned-romantic relationship. After all, you'll more likely maintain a healthy relationship in the future if it starts out that way from the very beginning.

63

How Good a Friend Is Your Lover?

Lovers can and should be friends. But how do you know if your lover really is a good friend to you?

Start by reviewing your best friends in life, male or female. How would you describe them? What adjectives come to mind? You're probably thinking some combination of the following qualities: open, honest, supportive, caring, compassionate, close, loyal, makes me feel like I'm part of a family, wants the best for me, likes to do fun things and spend time with me, stands up for me. Does your lover measure up as your friend?

Also think about the most important life experiences that you've encountered, and the friends you shared those experiences with. Would you share those experiences with your lover? There are loads of questions you can ask yourself to get a better sense of what kind of friend your lover is; start with the questions I list in the following "The Test of Friendship."

The Ten True Tests of Friendship

My bottom-line message is: You should impose the same standards of friendship on your lover as you do on your friends. I'm always surprised when people accept behavior from lovers that they'd find intolerable in friends. Too many times I've heard women complain, "He's always late, he never calls, and he never pays attention when I talk … but I love him anyway." And I always ask, "Why?"

Dr. Judy's Rx

Men and women who can maintain friendships with people of the opposite sex are often better candidates for healthy love relationships since the ability to trust someone of the opposite sex is essential for cultivating lasting love. A man who has never had a platonic relationship with a woman may have a hard time relating to women emotionally or allowing themselves to get close, and may even see women only as sex objects. But beware: A man who has many female friends but who never made a love commitment may not be able to see women as a friend *and* lover. The same is true for women with many male buddies.

Would you bother maintaining a friendship with someone if she were always late if he never called or hardly listened when you talked? Doubtful. So why should you put up with a lover like that? If anything, you should be *more demanding* of your lover, and insist that he live up to all those qualities I described earlier.

So how good a friend is your lover? To figure it out, ask yourself the following questions:

The Test of Friendship

1. Is my lover reliable (does she do what she says, does he keep promises)?

2. Is my lover "true"—is he there for me in good times and bad?

3. Do my lover and I share both laughter and tears?

4. Is my lover honest with me?

5. Does my lover treat me with courtesy and respect when we're not making love?

6. Does my lover listen when I talk?

7. Does my lover give weight to my opinions, whether we share them or not?

8. Does my lover help me out when I need it, when it really counts?

9. Does my lover accept me for who I am, faults and all?

10. Do I see my love relationship lasting forever, as my friendships might?

Clearly, your answers to almost all these questions should be yes. You certainly wouldn't expect any less from a friendship. As I mentioned earlier, if anything, you should be a little more lenient with your friends than with your lover. Think about it this way: You invest more time, energy, and emotion in a love relationship than you do in a friendship. If this love is going to last, the stakes will be higher—you need to raise the bar on your expectations.

How Friendship Changes as Love Grows

Whether you started as friends, or as lovers who became friends, the friendship can change as the love relationship does. Hopefully the friendship will grow as you share more experiences and endure more crises together and learn to enjoy, trust, and lean on each other.

Unfortunately, the opposite can also happen. The longer people stay together, the more their friendship might continue to fade. The couple might start becoming closer to their other friends, sharing their deepest feelings with them instead of with their mate. Often, this happens because people fear they'll lose their loved one if they let their real feelings out. How ironic! The best solution to this is to keep monitoring yourself; make a continual effort to be honest and open with your mate and keep your relationship close. If you find yourself always turning to your friends instead of your lover for support, you should stop and reassess where your love relationship is going. In fact, that might be the perfect time to get close to your mate again by having a heart-to-heart about your concerns.

Healthy or Unhealthy?

Should your mate be your best friend? In short, the answer is yes. You can certainly have other close and "best" friends, but in a healthy relationship, your mate should ideally be the one you feel the closest to, the person you can turn to the most. The biggest danger in becoming better friends in a love relationship is that the sex fires die, and you become more like siblings or buddies than the exotic lovers you were when you first met. Read Chapter 17, "Keeping the Sex Fires Burning," for ways to prevent this.

Ask yourself this: If your lover is your best friend, can you also continue to see him as sexy?

Yes. But you might have to work at it. If you find that you're becoming *too* good friends with your lover—so friendly that you stop having sex—try using the following tactics to end that trend:

➤ Acknowledge to yourself that you are withdrawing from the erotic side of your relationship. Catch yourself when you are resisting and purposefully do something erotic or sexual.

➤ Get in touch with some of the deeper dynamics and fears causing your resistance to sex, such as fear of intimacy or commitment.

➤ Purposefully work at being more romantic with each other (follow the suggestions in Chapter 12, "Making the Honeymoon Last").

➤ Use fantasy. My favorite technique for continuing to feel sexy toward your lover when you have become "just friends" is to purposefully insert him into your sexual fantasies (see Chapter 14, "The Art of Seduction").

➤ Be nostalgic and remember all the reasons why you fell in love in the first place.

➤ Act "as if." Act toward your "best friend" lover as you would toward the most exciting lover you can imagine. This will augment your own excitement, making it more likely you *will* get turned on to your mate, and will also give him or her the chance to act in that sexy way you prefer.

Some couples tell me that they've known each other so long and so well that they're just bored with the same old sex with the same person over and over. Or they simply become incapable of finding their mate interesting or appealing anymore, no matter how many romantic situations they put together or how many fantasies they have about their mate. The fact is, if you really work at it, these techniques will work. If you don't, it may be time to part ways.

When It's Either/Or

In certain situations, it's not the friendship that kills the sex, but your black-and-white view of men or women that prevents you from ever mixing the two to begin with. This can happen to men or to women. The most common examples of this are described in the following syndromes.

The Madonna-Prostitute Syndrome

In this syndrome, men "split" women into two types: the "nice girl" or Madonna type (as in the Virgin Mother, not the Material Girl) and the wild, erotic "prostitute" type. Men who do this put women into one category or the other, never both; the Madonna types are sweet, pure, and untouchable, while the prostitute types become the object of the man's sexual desires.

The only way a man can resolve this split is to force himself consciously to allow his sweet woman to also be sexy. As described above, he has to plug her into his wildest sexual fantasies, and allow himself to act some of them out with her. By treating her like a desirable, erotic lover, he will also encourage her to see herself that way and to act accordingly.

The Daddy–Don Juan Syndrome

I was the first psychologist in the media to point out how some women suffer a syndrome equivalent to the Madonna-Prostitute syndrome in men; it's called the Daddy–Don Juan syndrome. Like men with the Madonna-Prostitute syndrome, these women separate sex and love and "split" men into two types: the "nice guy" or Daddy figure, who they treat as a friend and not a lover, and the Don Juan type who wines, dines, and then drops them but whom they wildly desire.

To get over the Daddy–Don Juan syndrome, the woman has to stop living *through* a man to find excitement and create that excitement herself. Reexamine and consider changing what you consider important qualities in a love partner. That means, stop thinking *exciting, dangerous,* and *hard-to-get;* start thinking *reliable, loving,* and *supportive.* Face and overcome any unconscious conflicts like fears of intimacy and commitment. Turn your "nice guy" into a sexually desirable and satisfying man by imagining him in your most erotic fantasies. Remember, when you treat him as you would the most exciting lover, you give him a chance to be that way!

To learn more about these unconscious or deeper fears of intimacy and commitment and how to recognize and deal with them, check out Chapter 11, "Commitment—Warming Up Cold Feet."

Ask Dr. Judy

I was asked the following question by Ann, who has a typical case of the Daddy–Don Juan syndrome: "My boyfriend and I have been together for four years. We never really have great sex, but he's very sweet and funny. I can see he'd be a good father and it would be nice to grow old with him. But lately I haven't been able to stop thinking about all my past lovers, who were much more exciting. One guy in particular was so hot that he made all my friends jealous of me. I can't stop thinking about him even though he always did things that made me cry. What do I do?"

The problem in Ann's case, and in most other Daddy–Don Juan situations, is that she just isn't mature enough yet for a lasting relationship. Younger women often go for the Don Juan type; they're attracted to a man in superficial ways, concentrating on his physical appearance, his car, or how much he stirs up their girlfriends' envy. Deep down, these women are insecure, and in order to prove that they are worthy or desirable, they become addicted to the challenge of making that bad-boy type want them. As they mature, though, they learn that the short-lived adrenaline high of being with a hot but unreliable or insensitive man just isn't as special as the lasting intimacy and stable love that the "nice guy" offers.

Hopefully, as women grow up, they learn the same lesson that Sally Albright (played by Meg Ryan) does in the movie *When Harry Met Sally*. After years of dating noncommittal hunks and an assortment of other losers, she finally realizes that the perfect man for her has been right under her nose for years—her best pal Harry (played by Billy Crystal). He's less handsome and exciting, but he was the one who listened to her, comforted her, and stuck by her over the years, and proved time and time again how much he really cared for her.

While researching my book *How to Love a Nice Guy,* I encountered innumerable real-life "Sallys," women who would dismiss the "nice guy" as not being their type, but would then fall deeply in love with him (sometimes within weeks), as he continued to care about them and make them laugh. Remember that choosing the nice guy doesn't mean that you're settling for less; rather, you're expecting to be treated well, and that means you have higher self-esteem.

The Least You Need to Know

➤ Friendship is a critical and necessary element of a lasting love relationship.

➤ Expect your lover to be as good—if not better—a friend to you as your other friends; your lover should be honest, dependable, and respectful.

➤ Turning a platonic friendship into love is tricky, but possible. Consider the risk worth the potential reward.

➤ Be careful not to become such good friends that you forget to also be lovers.

Chapter 6

The Importance of Matching Your Love Styles

In This Chapter

➤ A quiz to determine your love style and your partner's

➤ The four love styles and their characteristics

➤ Why being an extreme love "giver" is just as bad as being an extreme love "taker"

➤ Resolving love style conflicts

Hopefully your relationship is clicking and your gears seem to smoothly fit. But maybe something's gone wrong with the romantic part of your relationship and you're not sure what it is. You've been trying. The romantic dinners and seductive gestures aren't working. Your mate doesn't even notice when you flirt. Lately, nothing seems right in the romance department.

Don't rush to conclude that it's all over. At this point in the relationship, too many couples reach a silent compromise. They evaluate their mate's good qualities. With a wistful sigh, they decide to give up on romantic fantasies and keep this reliable, trustworthy, kind, and considerate partner in their lives.

Is that a choice you have to make? No. You can have the romance and the rest of it, too. Often the romance stops working because two people fail to recognize and respond to the differences in their love styles.

"How Do I Love Thee? Let Me Count the Ways ..."

Those lines are the beginning of a poem by Elizabeth Barrett Browning. I remember my mother always recited them when I was growing up. It suggests appreciating a lover's qualities. For me, it also suggests that everyone loves in his or her own way.

How you think and behave in romance and seduction is an extension of how you think and behave in other areas of life. The key to making romance and seduction work is understanding and adapting to your mate's style. A man brings the traditional roses home to his lover who is not the traditional type and is surprised when the expensive blooms elicit little more than a polite response. A woman buys black lace lingerie to seduce her husband and is hurt and disappointed when he pays little attention—without realizing that it's not his "thing." In both cases, the partner who was trying "to put a little romance" back into the relationship feels discouraged and rejected.

But what looks like indifference, even rejection, is often nothing more than different preferences for what is romantic or seductive. Even though they are potent cultural symbols of romance and seduction, not all women melt over a dozen long-stemmed red roses, just as not all men are aroused by black lace lingerie. In the beginning of the relationship, these effects may have worked because they are universal signals everyone expects to be associated with seduction. And in the beginning, you aren't expected to know a partner well enough to get the details right. As you can see, using the stereotypical symbols may have the desired effect, or may leave both people feeling misunderstood and disappointed.

"Why doesn't my lover know what I want?" you may ask yourself. "After all this time, why doesn't he/she know ... I don't care that much about roses/I would rather see her in white cotton undies than black lace/I prefer sardines on crackers to caviar on toast points?"

Pay attention to who your partner really is. The romantic gestures and seductive moves may not be working because you aren't taking the time to personalize them to his or her love style. When these things don't work, most people withdraw and wait to be approached. If your mate is feeling as unappreciated as you are, it could be a long wait. The following quiz will help you get back on track by identifying your styles. It's based on research on brain styles developed over 30 years by the Ned Herrmann Group in Lake Lure, North Carolina, and adapted by my work, also over many years.

What's Your Love Style?

Take the following quiz yourself and ask your mate to answer it as well. Even if you think several answers apply, choose the one that applies to you most of the time.

A Love Style Quiz

❏ My most romantic qualities are ...

    a. Ability to engage my partner intellectually.

    b. Efficiency in organizing a special dinner or weekend getaway.

    c. Sensitivity and ability to express my love and admiration for my mate.

    d. Spontaneity and creativity in the way I show my love.

❏ If I fulfilled my idea of setting up the perfect seduction, I would ...

    a. Get tickets to a sold-out dramatic play and analyze it over dinner.

    b. Re-create a time when things worked out perfectly.

    c. Pull out all the romantic stops: flowers, candles, wine, soft music.

    d. Plan a fantasy and put together the props, including costumes.

❏ I would love it if my partner ...

    a. Signed up for a class on art appreciation with me.

    b. Arranged to have all our closets organized.

    c. Hid a love letter in my overnight bag when I am going out of town on business.

    d. Called me one afternoon and said, "Let's meet at a hotel now."

❏ When my partner and I have an argument, I ...

    a. Try to look for ways we can both change.

    b. Need to get out my feelings and talk about problems until they're re-solved.

    c. Would rather put it behind us and avoid the conflict.

    d. Think about what really happened to cause it.

❏ The cost of romantic evenings should be ...

    a. Varied, according to how the relationship is going.

    b. Within the budget, no matter what.

    c. Whatever you can afford to spend to create the right mood.

    d. Inconsequential—sometimes you don't need to spend anything at all and sometimes you want to be extravagant.

❑ I respond to my partner's failure to be romantic or seductive by …

    a. Deciding whether the reaction is reasonable; if so, I accept it; if not, I confront the problem.

    b. Going about "business as usual" to keep things going smoothly, until change happens.

    c. Crying and feeling sorry for myself.

    d. Coming up with something irresistible, like a nude picnic in bed.

❑ My idea of a perfect seduction scenario would be …

    a. Entirely dependent on the circumstances. (Are we at home or on vacation? What is the season? What is the status of the relationship?)

    b. A scene from an old black-and-white film in which we are both elegantly dressed, dancing to Gershwin, and recalling wonderful times.

    c. A scene from a romance novel, where our eyes meet and we melt into each other's arms.

    d. Having my partner blindfold me and lead me through an evening of sensual surprises like exotic foods and new lovemaking techniques.

❑ I sometimes think I could have a better relationship if …

    a. I were less controlling or opinionated.

    b. I weren't so stubborn.

    c. My feelings weren't so easily hurt.

    d. I didn't need so many new experiences and stimulation.

❑ On a vacation, I would like to …

    a. Take a study tour to Russia or Rhodesia.

    b. Revisit a favorite place or tour a historical site like Gettysburg.

    c. Stay at a romantic hideaway like Mt. Airy Lodge.

    d. Go on an exciting adventure like hiking in the Himalayas.

❑ When it comes to lovemaking, I'm most comfortable when …

    a. Everything is under control.

    b. Things go as well as they have in the past.

    c. We feel like the only two people in the world.

    d. It is playful and different.

To calculate your score, record the number of answers for each letter you selected:

	My Answers	My Mate's Answers
a.	_____	_____
b.	_____	_____
c.	_____	_____
d.	_____	_____

In the next section, we'll look at the four love styles that this quiz covered and what your score says about you and your mate.

The Four Love Styles

If you (or your mate) had mostly **d** answers, you are a Creative Lover; mostly **c** answers, an Emotional Lover; mostly **b** answers, a Conservative Lover; and mostly **a** answers, an Intellectual Lover.

Healthy or Unhealthy?

What if you and your partner answered most of the questions differently? Don't be concerned—it's unlikely that both of you will have answered every question with the same lettered response. Because most of us are a mixture of personality types, most people also have a mixture of love styles. But you will likely have one that stands out. That's your predominant love style. It refers to how you prefer to behave, not necessarily the way you do behave under all circumstances.

In general, men tend to be Conservative or Intellectual Lovers (both left-brained tendencies) and women tend to be Creative or Emotional Lovers (right-brained). This fact has been corroborated by extensive analyses of computer tests of brain dominance in thousands of men and women conducted by world-renowned Herrmann International, a consulting and training group at www.hbdi.com. But keep in mind that not all men and not all women fit these patterns.

Easily bored and often impatient, *Creative Lovers* are free-spirited, intuitive, impulsive, imaginative, and fun-loving people who appreciate beauty and fantasy a little more than the average person does. They thrive on exploring, taking risks, and projecting into the future. Not at their best with details, they see the whole rather than the parts.

Visually oriented, Creative Lovers often express themselves through drawing, designing, or, on a personal level, dressing imaginatively. They love excitement and innovation. You can reach them romantically or seductively by planning a fun, even

Dr. Judy's Rx

Has your Creative Lover been remote lately? Be unpredictable. Laugh a lot. Whisper what you plan to do in her ear before you do it. Come up with new activities to share. But also give him space and don't try to rein him in with details, specifics, or demands.

Dr. Judy's Rx

Has your Emotional Lover been disinterested in loving? Talk things over. Ask, "How does that make you feel?" and start sentences with "I feel …." Listen attentively while you hold her. Offer a lot of reassurance without conveying the notion that you are judging her feelings or condemning her for being "oversensitive" or "needy."

outlandish, experience or buying an unusual and intriguing gift. Cost is not nearly as important as imagination.

Emotional Lovers are expressive, spiritual, and humanistic. They thrive on relationships, communication, and touching. These people focus on how they feel about what is happening, not so much on what is actually happening. That is why they respond to classic romantic gestures as fully as they do. Whether roses are her favorite flower or the dinner she's carefully prepared is really his favorite meal matters less than the feelings these romantic and seductive gestures elicit.

Emotional Lovers value sharing and sensual experiences. If you want to make the relationship closer, use "we" a lot, talk a great deal, and participate actively in the joint decisions such as selecting a sofa. To appeal to an Emotional Lover's sensuality, choose gifts that trigger the senses.

Conservative Lovers are most comfortable with what they know or have done in the past. They like tradition—in romance and seduction as well as in clothing, furnishings, and careers. Practical and economical, they value planning, punctuality, and reliability. Introduce creative loveplay or fantasy carefully and gradually. Detail-oriented (sometimes in the extreme), Conservative Lovers thrive on being safe and going by the book. They have excellent memories and are fiercely loyal, so they will notice if you change your way of doing the smallest things.

Intellectual Lovers are analytical, rational, and logical. They are reasonable people who are good at winning arguments and solving problems. They love intellectual challenges—puzzles, chess, even figuring out the directions for the new VCR.

Intellectual Lovers value good judgment, so ask for their opinion often. If you disagree, don't spill your feelings randomly. Discuss differences rationally. Ask, "What do you think?" rather than "How do you feel?" When you think they're right, let them know it. Allow them a lot of time to think things through, particularly if you have reached a relationship impasse. Instead of talking about "the relationship," talk about current events, politics, art, and culture.

Resolving Love Style Conflicts

Keep in mind that any combination of love styles can work—if you work at it. While similar styles usually find it easier to get along at first, they can seek the stimulation of someone different. For example, two Emotional Lovers may revel in sharing feelings, but then one may feel overwhelmed and seek the practicality of an Intellectual Lover. And clearly, opposites can attract but then clash. For example, a Creative Lover who is spontaneous may be attracted at first to a Conservative Lover, but quickly become bored by his caution and wariness.

If you and your lover have different love styles, recognize that the differences help you complement each other, as well as cause occasional frustrations. Your partner is not deliberately trying to frustrate you. When you learn to be more in tune with each other's love styles, you'll find accommodating the other becomes easier. Suddenly it's not a power struggle anymore.

Take these steps to try to reconcile your differences when it comes to romance and love:

➤ **Identify the differences.** Then accept them without judging. Focus on what you can learn from each other as well as about each other. Maybe the Conservative Lover can learn to be a little more spontaneous, while the Emotional Lover can benefit from becoming a little less sensitive.

➤ **"Speak" in your partner's style.** A romantic or seductive gesture means so much more when it's "spoken" or delivered in the lover's language. For example, an Intellectual Lover would make an effort to please his Emotional Lover by taking her to a romantic movie instead of insisting on an action adventure that he would normally prefer.

➤ **Trace the history of your love styles.** What were the influences on your style? Family, media, socioeconomic factors, and cultural influences all affect our love styles to some extent. Sometimes these influences cause us to adapt styles that are not what we would

Dr. Judy's Rx

Has your Conservative Lover stopped responding to your romantic overtures? Make explicit plans together. Don't spring romantic surprises on him. Don't be vague, unpredictable, or spontaneous. Once you've made the plans, be punctual and follow through to the last detail.

Dr. Judy's Rx

Has your Intellectual Lover cooled to your touch? Don't be overly demonstrative of your feelings. Forget about public displays of affection. Don't complain that he doesn't give, share, or talk enough. Instead, pose intelligent questions requiring deep thought.

truly prefer if we could choose freely. Imagine what you would be if you were free to choose without these influences. Are you the lover you want to be?

➤ **Ask questions about your partner's preferences.** Avoid misunderstandings by getting things clear. It's okay to ask your mate to describe his or her idea of a perfect romantic evening or seduction scenario. You don't have to be a mind reader.

➤ **Share your preferences.** Don't wait to be asked. Make it easy on your mate by telling him or her what you consider romantic or seductive.

➤ **Compromise.** Sometimes you do things her way, sometimes his. And sometimes you can take elements from each other's love style and create a passion collage.

Love Lookout

I caution against analyzing a person's love style on the basis of their business behavior. Some men and women act one way in intimate relationships and another way at the office. This is especially true of working women today. Some women are logical, analytical, and controlled at work, but are very emotional when it comes to love and want to be "swept away."

Are You a Giver or a Taker?

The balance of give and take in your relationship is critical to your happiness. Being an extreme love "giver" can present just as much of a problem as being an extreme love "taker." Human relationships are not mathematical equations; in any relationship, one partner is more often the giver than the taker. But in relationships where a serious imbalance exists, there will be trouble eventually. The giver will become resentful, angry, and frustrated. Surprisingly, so will the taker, whose resentment, anger, and frustration of the supposedly "good" and martyred giver will likely be hidden.

In our society, women have been encouraged more often to be love givers than takers. Women who look out for their own interests are considered selfish and at worst even labeled nastily as "bitchy," while men who look out for their own interests are admired. These stereotypes are unfortunate. Really, there is healthy "taking" and unhealthy "giving" for both genders.

Often, giving comes with strings attached. Yes, women give in love, but in return many expect to be supported financially and indulged emotionally. Yes, men have been raised to give financially, but often they think that controlling the money entitles them to control the relationship. In a good relationship, the balance between giver and taker is a fair one, at least most of the time.

✓*If You Give Too Much*

Achieving a balance between giving and taking can require work and concentrating on behaviors that don't immediately come naturally. But learning to receive when you give too much is worth the effort. If you find yourself giving more than you receive, try the following suggestions:

➤ Learn to become more selfish. Think about what you want to do instead of what you need to do to please your partner. Put your needs first sometimes.

➤ Start saying "no" to small things. If you ordinarily answer "yes" to your partner's requests for favors or restaurant picks, start objecting once in a while. If you don't have time to pick up his cleaning or really don't want to eat at the restaurant of her choice, risk declining.

➤ Realize that part of giving is taking. By letting your mate give to you sometimes, you are letting him or her have the pleasure of satisfying you.

➤ Don't label "giving" as being "good" while "taking" is "bad."

✓*If You Take Too Much*

Resisting the impulse to take also requires effort, but it's worth it in the long run. If you find yourself taking more than you give, try the following suggestions:

➤ Recognize how much taking makes you feel guilty. Most takers secretly know they are taking advantage and feel guilty about it. Guilt does not inspire romantic behavior.

➤ Say "no" to one small thing a day that is offered to you. You don't have to accept everything the giver wants to give you.

➤ Assume responsibility for your part of the relationship. Start giving your share. Keep a mental tally sheet for the time being, so that for every time your partner gives to you, you give something in return.

➤ Don't fear that if you don't take, you'll end up deprived.

Correcting an imbalance will be difficult initially. You and your partner have found a pattern that is comfortable. Changing it inevitably causes some discomfort. But you will both be rewarded by the effort.

The Least You Need to Know

➤ Pay attention to who your partner really is. Target your words and gestures to your partner's love style.

➤ There are four basic love styles: creative, emotional, conservative, and intellectual. No one style is inherently superior to another. In general, men are more often conservative or intellectual in their style and women are more often emotional or creative. Most of us blend some elements of another style into our predominant one.

➤ Being an extreme giver in love can create just as much of a problem as being an extreme taker. In the best relationships, the balance between giving and taking is fair most of the time.

➤ You can resolve love style conflicts. The differences in your styles help you complement each other and lend balance to your personal lives as well as your relationship.

Part 2

The Secrets of a Healthy and Lasting Relationship

The wish for lasting love is a wish shared by the overwhelming majority of people who enter into relationships. Of course you want it to work. Despite the reality of high divorce rates, hope springs eternal. The fantasy of growing old together is still strong, with many couples hoping to be able to see past the lines and wrinkles to the soul of their beloved inside.

In this part, we'll examine in depth the important qualities that make love last. In Chapter 7 you'll learn how having a healthy self first will lead to a healthier relationship, and in Chapters 8 to 10 you can test whether you have the four C's necessary for a healthy relationship: compatibility, cooperation, communication, and commitment.

A Healthy Self First

In This Chapter

➤ The importance of self-love

➤ Taking care of your body and mind

➤ Writing your love script to ensure love

➤ Facing your fears

In order to have a healthy relationship, you need two healthy individuals. That means each of you has to be healthy on your own. Ideally, you should be healthy on all eight dimensions: physical, mental, emotional, familial, financial, sexual, spiritual, and technological.

I'm sure you've heard the phrase, you have to love yourself before you love anyone else. So true. Learn how to love yourself first before you worry about whether your relationship will work.

Building Up Your Confidence

Studies show that over eight out of ten people despise something about their bodies. Even actor Kim Bassinger and Aerosmith rock star Steven Tyler repeatedly hated their "big" lips, now considered by many as the ultimate sign of sensuality. And Cindy Crawford hated her mole that later became her signature of beauty. That includes even the sexiest stars and most envied models. Feeling good and confident about your body is fundamental to self-esteem. It breaks my heart to hear so much distress about appearance. In a survey of over three thousand listeners to my *LovePhones* radio show, nearly one in five had a question or complaint about their body, from their toes to their hair to their sexual parts.

Confidence in yourself is equally important. Look at yourself in the mirror and appreciate the parts of your body. Focus on the positives instead of dwelling on the negatives. Positive self-talk will help you build self-confidence. Monitor what you tell yourself in your mind. Make sure it's encouraging and positive, rather than critical or negative. Be as encouraging to yourself as you would a child. Confidence also comes from setting goals and achieving them. Be aware of even the smallest things you want to accomplish, like cleaning the garage, rearranging your furniture, or preparing a report. Take delight in completing discrete tasks.

Are You Fit for Love?

Dieting is a billion-dollar industry in America. You've probably been unhappy with your weight at some point in your life. Unfortunately, this unhappiness is often the source of many failed relationships.

Dr. Judy's Rx

There are simple things you can do to include more exercise in even the busiest life. Take the stairs instead of taking the elevator. Do side leg lifts while you're washing dishes. Move your arms while you're watching TV.

A healthy body is necessary for a healthy mind and a healthy relationship. Find an exercise routine that fits into your enjoyment and lifestyle. Being tired or feeling out of shape deflates your self-esteem and your mood. Remember, when you feel physically unattractive, you don't feel good about love.

My cosmic sister, health guru High Voltage, presents an excellent program for total health in her book, *Energy Up!* (Putnam, 1998). In the book she talks about devoting an hour every day to fitness, including mental health (loving yourself), and making healthy food choices. Voltage is passionate about her three "no nos": no sugar, no salt, no flour.

Don't just focus on dieting. Instead, make a life change and a commitment to eating healthier. A new eating plan should focus on what you can eat rather than what you *can't*. Also follow this rule: Never call yourself "bad" for "cheating."

Time for an Attitude Adjustment

Just as you clean your house, clean your brain of any self-criticisms and thoughts that are negative or that cycle what I call "bad energy." You'll notice these make you furrow your brow and grimace. If you have to consider negative things to solve a problem, that's fine. But don't dwell on or brood over such negativity. Always balance it with a higher proportion of positive thoughts.

If you need inspiration for positive thoughts, just look out the window at the sky, trees, buildings, or other people. Replace emotional thoughts with observations (about colors, shapes, and sizes). Keep inspirational books and audiotapes around. I like all of Robert Schuller's books, and also like Dr. Emmett Miller's audiotapes put out by Source Learning Systems in Stanford, California.

To help you achieve a more positive outlook, find a supportive environment. Surround yourself with pleasurable people and things. Make your home into your nest, where you feel comfortable. End relationships that bring you down. Spend time with people who make you feel good, and who feel good about themselves.

In addition, maintain a positive lifestyle. Strive for a balance in your life between your responsibilities and your pleasures. Make time for doing what you enjoy. Strive for the ideal: enjoying your work as well as your play.

Love Lookout

Don't fall prey to the "beauty myth" that you have to look like some media ideal—as thin as model Kate Moss or as studly as actor Brad Pitt, for example.

Your Love Script

Love scripts are like movies in our head of the way we think, desire, or fear—how our personal love story goes. Whatever we expect to happen is more likely to happen. The more you are aware of your love script, the more you can change how it plays out in real life.

Dr. Judy's Rx

End bad habits, from simple ones like nail-biting to serious addictions. Such behaviors serve as escapes from dealing with feelings and relationships.

Consider the stories on the next page. Describe what's happening right now, what each of the two people think and feel, and what will happen in the next six months. Write down your thoughts in the appropriate columns. Use a separate sheet of paper if necessary.

Some of these stories relate to the obstacles to a healthy relationship that are described later in this chapter and in greater detail in coming chapters.

In reviewing your explanations of these stories, examine the themes. Is your description more like a comedy or a tragedy, an adventure movie (where there's lots of action), or a romance novel (with heroes and heroines or damsels in distress)?

Love Scripts				
Story	Today	He Feels	She Feels	Six Months Later
1. After they got married, Peter and Susan argued constantly.				
2. After only six months of seeing each other, Ron and Sandra were happier than any of their friends.				
3. Sally found out Paul cheated on her right before their wedding.				
4. Pam couldn't bring herself to tell Ken she'd fallen out of love with him.				
5. The real life story of me and my mate.				
6. The perfect love story of me and my mate.				

For you and your mate to get along, you must both to some degree fit the roles in the love scripts that each of you have. Imagine if your love script follows more along the storyline of the movie *When Harry Met Sally,* where good friends played by Meg Ryan and Billy Crystal fall in love and live happily ever after, versus a love script that casts you as constantly at each other's throats, like the characters Elizabeth Taylor and Richard Burton play in *Who's Afraid of Virginia Woolf?*

Have your partner do the previous exercise. Examine where you both see similar or different dynamics in a relationship. Use your answers as a jumping-off point to discuss how you see relationships working out and where the trouble spots are.

Are You Scared?—Face Your Fears

Fears stop you from fully being yourself and expressing yourself. These fears can be about yourself, your partners, or love in general. Some common fears people have when in love include the following:

➤ Fear of reliving old hurts

➤ Fear of something happening to one of you

➤ Fear of not being able to keep your partner interested

➤ Fear of abandonment

➤ Fear of your mate finding someone who's "better" than you

➤ Fear of inexperience

➤ Fear of failure

➤ Fear of inadequate sexual performance

It's important to identify and admit to these fears in order to dissipate them. Then you can think through a more realistic scenario or outcome ("I will not be abandoned, because he loves me") or make affirmations ("I am a good sexual partner"). Let's examine two other popular fears.

Fear of Intimacy

People who can't commit usually have a tremendous fear of intimacy, either because they have a history of failed relationships or they grew up with painful examples of love going sour. Like Dave, who told me: "I've always had problems getting close. Sex means nothing to me. I've asked a lot of girls out and got rejected, so now I just go for the bar pigs and booze hounds that I can make and drop. I act like a jerk and it doesn't matter." Dave, like too many others in the dating world, is keeping himself safe, but he's also miserable!

Kevin wanted to know: "Is it possible to go out with someone for six months and not have any feelings for them?" Like Dave, Kevin is cutting himself off from his feelings. He has fears of intimacy and rejection, so he bides his time and keeps company without being invested in the relationship.

If you feel badly about not feeling anything, that's a sign that you need to work on being more in touch with your emotions and your desire for love. Pay attention to small feelings and bigger ones will grow. Be up front with your dates so you don't mislead anyone into thinking you care more than you do.

Fear of Missing Out

A girl who logged onto my Internet chat show said she fell in love and told the guy she was ready to get married, but was sorry she rushed into it because she's only 20 years old and this was the first time she had ever been in love. She feared that by committing to one person, she would miss out on other life experiences she really wanted. Facing her truth made her tell him the truth as well, and save them both unhappiness and disappointment later.

Mark has a related problem. At 35, his wife of eleven years left him because she felt that she married and became a mother too soon, causing her to lose her youth. Mark is now dating a 20-year-old girl who wants to marry him. She has a three-year-old girl. Mark is wise to be wary. It sounds like he's repeating his pattern—marrying another young girl, with a child, risking that a few years down the road, she, too, will end up saying that she missed her youth. She may want the security of a man taking care of her now, but later this may change.

Setting Yourself Up for Failure: Fear of Success

The opposite of fear of failure can also get in the way of your love lasting. You can have a fear of success—in love or sex, as well as work or other aspects of life—and not even know it. Basically, a fear of success means you sabotage yourself by not allowing things to work out well. When you're close to having it all, you "blow it"—whether it's getting sick before the play that you're starring in opens, losing your notes before a major presentation, or making your relationship go sour just when your career takes off.

Ask Dr. Judy

Lisa has a fear of success in sex. Although she's married to a wonderful man and has two beautiful children, a lovely home, and a satisfying part-time job, every time friends remark about how perfect her life is, Lisa blanches and protests that sex with her husband is a disaster. A lot of men and women won't let sex be as exciting as it can be with their mate because they're really afraid they won't be able to keep upping the ante. So they never really give it their all. It sounds so self-sabotaging, and so silly, but it's so common that it's shocking.

Lisa's mother warned her it was impossible to work and be a good wife and mother, so Lisa had to prove her mother right by being unhappy in one area: bed. Although it seems to make no sense, the psyche makes unusual accommodations.

Once I pointed out to Lisa just how and why she had a fear of success in love and sex, she was able to start working on overcoming it and reclaiming her "perfect" life as wife, mother, friend, and lover.

To help tell whether you have a fear of love or sex success, review how you answered the second love script earlier in this chapter. The story was about Ron and Sandra being happier together after six months than any of their friends. People who have a fear of love success make statements like, "Their friends didn't want to see them anymore," or joke, "Peter had an affair with Sandra's best friend," and "Sandra had a baby, lost interest in sex, and things went downhill from there."

To get over a fear of success, change your thinking—from the belief that things can never get better, to trusting that more is yet to come and that there's always room to grow. Avoid friends who enjoy hearing about your love troubles and favor ones who relish good reports. Don't believe those who say you can't have it all; you can. Don't even the score or protect others (from shame, guilt, or jealousy), by being less than you can be. Give up your superstition that if things get too good, they will turn bad. Engage in endlessly exciting experiences. Success is healthy, sexy, deserved, and attainable; go for it!

Love Bytes

A famous Greek myth that tells how Icarus flew too high and got burnt by the sun warns that blazing ambition can lead to self-destruction. In modern day fear of success, you're similarly afraid that if you achieve what you want, you stand to lose something. So you sadly allow your life or love to be less than it could be.

The Least You Need to Know

➤ A healthy self spells healthier relationships.

➤ Turn criticisms into calls of action to change.

➤ Recognize your fears about relationships and focus on overcoming them.

➤ Everybody has their own idea of how love stories play out. Learn from your "scripted" views of relationships and change self-fulfilling prophecies that doom relationships to those that foresee happiness.

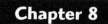

Are We Compatible?

In This Chapter

➤ What it means to be compatible

➤ The 12 major areas of compatibility

➤ The Compatibility Quiz

➤ Roadblocks to compatibility and five ways to handle them

➤ Resolving sexual incompatibility

➤ Kicking habits—when his or hers makes you crazy

Early in a relationship, couples may seem more compatible than they really are; as new lovers, you tend to smooth over your differences. To please and impress your new partners, both men and women may pretend likes and dislikes they don't actually have. He goes cheerfully to the ballet, she to the football game, because they're infatuated with each other. He never wears the worn-out socks that annoy her, and she agrees to sex more than she would really like to because they want to please one another.

Eventually, though, those rose-colored glasses come off, and with them go earnest efforts to win each other over. No longer on their best behavior, they might end up looking at each other thinking, "Do we really have anything in common?" Or, after a while, they might think, "We've already put so much into this relationship, we really don't want to know the ways we don't get along or deal with the fact that we may not make it." There comes a point, however, when all those issues that have been willfully ignored become unavoidable—like the elephant in the room you can't pretend not to notice.

What Is Compatibility?

Compatibility means being able to exist together in harmony. You might have similar likes and dislikes—which always makes getting along together easier—but even if you don't, you still enjoy, appreciate, and accept one another. Being together just seems to flow.

Dr. Judy's Rx

If you're a new couple, imagine your relationship with less sex than you're having now (or had when you were still in those early "honeymoon" stages). Would the two of you still get along?

It's rare for two people to exist together in harmony *all* the time. In fact, it would be unrealistic to expect to be happy with every single thing your partner does and says. That said, couples with healthy, happy relationships do feel that harmony, that magic of being a team, most of the time. Sure, you may have differing views on many issues, but regardless of your differences, hopefully you're able to respect each other's opinions.

Although it's perfectly fine to enjoy your differences, research shows that the crucial factor in healthy, long-lasting relationships is the couple's agreement on a core group of key life values. If you differ drastically on the issues that really matter (for example, your primary goal is to enjoy life while hers is to have a lot of money, or you want a house full of children while he prefers freedom for just the two of you), your relationship is in trouble.

The Twelve Major Areas of Compatibility

There are 12 major aspects of life about which you have personal views; these opinions can either agree or clash with those of your partner. Below, I'll outline these major areas, then give you a quiz that will help you and your loved one figure out how compatible you are. Later in this chapter, I'll point out the major sources of conflict, some of which include the following 12 compatibility areas:

1. **Physicality.** The importance you place on natural attractiveness, the effort you put into maintaining or improving your appearance, and your interest in participating in sports or athletic activities.

2. **Intellect.** Educational achievement and interest in culturally enriching activities, current events, and world affairs. IQ may also be considered important.

Ask Dr. Judy

People called me all the time on my radio show worried that their relationships might not survive because they and their partners come from different backgrounds, ethnic groups, or socioeconomic strata. My answer is that there's one factor that will determine your chances: Are you both willing to make the relationship work despite your differences? Some are reassured and inspired by this way of thinking. Others, like those single, dysfunctional friends on the hit TV show Seinfeld, have the opposite reaction and decide (consciously or not) to put up so many roadblocks to intimacy, that every person they meet becomes too difficult to have a relationship with: "Well, we don't enjoy the same television commercials. We're simply too different; it'll never work."

3. **Emotions.** The importance you place on feelings, and how you handle and express your feelings and emotions.

4. **Finances.** The priority that money holds in your life, how you handle your finances (from routine spending decisions to long-term financial plans) and attitudes toward money and spending.

5. **Individuality/Independence.** The space you need for personal growth, hobbies, and interests. Some people need time for themselves and their pursuits, others need to merge and be together constantly. If one person makes the other feel either abandoned or suffocated, the relationship is in trouble.

6. **Spirituality.** This includes concern for more spiritual (compared to practical or materialistic) ways, the belief in a higher being (God or otherwise), and the attendance to religious practices.

7. **Work.** Attitudes toward the importance of work, interest and priority set on attaining a career, and the commitment to a job.

8. **Sociability.** How much you want time alone versus time spent enjoying the company of others, entertaining, or partying.

Love Lookout

Even if you and your partner are compatible in a few areas—such as shared professional goals, similar educational backgrounds, or the same religion—don't ignore the areas in which you're not compatible.

9. **Communication.** How willing you are to discuss problems, and how good you are at expressing yourself and listening.

10. **Sex.** Your lovemaking style, level of desire, and sexual hang-ups—these are likely more important than your mastery of technique.

11. **Life habits.** He's a night owl, she's an early bird. He loves to watch TV to relax, she would love to throw out the remote control. She loves breakfast, he never eats it. She never drinks, he considers himself a wine connoisseur. How much do your daily routines and things you like to do differ?

12. **Family.** Along with your own desire to have and raise children, this also refers to your attitude toward visiting family members and living with family.

How Compatible Are You?

You and your partner are probably more compatible in some of the 12 major areas than in others. The following quiz will help you gain some insight into the areas you do and don't agree on.

Both you and your partner need to do this exercise. Each of you should circle the answer that is most closely true for you most of the time. Then plot your answers on the graph at the end of the quiz—this will show where and how much you and your partner agree or disagree.

The Compatibility Quiz

	Unimportant	Desirable but Not Crucial	Essential
I. Physicality			
1. Keeping up an attractive, put together appearance is:	1	2	3
2. Regular physical exercise is:	1	2	3
3. Healthy eating habits are:	1	2	3
4. Maintaining a youthful image is:	1	2	3
5. Not smoking and drinking too much is:	1	2	3
II. Intellect			
6. Achieving a level of formal education up to my standards is:	1	2	3
7. Having others regard my partner and/or me as intelligent is:	1	2	3

	Unimportant	Desirable but Not Crucial	Essential
8. Being well-read in literature and well-versed in the arts is:	1	2	3
9. Keeping up on politics and current events is:	1	2	3
10. Continuing to learn and be educated (through independent study, continuing education classes, etc.) is:	1	2	3

III. Emotions

	Unimportant	Desirable but Not Crucial	Essential
11. Being able to express and share feelings with my partner is:	1	2	3
12. Having a partner who can empathize with me—who will share my feelings whether I'm happy or sad—is:	1	2	3
13. Being able to understand each other's feelings without always having to explain ourselves is:	1	2	3
14. Having a partner who is not ashamed or embarrassed by tears (or by showing emotion in general) is:	1	2	3
15. Celebrating meaningful occasions like anniversaries is:	1	2	3

IV. Finances

	Unimportant	Desirable but Not Crucial	Essential
16. Paying bills on time, balancing the checkbook, and managing money is:	1	2	3
17. Having a partner who shares my long-term financial goals in investing and saving is:	1	2	3
18. Leading a comfortable lifestyle—spending freely on vacations, entertainment, other leisurely activities, and possessions—is:	1	2	3

	Unimportant	Desirable but Not Crucial	Essential
19. Sharing responsibility for money management is:	1	2	3
20. Being generous with family, friends, and each other is:	1	2	3
V. Individualism/Independence			
21. Having time to see my own family and/or friends alone is:	1	2	3
22. Having "me" time or time alone to do whatever I want without interacting with my partner is:	1	2	3
23. Having my own hobbies and/or interests, not shared with my partner, is:	1	2	3
24. Having my own interests and/or hobbies shared by my partner is:	1	2	3
25. Being free to develop my identity and lifestyle without fear of being criticized is:	1	2	3
VI. Spirituality			
26. Being in touch with my inner spiritual self is:	1	2	3
27. Having my religious or spiritual beliefs acknowledged and respected by my partner is:	1	2	3
28. Sharing my spiritual beliefs with my partner is:	1	2	3
29. Belief in God or a higher power is:	1	2	3
30. Attending religious services regularly and/or otherwise observing daily the tenants of an organized religion is:	1	2	3

	Unimportant	Desirable but Not Crucial	Essential

VII. Work

31. Being good at what I do and/or truly enjoying my work is:

| | 1 | 2 | 3 |

32. Putting a high priority on work (sometimes above family, friends, or relationships) is:

| | 1 | 2 | 3 |

33. Achieving a balance of work and other aspects of life is:

| | 1 | 2 | 3 |

34. Having a partner who encourages me in my professional goals and supports me when possible is:

| | 1 | 2 | 3 |

35. Achieving a high level of professional success and/or having a partner who does so, even if it means putting in long hours and weekends, is:

| | 1 | 2 | 3 |

VIII. Sociability

36. Being warm, friendly, and open to new people (including your partner's friends) and/or having a partner who is the same way is:

| | 1 | 2 | 3 |

37. Having fun in casual groups of family and friends is:

| | 1 | 2 | 3 |

38. Being able to move easily in large (or formal) social situations and/or having a partner who can do the same is:

| | 1 | 2 | 3 |

39. Having a partner who likes to stay home, cook dinner, and rent a movie is:

| | 1 | 2 | 3 |

40. Entertaining or treating others in or outside the home is:

| | 1 | 2 | 3 |

	Unimportant	Desirable but Not Crucial	Essential
IX. Communication			
41. Being able to talk easily with my partner about my feelings and have him share his feelings with me is:	1	2	3
42. Discussing ideas and intellectual positions is:	1	2	3
43. Dealing with anger openly and constructively—not by withdrawing, dissolving into tears, or resorting to screaming at each other—is:	1	2	3
44. Being able to discuss our differences and problems and work through them constructively is:	1	2	3
45. Accepting each other's style of communicating (both like to talk things through; one cries, the other doesn't) is:	1	2	3
X. Sex			
46. A good sex life is:	1	2	3
47. Having a partner who wants to make love as often (or as infrequently) as I do is:	1	2	3
48. Being skilled in sexual techniques is:	1	2	3
49. Being creative, experimental, even wild, in lovemaking variations is:	1	2	3
50. Having a partner who considers my sexual needs as much as his own and who is sensitive to the things that I like or that make me particularly uncomfortable is:	1	2	3

	Unimportant	Desirable but Not Crucial	Essential
XI. Life Habits			
51. Spending time together and doing things together (from going to the grocery store to going out to dinner, watching movies, or even going away on vacation together) is:	1	2	3
52. Getting up and going to sleep at the same time is:	1	2	3
53. Taking time off from work to be together is:	1	2	3
54. Taking care of our home together is:	1	2	3
55. Having similar daily routines (watching TV together, sleeping late on Sundays, eating breakfast) is:	1	2	3
XII. Family			
56. Getting along well with our respective parents is:	1	2	3
57. Spending time with each other's family members is:	1	2	3
58. Keeping in touch and visiting with family members is:	1	2	3
59. Having a family (children) ourselves someday is:	1	2	3
60. Spending time with our children as a family (having dinners together, taking them on outings, playing games) is:	1	2	3

To determine your score, add up the total numbers for each of the five questions in each category and average them. For example, if you thought each of the criteria in Section I was essential, your average would be a 3. Here's how that would be figured out:

5 questions × 3 ("Essential") =	15
÷ by total number of questions in the section =	5
Average =	3

Write down the averages for each section for both you and your mate in the following table.

Our Compatibility Quiz Scores

Areas of Compatibility	Me	My Mate
I. Physicality	_____	_____
II. Intellect	_____	_____
III. Emotions	_____	_____
IV. Finances	_____	_____
V. Individualism/Independence	_____	_____
VI. Spirituality	_____	_____
VII. Work	_____	_____
VIII. Sociability	_____	_____
IX. Communication	_____	_____
X. Sex	_____	_____
XI. Life Habits	_____	_____
XII. Family	_____	_____

Now both you and your mate should plot your answers on the blank graph on the next page. To make the differences obvious, use one color pen for your answers and a different color for your mate's answers (or one of you can use a pen and the other a pencil). Then connect the 12 dots to form a plotted figure. Use two solid lines in the different colors, or use a solid line for one of you and a dotted line for the other. For an example, take a look at the sample graph on the next page.

Now look at the patterns that your answers created. Notice where there are similarities or a large divergence in your plotted figures. If you and your mate's plots follow a similar pattern, you probably agree on most matters and don't have conflicts in those areas. Very erratic plots (in which one goes up on the scale while the other goes down) reveal considerable differences in what is important to you. Review these differences with your mate, since these are the areas that likely cause friction between you. Turn back to those sections in this chapter on that particular area of compatibility and discuss your answers.

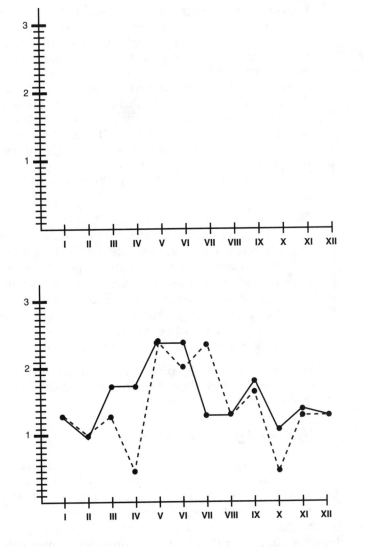

Plot your answers on this blank graph.

Here's a sample plot of a couple's compatibility quiz scores.

What Are the Big Compatibility Roadblocks?

Some of the 12 areas of compatibility (or conflict) are generally more troublesome than others for couples—among them are sex, money, and family. In the next few pages I'll talk about the major areas of couples' incompatibility, then cover some other common areas of conflict or anxiety, such as age gaps, political differences, and bad habits.

Sex Drive

Over the course of a relationship, both partners' sex drives will certainly fluctuate as a result of many factors, including stress, exhaustion, professional and other priorities,

101

Love Bytes

The honeymoon can end fast. One survey showed that nearly half of the 345 newlywed couples surveyed said they wished they had sex more often. The book *The First Year of Marriage: What to Expect, What to Accept and What You Can Change* reported that newlywed sex is hardly as romantic or as exciting as one would like to believe.

Dr. Judy's Rx

Some women think men are interested in sex in the morning because they wake up with erections. Contrary to popular belief, these erections don't necessarily signal sexual arousal; rather, they're a physical response to a part of their sleep cycle. So, don't worry, men aren't necessarily waking up "horny" and won't be depriving their bodies of anything by not having sex then.

fights with each other, illnesses, medications—the list goes on. Clearly, problems will arise when one person maintains his or her regular sex drive while the other person lags. You can weather these difficulties as long as both partners accept each other's occasional downward trends in desire, and trust that imbalances in sex drive can restabilize in a reasonable amount of time with effort. However, if the imbalance in a couple's sex drive lasts too long, or gets totally out of kilter (which can occur if the partner with the higher drive begins giving sexual satisfaction an increasingly higher priority), then the incompatibility can spell disaster.

Many couples start out fairly similarly in their sex drives, but over time, differences will probably emerge (regardless of external factors). These differences may have been repressed in the beginning when the desire to please each other was great, but surface later when the couple gets used to each other and, sadly, starts taking each other for granted. Women often complain of too little romance while men tend to desire more frequency and more playing out of their fantasies.

Married or not, couples often disagree about the frequency with which they would like to have sex and the type of sex they want.

When to Have Sex

He's a night owl, she's a morning glory. This can be physically determined by different circadian rhythms, or body clocks, which make people more alert either in the A.M. or P.M. Partners who differ have to find a middle ground—in the early evening or on weekends, for example. Or they'll have to compromise by switching off, having sex sometimes at her peak time and sometimes at his.

How Often It Happens

When couples fight over sex, it's often about the (in)frequency of it. Hopefully you both have compatible sex drives, or you accept your differences. In any case, both of you are bound to have fluctuations in your sexual mood and functioning. There will be times, therefore, when you feel less in synch than usual. Don't despair. Accept the normal ebb and flow of sexual desire that changes with major life transitions, such as before or after making a commitment, getting married, having a child, or changing jobs. But face sexual withdrawals that come from upsets between you by confronting the issues (anger, frustrations, arguments, hurts).

Be particularly wary when the more desirous partner keeps insisting on sex, since the less interested party will shut down further, physically and emotionally, feeling pressured and resentful about not being able to respond. Holding back and giving the less desirous partner a chance to build up interest can restore more equal desire. Remember that loving sex should always take both people's desires into consideration.

Attitudes about sex also affect your sex drive. Some women think they're supposed to act "proper," which inhibits their sex drive. And some men think they're always supposed to be ready and willing. They feel anxious when it turns out that they're not. Retrain your brain: Trade in those unpleasant, anxious thoughts for pleasurable ones. Confront and resolve real problems, like stress or anger, that are dampening your desire. Step back and give yourself time to get in the mood. Try to establish a "transition time" in bed, when, instead of jumping into sex immediately, you first share feelings or talk about events of the day. Hold and cuddle each other to heighten intimacy. Build each other's confidence with statements like, "I enjoy just being with you, no matter what happens."

Whatever the cause is, you can always compromise to get around an imbalance in sex drives. One solution: Alternate weeks where you each get your way. Or have the passive partner learn to increase desire, while the active one learns to drain off energy, exercising before sex, or bouncing around the bed more during it. However, you decide to resolve this problem, you should make sure you do it by compromise; the passive partner should never be expected to become like a filling station, where the active one just pulls up and says "fill 'er up" whenever he or she wants. If you can't overcome the

Love Lookout

A marriage certificate is not a license to free and continuous sex. If you feel that you should be serviced sexually whenever you want, you'll only turn your partner off. Relax and give your partner a chance to feel respected and to desire sex—and you.

Dr. Judy's Rx

Remember that you're always entitled to say no to sex; just do it in a sensitive way so your mate doesn't get upset. A flat "no" is rejecting and hurtful. Instead, reassure your partner by saying, "I love you and I love making love with you," and promise another time when you will be sexual. You can also identify the needs from sex that could be satisfied in other ways—by spending time together or expressing love for each other. Be clear; you can't expect your partner to know exactly when you want it and when you don't.

difficulties—that is, if the problems persist longer than a few months or interfere greatly with your life—I suggest you try seeing a sex therapist or marital counselor together.

Not Tonight, Dear, I Have a Headache

How many jokes have you heard about that old line? Clearly, unequal sex drives have been a problem since sex has been around. As the saying goes, though, many a truth is said in jest. That means sexual headaches can be real. Experts estimate that about half a million Americans suffer from what's called "benign sexual headache" (BSH). More men than women suffer from it, because men are more susceptible to the sudden or extreme change in blood pressure during sex which is associated with headaches. Unfortunately, all too many men suffer in silence because they're ashamed to admit to this problem.

A tension-type sexual headache (also called coital headache or orgasmic cephalgia) can happen after sex or during the excitement phase of the sexual response cycle, which is characterized by rapid increases in body tension and blood flow, altered breathing patterns, and muscle contractions literally from head to toe. For most people the headaches pass, but they can persist if you suffer from high blood pressure, stress, obesity, migraines, or heart disease. Taking an aspirin prior to sex can help.

"Exertional" headaches are caused by increased blood pressure from being too active, as in any exercise, and can last from seconds to hours. Seek medical advice. Danger signs that include nausea, vomiting, altered consciousness, or lasting pain can signal a stroke, or blood or spinal fluid leaks. Be wary of highly charged sexual activity, including attempting multiple orgasms.

Cultural Clash

Different ethnic, racial, or socioeconomic backgrounds can create problems for couples. Such couples may not share commonality of experience that sees many people through a relationship's rough spots. For example, her culture may require adherence to parental attitudes, while his does not; so he ends up resenting that she always seems to "listen" to her parents. These couples have to work harder than others to bridge their gaps and understand each other. With effort and determination, these problems can be resolved. Recognize where the differences come from. Explain how your background brings you to look at things the way you do. Appreciate each other's cultural perspective and make necessary compromises.

Religious Rights

Interfaith relationships can be successful, but they require tolerance on both parts. In dating, a major choice has to be made about overcoming any objections or disapproval that others may have about your connection. Once you become committed, decisions have to be made about where and how to have the wedding, what religion to raise the children with, and how to deal with relatives.

Ask Dr. Judy

Traditionally, it was always women who were thought to voice the usual complaint, "Not tonight, dear, I have a headache." Nowadays, some men are upset that their women want sex so often. One woman expressed her concern to me, "I know people joke that women claim to have headaches to get out of having sex, but in my case the joke's on me—my husband is the one who says he gets headaches during sex. We have a very happy marriage and have always enjoyed sex, but now we hardly do it at all. Do you think he really has headaches, or is there something suddenly wrong with me?"

First of all, no woman should attribute a man's lower sex drive to her not being attractive enough. Accept that women can and often do have higher sex drives than men. First, consider BSH (mentioned earlier); your husband really could have headaches. If he doesn't, you should try to identify any fears or worries he might have (for example, distrust, fear of rejection, or fear of pregnancy) and allay them; any anxiety or "holding back" in sex on his part could trigger physical failures, which in turn can escalate anxiety even further. Relax, allow yourselves to become sexual and establish trust. But keep in mind, studies show making love can also cure headaches by stimulating blood flow, reducing body tension, and releasing pain-killing chemicals!

Family Matters

If you're in a serious, long-lasting relationship, you'll probably talk about marriage sometime in the future. And once you've taken that leap to marriage, one of the first likely compatibility problems awaiting you will be about children. More importantly, you'll have to decide whether or not to even have kids. Although contemporary couples are increasingly deciding not to have children, if one of you wants a family and the other doesn't, you're in for big trouble. In fact, the chances are high that you'll end up breaking up so that the one who wants children can have them with someone else. For this reason, you should definitely resolve this issue before you get seriously involved.

Age Gaps

It's no secret that older men seek out younger women. Forty-something TV comic Jerry Seinfeld's relationship with a girlfriend 20 years his junior was a much-publicized example of this phenomenon. But the May–December relationship has been going on since long before Seinfeld became so popular. Thousands of years ago, aging kings kept many young concubines to balance their "yang" male essence with the women's "yin" female energy.

Love Bytes

Statistics show that nearly 25 percent of U.S. brides are now marrying younger men. For women aged 35 to 44, the number goes up to 41 percent. Author Victoria Houston reported in her book, *Loving a Younger Man,* that a 40-ish woman with a 30-ish man can be an excellent match, since she's likely to feel secure and mature, and he's likely to see her as an equal. Such couples described their sex life as "the best ever."

There's now a trend for younger men to be attracted to older women, whom they find more financially secure and emotionally mature than their younger counterparts. And older women, who are these days feeling better about themselves and are more physically fit, allow themselves to fall for younger guys—something that was previously frowned upon. Singer Cher and actresses Mary Tyler Moore and Susan Sarandon are shining examples.

A difference of more than five to seven years in age used to mean that couples would have significantly different cultural reference points. The music, movies, and world events that shaped one person during his or her youth would have been completely different from those that influenced the other. The bigger the age gap, the more likely the couple would suffer conflicts from different levels of experience and maturity.

To some extent, these gaps have been shortened in modern times. Younger people are often very aware of culture and history of all generations, not just their own, so they can more easily understand older people. There are also young people who are too mature to date people their own age and need to be with someone older. And there are older people who are still so youthful inside that they more easily relate to younger partners than those in their own peer group.

Expressions of Affection

Some people like big shows of affection, both in private and in public; others are very low key, or even kind of distant. Usually, the partner who wants to be treated more affectionately gets distressed, sometimes to the point of feeling deprived or unloved.

Ask Dr. Judy

Although age-gap relationships have proved successful time and again, they can still present some anxiety. One woman wrote to me, "I'm a divorcee in my 40s and I've fallen in love with a 22-year-old man. We have great fun, long talks, and lovemaking sessions like I've never known before. I'm planning to have him move into my apartment soon. The problem is that although I look and feel like I'm still in my 30s, I sometimes worry about his age—he's young enough to be my son. And though he works hard, he doesn't have much money, so I take care of everything. Am I silly to pursue this?"

For the relationship to work, you have to overcome your fears ("Will he still love me when I'm old and gray?"), embarrassment ("I'm robbing the cradle to feel young again"), and other people's criticisms ("Why can't you find someone your own age?"). Some older women enjoy "turning the tables" and supporting a younger lover as they dreamed would happen to them. Be careful of this, though—initially you might enjoy the power and control, but later tire of it. Make sure that you're not showering him with presents to buy his affection or submission, and that he's not with you just for the money and gifts. Decide if your love is true. If it is, accept age as a state of mind and prepare for your best love life ever.

One woman complained to me, "I need a lot of affection and the man I'm seeing says he is turned off when I hang on his arm, turn to make him kiss me, or jump into his lap. He claims I am too needy. Is this true, and how do I get over this?"

It would be ideal if your mate could give you "unconditional love," the kind of "true" love that allows you to express all your needs without judgment. People who are critical of a lover's neediness are often uncomfortable with their own needs; condemning such needs in their partner is a way of negating them in themselves. A kinder, healthier approach would be to admit this projection and say, "I'm uncomfortable with your neediness because I want to deny those feelings in myself, or forget experiences like that in my own past." Or, the critical partner could just indulge his or her lover a little, until that "neediness" passes.

If, however, your demands are a bottomless pit that catapults you into a vicious cycle of deprivation, self-doubt, and more demands that no partner could ever fill, the problem is within yourself. You may have even purposely chosen a withholding lover in order to force yourself to develop self-reliance. To preserve the relationship, you

107

need to end the cycle; instead of requesting a hug or kiss in a needy tone that begs for rejection, take a deep breath, remind yourself that you are lovable, look into your partner's eyes, and sense his presence. Then you can make your request in a confident tone, without demanding that your partner oblige. Such "nondemand" requests will more likely result in you getting what you want.

Five Ways to Handle Compatibility Roadblocks

Knowing that you can overcome any problems in compatibility should give you hope that you can make your relationship a happy and lasting one. Here are some tips to help you ensure the health of your relationship:

1. Acknowledge that roadblocks exist early on. Glossing over your differences or pretending they don't matter all but guarantees trouble.

2. Learn all about your partner's different ethnic or cultural background, religion, political ideals, age-based experiences, etc. Share yours with him or her. Get rid of any misconceptions or problems you might have based on these differences from the beginning.

3. Don't blame every disagreement on the compatibility issue. Even couples who don't have any of these roadblocks will disagree about where to have dinner, go on vacation, or how often to visit relatives.

4. Agree to disagree. Resist religious or political proselytizing. Mutual respect for the other's beliefs and experiences has to be the cornerstone of your relationship.

5. Find your common ground. Focus on the issues you agree on and strengthen that compatibility.

Other Trouble Spots

There are other areas of compatibility described below that can certainly create conflict but rarely go so far as to break couples up. People tend to gravitate toward people who are already compatible with them in these areas. But if you are not, you may still find yourselves able to resolve these differences with just a little effort.

Shared Chores

Surveys have repeatedly shown that one of the biggest complaints women have of their male partners (besides the fact that they don't express their feelings enough) is that they don't help out around the house. This usually doesn't cause a break-up, just endless tension and arguing.

Allie called my *LovePhones* radio show just after she and her fiancé had moved in together. She said that he was always complaining about her constant nagging about doing the chores. In this case, the problem wasn't that he didn't help at all, the problem was with *how* he helped. She said that he would do the vacuuming, but wouldn't put the vacuum back in the closet. She also said that he would make breakfast, but then leave the cereal box and milk carton open on the counter instead of putting them away.

To avoid Allie turning into a nag, my solution to them was to sit down and calmly point out the differences in their styles—she likes neatness and closure, he tends to leave things unfinished. Instead of resenting that parts of his chores are left to her—and making him feel wrong and resentful that she doesn't think he can look after things himself—they were to think of the household chores as a team effort. Figure out each other's strengths and weaknesses, and plan to redistribute the tasks according to each person's abilities and also for more equitable distribution, as if you were running a business. For example, break down vacuuming into three separate tasks: taking the vacuum out, doing the vacuuming, and putting the vacuum away. If he does only steps one and two, you do number three and reassign him a part of one of your chores. That way, you're both unemotionally and more appropriately assigned to do what suits you. More important, you nag less and get along better with your partner.

Politics

Liberals and conservatives have clashing viewpoints on more than the presidential elections. Politics permeate our lives in more ways than we realize. Are you for or against labor unions, affirmative action, handgun control, the death penalty? Are you pro-choice or a right-to-lifer? How much of your tax money are you happy to see go to welfare, subsidizing the arts, health care? Certainly, the much-publicized marriage of former Republican Party campaign leader (turned TV talk host) Mary Matalin to her Democratic counterpart James Carville proved that even political opposites can cultivate a bipartisan romance.

Bad Habits

Bad habits may not be as seriously detrimental to your compatibility as the roadblocks I discussed earlier. But some habits are more annoying than others, and even the most benign of bad habits can loom large after a while, or during times of conflict. They may not break you up, but they're usually difficult to change and they can cause a lot of irritation and aggravation unless they're resolved.

Minor bad habits can be divided into two categories: ones that directly impact a partner, and ones that the partner simply finds aesthetically unpleasant. Habits like chronic lateness, leaving dirty dishes in the sink, or using up supplies without ever replacing them create a problem for a partner. Others, like bad breath, spitting out fingernails, or wearing smelly T-shirts, might just make your mate cringe.

What about major bad habits? Some can be downright destructive, like driving too fast, drinking irresponsibly, or smoking. Smoking especially causes problems, particularly in today's social climate. The nonsmoker will complain about the stench of stale smoke in the air and in the fabrics and remind the smoker about the health dangers associated with secondhand smoke. The smoker will defensively cling to his right to pollute his own lungs and discount the damage to surroundings.

Ask Dr. Judy

Every year around the Super Bowl season, I'm questioned by some TV reporter for a story on "sports widows"—women whose husbands are so maniacally involved in watching their team that they make their wives feel neglected. The "widowhood" that results from a mate's obsession with another activity doesn't just apply to sports; these days it applies to a whole host of other activities, such as going online. Statistics show that the majority of online subscribers are men, and some of them spend so many hours on the Internet that their female partners complain that they no longer talk with each other, eat dinner together, or have sex.

A partner's serious complaint is one legitimate sign that your involvement with a particular activity is crossing the line from hobby or interest to obsession. You might want to step back and think about whether you're using that activity to escape intimacy or commitment. Consider your partner's needs, confront whatever latent problems you might have with the relationship, and make compromises about how to spend your time. Agree on the amount of time you'll indulge in your other interests, and promise another amount of time you'll focus on your partner. One sports widow, for example, gave up nagging, and followed the "if you can't beat 'em, join 'em" philosophy: She began sitting down to watch games with her husband, and would then slip into a sexy outfit during the post-game wrap-up.

When They Make You Crazy

Some bad habits become so irksome they provoke constant arguments. Different couples fight over different things; they might be anything from financial irresponsibility (like not recording ATM withdrawals in the checkbook) to having long telephone conversations while neglecting their mate.

To analyze the habits that annoy you and your mate, you should each make a list: You write down all of your own and your mate's annoying habits and have him or her do the same for you. Use the space below.

My Habits That Annoy My Mate

My Answers

My Mate's Answers

_____   _____

_____   _____

_____   _____

_____   _____

_____   _____

My Mate's Habits That Annoy Me

My Answers

My Mate's Answers

_____   _____

_____   _____

_____   _____

_____   _____

_____   _____

Review your list and determine how much each of the habits annoys you. Now go back over the list and circle the habits that each of you absolutely can no longer tolerate, and need to have changed. Cross out the ones that you can live with—ones that would be best ignored in the interests of getting along better—and resolve not to pester each other about them anymore. Now reexamine those habits that you have left. Are they really driving you to insanity? Can you accept them in the interest of preserving and improving your tolerance of each other and thus, your love.

Dealing with Your Mate's Bad Habits

Instead of either stewing about your mate's bad habits or nagging, take constructive action. Here are some suggestions about what to do:

➤ If the habit directly affects you, such as your partner's failure to perform a fair share of routine domestic tasks, get him to agree in writing to mend his ways— at least to some extent. And then don't let yourself do for him what he doesn't get done. For example, if he constantly leaves the cap off the toothpaste, just get two separate tubes of toothpaste and cap your own.

Dr. Judy's Rx

If your mate's habits are really making you crazy, give him space. Take a time out from being together. Go into another room. Take a walk. Lose yourself in a book or a movie. Later you can talk it out more rationally.

➤ Don't make yourself responsible for monitoring your partner's behavior. If she can't keep track of ATM withdrawals or checks, consider keeping separate checking accounts.

➤ Instead of berating your mate about a bad habit, ask him to stop but place your request in the context of how much you care about your partner. For example, gently remind her now and then that biting her nails is not only bad for her but painful for you to watch. Don't constantly criticize her about it.

➤ To avoid constant fighting, come to a compromise on more difficult issues. For example, in the case of smoking, you can agree to make most rooms of the house smoke-free zones.

Kicking Your Own Bad Habits

Show your concern for your mate's happiness by working on those habits of yours that are distasteful or distressing to him or her. Follow these steps:

➤ Identify the habits that annoy your partner.

➤ Resolve to make a change, controlling your urge for that behavior.

➤ Identify the motivations or feelings that lead you to engage in the habit (being too impatient to bother putting your clothes away, or being too inattentive or careless to bother hanging up the towels).

➤ Consciously choose a trigger word to remind you to stop the behavior.

➤ Purposefully do something in place of that behavior (to stop chewing your fingernails, chew on celery or gum, for example).

➤ Ask your mate to help you break a bad habit. For example, if you want to stop eating so much chocolate, you can ask your mate to be sensitive about it and not bring home a box of Godivas for your birthday, or refrain from stopping by the market on the way home from work to pick up a pint of Ben & Jerry's Cherry Garcia ice cream.

The Least You Need to Know

➤ No two people are compatible all the time. Don't exaggerate your incompatibilities but don't ignore them either.

➤ There are 12 major areas of compatibility. A strong connection in one or two areas early in a relationship can blind people to other serious differences, but strong connections in several areas typically indicate a high level of compatibility that portends smooth sailing ahead.

➤ Similar sexual desires, feelings, and fantasies can provide strong glue to a relationship. But when differences or conflicts arise, they can be worked through if you both really care to.

➤ Sometimes minor bad habits can cause as much tension as major compatibility roadblocks (such as age gaps and cultural differences). If you want to stay together, you have to be tolerant of each other's habits and not see them as flaws. Make it a habit to do whatever is necessary to accept and adjust to each other.

Chapter 9

Cooperation— Whose Team Are You On?

In This Chapter

➤ What is cooperation?

➤ Test your cooperation skills

➤ How gender-based stereotypes get in the way

➤ Avoiding competition in your relationship

➤ Dividing responsibilities fairly

When couples clash, they'll often attribute their conflicts to one of the big "C's": "We're just not compatible anymore," or "He won't commit," or "We can't communicate with each other." But there's another C-word, a big one, that couples rarely bring up: cooperation. Although couples certainly sense that cooperation is a major player in the success of their relationship, even something they complain about indirectly ("he won't help out around the house"), it remains a silent C-word.

Few relationships would last if the partners didn't know how to cooperate with each other. Even couples that seem incompatible or uncommunicative at first can work out their differences through cooperation. It hardly comes naturally, though, and sometimes, it takes concerted effort.

It's never too late to learn how to cooperate. Cooperation, like public speaking, is a learned skill; for most of us, it's not an innate ability. But without it, we'd all be stuck in frustrating relationships, paralyzed by our inability to work with our partner to move forward.

What Is Cooperation?

Cooperation—a necessity in any healthy relationship—occurs when both partners work together for a mutual benefit. That doesn't mean that one person gives in to all the other's wishes or demands; one person shouldn't end up doing all the chores and accepting an unfair burden of the responsibilities just to keep the peace or get the job done. Each partner has to contribute as much as he or she can. People who cooperate well with each other do so willingly, not just to avoid confrontation but to achieve their shared and individual goals. Cooperative partners also work together and feel like a team. They pitch in to accomplish their common goals, getting done whatever needs to get done by taking the initiative, or by just lending a helping hand.

Love Bytes

The *Virginia Slims Opinion Poll*, taken repeatedly over the last 25 years, shows that the biggest complaint women have about the men they live with is that they don't help out enough around the house. As their spokesperson for years, I heard this complaint over and over.

Compatibility Does Not Equal Cooperation

Review how you and your partner fared on the Compatibility Quiz in Chapter 8, "Are We Compatible?" Although being compatible doesn't necessarily guarantee cooperation, your compatibility does mean you have common views and goals, at least in certain areas, which in turn facilitate cooperation. In fact, your cooperation in those areas will seem to flow without your even thinking about it or making much of an effort.

On the other hand, if you discovered that you were incompatible in many areas, you'll probably experience difficulty cooperating on those matters. Not surprisingly, you'll probably have fights about these issues, too.

Love Lookout

It can be hard to tell from outward appearances if a cooperative effort is a true collaboration or just a case of one partner continually making concessions to the other. Think about your own relationship: When things are running smoothly, is one person more stressed, running ragged, and carrying the load more than the other? Even if neither of you is complaining, examine the balance of your responsibilities.

Take Peter and Veronica's situation, for example. They were essentially living together in Peter's apartment; Veronica, however, wanted to buy a house and move in together formally. But because Peter wasn't ready for that kind of commitment or responsibility, he wouldn't put aside his share of the money for the down payment. Veronica ended up angry and hurt that Peter not only didn't see eye to eye with her about their future together (they were incompatible on their life goals), but also refused to pitch in for the benefit of their future together (he wasn't cooperating on their future).

So, compatibility certainly makes cooperation easier, but as I said before, it's no guarantee: A couple can be compatible on a subject (agree in principle), but when it comes down to taking action, one or both partners seem to sabotage the results, or be uncooperative. Take, for example, a couple that agrees to have a baby or make a down payment on a house as soon as they save up enough money. One partner could sabotage the couple's efforts (as happened with Peter, whom I just mentioned) by continually spending the money that was supposed to be saved. Or let's say a couple really wants to get away together for a long weekend, but neither of the partners makes time to reserve a hotel, get airplane tickets, or clear his or her schedule.

The Seven Main Areas of Cooperation

Because issues of cooperation are often related to or are extensions of issues of compatibility, the major areas of cooperation will overlap with the areas of compatibility that you reviewed in Chapter 8. Here are the major areas of cooperation:

1. **Finances.** Even couples who aren't at the living-together stage still make joint financial decisions: Who pays for dinner? Who pays for the movies? If you are living together, there are countless other money questions: Do you split the rent equally? Who is responsible for actually writing the check? As for the other bills (electric, heat, cable TV, phone)—who's responsible for paying and sending them out? How much do each of you chip in for joint purchases, like a couch or a TV? How do you split the cost of a shared vacation? What about buying gifts for mutual friends?

Dr. Judy's Rx

Cooperation requires making compromises—mutual decisions in which both you and your partner give in a little, and concede a bit to the other in order to reach a decision that both of you can live with.

2. **Domestic details.** Even if you're only spending weekends together, you'll probably end up sharing some chores, like preparing dinner, doing dishes, and even walking the dog. And if you are cohabitating, you'll also have to decide who takes out the garbage, does the laundry, waters the plants, and decides on the décor.

Dr. Judy's Rx

Cooperation also requires sharing. If you think of yourselves as a team, then you should each contribute your resources. How much of what you can give are you willing to pool for your mutual benefit? Do you ever withhold your time, money, or attention?

3. **Romance/sex.** In the beginning, couples usually can't get enough of each other. After a few months, however, they might revert to their more natural lovemaking preferences; that is, one partner might end up wanting less sex or becoming less adventurous in sex. How much do you and your partner each contribute to keeping the fires burning and keeping you both equally satisfied?

4. **Entertainment/leisure.** Unless you and your partner are exactly compatible in what you like to do in your leisure time (for example, you both like going to the movies, attending concerts, or ordering in Chinese food), one of you will usually have to make a concession to the other about where to go and what to do. What is a reasonable concession, and how often should you be the one giving in? And what about vacations together—how do you decide where to go and what to do during that time off?

5. **Contraception/family planning.** Which one of you pays more attention to the issue of birth control and takes more action to be responsible about it? Do you agree on how you would handle an unplanned pregnancy?

6. **Family/friends.** How much time should you spend with your own family and friends? What do you do if one of you dislikes the other's family or friends? What do you do if your partner's family or friends can't get along with yours?

7. **Private space/individuality.** Some people need more private space and "me" time than others. How do you compromise when one likes a lot more togetherness than the other? How do you encourage and support each other's individuality?

How Well Do You and Your Mate Cooperate with Each Other?

Take the following quiz to get an idea of how you and your mate cooperate in the areas previously discussed. Both of you should answer the quiz questions; record your answers on separate sheets of paper, then log them in below (put your answers in the "Me" column, and ask your mate to put his or her answers in the "My Mate" column). Then look at both of your answers and check in the last column whether you agree or disagree. The final step, of course: Discuss your answers. Pay particular attention to the areas where you disagree so you can resolve your differences. But don't neglect talking about where you agree. Confirming your cooperation ensures that good feelings and good teamwork will continue.

Note: Sometimes the answer won't be crystal clear. In other words, none of these choices will seem correct, and you may think, "Well, it depends." In that case, pick the answer that applies most of the time. You can always raise the conditions of your cooperation when you discuss each item together.

The Cooperation Quiz

Area of Cooperation	My Answer Who's Responsible?			My Mate's Answer Who's Responsible?			
	Me	My Mate	Both of Us	Me	My Mate	Both of Us	Agree/ Disagree
Who pays for our dates?							
Who balances our checkbook?							
Who writes the checks and sends the bills?							
Who handles our investments?							
Who does the housework?							
Who decorates the house?							
Who does our home repairs (or arranges for a professional to come do them for us)?							
Who decides what we're going to do together for fun or for vacation?							
Who makes reservations for dinner, buys movie tickets, makes arrangements for trips, and so on?							
Who initiates sex?							
Who takes responsibility for birth control?							
Who pays for birth control?							
Who decides how to handle an unplanned pregnancy?							
Who makes the effort to include family in social events?							
Who makes the effort to get together with friends?							

Cooperation Problems and Solutions

Now discuss your differences and figure out why cooperation isn't happening where it should; sometimes not being cooperative is completely unintentional. If you feel your mate isn't pitching in enough, let him or her know what you need and how he or she could help you. Emphasize that cooperation will benefit both of you, and ask for help in the spirit of togetherness. Don't nag or complain or make your partner into the bad guy (see Chapter 10, "Communication—Can We Talk?" for more hints on good communication). The following are some reasons that your partner might not be chipping in, with some suggestions on how to solve these minor glitches in the grand plan of cooperation.

1. **Problem:** He doesn't know what to do.

   Solution: Don't expect him to guess. Give him your specific expectations and instructions. Spell out the kind of behavior you would like, the steps he should take to accomplish each goal, and deadlines to keep in mind.

2. **Problem:** She doesn't know how to do it.

   Solution: Explain how you see it can be done, and give her detailed instructions on how you would do it.

3. **Problem:** He doesn't know why he should do it.

   Solution: If he doesn't see the relevance in the same way you do, explain your perspective. If he still doesn't fully understand, ask him to cooperate with you to make you and the relationship happier—even if he wouldn't do it on his own.

4. **Problem:** She thinks her way is better.

   Solution: Accept your differences without making either of your approaches right or wrong. Then discuss which way is more efficient or easier for the time being.

5. **Problem:** He thinks he is doing it.

   Solution: Let him explain how he feels he is already contributing—you may be overlooking something. Acknowledge the behavior, show appreciation, and explain to him how you perceive his cooperation to be lacking.

   Review the above to see if any of these problems apply to you. For example, you may be the one who does not know what to do or how to do it. If so, apply the solution to yourself. Open communication and a willingness to change are key. These minor problems in cooperation can become serious if one of you refuses to discuss the problem or fix the imbalance. Remember, the goal is to alter behavior to achieve a better arrangement and a happier, healthier relationship.

A Major Cooperation Impediment: Gender-Based Stereotypes

Most contemporary men and women are more aware of gender stereotyping than their parents and grandparents were. In previous generations, men were expected to be the primary breadwinner of the family, and women were expected to assume the majority of household chores. Today, the dual-income couple is the norm, not the exception, and both men and women understand that one person can't do all the work around the house. More and more, couples are avoiding the trap of expecting women to do both a first and a second shift—doing all the household chores after working full-time. Consider that such expectations amount to double duty. That said, some gender stereotyping still does exist.

There are, of course, irrefutable gender differences: Men are generally stronger (physically) than women. But be careful not to confuse gender differences with gender stereotypes: Men are touted to be "left-brained" (logical, better at math) and women are supposed to be predominantly "right-brained" (intuitive, social, creative). Women have babies and men can't, but men can change diapers as easily as women can. Men are typically taller, heavier, and stronger; thus, they're the more likely choice for lifting a large box onto a high closet shelf. But being taller, heavier, and stronger doesn't make a man the ideal candidate for balancing the checkbook while the "little woman" loads the dishwasher. These issues aren't just the business of married couples; even couples who spend only odd weeknights or weekends together need to cooperate on handling the basics.

Love Bytes

Studies have shown that working women still do a greater percentage of household chores than men. Women also devote more hours to child care. In fact, more than 50 percent of married women working full-time regard child care as their responsibility. This is a source of strife in many relationships and can lead to continuing Chore Wars (see the following section).

The Chore Wars: Ten Gender-Based Questions

If you and your partner are struggling through the Chore Wars—you have problems cooperating in domestic and/or financial areas—take some time to examine your attitudes and prejudices. Maybe you're subscribing to stereotypes without even knowing it. To find out, answer the following questions honestly:

1. Does she constantly complain that he doesn't do his share of domestic chores, whether it's taking out the garbage, walking the dog, doing the dishes, cleaning, etc.?

2. When he does the laundry, does he fail to sort or fold the clothes? If she gets angry, does he retort defiantly, "If you don't like the way I do it, do it yourself!"?

3. When he cooks, is the meal a big production that results in a dirty kitchen, which he fails to clean?

4. Is routine meal preparation more up to her than him?

5. If you aren't living together, does he pick up after himself when he stays at your place? Or does she pick up after him regardless of where they stay?

6. Does he pay for all or most of their dates even though her salary is roughly equal to his?

7. Is he alone expected to provide all the accouterments of romance—flowers, candy, champagne?

8. Do you both defer mainly to his tastes in picking restaurants, movies, and plays?

9. Is it okay for her—but not for him—to be foolish or extravagant with money?

10. Whether you are living together or spending a lot of time together, who is more likely to pick up the other's cleaning or drop off the other's mail?

Dr. Judy's Rx

Research shows that in homes where both parents work, teenage daughters do three times as many hours of chores per week as their brothers. Training sons from an early age to do their equal share will prepare them for an enlightened sense of fairness that will bode well for healthy adult relationships. Not only that, they'll be better equipped to take care of themselves at college and in their first apartment. They'll know how to cook, iron a shirt, and clean up. It's good training for life!

Are You an Old-Fashioned Couple?

Discuss your answers to these questions. If your answers reveal that you harbor the sentiments I list here, you may be a bit more old-fashioned than you thought.

❑ She's the chief cook while he is the chef.

❑ She does the laundry "right," and he'll just never learn to sort and fold.

❑ She picks up his socks, drops off his laundry, and stands in line at the post office to mail his mother the Mother's Day gift she bought.

❑ His money is theirs while her money is hers ("play money" spent on frivolous extras, and good for a rainy day).

❑ He pays for dates and picks the restaurants.

❑ For him, love means bringing flowers, for her, it means accepting them graciously, or putting them in a beautiful arrangement.

Couples who can't let go of their misconceptions about what is a "woman's work" and what is a "man's responsibility" are doomed to battle indefinitely through the Chore Wars and continue to revisit all the problems that come along with them, including fights over money (see Chapter 20, "Dollars and Sense: A Healthy Couple's Guide to Handling Money Issues").

Call a Chore War Truce

Here are some things you can do to combat your lack of cooperation and avoid gender-based stereotyping:

➤ Sit down with your partner and create a comprehensive list of what needs to be done and how you'd like it to get done to ensure that your relationship runs smoothly. Your list should include examples of the seven major cooperation areas mentioned in this chapter: domestic chores, money management, decisions about entertainment, how much time to spend with family and friends, how to balance individual private time with couple time, sex, and family planning. Put your sexual issues aside for now because we'll be dealing with them in greater depth in Part 3, "How to Keep the Passion Alive."

➤ Underline the things you fight about, from cleaning up the kitchen to spending time with his friends. These are the areas in which cooperation is difficult for you. Give yourself credit for cooperating well in other areas (all the items you listed but did not underline). Can you apply some of the strategies that work in those areas to the trouble spots? Can you determine how gender stereotyping or other attitudes (feeling overworked, resentful, inadequate) create or intensify some problems that could be easily resolved?

➤ Make a list of your own strengths and weaknesses, and have your partner do the same (do this without discussion). Go over your lists together. Do you think your partner is being realistic? Does he or she think you are? Now match your strengths and weaknesses to the trouble spots in your relationship and assign chores. Say, for example, a couple fights about the clutter in the living room. Organization is his strong point, not hers. So put him in charge of eliminating the clutter and let her be responsible for something else.

➤ When you've finished assigning responsibility for tasks, check to see if the division is a fair one. If not, go over the lists again and make some changes. Each of you should feel like the other is doing his or her share.

A Unique Chore Plan

My favorite suggestion for doling out household tasks fairly is to make a list of the chores that need to be done and then consider that each task is really a professional job. Then you can assign each "job" an hourly rate in dollars and compare how much each of you contributes to your coupledom in terms of dollars and hours. This should help you decide on an equitable distribution of duties.

Task	Equivalent Career	Approximate Hourly Rate	Approximate Hours/Week	Gross Weekly Pay
Cooking	Chef	$30	10	$300
Housecleaning	Freelance domestic	$10	7–10	$70–$100
Driving kids	Chauffeur	$25–$30	7	$175–$210
Grocery shopping	Personal shopper	$10	9	$90
Running errands	Personal assistant	$15	10	$150
Other: _____	_____	_____	_____	_____

Still having cooperation problems? Review your lists again. Maybe you need to reconsider what needs to be done or who is best able to do what. If one partner consistently fails to live up to a cooperation agreement, the other has to decide how important the issue really is, weigh that against how well you are getting along in all other areas, and discuss the other larger issues of the relationship (commitment and compatibility).

The Friend/Roommate Test

If you're still having cooperation problems, try this: Think back to your college days and remember what it was like to live with a roommate (if you've never had a room-mate, imagine what it would be like to have one). What would you expect each other to do as roommates? I doubt either one of you would accept full responsibility for making sure there's toilet paper in the bathroom and milk in the refrigerator. More likely, you'd be expected to wash your own dishes and clean your own hair out of the bathtub drain. If something jointly owned or used broke (the TV or the knobs on the stove), you'd probably talk about who would handle getting it fixed instead of just as-suming one of you would do it. You should treat your love relationship in the same way—as two individuals agreeing on a plan for your mutual benefit. Remember, you're a team.

The Teflon Test

Another alternative is to apply the "Teflon Test," as my writer friend Donna Jackson calls it. That means if the woman is working full-time just like the man, the next time she hears a phrase that could easily trigger guilt, such as "Honey, what's for dinner?" then she should say a mental "no" to "Teflon Man" rather than assume that she should do everything and feel guilty. She should ask her mate instead, "How can you help me work that out?" Similarly, the next time she expects him to fix the stereo or hook up the VCR, he should hesitate and resist "Teflon Woman," and ask her what she can do to help.

Ask Dr. Judy

My favorite suggestion for resolving many of the relationship problems that people come to me with is the "Walk a Mile in His/Her Shoes" game. This exercise applies to most other aspects of a healthy relationship, including, of course, communication. By imagining yourself in the other person's shoes, you'll be able to clarify your own position and gain empathy for and a greater understanding of the other person's point of view.

Start with the simple process of imagining how the other person would feel in a given situation. To combat gender-based stereotyping, for example, you could each go through a set period of time (an evening, a weekend day) together, acting like the stereotypical male and the stereotypic female. This means that he rushes to open all the doors and she feigns inability even to change a light bulb. Then you reverse roles, and he acts like the stereotypical female, and she the stereotypical male. This means that she plops down in front of the TV and demands, "When's my dinner ready?" and sends him rushing into the kitchen. And he picks up the kids, rushes home, cleans up, and makes dinner.

You might think these two exercises sound silly, but couples who do them end up laughing and learning about how they truly see themselves and each other; then they make some real changes.

Save Competition for the Ring

Believe it or not, even lovers get competitive, and this competition becomes another major impediment to cooperation. Sometimes a couple doesn't even realize they're competing with each other. Examine your own situation: Instead of chipping in, does one of you ever purposefully refuse to do what the other asks or what's required of you? If your partner's reaction to your request for cooperation seems unreasonable or irrational, trust your instinct that something is wrong. Consider the underlying reason for the refusal: Is he in a bad mood? Is she just tired? Does he feel that doing what you ask is tantamount to being controlled by you, or believe that saying "no" proves he is stronger?

Ask Dr. Judy

Ken is a photographer who is dating a model, Julia. Ken was secretly envious of Julia's public position and the money, attention, and favors it afforded her. So whenever Julia made a suggestion to go somewhere or do something, Ken refused, making her feel upset and disrespected. Their relationship only improved when Ken admitted he wished he had the privileges Julia had—allowing himself to enjoy them with her instead of quietly competing with her over them.

Love Lookout

When lovers carry competition into the bedroom, each person might start trying to match the other's number of past lovers, experience, or success at flirting. Resist such impulses to compare or to score against each other.

Competitive social behavior in adults is usually rooted in childhood rivalries with brothers and sisters; it can also be a result of other life experiences and influences that taught people to place importance on winning rather than working with others toward a common goal. Do you or your mate act more like rivals than a team? Just by recognizing a pattern of competitive behavior within your relationship, you're already halfway to overcoming the problem. You can then begin to make concerted efforts to change. Eliminate the impulse to win out over your mate by understanding how you can work together to allow both of you to win. In other words, adopt a "win-win" attitude: Expect both of you to win, instead of having one person win at the other's expense. Achieving a "win-win" strategy is the secret to a truly successful cooperative team. That's what you should be striving for in a healthy relationship.

Five Tips to Team-Building

To facilitate cooperation, you and your partner should see yourselves as a team. In general, a good way to heighten your sense of cooperation and team playing is to apply certain exercises to your relationship. The following are some exercises, adapted from those used in the business world, that you can do together to boost your team morale.

There are no "right" or "wrong" answers. The key is to think about how you would approach each of these situations. For example, does one of you always give instructions, while the other follows? Do you seem to easily give each other a turn to take the lead? Do your styles please one another? If not, what changes are you willing to make?

1. **Imagine situations in which you and your partner would have to rely on each other to survive.** Discuss how you would deal with such a situation. For example, say the two of you are hiking in a canyon and end up straying off the trail and getting lost. You have one canister of water between you, and two hours before it gets dark. What do you do?

2. **Think about some of the items that you and your partner need or are planning to buy—anything from an electric toothbrush to a new car.** Pick one of these and go through the steps of researching choices, shopping, and purchasing the item together. Discuss what model you want to buy, who is going to buy it, and who is going to maintain it.

3. **Perform some domestic activity together, such as washing the car or cooking a meal.** Pay attention to the dynamics of your "working" relationship. Does one person tend to delegate tasks or give instructions about what's to be done? If so, does the other accept them readily?

4. **Exercise together.** Do an exercise that requires you to use each other's bodies, something that will give you the sense of working in tandem (see Chapter 28, "Keeping Your Love Exciting with New-Millennium Body and Mind Techniques," for some simple stretches you can do with your partner). For example, sit facing your partner on the floor; both of you should have your legs open and stretched out to either side. Now place the soles of your feet

Dr. Judy's Rx

Remember the game you used to play as a kid, where you and your friend would lie on your backs with your legs in the air and the soles of your feet pressed together, and you would begin to pedal? It undoubtedly gave you a feeling of working together and cooperating—that's partly why it was so fun. You can learn from these childhood episodes of sharing.

on the soles of your partner's feet and grab his hands. Take turns pulling each other; first he should pull you so that you're leaning forward, then you should pull him. You should also alternate pulling straight toward you, off to your right, and then off to your left.

Dr. Judy's Rx

There's a brilliant organization mentioned earlier in this book that I've been working with for 20 years: the Ned Herrmann International in Lake Lure, North Carolina. The group offers great training programs that teach a "whole brain" model for increasing creativity and team-building (this is the model on which I based my "Love Styles" quiz in Chapter 6, "The Importance of Matching Your Love Styles").

5. **Make a drawing of something together.** Here's a suggestion: Draw a new toy. Just make it up as you go along. Take turns drawing a line, and don't worry about whether it could ever be a real toy, or whether it even makes any sense. Each of you should use a different-colored pen or crayon so you can distinguish each of your contributions, and don't worry about your drawing abilities—that doesn't matter. The idea is simply to see how you and your partner interact on a common project.

To use this experience to learn about your cooperation skills, look at your drawing. How would you describe it? How would your partner describe it? How did you each feel doing it? Did you readily accept each other's contributions (a measure of your tolerance for differences, or appreciation of each other). If you got frustrated with your mate's lines and felt that they messed up your concept, this should send up a warning flag. Examine the real-life situations that require you to work with your mate or with others; maybe you need to be more tolerant of other's contributions.

The feelings and experience you take away from these exercises are typical of how you work with others on a project. What you discover about yourself could apply to anything you and your mate do together. What did each of you contribute? Did one of you seem to dominate the concept? Was it the person who seems to dominate your real-life decisions? Think about whether you feel comfortable with that division of power, or whether you would prefer to have more balance and an equal say in what goes on.

The Least You Need to Know

➤ Consider your relationship a team; for the team to succeed, it needs cooperation and balanced or agreed-upon contributions from each partner.

➤ Gender-based stereotypes interfere with cooperation (even some of the most modern couples might subscribe to some of these stereotypes without realizing it), but can be overcome.

➤ Expect your lover to be as cooperative and responsible as you would a friend or roommate.

➤ Do some activities that promote your conscious feeling of being "teammates" with your partner.

Chapter 10

Communication—
Can We Talk?

In This Chapter

➤ Why communication is so important

➤ How to actively listen

➤ What *not* to do for good communication

➤ The Communication Skills Quiz

➤ How to get a silent mate to talk

➤ How to speak clearly, listen well, and give good feedback

➤ Which secrets to reveal and which to keep

➤ How to talk about sex

I'm sure you've sat in a restaurant and looked over at other couples staring into space, looking aimlessly around, picking at their food, doing anything but talking to one another. Perhaps you have done this yourself. What a tragedy, when there is always so much to share. If only you knew how, and felt motivated to do it.

Ask some friends, "What's the best way to keep a relationship going?" I'll bet at least eight out of ten will say, "communication" (some others might say, "good sex"—for that, see Part 3, "How to Keep the Passion Alive"). Communication has become a buzzword for making relationships work. Certainly, if you've ever watched daytime talk shows with advice experts (and I've done hundreds of such appearances myself!), you know that at some point in the program troubled panelists will be advised to "communicate" with their partner. Everyone nods wisely as if the invocation of this word were a solution in itself. Books, magazine articles, and your best friend all preach the gospel of good communication. But it does take clarification and specifics to know exactly how to accomplish this.

The Importance of Communication

Not every couple communicates in the same way. Some are more verbal than others. Some choose their words with great care, while others are comfortable exchanging unedited information. How you communicate with each other is a reflection of your personalities, ages, backgrounds, and lifestyles. Two people who communicate in very different ways can learn to adapt to each other's styles.

Dr. Judy's Rx

Expand your definition of "listening" to include observing behavior. Pay attention to body language, gestures, and actions. An untalkative mate may actually be speaking volumes nonverbally.

To stay together you have to share information about yourselves. Two people who are unable to be vulnerable with each other can't help each other heal, get closer, or make a real commitment. We have to share our hopes and fears to be understood and loved. Sometimes we have to share our hurts, angers, and disappointments to get past them. Love isn't possible unless we can tell our partners how we feel about significant matters.

On a practical level, couples need good communication skills just to organize the details of their lives together. When both have jobs and other personal commitments, they have to exchange necessary information quickly and accurately. Otherwise they risk angry conversations beginning with the words, "But I thought you were going to …"

Love Bytes

Studies of married couples show that those who rate the communication between them as good are also more likely to report higher levels of satisfaction with their marriage in general.

Test Your Communication Skills

You might think your communication with your partner is good. That's great. But it is always helpful—and fun—to see just *how* good. Take the following quiz for a check-up. Circle the answer that most applies to you (even if others also ring true). Both of you should answer the questions separately and then compare each of your answers.

The Communications Skills Quiz

1. You've had an exceptionally bad day at the office. You …
   a. Tell your partner the details the minute you see her.
   b. First ask about your partner's day.
   c. Put it out of your mind and talk about happier things.
   d. Withdraw emotionally and/or physically and refuse to be drawn out.

2. You feel more strongly connected to your partner right now than you've ever felt to anyone. You …
   a. Say so, with an outpouring of emotion and adoring glances.
   b. Declare your love but then get on to other things.
   c. Assume she understands how you feel.
   d. Show your love through acts more than words.

3. Your partner is 30 minutes late meeting you in a restaurant and it's not the first time. You …
   a. Launch an emotional verbal attack as soon as she sits down.
   b. Express your anger in more restrained fashion, stating the facts.
   c. Say, "That's okay" through gritted teeth.
   d. Pretend you didn't notice or don't care and act distant for the rest of the evening.

4. Your partner has gained several pounds. You …
   a. Suggest a diet or exercise program.
   b. Mention the weight gain as diplomatically as possible.
   c. Deny you've noticed any added pounds if she asks.
   d. Refuse to talk about it, but mention you feel less attracted than you were before the added pounds.

5. You had dinner with an old lover recently. You …
   a. Tell your partner everything, including how you used to make love.
   b. Say you had dinner with an old friend.
   c. Say nothing.
   d. Have an alibi for your whereabouts that night, just in case your mate finds out you had dinner.

What Do Your Scores Mean?

If you selected mostly **a** answers, you have a strong need to spill out your feelings, no matter what. You feel something, you share it. Something happens, you tell it. You have a hard time containing your feelings. Maybe you don't always take time to temper criticism with kindness or determine if the secret you're sharing is something your partner has to know (such as the details of past love affairs).

Dr. Judy's Rx

The three essential C's for communication are: clear (state your points clearly without distractions or smoke screens); clean (state the points as objectively as possible, without blaming or attacking); and complete (don't be afraid to say what you really mean until you feel really satisfied that you get your full point across).

Mostly **b** answers? You're more reticent than the indiscriminate spillers and more inclined to think before speaking the harder truths. It will probably be easier for you to adapt your style to a partner's than it is for most others.

If you selected mostly **c** answers, you are the classic silent type who holds everything in and tries desperately to keep the peace. Some people who are like this fear being open and feel that sharing feelings, both good and bad, is a sign of weakness. You likely have trouble trusting someone enough to be vulnerable.

Mostly **d** answers indicate a possible passive-aggressive streak. At the very least, you avoid conflict, often at heavy cost. Rather than expressing needs or anger, you pull away. That behavior sends a conflicting message: Come closer and move away. Your "aggressive" part is seething with unexpressed anger, while the "passive" part expresses that anger in subtle ways, such as not wanting to make love with the person who has gained weight.

Is one communication style better than another? Not necessarily. Some combinations of styles may present more challenging problems, and those who are less extreme are more likely to work things out. But any two people can overcome natural tendencies and come to an understanding. Recognizing your own and your partner's styles is the first step toward improving communication.

Communication Techniques

There is no right or wrong way to express yourself, but some techniques will make communication smoother. Remember that communication is an ongoing process. Sometimes we focus on the "big talks" and forget that everything important doesn't get said at those times.

Direct Communication

Be clear and direct about your message. Whether you want a behavioral change, reassurance, companionship, support, lovemaking, or clarification of your partner's position on an issue, be clear. Your partner isn't a mind reader. Sometimes people are vague because they are uncomfortable asking for what they want directly or stating their positions unequivocally. The more honest and straightforward you are, the better. For example, saying "I'm hungry and I'd like to eat now. Are you ready to go out to dinner?" is preferable to "When would you like to go out to dinner?" because the latter approach requires your mate to intuit that you are hungry now. Unless your stomach is growling noisily, your message may not be received.

Even when you have a complaint about your mate, take responsibility for your statements by using what are called "I statements." That means, say "I want ..." or "I need ..." or "I feel ..." that puts the emphasis on you and takes the pressure off your partner that saying "You do ..." "You don't ..." or "You never ..." creates. The use of "I statements" is less threatening and more likely to elicit a helpful response. For example, saying "I have trouble talking to you about important issues" is better than "You never want to talk about anything important."

Frame your questions so they can be answered with the information you need. This is particularly important if your partner falls into the "silent" category described earlier. His tendency will be to give short (probably "yes" or "no") answers. If you ask questions that can be answered this way, you may not be getting all the information you want. And, if you are the less talkative partner, realize that the more information you withhold, the more you encourage the intrusive questioning you dislike. For example, demanding "I'm getting the message that you probably don't want to go to the party this weekend. Can you tell me why not?" is better than saying "Do you want to go to the party or not?"

Dr. Judy's Rx

Choose a good time to bring up an important issue. Approach your partner when he or she is most receptive and relaxed, and not distracted by TV, newspapers, work, or children.

Dropping hints, cajoling, saying one thing when you mean another, verbal manipulation—these are all barriers to clear understanding. Such indirect communication leads to misunderstandings and resentments. Why resentments? Because neither feels understood or truly accepted by the other.

Active Listening

One of the most important aspects of healthy communication is feeling that you've been "heard" and letting your partner know that you "heard" what she said.

A good listener does much more than wait patiently until it's his turn to talk again. He hears the speaker's words, notes the emotional tone in which they are spoken, and observes the body language and gestures accompanying speech. Sometimes our words are conveying one message while our body language is signaling another. When words and body language don't complement each other, ask yourself, "What's really

135

Dr. Judy's Rx

Resist the impulse to interrupt, but do ask questions like "What do you mean?" or "Can you give me an example?" when you don't understand what your partner is saying.

going on here?" For example, if he says "I love you" in a voice devoid of emotion, his eyes not meeting yours, his arms crossed over his heart, a reasonable interpretation could be: No, he's shutting me out. He's closed off.

An emphatic listener is able to identify with the speaker. That can't happen unless the listener is truly paying attention. Too often a conversation is really two people taking turns expressing their viewpoints, without really listening and responding to what the other says. If your response is formed before your partner has finished speaking, you can't be an emphatic listener.

Watch your own body language as you listen to your partner. Are your legs crossed, arms folded protectively across your chest? Maybe you're not open to the message being delivered. If you're sitting on the edge of the chair, you'll probably appear impatient and anxious for your mate to finish speaking. On the other hand, if you're relaxed, sitting back in your chair, but leaning slightly forward, you're encouraging communication and demonstrating your willingness to hear the message and respect your partner, whether you agree with his words or not.

Giving Feedback

Responding appropriately to your partner's message is as important as being able to state your own clearly and listen actively. First, determine what response is needed. Maybe you don't have all the answers to the questions asked or you're not ready to make a decision on an important issue, but your partner wants to know your reaction to his concerns, opinions, or desires. It's helpful to restate the other's words when you acknowledge them. Then give your reaction. For example, say "I understand that you want to have a wedding with 200 guests." Then add, "I'm not sure if I'm ready to commit to something that big, but I am willing to look at some figures and have another conversation about this later."

Giving feedback can be a simple matter of expressing your continuing love and support. If your partner has an ongoing problem, particularly one that you can't help resolve, such as a work crisis, indicate your willingness to be a supportive listener whenever needed. Say, "I care and I'm here for you," and add loving gestures (smiles, hugs) as you listen. Caressing a hand, arm, or shoulder gives supportive feedback, too.

When you do have an opinion to express or a solution to offer, state your case in clear, descriptive language. Limit your feedback to the subject under discussion. This is not the time to say, "And you also need to do [x] about [y and z]."

Show Appreciation

Acknowledge yourself and your partner for communicating. Show your gratitude in words and actions. Say, "I'm very glad we talked. Thank you for taking the time to discuss this." Allow your partner to feel as good about communicating as you do by reinforcing your words with affectionate gestures.

Eight Communication *Don'ts*

Besides what to do to communicate well, it is also important to know what not to do. Avoid the following:

1. **Jumping to conclusions.** Most conflicts arise out of misunderstandings. You may think you heard something, but take the time to find out the whole truth.

2. **Defensiveness.** People become defensive when they feel threatened. Your partner should know that you respect her opinion even if you don't agree. Listen to every idea offered.

3. **Aggressiveness.** You can resolve conflicts and get your needs satisfied without being overbearing. Aggressiveness is a battle for control; assertiveness is being definite.

4. **Argument for the sake of argument.** If you're not working toward a solution, you're wasting your time, proving nothing, and causing unnecessary rifts. If a conversation seems to be going nowhere, stop and rethink what you are really upset about. Approach it from a different point of view.

5. **Adversarial attitude.** An attitude that says one of you is wrong or out to hurt the other only creates defensiveness and distrust. One of the most important ways to keep both of you feeling good about communicating is trusting that you both care about making your relationship work.

6. **Raining on each other's parade.** It saddens me when I hear stories like this: Shari was really excited about an upcoming business trip, but when she told her husband, Jonathan, his response was, "Oh sure, they probably couldn't get anyone else to go." They ended up not talking to each other for days. The truth was that Jonathan felt threatened and haunted by fantasies about her meeting someone else. This fear overshadowed his being happy for her. Only when he acknowledged and admitted this fear to her were they able to resolve their argument.

7. **Prophesying doom and gloom.** A partner with a pessimistic outlook on life needs to make a real effort to keep that negativity under wraps to make the relationship healthy. Continual pessimism only drains energy and lowers morale.

8. **Playing games.** Some people delight in creating manipulative scenarios and thrive on discord. For example, Chip and Melissa were seeing each other exclusively for a year. Yet nearly every week, Chip would hedge about whether they

Dr. Judy's Rx

In the initial stages of dating, you certainly don't have to spill all the beans. But when you get serious, it's time to let your mate in on some things you may have been wise not to have shared earlier, such as family scandals, medical conditions, or financial trouble. Openness is crucial to good communication. But there are limits—for example, be careful about revealing details of past loves.

Dr. Judy's Rx

It's not necessary to tell someone you're casually dating that you have been abused. But once you care about someone and know that he really cares about you, it's important to let your mate know to allow him to understand you and to help you get past the pain.

would get together Saturday night. He teased that he might have something else to do, and baited her to beg that they be together. Chip didn't stop his game until Melissa stopped worrying about what he would do, ignored his resistance, and let him make plans or not. Eventually, he stopped taunting her and made active plans to spend the weekend together.

What Should You Tell—and When

I don't advocate game-playing—withholding information for the sake of manipulating another into a relationship or into a certain kind of behavior within the relationship. Other books may tell you not to express your real feelings or advise you to hide your real interests and intentions so you have the upper hand. But in my view, if you can't be yourself with your partner, then you aren't with the right person.

In a good relationship, the partners should be able to tell each other almost anything. The operative word is "almost." Complete honesty can be cruel.

Ask yourself, "Why am I saying this?" Do I want to get it off my chest, alleviating guilt for something I wish I hadn't done or thought? Am I looking for absolution? Does my partner need to know? Will sharing this strengthen our relationship or drive a wedge between us? Do I secretly want to boost my own ego or foster jealousy and insecurity in my partner?

Assess the impact of your confession on your partner before you make it. Maybe you betrayed him by having a one-night stand early in the relationship. The damage is done. What is to be gained by speaking up now?

Also ask yourself, "Why am I saying this at this particular time?" Do I want to slow down the relationship by confessing to my past now? Or do I want to be clear about the past at the beginning of a relationship before such a confession can cause real pain? Do I want to share my negative feelings (about family, weight, friends, habits, or our relationship) because I want to initiate positive changes that will bring us closer, or because I want more attention or revenge? Am I speaking up now because my partner is very strong and can handle the secret, or because my partner seems more vulnerable than usual?

Maybe the secret does need to be shared. But when you speak, and how you do so, can mitigate or increase the pleasure or pain your words may cause.

When a Mate Won't Talk

Consider this joke. A boy comes home from school all excited about getting the lead role in a school play. "What role did you get?" asks his mother. "I'm going to play the Father," replies the boy. "I thought you were going to get a speaking role!" exclaims his mother.

This joke pokes fun at men not communicating. Fortunately, more men today are keen on sharing their feelings, if they still have more progress to make. A major complaint women have always had about men is: "He doesn't talk about his feelings." This has been documented in many studies, including over 25 years' worth of Virginia Slims Opinion Polls.

Ironically, I hear some men today complain about women's reticence, like this man who told me: "I'm always asking my girlfriend what's wrong and she says 'Nothing,' but I think she's upset about something. How can I get her to open up to me?"

Dr. Judy's Rx

Be clever. Rather than nagging your silent partner to tell you what he's feeling be more specific about the acts or behavior you want. Use the word "think" instead of "feel." Ask, "What do you think about ...?"

Clamming up is one of the biggest problems—and complaints—in relationships. I could answer every person's question to me with: "Talk to her about it ..." It sounds so simple, but men and women alike resist doing it. Why? Because a host of fears get kicked up—hurting the other person, losing control, being vulnerable, facing unacceptable feelings. Yet you have to get over your resistance because talking together is essential. The silent one and the talker both have to make some adjustments to get the communication going.

What to Do If Your Mate Is the Silent Type

How do you get your mate to talk? Getting a partner to open up and share feelings takes time and trust. Use self-disclosure by talking about yourself first. Rather than feeling hurt or shut out when he won't talk, recognize that he may not be used to sharing, or has had bad past experiences with revealing certain personal issues. If the silence is not being used as a weapon, it's probably your mate's style. You can't blame a person for his or her style, but it doesn't mean the person can't change. Practice the four A's: Accept, Accommodate, Appreciate, and Agree:

Dr. Judy's Rx

If your mate uses silence as a weapon, refuse to be upset. Diffuse your anger with an activity. Separate your mate's withdrawal from your own painful past experiences in love or childhood. Let her cool off. Take deep breaths and switch your attention to doing something that makes you feel good. Come back to the discussion at some other time.

➤ **Accept** the way your mate is. If you have to be the one who talks more, or is more emotionally expressive, so be it. If you really wanted someone more expressive, you wouldn't be in the relationship to begin with. So value the other things you obviously chose you partner for.

➤ **Accommodate.** That means adjust or make changes yourself in a way that is more in alignment with your partner. There are several ways to adjust:

Approach your partner with a positive attitude. Don't fall into generalizing ("Men don't talk about their feelings").

Show by example how you like to be spoken to. Do the talking and then say, "I love talking to you like this, and I would love it if you talked to me like that, too."

Learn to communicate in other ways. Instead of using words, touch each other. Interpret actions as words. If your mate hangs up your shirt or brings you flowers, acknowledge those loving gestures.

➤ **Appreciation.** Give positive reinforcement for the behavior that you like. Follow one of my favorite principles: Train your mate by rewarding what you want repeated. As soon as he says the slightest statement you feel is personal, say, "It makes me feel so close to you when you open up to me," or "Thank you so much for sharing those personal feelings with me."

➤ **Agreement.** Once your mate is in a receptive mood, make a plan about when you can talk, even if you end up doing most of the talking. You'll feel better about the communication between you even when one person is just listening. During your discussion, make requests about what you would like. Say calmly, "I would really like it if you said you loved me. I know it's not your way, but it would mean a lot to me."

What to Do If You're the One Who Doesn't Talk

The burden of adjusting usually falls on the talker in a relationship. The silent types have to show equal effort to:

➤ Reassure your more talkative mate that you're not purposefully withholding, but just not comfortable expressing yourself.

➤ Ask your more talkative mate to be tolerant and patient with you.

➤ Examine your fears about talking openly. Are you distrustful of what people do with your personal information?

➤ Trace your silence to your childhood. Did you copy one of your parents (perhaps your father was quiet in contrast to your mother's openness)? Were you criticized for saying something, so you learned to keep to yourself?

➤ Review your past experiences with lovers. Have you been hurt by saying something personal in the past?

➤ Conquer shyness. Feel confident about what you have to say. Admit being shy and take a risk and say it anyway.

➤ Practice talking. Pick an experience or news event that you find interesting and say it to yourself (as you are driving or to a mirror) to hear yourself tell a story.

➤ Every day express one feeling in response to something your mate says ("I'm happy for you," "I'm sad to hear that," "I'm angry that happened").

Love Lookout

What are your fears about saying what's on your mind (that you will be judged, be wrong, or be misunderstood)? Whatever your fears, examine them if you want to be close to someone you love. Fears can be obstacles to healthy communication, and consequently, to a healthy relationship.

Talking About Sex

All the previous rules apply when you're in—as well as out—of bed. Communication is key to good sex. Review the guidelines and think about your sex life. Do you listen to your partner? Do you communicate your likes and dislikes in a gracious, nonthreatening, clear way? Do you give supportive and encouraging feedback?

Withdrawal or upset in sex can be a smoke screen for problems outside the bedroom. Ask your partner what those problems might be, and work toward dealing with them directly, so the bedroom does not become a battleground.

Love Bytes

More men than women need direction about their partner's sexual responses, since female sexual responses are generally more varied, idiosyncratic, and not as evident (as men's erections or ejaculations).

When Silence Is Not Golden in Sex

A woman sent me an e-mail that her husband is so quiet in bed, she worries he's not enjoying himself. "Am I doing something wrong?" she wondered.

I find it common that men and women alike are so quick to question their sexual skill, worrying that they are not doing some activity "right," and assuming that if their partner is not responding, he must be disinterested or displeased. Often it is not at all a partner's fault. Clarification and explanation are necessary to clear up the confusion and restore confidence.

One partner may be more vocal and verbal about sex than the other. Rather than displeasure, reticence is more likely due to inhibitions or personal style. You have several options: Accept your partner's quiet enjoyment while you express yourself freely (touching in various motions, pressures, and places, and with various body parts). Or verbalize how you feel and what you imagine your partner feels. Or request feedback and give your partner permission to make direct requests.

Ask Dr. Judy

One woman told me, "I've been seeing a man for three years and we just got engaged. I never knew he was dissatisfied with me in bed, but the other night when we were making love he turned the stereo up until the sound was deafening. When I complained, he said sarcastically that my silence was deafening him! We got into an argument and I nearly broke the engagement. I'm 32 and have only been with a few men before, but they never complained. Am I abnormal to be quiet in sex and am I right in being so upset?"

This woman's fiancé demonstrates how not to talk to your partner about sex. He should have whispered in her ear one night when she was feeling especially confident, "Honey, I love when you make noises. It lets me know you are enjoying yourself so I can feel good that I am pleasing you."

But she also has to understand his need for feedback—most lovers need some sign that they are pleasing. If making noise is not your style, give feedback in another way, like movements, facial expressions, heavy breathing, even sighs. To please your partner, can you learn to vocalize more?

Realize that more than technique, the most important element in pleasuring a partner is attention and attitude. Squash self-doubt by being totally immersed in what you are doing. Focus your attention ("tune in") on what your partner is feeling inside, so you will be sensitive to even the tiniest reactions that will guide you.

Asking for What You Want

Asking for what you like is essential for good sex. You may feel that discussing the specifics of lovemaking ruins its spontaneity and mystery. I've heard women say, "If he really loved me, shouldn't he just know?" It would certainly be a dream come true if you were so in tune with each other. Some partners are. However, while such sexual intuition is possible, it does not preclude that loving couples may still need to educate each other. Have the courage to ask for what you want. Obviously, the longer you know your partner and the deeper your trust, the easier it is to ask. But have courage to ask even in the beginning. The best way to get what you want is to ask without expectations or demands (called "nondemand" requests). That means simply stating what you'd like without implying punishment or inducing guilt, so the other person is free to give willingly or refuse without being defensive.

Dr. Judy's Rx

Make requests about what you like in bed, but avoid lengthy discussions about what you don't like. Stop an undesired behavior by directing attention to what you prefer (say, "I'd prefer you to ...").

Saying What You Don't Like

It is equally important to make clear what you don't like. The best way of doing this is by first telling your partner what you do like. Criticism only makes people feel defensive and deflated. Pointing out what they did wrong only reinforces the act. "I hate when you do that" only makes their mind focus on what they did wrong, not on what you want. Make their mind focus on what you want, since what the mind conceives is more likely to be enacted in real life. Telling your partner what you like motivates him to please: "I prefer it when you touch me softly there to when you pinch harder."

Love Bytes

Most people are afraid to tell a partner what they don't like about their sexual behavior for fear of hurting them. But if you don't say anything, your partner will just assume you like the act and continue the behavior. Silence compounds the problem; speaking up gives your lover a chance to truly please you.

Can't Say No

Consider this: You cannot truly say "yes" if you cannot truly say "no." That means you must set your limits without fear. If you really don't want to do something in sex—or at all—you have to be able to say "no." Maybe you don't really want to do it in a certain position, or on that particular night, or in a particular way.

Jacqueline can't say "no" any time her fiancé wants sex, even if she's not in the mood. "I'm so afraid he'll be upset," she told me. Fear of hurting or losing love is a common reason people don't speak up. Sometimes they go along with a partner's request because they don't ever want the tables to be turned—they wouldn't want to hear "no" said to them. If so, assertiveness training is in order. Acknowledge "I'm a people pleaser." Maybe you watched your mother be that way when you were growing up. You don't have to be like her. Affirm, "I don't have to please others," facing that you can bear the worst of their reaction (their anger, revenge, or even love withdrawal). Practice saying "no" to three requests a day that you would normally have said "yes" to, and feel the pride and self-esteem that comes from exerting your will without fear.

The Least You Need to Know

➤ Good communication is essential to a relationship.

➤ Good communication involves speaking directly, listening actively, and paying attention to tone of voice, body language, and gestures as well as words.

➤ Not everyone communicates in the same way and one style is not inherently better than another. Couples need to adapt to each other's style.

➤ Criticism can be handled in a positive way to help relationships grow and partners improve individually.

➤ Know why you're sharing a painful secret before you speak.

➤ Speak up about what you like in sex.

➤ The same rules for good communication outside of bed apply in bed.

Chapter 11

Commitment— Warming Up Cold Feet

In This Chapter

➤ The five dimensions of commitment

➤ A Commitment Readiness Quiz

➤ Reaching agreements about commitment and fidelity

➤ Recognizing "cold feet" and how to warm them

➤ Eleven events that push you towards a commitment

➤ Making long distance love work

➤ Ultimatums: Do they work?

Commitment—another of the big C's—is a promise you willingly make to follow a course of action. The word "commitment" has come to imply a long-term involvement, but actually can be specified for any amount of time. If you commit yourself to love one person forever, you promise to keep him or her in your mind and heart, for life. Even though relationships like this—ones that last forever—are becoming increasingly rare these days, most of us still cherish this ideal of commitment. Marriage vows still include this promise. Who among us doesn't want to feel secure in a lasting, forever love, trust, and fidelity to share with our partner?

If you and your mate have been dating a while, and if you're like most couples, you're probably either gearing up to discuss this big "C," or consciously avoiding the topic altogether. If you fall into the latter camp, you also probably know that no amount of denial will make the issue disappear—like a heavy scent, it hangs in the air.

The Nature of Commitment

For many people, commitment and marriage go hand in hand—often the first naturally leads to the second. For others, commitment doesn't necessarily include marriage. For example, actress Goldie Hawn has often publicly described her long-time devoted union and family life with actor Kurt Russell, although they are not formally married. Such couples can happily live together (or apart) and have a sexually monogamous relationship with their partner. In society today, you're increasingly free to define commitment almost any way you like, spelling out your own terms regarding mutual psychological, emotional, economic, and physical support.

Commitment is not a one-way street. To cultivate a true commitment, both people need to know what they want from the relationship, and from themselves. Ideally, both would be equally in love with each other. Also, ideally, you would share a real and unconditional love; you can't have a true commitment if your love is based on some fantasy image of your partner instead of real knowledge and acceptance, faults and all.

A committed couple acknowledges the strength and depth of their feelings for each other and pledges to be a continuing, significant part of each other's lives. Their feelings reflect true dimensions of commitment, consistent with the eight dimensions of a healthy relationship described in Chapter 2, "The Seventh Dimension of a Healthy Relationship: Spiritual Love."

Love Lookout

Although they're often linked in people's minds, marriage doesn't always mean commitment. Some marriages happen as a result of circumstance—situations like unplanned pregnancy, feeling desperate or alone, or needing financial support—rather than being a contract based on love and emotion. Commitment should be voluntary, as an act of faith made freely by each partner.

1. **Physical.** Just as with primitive societies and the wild west, commitment involves dedication to each other's safety.

2. **Emotional.** You and your partner should acknowledge that you are each the most important person in the other's life and that you are willing to make certain sacrifices to keep your togetherness intact.

3. **Intellectual.** Although you certainly don't have to agree on everything, you should have a solid shared core of values and beliefs. And you should respect whatever differences you have.

4. **Physical.** Traditionally, commitment meant being sexually monogamous. For most people today, it still does. For some, however, commitment doesn't necessarily entail an exclusive sexual contract. Whatever your view, your partner should agree to the same.

5. **Spiritual.** At the deepest level, commitment to each other reflects or devotion to nurture each other's spirit, support and share each other's spiritual journey.

What Makes You Want It?

Decide exactly what commitment means to you and why you desire it, if you do. Figuring out why something matters to you is always important, especially in a relationship. Your motives will determine how you behave in the relationship (for example, how driven you are about wanting to get your mate to commit) and how your partner will react (even if he or she isn't consciously aware of your motives).

Take Patty and Wesley's situation, for example. After six months of dating, Patty wanted Wesley to make a commitment to her, and although he didn't know why, Wesley was resistant to the idea. He loved Patty but somehow he felt "funny" about making a big commitment to her.

In talking to them both, we figured it out. Patty felt pressured to marry because she wanted to stick to the fantasy timeline that she'd set up for herself: Find a man with a stable job, get married by age 25, buy a house, then have a child right away. Patty had made what I call a "love casting call." She was looking for a man to fit her master life plan and Wesley seemed a likely choice. Without realizing it consciously, Wesley sensed something unnatural about being cast just to play a role in the movie Patty had written for her life.

Many women—and some men—experience a similar pressure to conform to such a timeline in settling down. Recognize this in yourself to prevent it from driving away potential lovers. Focus on the real people, rather than how they fit into your master plan.

If you, too, are looking for commitment from your partner, figure out why you want it: Is it to make your relationship even stronger or is it to settle down, please your family, make your friends jealous, or fulfill a fantasy?

Love Lookout

Marriage is a constantly evolving partnership that takes a lifetime of work. Although a wedding ceremony is an important public symbol of your love, it only marks the beginning of an ongoing process; it's not an end in itself. Expect the true test of your togetherness to begin when the wedding and honeymoon are over.

Dr. Judy's Rx

Give a relationship your all if you really want it. Pull out all the stops to make it work. Ask directly for a commitment and probe for the root of any resistance. If you're still not satisfied in a year, reconsider whether you are willing to continue the relationship without any dramatic progress.

Are You and Your Partner Ready to Commit?

So now you have a better understanding of commitment, and maybe you even want to establish commitment between you and your partner. But are you sure you're ready for it? Is your partner? Both of you should take the following quiz. Answer "yes" or "no" as best you can, realizing that you may have qualifying considerations. Pick the answer that applies most of the time and check the appropriate answer. Keep your answers to yourselves until you're both finished, then discuss your answers and your feelings. You'll notice the questions are divided into steps. These are the steps toward a commitment that I'll explain after you take the quiz.

The Commitment Readiness Quiz

	Yes	No
STEP I		
Do you enjoy being together?	___	___
Do you have similar interests?	___	___
Are you comfortable talking with each other?	___	___
Do you feel you "know" each other as people?	___	___
Do you look forward to seeing each other?	___	___
Do you enjoy introducing your partner to others?	___	___
Can you hardly wait to tell your partner about an experience?	___	___
Do you have fun together?	___	___
Do you care about how each other's day went?	___	___
Do you feel good after seeing one another?	___	___
STEP II		
Do you tell each other things you don't tell others?	___	___
Do you say "we" a lot?	___	___
Do you like feeling like a couple?	___	___
Are you tired of casual dating and the singles scene?	___	___
Do you prefer each other's company to anyone else's?	___	___
Do you enjoy being together when you're around other people?	___	___
Do you always spend nights together (at one partner's apartment), rather than sleep alone?	___	___
Do you find yourself less attracted to other women/men?	___	___
Do you care about your partner's happiness?	___	___
Do you make small sacrifices to please your partner?	___	___

	Yes	No
STEP III		
Can you trust your partner?	_____	_____
Do you feel like you're at "home" when you're with your partner?	_____	_____
Have you resolved arguments?	_____	_____
Do you always consider your partner when making decisions?	_____	_____
Do you feel like you've known your partner "forever"?	_____	_____
Do you have similar sex drives?	_____	_____
Are you totally comfortable with your intimacy?	_____	_____
Have you pictured what your kids might look like?	_____	_____
Have you stopped thinking about other women/men?	_____	_____
Do you live together?	_____	_____
STEP IV		
Do you always think of your partner first, over yourself and over others?	_____	_____
Would you do whatever it took to keep your relationship intact?	_____	_____
Is it impossible for you to imagine a future without your partner?	_____	_____
Have you argued over money and resolved your differences?	_____	_____
Have you introduced your families and been anxious that they get along?	_____	_____
Have you survived crises together (major losses, injuries, someone's death)?	_____	_____
Do you agree on how and where to live?	_____	_____
Do you already feel married?	_____	_____
Do you want a family together?	_____	_____
Do you imagine yourselves growing old together?	_____	_____

Look over your answers together. The further down the list your "Yes" answers go, the more ready you are for commitment. So, if the questions you answered "Yes" to are mostly clustered in Step I (and you answered "No" to most of the rest of the quiz questions), you fall into the "Casual Dating" category; that is, you're not quite ready for commitment.

If you answered "Yes" to the questions in Step II, you're in the "Serious Dating" phase and although you're closer to a true commitment, you might want to wait and see how your relationship evolves before taking the big step.

If you answered "Yes" to most of the questions in Step III, bingo! You've entered the "Ready for Commitment" stage of your relationship. If you haven't already, and if you want to, you and your partner should discuss the terms of the committed relationship you'd like to have (see the following section). And, finally, if you answered "Yes" to the questions in Step IV, you're not just ready for commitment, but you've reached the "Ready for Long-Term Commitment" phase—you might even want to think about marriage.

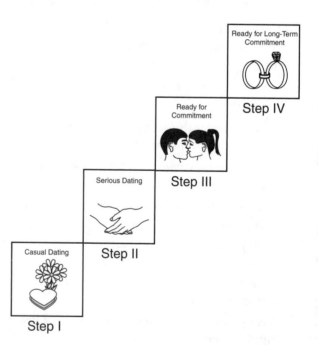

Terms of Commitment

If you and your partner have taken the quiz and feel ready to make the big "C" a part of your relationship, you need to now sit down together and iron out the details of what your commitment will entail.

Until Death Do Us Part?

If you decide your commitment is going to mean a long-term involvement, spell out what "long-term" means. Leaving the time frame of your commitment undefined allows too much room for misinterpretation and strife. She may say, "I want a commitment" and he'll panic as his mind flashes ahead to scenes of a wedding, a house full of kids, and mortgage payment pressures. Avoid this problem by being more specific about the nature and length of the commitment you want (through the summer, while you're in school or away at boot camp, or forever). That may sound unnatural, but if you set your initial goal to be committed for a defined period of time, it'll be easier to make the commitment. Then, as your relationship evolves, you can check in with each other periodically and make recommitments along the way.

What About Monogamy?

Many men and women are afraid that a partner cannot meet *all* of their sexual needs all the time. You might, however, want to *pledge* sexual exclusivity. This means that even when you don't feel 100 percent satisfied by your partner, you agree not to go outside the relationship for sex. Monogamy also implies that you expect your partner to try to satisfy you fully (and vice versa), or that you'll alter your own sexual expectations in order to feel satisfied by your partner. Generally, monogamy is a big part of a commitment package. (See Part 3 for more on the importance of sex.)

Many couples just assume that their relationship is sexually exclusive after they've been together for a while or have had sex several (or even a few) times. Instead of having a discussion and coming to a mutual agreement not to have sex with others, they just assume they won't. Assumptions like this can lead to a crisis if one partner later discovers that the other isn't being faithful. Is it fair to accuse someone of being unfaithful if a pledge of fidelity was never made? I don't think so.

Monogamy should be a choice, not a default position. The idea of monogamy has become more important these days as people become increasingly aware of the threat of sexually transmitted diseases (STDs). But even though it makes sense to stay monogamous, people aren't always going to act that way. Temptations and opportunities for sexual liaisons are all around you, so you and your partner should consciously and deliberately make agreements about whether and how you will be sexually faithful to each other. Doing so will lessen the likelihood of giving in to temptation or hurting each other.

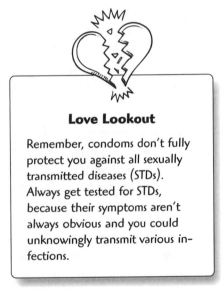

Love Lookout

Remember, condoms don't fully protect you against all sexually transmitted diseases (STDs). Always get tested for STDs, because their symptoms aren't always obvious and you could unknowingly transmit various infections.

Can You Be True to Each Other?

How capable of fidelity are you? What about your mate? You and your partner should both take this Fidelity Quotient Quiz and compare your results.

151

The Fidelity Quotient Quiz

	Yes	No
Are you comfortable with the idea of having sex with only one person (that is, your current partner) for the rest of your life?	_____	_____
Can you enjoy fleeting fantasies of being with someone else, but dismiss them easily?	_____	_____
Do you believe that monogamous relationships are not only possible but preferable to having several partners?	_____	_____
Are you comfortable with the fact that sexual desire will wax and wane in an ongoing monogamous relationship?	_____	_____
Do you believe that monogamous couples can rekindle their sex fire by being more creative as lovers?	_____	_____

If you answered "Yes" to most of these questions, you have a high fidelity quotient and are now, or will be, ready to have a sexual commitment. Only one or two questions? Monogamy might be a stretch for you, at least for now. Couples who understand that their sex life will go through natural ups and downs over time, and who may feel attractions to others but not act on them, have the best chance of staying faithful to each other.

Talking About Commitment

Here are five crucial guidelines for your discussion with your partner about commitment and monogamy:

➤ **Define your terms.** Each of you needs to ask the other how you view commitment ("What does commitment mean to you?") and fidelity ("How important to you is a monogamous relationship?"). You and your partner may have different ideas about the definitions of commitment or monogamy, and you need to get these out in the open before assuming anything. Does monogamy mean you both will have no other sexual partners or dates, or does it mean that any intimacy short of sexual intercourse with another person is acceptable?

➤ **Be honest.** Be forthcoming about your previous relationships and sexual history. Your partner has a right to know that you've had sexual experiences, but a body count and details aren't necessary.

➤ **Don't make promises you can't keep.** Maybe you aren't ready to match your partner's level of commitment. Maybe you aren't quite sure you're ready for monogamy. Don't feel pressured to go along for the sake of agreement or fear of losing the person.

➤ **Don't be critical of your partner's feelings and needs.** If you asked for or agreed to a straightforward talk about commitment and/or monogamy, that means you agreed to hear some things you might not have wanted to hear. Accept these without judging your partner.

➤ **Keep the door open for further discussions.** You may not reach an accord this time, but that doesn't mean you never will. Don't get frustrated. Just give yourselves some time to regroup and plan another discussion.

Agreement Plan

Once you've discussed the terms of your commitment, you'll realize that being committed means agreeing to a certain course of action. Beyond promising to be committed for a definite length of time or promising to stay faithful, there are many other implied agreements. What are they? Identify these behaviors specifically. You're asking for trouble if you ask your partner for a commitment, but fail to explain what kind of behaviors you expect from him or her. For example, she may expect that he spend every weekend with her because they're committed to each other, but he may have no intention of giving up his Friday night poker parties with the guys. To avoid any confusion or hurt feelings, spell out exactly what you want and/or are willing to do. New expectations will emerge all the time, of course, and you should discuss these as the relationship evolves.

> ### Healthy or Unhealthy?
>
> If someone says, "I don't want a commitment," believe it. If you don't believe this, you'll end up getting hurt, or at the very least, you'll be wasting your time.

After you and your partner have talked about each of your expectations regarding commitment, write them down in the space on the next page. You may have some expectations that your partner can't meet, and vice versa. Go over each other's list and see which expectations (for example, spend Saturday nights together, don't have sex with anyone else, visit each other's parents together) you can and can't agree to. Notice how many check marks you have under the "agree" and "disagree" columns. Whose expectations lead to the most agreements or disagreements? When you disagree, come to some kind of compromise; if you can't, at least agree to discuss these particular issues again later.

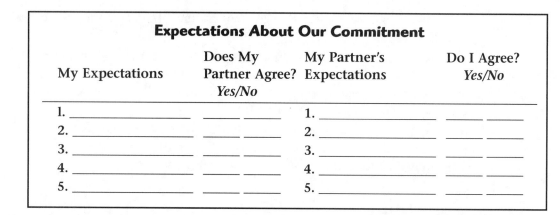

Expectations About Our Commitment

My Expectations	Does My Partner Agree? *Yes/No*	My Partner's Expectations	Do I Agree? *Yes/No*
1. _____ _____ _____		1. _____ _____ _____	
2. _____ _____ _____		2. _____ _____ _____	
3. _____ _____ _____		3. _____ _____ _____	
4. _____ _____ _____		4. _____ _____ _____	
5. _____ _____ _____		5. _____ _____ _____	

When Commitment Becomes a One-Way Street

In most cases—even with couples who have been dating for a while—one person makes a greater commitment to the relationship than the other. Most likely, one person is holding back or resisting a commitment out of fear. Perhaps he has been hurt before and doesn't want to make the same mistakes, or maybe she equates commitment with being trapped, or worse yet, a "jail sentence." These problems can be worked out given a little time and a lot of understanding.

You've definitely got a problem on your hands, however, if each of you is on a completely different wavelength. As Candy said, "I've been seeing this guy for two years, and all I think about is marriage—but I don't think he ever even gives it a passing thought." If you are still at odds about commitment after such a long time dating, you should start up a conversation about it. Each of you should decide what you really want and make your needs known. It's possible that one partner has no intention of ever committing—let alone getting married—which means that the other partner might want to rethink staying in the relationship.

Love Lookout

Honoring the agreements you make in life is essential to feeling good about yourself and nurturing a healthy relationship. If you don't follow through with what you say, other people will stop trusting you. Worse, you'll stop trusting yourself. Be clear and realistic about what you promise others.

Cold Feet: His and Hers

Sometimes when a partner can't commit, it's possible that he or she has "cold feet." Deep down, the person might want to have a fulfilling and committed relationship, but for some reason that proposition just seems frightening, unpleasant, or otherwise impossible. Many people fear commitment because they fear being hurt. Maybe they've been through a divorce or devastating break-up and they now fear becoming vulnerable to another person or making another "wrong" choice. If you can at least recognize why you're hesitating to commit, you're well on the road to resolving your problem.

Ask Dr. Judy

"I'm a nice guy and I'm seeing this woman who wants to marry me," said Dan. "I think I want a commitment, too, but I'm hesitant because I feel we just don't have enough chemistry in our sex life. I had a really passionate relationship before with a woman who was 10 years older than me. I didn't think that relationship would be permanent, so I enjoyed it freely. Could it be that I really liked the sex in that relationship because the pressure was off? Am I not enjoying the sex as much now because I have those cold feet?"

Good for Dan, for stopping to consider whether he had cold feet before writing his girlfriend off as "Ms. Wrong." If you're having similar second thoughts about your relationship, you should examine your whole dating history. Have you always seemed more committed when there was an "out"? If so, consider that your current boyfriend or girlfriend is someone with whom you're not interested in having a permanent relationship. By doing so, you might be able to relieve the pressure on yourself and "jump start" the passion.

Although men are generally the gender known for getting "cold feet," women are no less likely to exhibit their own brand of cold-footed behavior. But unlike her male counterpart, who may be straightforward about his desire to remain "free," the commitment-shy woman typically claims to want nothing more than to achieve a committed relationship. The problem? Usually she'll say that although she's met and dated a lot of men, she just can't find "Mr. Right." She laments, "All the good ones are married or gay." Her complaints are an excuse for keeping her uncommitted. Or she appears to set her standards so high, no man could meet them. She has a lot in common with the man who tires of the chase as soon as he has won the lady's heart. While he withdraws when the pursuit has been successful, she withdraws when actually being pursued.

Are you doggedly searching for that perfect mate—the elusive Ms. or Mr. Right—but keep coming up with people with flaws and imperfections you just can't handle? On the surface you say you're looking for "The One," but in reality, you might just be a "commitment-phobe," unwilling and unable to commit. If you've discarded many relationships because you didn't think any of your partners were suitable for commitment, you should stop and consider whether you're just using relationships as tests of your own desirability or ability to conquer, or whether you have unrealistic expectations of finding someone "perfect."

Dr. Judy's Rx

Broach the subject of commitment generally and impersonally at first. Mention a story involving a relationship that you heard about on, or rent a movie about a love affair or marriage. Gradually bring the conversation around to your mate's general thoughts about commitment, then to more personal thoughts about the two of you. Better yet, read this chapter together.

Dr. Judy's Rx

Sometimes holding on too tightly is the very thing that makes a lover choke and flee. Give your lover a little more leeway and some room to breathe so he feels he's with you willingly. Remember the popular saying: "If you love someone, set them free." What's truly yours, will come back to you.

Often, noncommittal men and women are attracted to those who really want a relationship. As I express in my "Mirror Law of Attraction," a concept I discussed in my previous book, *The Complete Idiot's Guide to Dating,* people tend to be attracted to others who reflect a part of themselves. For some, that part may be the fear of commitment. Neither partner may be aware of his or her own fear, or conscious that this is what is creating (at least partly) the attraction. If you or your partner swear you want a commitment but keep finding excuses not to make one to each other, you may be this type of match.

Can Those Cold Feet Be Warmed Up?

"I'm 28 and my boyfriend is 55 and has never been in a serious relationship. We've been together a year. Is there any chance he'll marry me?" Christy wanted to know.

"My girlfriend and I have been together on and off for four years now," Russell said. "She can't seem to make up her mind about whether she wants to stick with it. Will she ever commit?"

How can you tell the difference between an entrenched commitment-phobe and someone whose cold feet can be warmed? Here are some helpful clues.

➤ Look at your partner's relationship history. Does it consist of a series of affairs or is it marked by one or two significant loves that were lost? Someone who has endured a series of short affairs (a "love floater") is less likely ever to commit than someone who has loved and lost (a "love sufferer") who is capable of committing, but frightened of losing again.

➤ Learn about the kind of marriage your partner's parents have or had. Children of couples who had an extremely unhappy marriage tend to be determined not to repeat that pattern by either never marrying or ensuring they have a very happy marriage themselves. Those whose parents were devoted may want an equally idyllic pairing, or despair of ever equaling that ideal.

➤ Determine whether your partner has what I call a "hidden commitment"— something or someone else he or she is already committed to, something not obvious or conventional. This could be an attachment to a job, an ill parent, or an ex-love.

➤ Examine your partner's commitment in other aspects of life. Would/does he own a pet or take care of plants? How long has your partner stayed at her current job (or other jobs)? How long has your partner been in the same apartment? "Drifters" or "loners"—people who cannot commit to anything— are usually a bad bet in love as well. Being free is likely their preferred lifestyle.

➤ Think about how good your partner is at decision-making. How does he or she handle questions like, "Where would you like to go for dinner?" or "What's your favorite movie?" or "What do you really want to do with your career?" People who have trouble choosing between conflicting options ("vacillators") will likely continue entertaining options in love as well. Those who linger in the middle, wanting a little of everything ("fence-sitters"), or "passives" who defer decisions to others will be more susceptible to your (and other people's) influence.

As it turned out, Christy's 55-year-old, never-married boyfriend had a "hidden commitment." As sad as it was to realize, he was so entrenched in caring for his ill mother and so emotionally attached to her that it was unlikely he would ever commit to Christy while his mother was still alive. My prediction for Christy was that her boyfriend might finally agree to marry her after his mother's death, but then would turn Christy into a substitute mother. Could she be satisfied with that? Once she was prepared, and aware of this potential, she could face confronting her boyfriend to change this outcome.

Russell, on the other hand, finally convinced his girlfriend to get engaged to him—after which she had an affair. Talking someone into commitment is tenuous; only if she wants it herself will it really last.

Love Lookout

Sometimes the problem doesn't lie with the partner who seems unable to make a commitment. Maybe you're a "premature committer." Are you trying to move the relationship along too quickly? If you've frequently been involved with and left by people who weren't ready to commit, you may be the problem, not them.

Their Feet Are Frozen

It's easy to say that someone who won't commit is unhealthy, or has some problem—especially when you're the one left wanting a commitment. But you shouldn't be so quick to judge. For some people, flying solo is the best way to go, whether it's for life or just for certain periods of time.

General commitment-phobes or "floaters" feel trapped making a lasting agreement to just about anything. Selective commitment-phobes, however, might commit to some things in life, like buying a house or stocks, or owning a pet, but balk at boxing themselves into one intimate relationship. If you're the one trying to get such a resister to commit, you probably object to this kind of free lifestyle. But if these people are truly happy on their own, with no ties—even if others object and even if they might be missing out on certain joys of life—you cannot judge them as altogether unhealthy.

Timing Is Key

Maybe it's not that your partner is a commitment-phobe or that you are a premature committer. It's possible that neither of you have hidden commitments problems with monogamy.

Then what's the hold-up?

It's all about timing. I've heard countless versions of the following story: A woman calls me to complain, "I was madly in love with this guy and wanted to marry him, but he told me he wasn't ready to make a commitment. So we broke up. Some time later I found out he got married to someone else." In many cases, it's not that the two people are wrong for each other; rather, it might be that their timing is just off.

Eleven Considerations Along the Commitment Timeline

Ideal timing can be based on several factors. Jeff, a 25-year-old, just got engaged to Anita. He talked about caring for her but I noted that he didn't express any great enthusiasm. "Why did you propose?" I asked him. "I'm 25," he replied, "and it's time to get married. I'm tired of being on the circuit." Jeff's situation proves that factors other than true love can motivate the timing of marriage and commitment:

1. **Age.** Ideally, what age would you like to be or what age do you feel you should be when you settle down?

2. **Wanting children.** Although women are prey to the infamous biological clock, which increases their desire to bear children, experts have recently recognized that men also have a "father urge." Men are becoming more in touch with their desire to parent and are more willing to make a commitment to a woman in order to start a family.

Ask Dr. Judy

Consider this woman's story: "I like my current boyfriend, but I'm not ready to make a commitment to him. I was married for many years and just got divorced three months ago. Now I want to play the field a bit. My boyfriend and I are both in our 50s. He's never been married before and keeps threatening to leave unless I commit to him. Is it wrong of me to hold out? What if I lose him?"

If you're ever in this kind of situation, you'd be entirely correct to give yourself time not only to heal from your divorce, but also to rebuild your independence after having been married for many years. A strong sense of inner security is the best basis for any new relationship. Research shows that people in rebound relationships risk repeating problematic patterns. Spend some time evaluating what went awry in your marriage (or last relationship) and what you could change in yourself and in your interactions to make your next relationship a smooth and lasting one.

That said, you should be prepared to lose your boyfriend or girlfriend if you refuse to commit when your boyfriend or girlfriend is "ready." If that happens, though, you'll know that he or she didn't care enough to wait for you. Besides, you will have found (and will never lose) yourself—which is most important to your future happiness with or without a partner.

3. **Tired of "playing the field."** Dating around requires having pools of emotional and financial resources, which won't last forever. It can get frustrating to have continual casual relationships without depth.

4. **Pressure from your partners.** Pressure can come from the person you care about. He or she may insist you commit or threaten to leave.

5. **Inner pressure.** I often hear the story, "I'm not ready to get married, but I love her and don't want to lose her." Self-imposed pressure may come from this fear of loss or the pressure you put on yourself ("All my friends are married").

6. **Pressure from family or friends.** Other important people in your life may keep teasing or taunting you about settling down. Maybe you want to please your parents.

7. **Impending separation.** Moving away (for school, a job, even vacations) can create a desire for closeness and the security of a commitment.

8. **Threatening events.** Crises can make you reevaluate how precious and short life is. These can be personal (like a death (yours, your mate's, a friend's, or a family member's) or someone's illness or even hearing about an environmental crisis (earthquake, tornado, or floor) on the news.

9. **Events signifying birth or beginnings.** Similarly, a friend's wedding or the birth of a baby can motivate you to cherish precious moments in life and want to solidify your own participation in joy.

10. **Your own bad news.** As in the case of threatening events, bad things that happen to you (losses of any kind) make you want to reaffirm something good, like love.

11. **Your own good news.** As in the case of events signifying birth or beginnings, good things that happen to you (financial gains, promotions, success) can boost your ego and enthusiasm so much that you feel confident and excited enough to commit and share your good fortune.

On Different Wavelengths

There is truth to the saying that "Timing is everything." What this means is that your needs and your partner's needs may be different at different periods of time; when both your needs don't converge, your relationship may not work out.

One woman asked me, "What do you do when you and the person you love are at completely different stages in life? My boyfriend and I love each other, but he's ready to settle down and I'm not. He's older, has a steady job, and knows what he wants out of life. I don't. But if he really is Mr. Right, I don't want to pass up my chance."

The bottom line is that if you're not ready now, then he's not Mr. Right. Maybe if you were 10 years older, he would be "The One"—the point is, however, you aren't 10 years older. Granted, later on you may regret letting him go, but you have to do what feels right to you now. If your problem is a fear of commitment, then by all means address it and work through it; don't let a good thing walk away. Otherwise, accept that you love your partner, but that other circumstances are more important to you at this time in your life.

Making the Dreaded Ultimatum

If you truly feel that your mate loves you and is ready to commit deep down, but needs a nudge to take that leap, you can always give him or her an ultimatum. It's certainly a risky move, but it can work, as long as you stick to your guns.

Marnie told me, "I've been seeing this guy for five years and he keeps saying he loves me, but he still hasn't asked me to marry him. I've broken up with him several times because he refused to propose, but then I always ended up going back to him. How can I finally get him to propose?"

When you decide to pull out all the stops and make an ultimatum—"Make a commitment or else it's over" or "I want to get engaged by the end of the year or else I'm leaving you"—you have to be willing and ready to end the relationship if your terms aren't met. Otherwise, you've just cried wolf, and your words, threats, and desires carry no weight. You have to maintain your credibility by following through with your terms. If that means breaking up and staying apart, so be it. Getting back together would likely not get you what you want because the other person will have seen how desperate and easily manipulated you are.

Four Major Commitment Mistakes

Since commitment is so important and so coveted, people often fall into some common traps in their rush to find it. Don't let yourself be swept away by your own blind eagerness. Be cautious about the following four traps:

1. **Manipulating your partner into commitment.** Forcing a partner into a commitment may get you what you want in the short run, but just remember that what is not given voluntarily is often rescinded. Phillippa got pregnant and used the baby to corner James into marrying her; but he resented and distrusted her ever since. Ten years later, once the children were settled in school, he couldn't wait to divorce her.

2. **Making threats or dealing low blows.** For example, saying, "You'll never find anyone." Trading in on your partner's insecurities might get you a temporary stay, but he or she will likely not love you willingly, which is what you really want. In fact, your partner will probably grow tired and resentful of your harshness.

3. **Setting artificial timelines.** Relationships have a natural flow. Events—like finishing school or securing a good job—will determine whether the timing is right, and sometimes these conditions aren't entirely within your control. Most of the things that happen in life don't completely conform to whatever timeline you've set for yourself, so you have to learn when to make exceptions.

4. **Falling too quickly.** Some people fall in and out of love at the drop of a hat. If you're one of these people, you'll likely be expecting a commitment by the time

Love Lookout

Many couples let their relationships go on for years—all the while, one person has no intention of getting married and the other is patiently waiting for it to happen. Take inventory every three months about where you both stand on the issues of commitment and marriage, so the person who wants more does not end up disappointed or devastated.

161

the waiter comes back with your coffee. Get to know someone well before you ask for a commitment.

Long-Distance Love: When Separations Threaten Commitment

Many people have called me on my *LovePhones* radio show who are in love and exclusively dating someone, but who find themselves separated by distance for some reason. Perhaps one person got a job in a new city, went off to school, or joined the army. For example, Scot's girlfriend went to Seattle for basic training and he's back in Virginia, missing her and the great sex they were having before she left. He's wondering, as do others in similar situations, whether he can "hold out."

I always reassure couples that there are many ways to maintain your commitment during long-distance separations. With such advanced communications technology today, there's no shortage of ways to stay in touch with someone who's far away. Call or e-mail each other frequently. Fax sexy photos of yourself to your lover. Send overnight love packages. Most importantly, make sure you periodically reaffirm your commitment, so you both know what the other is feeling about your commitment while you are apart. Too many people end up feeling needless angst and worry, when talking about it would clear the air.

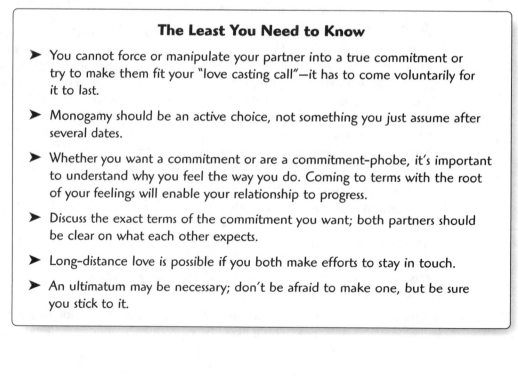

The Least You Need to Know

➤ You cannot force or manipulate your partner into a true commitment or try to make them fit your "love casting call"—it has to come voluntarily for it to last.

➤ Monogamy should be an active choice, not something you just assume after several dates.

➤ Whether you want a commitment or are a commitment-phobe, it's important to understand why you feel the way you do. Coming to terms with the root of your feelings will enable your relationship to progress.

➤ Discuss the exact terms of the commitment you want; both partners should be clear on what each other expects.

➤ Long-distance love is possible if you both make efforts to stay in touch.

➤ An ultimatum may be necessary; don't be afraid to make one, but be sure you stick to it.

Part 3

How to Keep the Passion Alive

Certainly romance and seduction play a crucial role in the beginning of a relationship. But do romance and seduction eventually die?

The answer doesn't have to be a scary or disappointing NO. Romance and seduction are certainly triggers for your attraction. But they need to thrive—and escalate—along the way, or your passion and commitment will peter out.

Studies show that what women want most in their relationships is more romance. Fortunately, men are increasingly seeing the value of romance. When men and women stop being romantic with each other (or no longer take the trouble to seduce one another), they feel taken for granted and their sex life is doomed to become predictable and boring. Romance and seduction are key ingredients to lasting love—as important as the four C's we've just reviewed: compatibility, cooperation, communication, and commitment.

Don't confuse romance with the first blush of new love and think you can't re-create that feeling with a known and trusted partner. True, lust and passion can cool over time, but you can keep your sexual chemistry cooking if you work at it. How? There are lots of wonderful suggestions in the pages that follow.

Chapter 12

Making the Honeymoon Last

In This Chapter

➤ Rules about continuing to date and what to do together to keep it exciting

➤ The importance of coming up with new ideas to do together

➤ Ten good ideas about what to do

➤ Identifying your mutual interests

➤ Making time for togetherness

When you first started dating, I'll bet you'd lie awake at night fantasizing about the exotic and fascinating places you wanted to run off to with your new flame. You'd probably just dream about spending time with your lover—maybe not doing anything particularly adventurous, but feeling warm and fuzzy just enjoying each other's company.

Even though your new beau has now turned into your steady special someone, you still need to continue fueling those passionate fires. Do you and your partner often find yourselves stuck with no plans on Friday night, and end up zoning out to bad B-movies on TV? Or maybe you're one of those couples who spends that valuable weekend time off continuing to work, or doing endless chores, separately. Instead, you should be taking advantage of your time together and maximizing any opportunity to bond with your mate. Think back to all the fun things you used to do way back when you were first seducing each other.

Keep Dating!

Remember: To keep up a lasting and healthy relationship, you have to keep dating each other with enthusiasm and passion—just like you did when you were first trying to win each other over. Remember this advice and use it when you both find yourselves too "tired" (that is, lazy) to go out and do something fun with each other on a Saturday night.

Rule One: Do Something You Both Enjoy

Because it's so important to dating couples to have fun together, they put effort into thinking of things that they both like to do. Maintain the same attitude with your partner now, and you'll notice that it strengthens your relationship in several ways. When you're doing something that both of you find enjoyable and exciting, your individual excitement will spill over and become excitement for the person you're sharing the experience with—your partner. This excitement is key for passion and sex appeal; as you both get excited by what you're doing and whom you're doing it with, you'll come to appreciate each other more and find each other more appealing. Doing something together also gives you the opportunity to bond, share, have a meaningful conversation, and strengthen your commitment.

Dr. Judy's Rx

Days off come around very regularly—there's no reason to let them sneak up on you. Don't spend that time just catching up on chores or lolling around with nothing to do (unless, of course, this leads to a day spent enjoying each other's company in bed). Plan something interesting to do together.

Sit down with your partner and talk about interests that you both share. Then, brainstorm together about where you could go to pursue your common interests. Use the following chart to write down the things you think of. If you're having trouble getting started, check out some of my suggestions, which follow the chart.

	Interest	Where to Go
1.	_____	_____
2.	_____	_____
3.	_____	_____

Here are some examples of interests and the places you can go to enjoy them.

Ideas on What to Do

If Your Interest Is	Consider Doing These Things Together
Sports	Schedule weekly games; take lessons in a sport neither of you has tried—anything from tennis, skiing, or golf to horseback riding, yoga, or tai chi (or how about rock climbing for you adventurers?)
Dancing	Take dancing lessons; go to nightclubs
Art	Take an art course; visit museums, especially for special exhibits; browse art galleries or go to openings
Music	Learn to play a new instrument; go to concerts
Health	Join a health club; go to a spa
Personal growth	Take self-improvement classes; learn meditation
Improving your relationship	Sign up for encounter groups; take communication training classes
Other	_____

Rule Two: Do Something Your Partner Enjoys

Pick an activity that you really don't like to do, but that your partner particularly enjoys. If he likes to watch basketball, but you hate it, sit yourself down and watch a game with him. Amuse yourself any way you can—critique the uniforms, concentrate on the cheerleaders or the fans, pay attention to anything that will entertain you. If she likes to dance but never suggests it because you hate clubs, surprise her and take her out dancing for a night. Do it for her. As much as you dislike dancing, consider this night an investment in your love. Try to have a good time while you're at the club; let your partner teach you new dance moves or amuse yourself by people-watching. Just make sure your partner is happy. Doing something you don't like for your partner makes your relationship better: You demonstrate your thoughtfulness and unselfishness, and your partner feels cared for and considered.

Dr. Judy's Rx

Check out my previous book, *The Complete Idiot's Guide to Dating*, for lots of great tips on things to do to enjoy each other's company.

In the following space, list six activities—three that your mate enjoys, but you dislike, and another three that you like, but your mate does not:

	What My Mate Enjoys (But I Don't)	What I Enjoy (But My Mate Doesn't)
1.	_____	_____
2.	_____	_____
3.	_____	_____

Now, promise to take your mate out sometime to do one of the activities on his or her list. Your mate should promise the same to you. Promise each other that over time, you'll do everything on the lists together. This is a true test of caring for each other by sacrificing your own tastes and appreciating your partner's.

Rule Three: Make Time

You can always find excuses for not having enough time to get to the gym, read a good book, or prepare a well-balanced meal (that is, not to resort to gulping down a quick bowl of cereal standing over the sink). Likewise, couples always find excuses for not having enough time to spend with each other. That's precisely why you have to make time. Certainly, making time for each other is easier said than done (who isn't busy these days?), but with some brainstorming it can be accomplished.

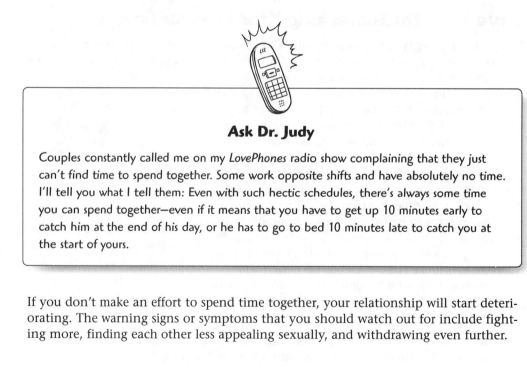

Ask Dr. Judy

Couples constantly called me on my *LovePhones* radio show complaining that they just can't find time to spend together. Some work opposite shifts and have absolutely no time. I'll tell you what I tell them: Even with such hectic schedules, there's always some time you can spend together—even if it means that you have to get up 10 minutes early to catch him at the end of his day, or he has to go to bed 10 minutes late to catch you at the start of yours.

If you don't make an effort to spend time together, your relationship will start deteriorating. The warning signs or symptoms that you should watch out for include fighting more, finding each other less appealing sexually, and withdrawing even further.

Make the effort. If you and your partner have jam-packed schedules, plan your time together and write it into your datebooks—right there along with all your other important appointments and staff meetings. Treat your scheduled moments together—no matter how brief—as seriously as you would any of your other commitments. Certainly your relationship warrants that priority. I know it seems awfully unspontaneous and unromantic, but if you don't actually schedule yourselves in with each other, you might both end up blowing the other off for any one of the dozens of other things to do that inevitably come up every day.

Dr. Judy's Rx

Think of nontraditional times you can spend together during the day. How about around noon? Some might call a meeting for a lunch-time date (the old "nooner") a cliché now, but if you've never done it, a midday rendezvous might just be the spark your love life needs.

Reality Bites: Do You Ever See Each Other?

To get an idea of how much—or how little—time you're actually spending together and what activities you're sharing, check your memory or your diary and fill in the following calendar (use another sheet of paper if necessary). Write down everything you've done together in the past week (watched TV, walked the dog, planned an evening out, made love).

Our Time and Activities Together							
	Mon	**Tues**	**Wed**	**Thurs**	**Fri**	**Sat**	**Sun**
Before breakfast							
Before work							
Lunch time							
After work							
After dinner							
Bedtime							

How Often Would You Like to See Each Other?

Now that you've figured out how little you get to see your mate, think about how much you would ideally like to see him or her, if you could (assuming that you couldn't just quit your job and stare dreamily into each other's eyes all day long). Fill in the following calendar with the activities you would share in a hypothetical week (use a separate sheet of paper if necessary).

Our Ideal Time and Activities Together

	Mon	Tues	Wed	Thurs	Fri	Sat	Sun
Before breakfast							
Before work							
Lunch time							
After work							
After dinner							
Bedtime							

Look over your hypothetical calendar and think about which of these "dates" you'll actually be able to keep with your partner. Write them into your datebook and be sure not to miss them.

In couples' therapy, I usually advise setting aside at least an hour three times a week for time together, and spending a minimum of one whole day together at least twice a month. More is certainly advisable.

What to Do Together

Remember my principle that the secret to a healthy and lasting relationship is to continue to date. That means to do all the fun, creative, and interesting things you did when first trying to impress and seduce each other. In the following sections are some of my favorite ideas—for staying in and for when you're on the go.

Staying In

Remember the 1990s that were criticized as the Age of the Couch Potato. All too often I listened to people complain that their partners ignore them in favor of the TV and will just sit for hours a night, zombie-like, in front of the boob tube. Some couples are couch-potato pairs—like Adam and Lisa who, after only three months of being together, ended up spending their nights mindlessly watching TV before finally falling asleep. Technically, they were spending a lot of time together, but let's face it, they were more "wasting" their time together than actually "spending" it with each other. The new millennium version of this is "Net-neurotics" who sit at their computers for hours, surfing the Internet, ignoring their partners.

Although watching television is usually a solitary activity, you can turn it into a bonding experience. Watch thought-provoking dramas or educational documentaries, a video, or a romantic movie. Discuss what you're watching during the breaks or commercials. Don't focus your conversations just on ideas, but personalize your talks and use them to learn about each other. Watching TV can be especially cozy if you curl up on the sofa together under a warm blanket, or give your mate a footrub as you watch. You might even inspire your mate to click off the TV!

But given the desire and some creativity, you can make staying home just as stimulating, fun, and bonding as going out.

Just Kick Back

You don't always have to be doing something. You can enjoy each other's company just by sitting around, appearing to be doing nothing at all, but really relaxing together. Being able to relax in each other's company—without the distraction of a TV or radio—is a sign of being comfortable with each other, which in turn is a sure sign of a healthy relationship. Cuddle up on the couch and listen to music while wrapped in each other's arms.

Or Get Busy

If you're not in a quiet, relaxed mood, then get busy indoors. If you have chores or home repairs, do them together and turn them into a fun project. Cook together. Call your family or friends together. Redecorate a room together. Help each other with the work that you both brought home from the office or do that dreaded paperwork in each other's company. Work can be very inspiring (and cozy) when you know that your loved one is in the room equally occupied. You can even watch TV.

Having Fun Right in Your Own Backyard

Sometimes couples get bored because they just can't think of anything to do or any place to go. But you'd be surprised at how many activities and experiences your own town has to offer. Sure, you might not get to spend the day hang gliding over the Alps, but you and your mate can make any activity fun for each other. And there's really never a shortage of places for you to just enjoy your partner's company or learn something—about yourself, your mate, your relationship, or life in general. The important thing is that you are spending time together.

No matter how well you think you know your own town, undoubtedly there are attractions you've walked by a thousand times but never thought to visit, or restaurants you've been meaning to go to but have yet to try. Most sizable towns also host countless public events, such as openings of museums, community centers, or health organizations—these can be free-to-all events, invitation-only galas, or expensive fund-raisers. You can also attend conventions, shows, or association conferences—which sometimes have unrestricted admission—in your city. Every year, I love to drag my partner to the car show. Get information and schedules from the Chamber of

Dr. Judy's Rx

Learn about your neighborhood with your partner. To get to know where you live, take tours (walking or bus) of the area. Explore new places with your partner and talk about what you learned.

Commerce, the concierge at local hotels that often host such events, and the large convention and concert halls in your area.

Here are seven good suggestions for coming up with ideas on what to do:

1. Call your friends and ask them what they're doing or where they're going.

2. Peruse the newsstands for magazines and local or neighborhood newspapers that have special sections on local activities and events. Some of these publications are free. If you can't find any at the newsstand, check in apartment building lobbies or on freestanding racks in bookstores. Or subscribe to publications (such as the weekly *Time Out* in New York) that specifically cover entertainment and events in your city.

3. Think like a tourist. Pretend you're on vacation in your own town. What would you do to find out what's going on? I always pick up brochures and booklets at airports. I also check out the pamphlets in hotel lobbies; hotel rooms also have copies of books or magazines (usually called something like "Around Town" or "Where") that feature local events and attractions. You can find many of these online on the Internet. You can also call or write to the Chamber of Commerce in your city for tourist brochures and pamphlets.

4. Pretend you have guests coming from a foreign country whom you have to entertain. I once did this and discovered a great "Rock and Roll Tour of New York." It's a bus tour of apartments, clubs, and sites related to rock music, including, for example, the street where John Lennon was shot.

5. Look in the Yellow Pages or Classifieds under "Clubs" or "Centers for" and see if there are any organizations or groups that might interest you.

6. Put your name on mailing lists for various museums, clubs, and organizations.

7. Be creative. In quiet moments, dream of something you've always wanted to do. For me, it was scuba diving, which I finally convinced my partner to try with me.

Musical Affairs

Given that my *LovePhones* call-in advice radio show was broadcast on many music radio stations around the country, I spend a lot of time at music festivals. And no matter what kind of music the festival is featuring, I was always surrounded by couples holding hands, hugging. As the music plays, you begin feeling at one with everyone else, which helps you feel at one with the person you're with. If you've ever taken your lover to a musical event—be it a country music festival, a rock concert, a jazz performance in the park, a karaoke club, or a piano bar—you know what I mean about wanting to hold that person close, as you lose yourself in each other and in the beat of the music.

If you and your mate have similar tastes in music, or maybe even the same favorite band, get a concert schedule (you can check with your local record store, look in music magazines, newspapers, or call a ticket agency) and find out if the band's touring and if it will be in your area. If there aren't any big concert arenas near your home, check the clubs or bars; often, smaller venues host great undiscovered local bands (and sometimes big names, too), which can make for a fun and interesting evening. And smaller places tend to have a more romantic and intimate atmosphere.

A Volunteering Heart

Another way for you and your partner to get to know your community is to find out about the issues that your neighbors, the building, or the block association care about—issues that your community holds meetings or lobbies the local government about. If you and your mate are passionate about these issues, you shouldn't hesitate to help out. Caring about your community not only benefits the community itself, but can also intensify your commitment to your home. In addition, the time you and your partner spend improving your community will bring you even closer together.

Helping others unselfishly will also increase your mutual respect and inspire you to be equally giving with each other. Beyond your community, there are statewide or even national causes that need help. Get active about a political or environmental issue. Or volunteer for a nonprofit organization and help raise money for the local zoo, museum, child-care center, hospital, home for the aged, or AIDS organization. There's no end to the list of museums, art galleries, dance and theater groups, or Big Brother/Big Sister organizations with which you can get involved together.

Love Bytes

Research proves that when you listen to music, certain chemicals are released in your body causing either relaxation or excitation (depending on the music), which in turn facilitates your experiencing feelings of love.

Love Bytes

Volunteerism has been proven to boost your immune system. Also, when you help others, chemicals that actually lift your emotions are released in the body, making you feel good. If you make volunteering a regular activity that you share with your mate, you'll be able to interact with each other while experiencing the same improved health and mood—resulting in a healthier, closer relationship.

Shop for Love

Shopping is one activity nearly every couple can do together right in their own hometown. Men: Don't think of yourselves as being "dragged along" by your

Love Bytes

If you want to be able to stick with it, pick a cause that you both feel strongly about and that has some meaning to your life. If his father suffered a heart attack, for example, find out how you can help raise money for the American Heart Association. If you both love children, spend every Saturday visiting a foster care center.

Dr. Judy's Rx

Malls today are almost like amusement parks; not only can you spend money in them, you can also browse, eat at the plentiful restaurants and food courts, people-watch, play video games, and sometimes even listen to live entertainment or ride a carousel. You'll notice many couples and families that make going to the mall a special trip on a weekend afternoon.

girlfriends to go shopping. Consider that maybe you've been missing something all this time: Shopping can be fun. Change your attitude. Figure out something that you both need—like a new TV or a gift for a mutual friend—and go shopping together to pick it out. Consider the trip a fun expedition instead of a chore.

Even if you don't need something right away, consider going window-shopping for something you would both enjoy having or plan to have someday. Treat your browsing like an interesting cultural experience—like going to a museum together. Have you ever dreamed of owning a Porsche? Why not take a test drive one Saturday afternoon? Are you electronics buffs? Why not go to an electronics store and check out the latest models of stereos, video cameras, and home entertainment systems?

I know a couple who stays in bed Sunday mornings to peruse the Real Estate section of *The New York Times* together. Although they're not ready to buy now, they still pick out apartments they'd love to live in and make appointments to visit some of their dream houses. Not only do they have great fun, but they're also getting more and more prepared for the day they really are ready to make that purchase. By window-shopping for things that you aren't quite ready to purchase at the moment, you can motivate each other to save money and plan together to buy things you both need or want.

Work It

If you and your mate both work out regularly or are thinking about starting an exercise routine, plan to work out together and reap an added benefit from it: a healthy relationship. The couple that works out together is more likely to have their relationship work out, too, so take up a sport you can participate in with each other—anything from golf, tennis, in-line skating, jogging, or shooting hoops to scuba diving or rock climbing. Join the same gym if you want to pump some iron or take fitness classes together, or set aside a time to exercise at home with a workout tape and some weights.

Love Bytes

Bookstores are becoming another interesting place for singles, couples, and families alike to spend an afternoon. More and more bookstores sport full-service cafés, plush easy chairs, peaceful music, and schedules of guest speakers and author readings or lectures. I've certainly given my own fair share of such bookstore seminars and lectures; many couples come to them together and make an afternoon or evening out of the event.

Pumping up your muscles pumps up your self-esteem. As you become more pleased with yourself, you'll transfer your positive attitudes to the people around you, including your mate. Working out together will also give you new topics of conversation, from workout routines to nutrition. Playing a sport together not only gives you time to spend with each other, but also intensifies your sense of being a team.

If you're both more observers than players, get season tickets to see your favorite team. If you can't get hold of those, head out to a sports bar where you can watch the big game on a giant-screen TV, have dinner and drinks, and maybe even do a little dancing. Of course, there's nothing wrong with staying home. You can cook up a romantic dinner, get cozy, and root for your team together on TV.

On the Go

Maybe you'd rather not stay in town—maybe you're one of those people suffering from a perpetual case of wanderlust. If you've got the traveling bug, turn your journeys into romantic interludes. Get away as much as you can for overnight or weekend trips. If you have more time, plan longer, exotic trips. If you suddenly come into some free time and can afford last-minute getaway, check out different newspaper ads or airline sites on the World Wide Web. These periodically have postings for discounted getaways, especially for last-minute trips.

Dr. Judy's Rx

If you're not too keen on hard-core athletics, but would still like to take part in some physical activity, why not join a "marathon" for charity? Watch for flyers or ads advertising a local "walk-a-thon" or "dance-a-thon." You can get exercise and have a load of fun spending time with your mate.

Going Back to School

A great way to spend time with your mate is to take a class together. Choose something you would both enjoy learning about—music, art, foreign languages, photography, Zen, investing. Then check out the local community college (and even the high schools) for catalogs on extension courses or adult-education courses. You can also find classes offered at religious centers, the local YMCA, and adult-ed centers like the Omega Institute, Seminar Center, or Learning Annex. Check the freestanding boxes on street corners, bookstores, music stores, newsstands, convenience stores, health-food stores, doctors' offices, school lobbies, and libraries. Everywhere you look, you'll find free publications with all kinds of course listings. You'd be surprised at the number of opportunities you have to learn something new.

Dr. Judy's Rx

Many religious institutions are eager for couples' attendance at the various activities they offer. If you're interested, stop in and get a flyer detailing their lectures, theater parties, study and discussion groups, dances, and holiday services.

For college grads, join the local branch of your alumni association and subscribe to your alma mater's magazine or newsletter. Most colleges offer activities for their graduates from local social gatherings and vacation trips to museum visits and theater parties.

Note, too, that you don't always have to be an alumni to join a school's activities. Call up a school in your area to get information on how to get involved with its programs. Check high schools, extension or adult-education schools, trade schools, colleges, and universities.

Business and Pleasure

Like schools, many companies offer activities and fun opportunities for their employees and employees' partners. I once worked for a radio station owned by a Disney-owned company, who offered employees the opportunity to take advantage of company discounts at all of Disney's attractions—including Disney World, of course.

Even if you're not able to jet off to an exotic location, you can still bring your mate along on business trips, industry-related seminars, and professional conferences or conventions. Take an extra day on these trips to sightsee in the area together. In fact, many businesses offer such opportunities, like golf days or family days. These trips will bring you closer to your partner. He or she will learn more about your career, and you'll also get to explore a new place together.

Ask Dr. Judy

My favorite place to go with my partner is an amusement park. Not only are amusement parks fun, but they're also conducive for falling in love (it's true; I even developed my "Theme Park Therapy" for Universal Studios Florida based on this concept). The chemicals that are released in your body as you get excited on the rides make for a powerful love concoction. Psychologically, having fun and feeling like a giddy child puts you in a great mood and in the right frame of mind for being in love.

Improving Yourselves and Each Other

If you haven't tried it, you might think it sounds a little hokey. But take it from me, there's hardly a better way for the two of you to bond and learn more about yourselves and each other than to take a self-improvement workshop. You can find groups on myriad topics, including communication, intimacy, and even sexuality. A lot of couples find it easier to reveal their deepest feelings, fears, and secrets in an organized workshop setting—it's safe, supportive, and supervised by experienced guides. Being surrounded by other couples equally motivated to grow is not only inspiring to your own togetherness, but it can also provide the right setting for cultivating a new network of friends.

For more information, flip to the back of the free publications and booklets distributed in various convenience stores, bookstores, supermarkets, and freestanding newspaper boxes on street corners; you'll find scores of advertisements for relationship and self-improvement courses. More advanced couples into "tantric" love should check out the relationship-enhancement workshops and spiritual retreats that I've listed in Appendix C, "Resources." Some of these programs last just a day and others last a weekend or longer. You can find a program to suit your schedule.

Dr. Judy's Rx

If one of you is involved in a support group, it's important for the other to attend the group also (if allowed) to increase your understanding of each other. Or perhaps there's a sister group that the partner can attend. If one of you belongs to an AA group, for example, the other can go to the corresponding Al-Anon group.

Don't feel that you have to limit yourself to couples groups only. Self-improvement courses designed for individuals can also be beneficial for you to take with your mate. Many of these are offered by local colleges or specific learning institutes. Any way you can learn more about yourself will also benefit your partner and your relationship by building your self-esteem and improving your ability to communicate. Try courses on the study of yoga, meditation, spirituality, and philosophy.

Ask Dr. Judy

An extremely transformational experience you can have is at the weekend or week-long couples' seminars called "The Art of Conscious Loving," run by the Hawaii-based Tantric masters Charles and Caroline Muir. The course includes yoga, communication exercises, and instruction on healing and pleasuring techniques. Couples are also given "homework" to do at night to practice the communication and pleasuring techniques taught in class. In beautiful locations, couples participate in lectures, and in free time, can hike, ride horses, get professional massages, or swim in waterfalls. The lectures, the activities, and the atmosphere in general all conspire to heighten couples' love connection.

The Least You Need to Know

➤ Continue to "date" to keep your love alive.

➤ There's always something you can do together, and you can make anything you choose fun for each other.

➤ Being involved in activities together increases your togetherness.

➤ Scheduling "meetings" with each other in your datebooks will increase the amount of time you get to be together.

➤ Identify the activities you both enjoy doing and pursue them together.

➤ Make an effort to do things together that one of you enjoys and the other does not.

➤ Be resourceful and creative when thinking of ways to spend time with each other: Check newspapers and magazines and ask friends for ideas.

Chapter 13

Resurrecting Romance

In This Chapter

➤ The real meaning of romance

➤ The importance of keeping romance alive

➤ A romance surprise calendar

➤ Five tips to keep long distance love alive

Being romantic in the early stages of your relationship can seem easy or come naturally. He brings her flowers and lights the candles as she prepares a cozy dinner for two. She greets him at the door with kisses and lures him inside for more. After time passes and life's stresses increase, couples become more familiar with each other and such gestures and excitement seem to come less naturally. You start feeling like you have to "work" on the relationship. Love suddenly becomes serious business, leaving no time for frivolity. The flowers get saved for Valentine's Day. The kisses become more rare.

But romancing and seducing one another aren't dispensable frivolities. Keeping those qualities alive and fresh in a relationship takes time and requires ingenuity. You can have a continuously exciting love life—if both you and your mate care enough to make it happen.

The Importance of Keeping Romance Alive

If either of you need to be convinced of the value of being romantic, consider the following:

Dr. Judy's Rx

When your partner says "I love you" or brings you a small, unexpected gift, be extremely appreciative and enthusiastic in words, smiles, or gestures of your own. Never be too busy or harried to acknowledge a romantic gesture in your life.

➤ Romantic gestures trigger the memories of falling in love. Initial romantic euphoria typically diminishes in three to six months of being together. The best way couples can hope to regain glimmers of the early glory days is by repeating some of the romantic behavior that came naturally in the beginning.

➤ Romance is the "show and tell" of true love. Songs have been written in which women equate the loss of love with the absence of flowers for a good reason. When Barbra Streisand sings "You don't bring me flowers anymore," she's saying, "You don't show you love me anymore." How do you know you are loved by your partner if he doesn't show you? Women may need the displays of romance more than men, but men need them, too.

➤ Behavior can affect feelings, changing negative to positive. Maybe you aren't feeling particularly romantic, but take the time anyway, for example, to stop at a music store, buy the new CD your partner wants, and have it playing when she comes in. Acting in a romantic fashion will stimulate her feelings of love and tenderness toward you. That will likely arouse some of your own feelings as well.

➤ By being romantic in the ways your partner appreciates, you will get him to pay more attention to your needs and desires.

Healthy or Unhealthy?

In a healthy relationship, do you think you can finally relax and not have to worry about what to do together? Wrong! While you can certainly feel more secure and less nervous about whether the other person wants to be with you or whether you enjoy each other, it's important to keep coming up with new ideas about how to spend your time together and keep your relationship fresh.

The Real Meaning of Romance

Romance is the expression of love through words, gestures, and actions. The love behind the words, gestures, and actions makes them romantic. Otherwise, they might be tools for manipulating a partner or creating a "relationship" that satisfies your ideas and fantasies of how one should be. Romantic behavior, without feelings of love, feels empty.

When's the last time someone did or said something that made you sigh? That was likely a true romantic act. The act may seem corny, but the sensitive thoughtfulness behind it can touch your heart anyway. Consider the classic example of one diplomat who handed a woman a rose, saying, "The beauty of this rose only pales when compared to you." You may groan, but can you escape the sweet compliment?

Love Bytes

In the initial stages of love, the brain produces a powerful love hormone, phenylethylamine (PEA). This hormone creates the natural high associated with falling in love. Excitement and risk also cause the brain to produce PEA, which helps explain why some people find activities like mountain climbing or motor biking so appealing and even addictive.

True romantics are empathic. That means you can put yourself in your partner's place and feel what he is feeling. Empathy makes it possible for you to choose the right words, gestures, and actions to show your love. A true romantic knows that his partner prefers orchids to roses, or chocolate chip cookies to chocolate-covered strawberries. Nothing is more romantic than thoughtfulness. It says, "I love you enough to know who you really are." It really is the thought that counts.

Here are six good ways to express romance your partner:

1. Show the kind of physical affection your partner likes. Does she like having you massage her feet? Does he enjoy having his back rubbed? At the end of a long day, when you're sitting together on the couch in front of the TV, touch each other in the ways you each enjoy.

2. Being romantic in public says, "I want everyone to know how much I love you." Hold hands while you're walking. Give each other a light kiss or caress.

3. Do something romantic every day. It can be as simple as saying "I love you." Changing the kitty litter or putting the laundry away when it isn't your turn because your partner is unusually busy is also a romantic gesture.

4. Be nice to your partner's mother, father, sibling, best friend, or annoying aunt. Being considerate of people who matter to your partner is a show of thoughtfulness and love.

181

5. Show genuine concern if she had a problem at work or he is concerned about a family situation. The worry hasn't necessarily disappeared just because your partner has stopped talking about it. Show your love by asking how things are going.

6. Don't nag your partner about a bad habit or an ongoing problem, such as weight gain. Do something positive to help instead. If he's gained weight, prepare low-fat meals together that you can both enjoy. If she's out of shape, plan physical activities you can do together. Don't say, "Let's go for a walk because you need to get more exercise." Say, "Let's take a romantic walk together."

The Four "F" Words of Romance

Consider these four reminders on how to keep your romance alive. If you practice the four F's and follow the advice in these chapters, your love life will never grow stale:

➤ **Feelings.** Remember to express your feelings and pay attention to your partner's feelings.

➤ **Facts.** Become knowledgeable about differences between men and women. Stay abreast of the ways in which health and aging affect sexuality. Keep track of the details of your partner's history, experiences, and schedule.

➤ **Fantasies.** Allow, accept, and enjoy your fantasies. Discuss which ones you both feel safe about exploring.

➤ **Fun.** Being in love and having sex should be fun, not a chore. When was the last time you really enjoyed yourselves? Having fun together is a wonderful bonding experience.

Love Lookout

Don't get so caught up in planning romance that you forget to be spontaneous. The most romantic gestures are often the ones not planned in advance. Unfortunately, many couples sacrifice spontaneity to the demands of their highly scheduled lives.

Your Very Own Romance Surprise Calendar

At the beginning of a new year, many people mark family birthdays and anniversaries in their new datebooks or calendars. Why not schedule some romantic surprises in there, too? Your partner's birthday and the significant anniversaries you share are obvious "Romance with a capital R" days. Create a romantic surprise by planning a romantic day on a date that has no prior significance in your life together.

Consider the ideas I offer to get you started on the romance calendar.

Are Time and Distance Romance-Ruiners?

Time and distance certainly can ruin your romance, but they don't have to. Time is the natural enemy of romance because it breeds familiarity, comfort, and security. While those are all good feelings, they run the risk of being potential romance-busters. In time, the euphoria of love may cease being a natural high. But remember, it is a high you can reach again and again in your life if you make the effort together.

Distance presents other special challenges. Depending on how far the relationship has progressed when a couple begins a prolonged separation, distance can make the heart grow fonder or simply wander. A little absence at the right point can influence your lover to realize how much you matter and to consider a commitment appealing.

Some couples build their lives together around the geographical distance separating them. Can that possibly work? It can, if both partners are committed to each other. Some people are better suited to this type of relationship than others. Those who need a lot of closeness and reassurance probably will feel discontent a great deal of the time. More independent types can thrive. Any couple can drift apart if they fail to have enough reunions or neglect to reassure each other. They end up developing lives that are so separate there seems to be no place in one for the other.

Dr. Judy Rx

Don't ever lose the ability to "play hooky" from duties and responsibilities to make room for romance.

Try the following five suggestions for some long-distance CPR:

1. Keep in touch several times a week, if not daily, through phone calls, faxes, e-mails, letters, or cards. The communication need not be a lengthy one. Scribble "I love you" on a postcard reproduction of a favorite painting. E-mail a brief hello from work. Call at the end of the day just to say good night.

2. Plan reunions often enough to satisfy your needs for closeness. Make the reunions a priority once the plans are made. Don't fall into the habit of canceling when work pressures or other obligations pile up.

3. Reassure each other often about your love and commitment to one another. Don't take that commitment for granted.

4. Keep each other informed about your friendships and activities in your city. Continue to share your lives with each other as if you were together.

5. Trust each other. Make an agreement on fidelity and then put your faith in your partner's word. Angry questions like "Where were you when I called last night at midnight?" create suffocation and distrust and lead to an emotional distance that will eventually be greater than the geographical one.

January Declare a snowy day love-in. Build a fire, add some brandy to the hot chocolate, and turn off the phone.	**February** Everyone celebrates Valentine's Day. How about turning President's Day weekend (that usually gives you a day off from work) into a romantic getaway?	**March** Celebrate the first day of spring by inventing your own version of a Pagan love ritual.
April Buy each other a piece of spring clothing, preferably something frivolous like a hat or outrageous golf socks. For extra excitement, model the gift wearing nothing else.	**May** The month of blooming flowers should inspire romance. Write a sonnet with a flower theme. Spread rose petals all over your bed or in a bath.	**June** Make your way to water—if not the ocean, then a lake, river, or pond. Walk at the water's edge. Dip your feet. Take a boat ride.
July Celebrate July 4th with your personal fireworks display—by sparkling yourselves indoors. Or take a walk together in the middle of the night or star gaze with a telescope from your window.	**August** Embark on a learning experience together. Sign up for a craft or cooking class, a seminar on film or art appreciation, or a workshop in archaeology that you will take together.	**September** Take a love holiday on the first day of autumn. Do something together that puts you both in the mood for the change of seasons. Visit an apple orchard and pick some apples.
October Halloween is for lovers, too! Have a private costume party and each dress as the historical character you think most resembles your mate.	**November** Take a day away from the families on Thanksgiving weekend and spend it alone together. Feast on each other as you would the holiday meal.	**December** Do something to make each other's holiday burden a little lighter. Help address your partner's Christmas cards, or buy a present for your partner's co-workers or impossible-to-please relative.

Create your own romance surprise calendar.

Ultimately, the goal is to eventually be together in the same place. One person will eventually have to make a decision that the relationship is more important than career or geographical familiarity. Any time you fall into a rut about being apart, focus instead on your future plans to be together.

Keeping Romance Alive with Kids Around

It's an all-too-common complaint that the sex goes out the window when kids come into the house. But romance and sex shouldn't die! It's even more important to keep this part of your relationship going when kids are in the picture. Children benefit by seeing a model of a love connection between their parents. So do it for their sake and for your own. Make time for each other. Put a lock on your door. Send the kids off to a friend or family member, or hire a baby-sitter, and go out. Concentrate on acting like lovers as well as parents.

The Least You Need to Know

➤ If the romance has gone out of your relationship, you can put it back in through loving words, gestures, and actions.

➤ Nothing is more romantic than a thoughtful act that demonstrates empathy for your partner.

➤ Planned romantic surprises and spontaneous acts are both key to maintaining a rich and fulfilling love relationship.

➤ Time and distance don't kill love. They present challenges that true love can surmount.

➤ Make time for you and your partner apart from children to keep your romance alive.

Chapter 14

The Art of Seduction

In This Chapter

➤ The continuing importance of seduction in healthy relationships

➤ Ten seduction tips

➤ How to flirt with your partner

➤ When love's on the menu: sensuous suppers

➤ Whispering sweet nothings in her ear

➤ The seductive power of physical fitness

Before you knew if the two of you would become lovers, you each put considerable effort into seduction. You flirted with one another over lengthy restaurant meals, gazed into each other's eyes as you spoke, and touched hands, arms, shoulders frequently. You held hands on the street.

Until you became sure that sex would take place on a regular basis, you continued to seduce each other. Romantic dinners at home, new lingerie, flowers, candles, scents, and maybe even a bubble bath were part of your life together. How long has it been since you lit the candles, turned down the overhead lights, and shared a romantic dinner wearing elegant loungewear?

Maybe sex is such a foregone conclusion in your relationship that you cut to the chase all the time now. "Let's do it" he says, and you do. But where's the exciting buildup?

There's nothing wrong with initiating sex this way sometimes, but not all the time. If that's the only way you begin lovemaking, or only one of you initiates it all the time, you're headed into a sexual rut. Both men and women want to be seduced occasionally, no matter how long they have been together.

Seduction in Healthy, Lasting Relationships

Seduction is more than the effort exerted to get the other person to say yes to sex. A successful seduction sets the mood for hotter than normal sex or for lovemaking that brings the partners to a deeper level of intimacy. Seduction carries love to higher levels in a way that the initiation of sex via routine signals probably won't.

Love Bytes

Seduction styles vary greatly from one person to another, but women generally use clothing, fragrance, lighting, and food to get their message across. They place themselves in seductive settings and sometimes strike alluring poses accentuating their best physical traits. Men tend to seduce actions (like taking her to a nice restaurant) or compliments.

Dr. Judy's Rx

Men can seduce women by paying close attention to their partner's needs. They should listen closely, offer compliments, and caress lightly.

When you seduce your partner, you're saying, "I really want to make love to you." On the other hand, the quick clinch followed by a nod in the direction of the bedroom can be interpreted as, "I really need sex." Who wouldn't be touched, flattered, and aroused by their mate's specific desire, versus the generic desire for sexual activity? Seduction, like romance, personalizes the erotic connection between lovers and keeps them from becoming just two bodies who meet in bed.

If you aren't comfortable behaving seductively, you may associate negative connotations with the word. Seductive behavior isn't manipulative, tricky, or false. It is one of the most sincere compliments lovers can pay to one another. By taking the time to create an enticing mood, you show how much you value making love to your partner. Here are 10 seduction tips to give you some good ideas.

Ten Seduction Tips

1. Get closer. Most of the time people respect what's called "safe personal distance," about two to three feet apart. Move in closer and linger there. Then step back a little, encouraging your partner to advance.

2. Mirror or copy your mate's responses and positions. If he puts his hand to his mouth, do the same with yours.

3. Show you care by repeating what your mate said earlier in the conversation and also by using his or her name frequently.

4. Wear something your mate considers sexy. He might be more aroused by the sight of her in a man's white shirt than in a garter belt and stockings. She might like to see him in an open shirt and snug jeans.

5. Perform selected grooming or dressing acts in front of your partner. Putting on lipstick can be very seductive. Greet him at the door fully dressed except for shoes. Slip into high-heeled sandals while he watches. Let her watch you shave. Ask him to zip your dress or ask her to adjust your tie.

6. Tell your partner something very personal about yourself that you've never told anyone else.

7. Make nonsexual physical contact. Run your finger down her cheek or the curve of her throat. Rub your thumb across the inside of his wrist.

8. Use scent. Many of the new women's fragrances contain a hint of vanilla, found by researchers to be particularly attractive to men.

9. Take care of your partner. Do his or her chores. Run an errand you weren't asked to run. Be tender and comforting.

10. Do something utterly frivolous, like making snow angels or cutting out a string of paper dolls from colored paper to give your mate.

Heightening Your Senses

Maybe you've never allowed yourself to be sensual. Sensual people are good lovers because they use their senses to heighten their awareness and their partner's pleasure during seduction as well as lovemaking. Some ways to feel more comfortable with seduction by increasing your sensuality include:

➤ **Awakening your senses.** Sensual people revel in all the senses: taste, smell, sight, touch, and sound. Take the time to develop and appreciate your own five senses. Experiment with food spices and new flavors. Burn scented candles. Introduce new colors into your home and wardrobe through accessories and small items.

➤ **Pay more attention to your surroundings.** How many people miss the first buds of spring, the first leaves of autumn, or the beauty of ice-covered branches because they are rushing past too quickly to see them? You may become more comfortable with the elements of seduction once you've increased your awareness of the sensual elements of the natural world.

➤ **Really feel when you touch.** Close out everything else and concentrate on your lover's skin when you caress his or her hands, arms, or face. Expand your touch awareness by stroking the petals of flowers, fabrics, and other everyday items.

These simple exercises will help you feel more sensuous and will also enliven your seductive skills.

Wink, Wink, Nudge, Nudge: How to Flirt with Your Partner

Smiles, direct eye contact, and double entendres are all classic flirting ploys. Flirting is light-hearted. It's a fun form of communication between men and women that is more often practiced by people who aren't in relationships than those who are. What a shame. Why should committed lovers be excluded from playing this traditional love game?

Whether conducted with a lover or an acquaintance, flirting is not just about sex, but about feeling good—about yourself and the other person. When you flirt, you let the other person know that he or she is attractive and desirable. There doesn't have to be a promise of sex, obligation to respond.

Dr. Judy's Rx

Don't be shy about flirting with your mate in front of others. Couples who are admired and envied by their friends for the quality of their relationship never stop having fun with each other. They never stop flirting, either.

The biggest resistance to flirting before men and women are involved with each other is fear of rejection. Once they are involved, they stop flirting because they don't think they need to do it anymore. Recognize these resistances, so you overcome them.

Flirting is certainly part of a successful dating ritual. For details on doing it well, check out my previous book, *The Complete Idiot's Guide to Dating* (Alpha Books, 1999).

When should you flirt with your partner once you're beyond those first stages of your relationship? At every opportunity! Romantic settings, such as the beach at sunrise or a picnic in the park, are natural backdrops for flirtation. Flirt when there is no time or opportunity for sex, such as standing in line at the movies, on the way out the door to work in the morning, or waiting for your table at a restaurant. Flirting increases energy, allows you to flex your sex appeal muscle, and acknowledges the continuing appeal of your partner. And it may lead to seduction later when there is both time and opportunity.

Basic Flirting Techniques

Basically, flirting involves flattery (expressing admiration, appreciation, and desire), paying close attention, and being alluring and suggestive. Five specific techniques include the following:

➤ Meaningful eye contact

➤ Touching (parts of his body, or parts of your own that you would like him to stroke)

➤ Suggestive body language (uncrossing your arms and legs, leaning toward your partner)

➤ Asking questions or talking in whispers

➤ Coy teasing remarks or double meanings

Dr. Judy's Rx

An "eye lock" is a technique whereby intimate lovers continue to look into each other's eyes for as long as they can. The goal is not to stare each other down, but to "see" into each other's soul.

Sensuous Suppers and Other Seductive Feasts

The sensuous repast is deliciously different from a merely romantic meal. Every aspect of this meal is designed to awaken pleasure in mind and body. The word "sensual" promises that all your senses will be stimulated and satisfied. They will be if you plan your meal to follow the curve of a sensual lovemaking encounter from arousal through resolution.

A late-night supper for two is the most common scenario, but Sunday brunch can be a sensuous opportunity as well. Time is the deciding factor. This is an experience that cannot be rushed. Being truly sensual means taking the time to relish every moment. In our busy lives, time is the ultimate luxury. Consider allowing a lavish amount of time on a meal with a mate as the equivalent of buying your loved one a luxury gift.

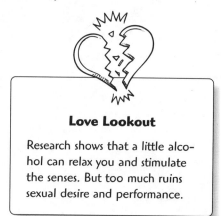

Love Lookout

Research shows that a little alcohol can relax you and stimulate the senses. But too much ruins sexual desire and performance.

Here are the five elements of the sensuous supper:

➤ **Setting.** Indoors or outdoors? What can you do to make the setting match your fantasies? One couple might choose to share an elaborate meal in bed, perhaps naked, feeding each other with their fingers. Another might drape the dining alcove in printed sheets to simulate the inside of an Arab tent. Be creative.

➤ **Planning.** Your sensuous repast should involve some foreplay. Make sure the timing is good for both of you. Do the shopping and cooking together. Take time to pick the best peaches and admire the artichokes.

Dr. Judy's Rx

The food can be a prelude to lovemaking. But I often point out the advantages of making it a postscript—eating after love-making. Your stomach won't feel too full for sex. He will be hungry, so he won't fall asleep right after sex. You can also take a love-making break between the main course and dessert. (There's something you can't do in a restaurant!)

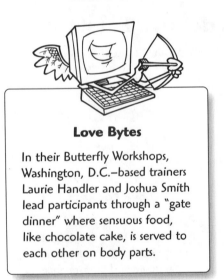

Love Bytes

In their Butterfly Workshops, Washington, D.C.–based trainers Laurie Handler and Joshua Smith lead participants through a "gate dinner" where sensuous food, like chocolate cake, is served to each other on body parts.

➤ **Food.** Some foods are reputed to have aphrodisiac qualities, but your response to them can have even more effect. What do you and your partner consider sexy food? Chocolate, oysters, and strawberries rate high on many lists. Avoid greasy, salty, heavy, or commonplace foods, like burgers and fries. The smell of the food as it is cooking influences people in different ways. Shapes and colors of food are suggestive, too. Keep all the senses in mind when you select the menu.

➤ **Drink.** Unless you are nondrinkers or in recovery, wine or champagne can be a part of the meal. These have a reputation for being sexy drinks, compared to beer or soda. (But remember, never overdo it!)

➤ **Atmosphere.** Play your favorite music softly in the background. If you aren't an aficionado, ask for a recommendation from someone at a music store. They may point you to the jazz section or CDs by a romantic vocalist. Wear clothing that is both comfortable and arousing to you and your mate.

Most of all, keep your sensuous meal light and playful. Savor each bite and linger over each course.

How to Pillow Talk

Silence may be golden but when it comes to love, whispering sweet nothings at the right time can have passionate payoffs. Couples who talk in bed have more than good communication. They have happier relationships.

Perhaps you've fallen into the habit of watching TV or reading side by side silently in bed every night. Conversation takes place when one wants to initiate sex, make some comment about the program or book, or reminds the other about something that has to be done the next day. Don't slip into this habit. Rekindle sexy pillow talk. Remember the days when you cuddled together and whispered your love, your secrets, your wishes and dreams? The intimacy created by these words was as important as physical lovemaking.

Since the days of Cyrano de Bergerac wooing Roxanne with eloquent words about her beauty and charms, lovers have used language to seduce. You don't have to be as verbally gifted as Cyrano was. *What* you say can be less important than *how* you say it. Simply expressing yourself in a tender way when you're close to your mate is seductive.

Pillow talk need not always lead to sexual contact. In addition to being specific erotic talk, it can also be loving talk. Men as well as women like to hear how much they are loved or appreciated.

Dr. Judy's Rx

Pick music for your sensuous super that isn't too fast (causing you to rush), too loud, or distracting. Some of my favorites are the Chamber Latin Jazz group Eye Contacts (www.jazzcorner.com/swartz), or the soothing "Music to Disappear In" by Musicians, Raphael and Kutira, 877-524-8250, or love songs from www.earthschild.com or classical violin or Hideko Udagawa (www.chandos.net).

What Is Your Mate's Pillow Talk Style?

There are different types of love talk. Based on my collaborative work with the Ned Herrmann Group in Lake Lure, North Carolina, that I have described in Chapter 6, "The Importance of Matching Your Love Styles," I have identified four types:

➤ **Creative Love Talkers.** They have active imaginations, such as artists and entrepreneurs, and enjoy unique and vividly described fantasies. Play charades with this type and spin exciting tales filled with promises about future love encounters.

➤ **Romantic Love Talkers.** These people, more often women than men, blossom on intimacy, shared feelings, and dreams. They ask, "How do you feel (about us)?" and speak more of love than sex.

Dr. Judy's Rx

Never have troubling conversations in bed. Save that place for pleasure. A partner can feel trapped and sabotaged by an attack in bed.

Love Lookout

In one major survey on sex, 35 percent of men and 23 percent of women agreed that making love is the best way to make up after an argument. Don't get into that habit, or you could start arguing just to get turned on.

➤ **Conservative Lovers.** These people are uncomfortable talking about feelings. But they need security, so you can do the talking, reminding them of past wonderful times together, and reassuring them that all continues to go as planned.

➤ **Intellectual Talkers.** Stimulated by lively debate, they can be excited by banter, even statements of opinion contrary to theirs. More often men than women, they want to hear they are loved but like to believe they are also appreciated for their quick minds.

What to Say—and Not Say

In an informal survey of callers to my *LovePhones* radio show, 9 out of 10 men and women said the most pleasurable pillow talk is hearing their own name. Using your lover's name increases attention and solidifies rapport. Pet names can add intensity to intimacy, unless your mate objects to the name. If a man calls all women "honey," he should call his partner something else.

Compliment and reassure your partner. "You're so funny," or "You feel so good" sound even better when you're cuddled close. Everyone feels insecure at some point about relationships or life in general. If your partner is going through an insecure phase, say, "I find you as exciting as when we first met," or "I have so much confidence in you that I know you will work everything out fine."

Don't criticize your partner. Intimacy allows you to share fears and anxieties, but is not a license to harp on your mate's inadequacies. No one likes to hear a barrage about their character flaws, bad habits, or sexual problems.

The Seductive Power of Being in Shape

Physical fitness has an added bonus: better sex. Exercise is an aphrodisiac for several reasons. Being physically active makes people both relaxed and energized, the very same conditions for feeling seductive. Exercise also enhances sexuality by building strength and endurance, helpful in long lovemaking sessions. Physical exertion releases pleasure chemicals (endorphins) in the brain. Read more about the helpfulness of exercising together in Chapter 28, "Keeping Your Love Exciting with New-Millennium Body and Mind Techniques."

The psychological benefits of fitness are as important as the physical ones. Many women and some men are sexually inhibited by being self-conscious about their bodies. Heavy thighs, pot bellies, and love handles can diminish desire as much as self-confidence. When people feel good about their bodies, they project both desire and desirability.

People do tend to put on weight once they are in committed relationships. In the beginning of a romance, couples don't usually overeat in front of each other. They pay more attention to how they look because they want their body to be accepted and admired. Unsure at first of their partner, they put their best foot—or other body part—forward until love becomes a sure thing.

Love Bytes

A survey of over 8,000 exercisers found 8 out of 10 women credited their workout with boosting their self-confidence, 4 in 10 felt more sexual arousal than before, and 3 in 10 were making love more often.

If you and your mate have become too relaxed with each other, start exercising together. Begin with easy walks. Build up to a joint gym membership or shared activities such as tennis, golf, or swimming. Working together to look and feel your best will make you sexier to each other.

The Least You Need to Know

➤ Seduction isn't just a game for new lovers. It sets the mood for better sex, deeper intimacy, and greater understanding between committed partners.

➤ Awaken all five senses—sight, touch, taste, smell, and sound—to be more sensuous and seductive.

➤ Keep flirting with your partner. If you want to maintain a little mystery in the relationship, flirting will do the trick.

➤ Sensuous meals are more than romantic dinners. They help create an environment in which sexual attraction builds.

➤ Whispered endearments are as important as good kissing skills. Couples who engage in loving pillow talk in bed have more satisfying relationships.

➤ Exercise is a aphrodisiac. Couples who stay in shape together reap sexual as well as health benefits.

Why not just ask "How important is air?"

Chapter 15

How Important Is Sex?

In This Chapter

➤ Making the decision about when to have sex

➤ Important ways that sex is good for you individually and together

➤ The role of chemistry in good sex

➤ Six signs of a sex-starved relationship

➤ Six ways to boost your sexual self-confidence

➤ The "Men vs. Women in the Bedroom" Quiz

Every couple has to decide how important sex is for them. For most couples, sex does matter. Relationships do break up over sexual incompatibility. Both men and women sometimes stray because their partners can't or won't meet their sexual needs. In this chapter, we'll look at how an unresolved sex problem or conflict can drain the joy from a relationship. We'll also see how good sex can sustain you through difficult times and help you grow together.

The Waiting Game: When's the Right Time?

Since casual sex and one-night stands have come under great scrutiny since the age of AIDS and sexually transmitted diseases (STDs) began in the last decade, the question of when to have sex has become more important.

A recent women's magazine survey showed that the majority of women thought that the third date is the right time to have sex. At that point, they think they "know"

Love Bytes

In radio, trends are tracked month to month, but a rating period—giving a substantial measure of how much the audience is listening—comes out once every *three* months. That's a good period of time to assess your relationships, too. Of course, there's no magic number. You'll have to decide what's right for you.

Dr. Judy Rx

One couple decided to make sex after marriage special by wearing a condom until the night of their honeymoon.

their date well enough to become intimate. I have often proposed an "observation period" with a "six-date minimum," on the basis that you can't even begin to entertain the question—much less have sex—until you know at least a few crucial things about a person. The person's character will become evident only after you have observed a *trend*—which requires at least six dates. Those crucial things may include the following observations: Has he been honest? Does she follow through on her word? Does he answer my calls? Does he listen to me? This observation period is also for you track your own behavior. Am I really seeing this person for who he is? What do I really want out of this relationship?

Hopefully, you will use these four guiding principles when deciding to have sex:

➤ Make love, as the word implies, when you feel love, and when you feel it is coming back at you.

➤ Make your own decision, rather than feeling pressured by anyone.

➤ Trust that you are entitled to say "no" and realize that saying no requires security and self-confidence.

➤ Always feel free to change your mind when new information comes to you.

These days, while most couples will have sex before they marry, a few are still waiting. There is nothing wrong with these "later-life virgins." I've had 27-year-olds call me worried that something is wrong with them that they haven't had sex yet. But they also haven't found the right partner. If you're not avoiding sex, but instead haven't found the right person, feel proud knowing that you expect nothing less than the best for yourself.

I've known couples who agreed not to have sex for a few weeks before their wedding to make their honeymoon a more special experience. Just because you've had sex together doesn't mean you can't stop for a while. Starting again makes it special.

Ask Dr. Judy

In one situation, however, stopping sex signaled trouble. As soon as Mason and his girl-friend got engaged, she told him she wanted to stop having sex until after they were married. He was upset, but decided to respect her wishes and go along with her. After the marriage, though, she would come up with other excuses not to have sex—she was tired, it was the wrong time of the month, she had to get up early in the morning. In retrospect he felt tricked that her having sex in the beginning was just to trap him into making a commitment. Mason and his wife needed intensive marriage therapy to work on this problem. After a year she was becoming more responsive to Mason, but he was still disappointed. The lesson: Reasons behind decisions about sex or no sex need to be clear.

Why Sex Is Good for You

When you and your partner decide that the both of you are ready to have sex, keep in mind that good sex offers many health benefits. Medical doctors, psychologists, and researchers have said that regular sex, particularly culminating in orgasm, is beneficial to both men and women. Good sex can have a significant impact on your health, happiness, and other aspects of your life outside your relationship. The post-coital energy boost, increased self esteem, and reduced anxiety all contribute immeasurably to the quality of life.

Here are six specific ways in which sex is good for you:

1. **Sex reduces tension-related stress.** People who report satisfaction with their sex lives are generally less anxious, tense, depressed, or hostile than those who are dissatisfied. An orgasm has the calming effect of a tranquilizer with none of the drug's drawbacks.

Love Bytes

A Rutgers University study found sexual activity and orgasm to be as effective as two aspirin in curing headaches. And people suffering chronic pain from arthritis, injuries, and other causes reported their symptoms were alleviated for half an hour following orgasm.

199

2. **Sex relieves minor pain.** Got a mild headache or premenstrual cramps? Make love. Orgasm releases chemicals in the brain known as endorphins, a natural analgesic. It also helps reduce premenstrual fluid buildup in the pelvic area.

3. **Sex regulates female hormones.** Research shows women who have intercourse at least once a week are more likely to have normal length menstrual cycles. They also have significantly higher levels of estrogen in their blood than other women. Estrogen keeps the cardiovascular system healthy, lowers bad cholesterol, raises good cholesterol, maintains bone density, helps prevent depression, and helps the skin stay supple.

4. **Sex boosts your immune system.** Orgasm boosts the production of infection-fighting white blood cells, in some cases by as much as 20 percent.

5. **Sex improves physical fitness.** Vigorous sex burns calories. Regular sex can help tone the muscles of the entire body.

6. **Sex improves mental health.** Orgasm leaves you with a feeling of well-being. This bolsters the ego and helps you deal with life's problems.

Why Sex Is Good for Your Relationship

Relationships are hurt from the outside by time and money constraints and the demands of work and family, and from the inside by the constraints and demands that each partner puts on the other. Good sex smoothes the rough edges that all the stresses leaves. It softens attitudes of resentment, anger, and boredom that might otherwise harden into walls between partners. It fosters the growth of love and the deepening of intimacy.

Few couples will make and sustain a strong commitment to each other without sharing a strong sexual connection. Wise couples want their lovemaking to be a deeper, more emotional experience. An increasing number are turning to the Eastern sexual arts for guidance. Others take marriage encounter courses or weekend seminars. Whatever they do to enhance sexuality, they do it as much for the emotional sustenance they receive from lovemaking as for the physical pleasure.

A man and a woman rarely come closer to each other than they do during truly intimate sex. Even people who profess minimal interest in sex unconsciously know this. When women (or less often men) sometimes say, "It isn't the sex I want but the closeness," they are really saying, "It isn't the physical pleasure I want, but the feeling of being intensely emotionally connected to my partner that I can get during sex."

Partners who can satisfy each other sexually continually generate mutual feelings of warmth and gratitude. In addition to experiencing all the individual physical and psychological benefits of lovemaking and orgasm, they reap the biggest rewards as a couple: Their relationship thrives and deepens.

Sexual Chemistry

You've probably heard a friend say this about a relationship, or maybe you've felt it yourself: "There's no chemistry between us" or "The chemistry is gone." If you've had this elusive thing called "chemistry," can you really lose it? Can you ever get it back?

Chemistry is hard to define but easy to recognize when you feel it with someone. It is that sense of being powerfully physically attracted to another person, which can happen instantly or develop over time. It is that feeling of being "home" in the embrace of another. The scent of your partner's skin, her taste, and his touch all seem right, familiar, and welcome. This chemistry is partially based on the real thing—chemicals in the body. Our physical response to certain individuals is triggered by the scent of pheromones, the love chemicals everyone produces.

Love Lookout

Studies have shown that couples who get together without ever feeling any sexual chemistry are setting themselves up for serious relationship problems if sex is important to either of them. One or both partners may have some deep or hidden sexual conflict that has to be resolved.

Chemistry is also based on mental, emotional, and spiritual connections, making it more complicated than the simple experiments done with chemicals in Chem. 101. Over the course of a relationship, the sexual chemistry between any two people can naturally fluctuate as does the level of desire. When you are feeling close to each other, the chemistry seems to increase. When you are angry at each other, it seems to decrease.

A couple who has built up a wall of anger and resentment between them will probably find the chemistry is gone. How could it get through that wall? A couple who fails to communicate or make time for each other may also sense the chemistry slipping away even if they don't have anger or resentment toward one another. Feel better knowing you can lose the chemistry, but you *can* get it back. These chapters are meant to help you do that!

Six Signs of a Bad Chemical Reaction

Tensions between you and your partner that are related to sex can be avoided if you recognize the factors that are causing the tension, and if you act on them right away. Here are six critical warning signs to pay attention to:

1. **Negative thinking.** You blow little problems out of proportion. Frustration makes you think poorly about yourself, and doubt your attractiveness and desirability, and leads to question yourself in other areas of life.

2. **Irritability.** You snap at colleagues as well as your partner and have difficulty curbing your frustration in everyday situations such as long lines at the grocery or ATM machine. Unless you've always been this cranky, your frustration may be sexual.

3. **Fatigue.** Are you always too tired to enjoy anything when the workday is over? A persistent feeling of lethargy could indicate you're not making love often enough. Remember: Sex is energizing, not energy depleting.

4. **Criticizing or blaming your partner.** She isn't interested in making love because he is doing something "wrong" in bed. He says she doesn't turn him on anymore because she's gained weight. If the sex were satisfying and frequent, you wouldn't be so harsh with each other.

5. **Workaholism.** One or both of you are sublimating your sexual desires in work (or childcare, family problems, or other activities). Chronic workaholism can signal sexual trouble.

6. **Recurring arguments.** You constantly fight over the same issues that never get resolved. You might be choosing to focus on these issues rather than talk about why you rarely have satisfying sex.

Just knowing the cause of the problem is a big step toward feeling relief and toward focusing on solutions to the problem.

Chemistry and Self-Confidence

The art of making love is not the easiest, most natural thing in the world for most people. Baring body and soul in the bedroom or adding a new sexual twist to a relationship can shake almost anyone's self-confidence. Some people tend to run short on sexual confidence—and not all lust women. While women more readily voice their insecurities, men have a lot of doubts and fears about their sexual abilities and attractiveness to their partners, too.

A little anxiety can have a positive effect on sexual performance if it motivates you to solve a problem. But excessive worrying does not help. If she can't get past the idea that her breasts are too small or hips too wide, or if he can't get past fears about his penis being too small or his technique below par, they aren't likely to light any major sexual fires.

Those anxious, invading, pleasure-sapping internal voices that whisper "you're not good enough" can be tuned down. Here's how:

➤ **Understand that your partner has worries, too.** Women are all too often self-conscious about their bodies, insecure about their attractiveness and sexual technique, and concerned about whether or not they have an orgasm or take too long to have one. Men are self-conscious about their size, insecure about their ability to please, and concerned about the ebb and flow of their desire.

➤ **Help your partner build self-confidence and allay fears.** This is not purely altruistic. As a man's fear of failure or performance anxiety fades, he feels less defensive and more open to new ideas about lovemaking. A woman who has overcome most of her own fears is a more enthusiastic lover, too. Compliment each other where you can. Show your partner what feels good and respond enthusiastically when your partner gets it right.

➤ **Don't feel pressured to perform or please.** To please your partner, you don't have to try sex acts that make you feel uncomfortable. A woman shouldn't feel she must reach orgasm every time, and a man shouldn't feel obligated to provide erection on demand. Being able to say "no" without shame or guilt boosts self-confidence.

➤ **Learn to like your body.** Take off all your clothes and take a good look in the mirror. Don't be so critical. Find something to admire.

➤ **Take the "shoulds" and "should nots" out of sex.** There are fads in sex just as there are fads in hemlines and haircuts. No matter what you've read, it is not healthy to consider one type of orgasm—clitoral or vaginal, by hand or by intercourse—superior. Any orgasm is a good orgasm. Multiples should be a happy event, not something that must be achieved like so many reps on the weight machines. Appreciate your own pleasure level.

➤ **Be responsible for your own pleasure.** This is particularly important for women. All the books, magazine articles, and talk show segments devoted to sex information haven't completely dispelled the myth that men are responsible for "giving" women orgasms. Both men and women have to communicate their needs to their partners. Sometimes you may have to take pleasure into your own hands.

Healthy or Unhealthy?

Joking, thinking, and talking about sex can indicate sexual frustration. But the opposite is also possible. Having as many or more sexual fantasies and dreams as when you were celibate and hungry, is not necessarily a sign that you aren't having enough or satisfying sex with your partner now. In fact, fantasies can increase with more activity and satisfaction, as you become attuned to sexuality and more comfortable with expressing your desires.

What Men and Women Really Want

In Chapter 16, "What's Healthy Sex for Couples?" we'll look at how you can get back the sexual chemistry in your relationship. But before that, let's look at sexual preferences and their differences and similarities between men and women.

Dr. Judy's Rx

Don't assume "men like this" and "women like that." Ask your partner, "How do you feel about ...?" Ask if he considers the occasional "quickie" essential (some women wouldn't mind), or if she likes a man with a slow hand (some women like the pace to vary after initial touches).

First, both men and women want to give and receive pleasure. You might be surprised, and certainly would be pleased, at the numbers of men who called my *LovePhones* radio show saying that they consider their partner's pleasure more important than their own, or that they get pleasure from pleasing a woman.

Both men and women want to feel desired by their partners and be admired as good lovers. But there are certain innate differences in male and female sexuality. Don't ignore those differences or bash one gender for not being like, or as good as, the other. Good sex depends on mutual understanding, acceptance, and respect.

Test your erotic gender knowledge with the following questions. Answer "true" or "false." Have your partner take the quiz, too. These are not the only areas of difference between men and women. You'll read about more in lovemaking tips in the following chapters. Hopefully, these questions will start you thinking about ways in which you can use the differences to surprise and delight each other.

The Men vs. Women in the Bedroom Quiz

	True	False
1. More men than women feel responsible for their partners sexual pleasure.	_____	_____
2. Both men and women close their eyes during kissing most of the time.	_____	_____
3. More women than men prefer the missionary position.	_____	_____
4. Women like to cuddle more than men do, especially after sex.	_____	_____
5. Women have a greater capacity for sexual pleasure than men do.	_____	_____
6. Men are always ready for sex.	_____	_____
7. Women care more about penis size than men do.	_____	_____

Here are the answers. Some may surprise you.

1. **True.** Many men will admit they care about pleasing their partners as much as pleasing themselves. Why? The female orgasm is the number one indication of his sex performance. Invariably, guys ask me, "How do I give her an orgasm?" (even though it's up to her, and he only helps). If a man fails to "give" his partner an orgasm, he may give himself a failing mark as a lover, too. The male orgasm is more inevitable. Women don't feel as much pressure to "give" their partners pleasure.

2. **False.** Women close their eyes far more often than men do. Men's excitement is more dependent on what they see. They want to make love with the lights on, are more easily aroused by visual stimulation, and more likely to keep their eyes open during kissing.

3. **True.** The female superior, or woman on top, position has become more popular with modern men. They like having a better view of their lovers this way. And they also like having a woman be active and take charge of the lovemaking. In surveys, women actually chose the missionary position as their favorite more than men did because they considered it intimate, enjoyed the feeling of the man being in control, and were often embarrassed being on top.

4. **True.** During lovemaking, the brain's pituitary gland secretes oxytocin, a neuro-hormone nicknamed the "love chemical" because it makes you feel warm and cuddly. Women produce much more of this bonding hormone than men do.

5. **False.** You might readily think that women are generally capable of greater sexual pleasure because 1) they last longer and are more readily multi-orgasmic than men (unless men *learn* how to do these things). 2) Men may have orgasms more easily and more often, but women can have several orgasms without stopping more readily than men. And 3) most men, even at young ages, need a refractory, or resting, period in between. *But* the "capacity" for sex and pleasure is as great in men—if they would only learn to enjoy the emotions and sensations rather than the performance.

6. **False.** Until recent times, women didn't initiate sex so they never had to find out that men weren't always in the mood. Now that men and women share more responsibility for sex, women have to come to understand that men aren't always ready, willing, and able to make love. More men today have to learn how to be more comfortable asking for sex when they want affection, reassurance, and communication.

7. **False.** Studies have repeatedly reported that men are more concerned about penis size than women are. Many men don't think they are big enough and mistakenly equate size with sexual prowess. About only half of women care about size, and given a hypothetical choice, most women prefer "average" over extra-large.

The Least You Need to Know

➤ Sex and orgasm offer many physical and psychological benefits to men and women alike.

➤ Good sex can be the glue that holds a relationship together over the years and throughout inevitable difficulties.

➤ If you had sexual chemistry once, you can have it again.

➤ Partners in a sex-starved relationship exhibit behaviors such as irritability, tiredness, and criticizing one another.

➤ Men and women are more alike than different where sex is concerned, but there are real gender differences. Understanding, accepting, and accommodating to these differences will improve lovemaking.

Chapter 16

What's Healthy Sex for Couples?

In This Chapter

➤ The "Is It Healthy?" Sex Quiz

➤ Five wrong reasons to have sex

➤ Identifying your decision style in sex

➤ Ensuring safe sex and contraception

In the movies, a man and a woman may fall into each other's arms and have perfect sex. They never discuss safe sex or birth control or timing or problems of any sort. In real life, a man and a woman have hard decisions to make about sex, starting with "when?" moving quickly to "how often?" At several points in your relationship, you will likely also wonder whether a specific type of sexual behavior is right for you.

It would be nice if there was a great deal of natural overlap between you and your partner about what you want in sex. Obviously the more sexually compatible you are, the fewer tensions and disagreements you will have. But since two people, no matter how compatible, rarely have precisely the same interests and opinions, why should you expect yourselves to have precisely the same levels of sexual desire, and the same preference for sexual positions and activities *all* the time? In this chapter, we'll explore the sexual choices and decisions you may have to make along the way to a healthy relationship.

Making Decisions About Sex

Sexual satisfaction can result from many different techniques and practices. Whether something is "right" or "wrong," "normal" or "abnormal," "healthy" or "unhealthy," is not as important as whether it is right for you and your partner. Refer to the chapters in this book on the four C's: compatibility, communication, commitment, and cooperation, to review how to ensure that you get along with each other. How you make agreements outside of bed will affect how you make agreements in bed.

Take the following quiz to see how you view sex in relationships—whether you feel certain aspects are healthy or unhealthy. Read each question and circle "Yes" or "No." Your answers will affect the decisions you currently must make or will have to make in the future about sex in your relationship. Have your partner also take this quiz. The answers you both come up with may point out how you both feel about the role of sex in your relationship. See where you agree or disagree and discuss your answers together. Then check your answers against the answers in Appendix B.

The "Is It Healthy?" Sex Quiz

	My Answers	My Mate's Answers
1. Do you have to have sex to have a healthy relationship?	Yes No	Yes No
2. If you have to schedule sex into your life, is that healthy?	Yes No	Yes No
3. Do you have to be automatically turned on for healthy sex?	Yes No	Yes No
4. Can sex be healthy if only one person is turned on?	Yes No	Yes No
5. If the woman takes the lead, is it unhealthy for the man?	Yes No	Yes No
6. Are fantasies about others unhealthy?	Yes No	Yes No
7. Should you have to tell your mate what to do to make you feel good? Is that healthy?	Yes No	Yes No
8. If you don't have intercourse, is that unhealthy?	Yes No	Yes No
9. Is it healthy to stop having sex so you can appreciate it more?	Yes No	Yes No
10. Is it unhealthy to have a lot of sex?	Yes No	Yes No
11. Is it healthy to want sex whatever age you are?	Yes No	Yes No
12. Is it unhealthy if you don't have a high sex drive?	Yes No	Yes No

	My Answers	My Mate's Answers
13. Is being turned off after marriage normal?	Yes No	Yes No
14. Is it healthy for the woman to have sex during pregnancy?	Yes No	Yes No
15. Is it unhealthy for a man not to want sex when his wife is pregnant?	Yes No	Yes No
16. Is wanting too much sex unhealthy?	Yes No	Yes No
17. Are day-long sex marathons unhealthy?	Yes No	Yes No
18. Are sex toys healthy?	Yes No	Yes No
19. Are vibrators healthy to use with a partner?	Yes No	Yes No
20. Are sex games healthy?	Yes No	Yes No
21. Are sex videos healthy?	Yes No	Yes No
22. Is it healthy to blame yourself when a partner is not interested in sex?	Yes No	Yes No
23. Is it unhealthy to be turned off if a partner gets very overweight?	Yes No	Yes No
24. Are sexual fantasies healthy?	Yes No	Yes No
25. Is it unhealthy for a man not to ejaculate during sex?	Yes No	Yes No
26. Does a woman have to orgasm to be healthy?	Yes No	Yes No
27. Is faking orgasm unhealthy?	Yes No	Yes No
28. Is masturbation healthy if you have a partner?	Yes No	Yes No
29. Is sex during a woman's menstrual period unhealthy?	Yes No	Yes No
30. Is oral sex during menstration healthy?	Yes No	Yes No
31. Is crying after or during sex healthy?	Yes No	Yes No
32. Are quickies healthy?	Yes No	Yes No
33. Is keeping something about sex to yourself, instead of sharing it with a partner, unhealthy?	Yes No	Yes No
34. Is it healthy to always fall asleep immediately after ejaculation?	Yes No	Yes No
35. Is it healthy for a man to turn off your sex drive?	Yes No	Yes No
36. Do you have to have mutual orgasms to have a healthy sex relationship?	Yes No	Yes No
37. Do both people have to be satisfied in sex?	Yes No	Yes No

209

The Wrong Reasons to Have Sex

Let's now look at when saying no to sex is always the right answer. No matter how long you and your partner have been together, there can be times when not having sex is the right thing to do. Do you often feel disappointed or let down after sex? Maybe it's your mood, disappointment with your partner over something other than sex, or outside factors (stress, frustrations at work, arguments with family). In that case, you might be using sex to fulfill nonsexual needs.

Sometimes sex can help satisfy those needs and make you or your partner feel better. But over time, emotional needs can't be addressed effectively by sex alone. Here is a checklist of five common emotional scenarios:

➤ Using sex to get something tangible from your partner. Saying things like "I'll have sex with you if you'll take my car to the shop [or visit my parents this weekend]" uses sex as barter—a bad idea. It demeans lovemaking and sets a precedent in the relationship that you'll both eventually regret.

➤ Using sex to get affection or attention. If you want to be held and caressed, don't be embarrassed to ask for that. Set aside regular time for sharing conversation and simple affection.

➤ Making love only to please your partner or only in the way your partner wants to be pleased. In a good relationship both partners compromise—one isn't always in the mood but still may want to satisfy the other. But a persistent pattern of one person appeasing the other is not healthy. Eventually, sexual desire will diminish.

➤ Using sex to end arguments. Many couples do make love after a fight. Venting anger enables them to feel more loving toward each other. But using sex to stop the argument before anything can be resolved only drives the anger underground—beware, it will resurface.

➤ Using sex to avoid intimacy. Some couples feel close only during lovemaking. They haven't learned how to share their thoughts and feelings with each other. Do not expect sex alone to create and sustain intimacy.

Four Different Approaches to Sex

Recall the four love styles discussed in Chapter 6, "The Importance of Matching Your Love Styles." These four styles will affect decisions you and your partner are going to make about sex. Let's look at how each style may view sex. What category do you fit in?

Since Creative Lovers are open-minded, imaginative, and impulsive, they will most likely be open to any suggestion about sex that you have. They'll consider all the options and want both of you to be satisfied with whatever happens. Creative Lovers, who are impulsive and make decisions on the spur of the moment, can clash with Conservative Lovers, who want to do only what's safe, or Intellectual Lovers, who dwell on whether it's the right decision.

Recall that Emotional Lovers care most about feelings, so they will make decisions about sex on the basis of how it makes them feel. Your actions could easily make them either very happy or very hurt. Because Emotional Lovers care so much about emotions, and because they often try to please others too much, Emotional Lovers always ask, "How do you feel about that?" or "How does this make you feel?"

Conservative Lovers play by the rules and go by the book, so in making decisions about sex, they'll always make the safer choice, and repeat what's worked before. Give the Conservative Lover all the details about a sexual issue (which condoms work best, how many people engage in a certain sex act, and so on).

The analytical Intellectual Lovers value good judgment, so they like to reflect on all sides of an issue before they make a decision. They like to be "right" about sex, as with anything else. Since Intellectual Lovers like to be in control, they may be overbearing, especially to an Emotional lover who may end up feeling neglected or discounted.

You may find that your lover's style may conflict with your own. Maybe you are a Creative Lover and your partner is too analytical. Is it the end of your relationship? No! However, this is a time for discussion of wants and desires. It is also a time for give and take, mix and match. Whatever your love styles may be, try to reach a common ground that gives you both pleasure.

Love Lookout

Unless you are both tested for STDs, you can't be sure one or both hasn't been long infected. It does happen that women discover an STD during a routine gynecological exam or fertility testing. She may immediately blame her partner for having an affair, when the STD may well have been present in her body for years. Get tested.

The Ultimate Decision: Safe Sex and Contraception

Birth control and safe sex are topics I covered at greater length in *The Complete Idiot's Guide to Dating*. Hopefully you are constantly aware of the importance of birth control, sexually transmitted diseases (STDs), and how to make love as safely as possible. The following points should refresh your memory:

➤ Condoms are highly effective in preventing the transmission of most, but not all STDs (with some STDs, like herpes, the sores or infected areas may not be covered by a condom). However, they must be used properly and consistently. And they do sometimes break.

211

Love Bytes

Some STDs (herpes, warts, yeast, chlamydia) can be present in one partner without any symptoms or with masked symptoms. The couple then passes it back and forth, called "ping-ponging." To prevent this, it is important for both partners to be treated.

➤ Stick to name brands, such as Trojans, that you can trust for durability and effectiveness.

➤ A couple should continue using condoms and practicing safe sex until they have made a monogamous commitment to each other and have tested free of STDs. Some people do get tested for HIV these days, but fewer ask their doctors to test them for the full range of STDs, including chlamydia, that is an increasingly common infection. Chlamydia and other infections are easily treated when diagnosed. Often asymptomatic, they can lead to sterility in both men and women if left untreated.

➤ The choice of a birth control method should be shared by a couple in a committed relationship. Make sure you understand the failure rates and possible side effects of every method. Talk over the options before deciding on one.

The Least You Need to Know

➤ In every sexual relationship, decisions have to be made about contraception and when, where, how often, and how to have sex.

➤ The four love styles will affect the way you and partner view the role of sex in your relationship.

➤ Sometimes not having sex is the right thing to do. Don't use sex as barter or appeasement, to get affection, or to avoid intimacy.

➤ Before you throw the condoms away, have a mutual agreement to be monogamous, and be sure both of you have tested negative for HIV and other sexually transmitted diseases.

Chapter 17

Keeping the Sex Fires Burning

In This Chapter

➤ How often is often enough?

➤ What to do in the face of fluctuations in desire

➤ Using variety to spice things up

➤ The five common sex fantasies and what they mean

➤ How sharing sex fantasies can help your sex life

➤ Learning how to negotiate for better sex

Do you have to have good sex for a relationship to be healthy? Yes, if having good sex matters to at least one of you. Sexual incompatibility can erode your relationship. The one who gets less than he wants feels frustrated, deprived, and angry. The one who wants less feels guilty and pressured. In the healthiest relationships, partners have an understanding about the role of sexuality in their lives. They can adjust to ups and downs, but basically stay in touch with each other's desires and are able, more often than not, to feel both considered and fulfilled. In this chapter, we'll explore how you can maintain sexual excitement in your relationship. Remember, sex is not for one of you—it's for both of you and hopefully, it's also mutually pleasurable.

A Question of Timing

Both men and women inevitably have fluctuations in their sexual moods. A couple who starts out with well-matched levels of desire can eventually find themselves out of synch at some point, due to normal fluctuations that are almost inevitable. And

Dr. Judy's Rx

Timing can affect sexuality. For example, early birds may experience greater desire in the morning, compared to night owls who prefer sex in the evening. Be flexible and make compromises about making love in the morning, the afternoon, evening, or even middle of the night.

couples who aren't as well matched from the start will find these fluctuations even more challenging to their relationship.

In some cases, a disparity of desires doesn't become obvious until a couple has been together a while. In the beginning, the partner with the naturally lower level of desire may appear to be more interested in sex, partly because the relationship is new and the feelings intense. After the couple has been together for several months or longer, that partner can display a decline in the level of interest that may have nothing to do with the relationship but more to do with her true level of desire. Consequently, the partner who wants more sex feels hurt, rejected, and cheated.

Sometimes changes in desire occur at identifiable stages, such as just before or after marriage, the birth of children, career changes, or family events. The birth of a first child typically triggers physical and psychological adjustments. Some factors that put a couple out of sexual synch are beyond control, such as changing hormonal levels in the body or medications.

Sex drive can swell with the thrill of success at work or sport, or with taking up a new form of physical activity. As blood and adrenaline flow, you are physiologically and psychologically more activated. Your sex drive can also deflate with stress, fatigue, illness, job or family problems, or depression. Being fired from his job often renders a man temporarily impotent.

Finally, attitudes also affect sex drive. A woman who has a baby and believes that being a wild lover is inappropriate for a new mother will start to act more primly in bed.

If frequency is an issue in your relationship, take the following steps:

➤ **Don't worry if the frequency of your lovemaking is below the figures cited in magazine articles or reported in studies of sexual behavior.** Normal sex drive, according to psychological standards, depends on what's satisfying to both partners. If the two of you are happy with twice a month or seven times a week, those numbers are neither "too little" nor "too much." They are right for you.

➤ **Accept changes in your own and your partner's sex drive.** Confront the underlying problems instead of focusing on how often you have sex. Can you do anything to help alleviate your own or your partner's stress, anger, frustration, or exhaustion?

➤ **Recognize that changes in desire and sexual performance upset men even more than they women.** Men need to realize that occasional problems with arousal, erection, or ejaculation are common. Worrying only perpetuates a vicious cycle of self-consciousness, anticipation of failure, increased fear and shame, decreased confidence, and impaired performance. Women shouldn't take a man's occasional problem as a reflection on their desirability. Both men and women have to be careful not to overreact.

➤ **Alleviate the pressure to perform sexually for both genders.** Switch anxious thoughts to pleasurable ones. Give yourself time to get in the mood. Many couples need a transition time in bed before they become sexual. Hold each other, cuddle, and talk about the events of the day.

➤ **Allow the partner who feels less sexual to participate only partially in the sexual encounter.** If one is disinterested and the other wants to make love, the interested partner can pleasure him or herself while lying beside and caressing the other. Occasionally one partner might want to satisfy the other manually or orally.

➤ **Offer reassurance of your love when you aren't interested in sex.** Build your partner's ego with statements like, "I'm not in the mood, but I do love you."

➤ **Give an explanation if you are feeling too tired, tense, distracted, or worried for lovemaking.** Don't just say "no!" This helps your partner understand why you aren't interested in sex rather than feel rejected.

Concerns and fears generated by frequency issues can be helped greatly through understanding, by permitting the partner with the higher drive to be sexual, and by accepting differences between both partners.

Variety Is the Spice of Good Sex

Routine can be just as boring in bed as it is in other areas of life. You don't eat the same dinner every night, wear the same outfit day after day, or rent the same video every time you go to the video store. But many couples make love in exactly the same way time after time. Then they wonder why the excitement seems to be disappearing from their sex lives.

What can reinvigorate your lovemaking? Try new positions and techniques. Go out together and purchase erotic aids such as vibrators and sexy videos. Experiment with fantasy role play. Stimulate different parts of the body. Devote more time to those activities traditionally considered foreplay, such as fondling and caressing with hands and mouth. The sign of a good lover is an eagerness for experimentation.

Sexual variety can bring unlimited rewards. It can quicken the pulse of a sluggish relationship and reawaken that wonderful rush of passion. As you explore sexuality, you reinvent your relationship. You learn more about your mate, intensifying the bond between you and refining your intimate knowledge of one another.

Couples get into trouble when one partner favors a position, practice, or technique the other finds unexciting or inappropriate. It can take courage to say you don't like certain sexual activities you are "supposed" to like, such as having your breasts fondled or nipples sucked. It can also take courage to say you do like other activities that you are not "supposed" to like, such as being spanked or pretending to be the opposite sex. Speak up. How can you get your needs met and your desires gratified if you can't articulate them?

Love Bytes

Although we think of men as being the more sexually adventurous gender, this isn't necessarily true. Research has shown that women are as likely as men to complain about lack of variety in lovemaking. Women more often buy sex advice books and introduce new ideas into old routines than men do.

Love Bytes

The ancient Eastern text on sexuality, the Kama Sutra, presented hundreds of sexual positions couples can enjoy.

What pleases you doesn't always please your partner, so you may be disappointed when your lover doesn't respond enthusiastically to your confessions of desire. Compromise is a sexual skill. No one should have to perform acts that are painful or feel demeaning. But if what you or your partner want is neither painful nor demeaning, why not give it a try? Don't pretend to enjoy something you don't, but don't write off something different, such as making love in the kitchen, before you've relaxed and given it a chance to move you.

Remember, lovemaking is more than kissing and stroking followed by intercourse. The following are four of the most common ways to create sexual variety:

➤ **Oral sex.** Couples today consider this an essential part of their lovemaking repertoire. As liberated as our society is, however, oral sex still causes anxiety for some people. Some chief areas of concern include hygiene (or freshness) and technique. Women in particular worry that they aren't "clean" or don't taste or smell good enough. These fears may reflect a deeper feeling that she is not appealing or that certain kinds of sex are "dirty." Bathing or showering before lovemaking should make anyone clean enough for oral sex. In addition, both men and women sometimes hesitate to perform oral sex because they fear doing it wrong, not because they find it distasteful. For now, keep in mind that a light touch is generally better. Be guided by your partner's responses as to what is pleasing.

➤ **Positions.** The two most frequently used positions are missionary (man on top) and female superior (woman on top). In addition, a couple can make love lying side by side, sitting in the middle of the bed with her legs over his, or rear entry (with the man behind). There are many variations on these themes. More agile partners can try making love standing up with the woman's back braced against a wall. Many men find that switching positions helps them to last longer.

➤ **Sexual paraphernalia.** Sex aids include oils and lotions, books, magazines, videos, vibrators, and other items. You aren't weird if you use sex aids. They are tools for expanding your sexuality and injecting a note of play into lovemaking. Some people are too embarrassed to purchase them or even to let their partner know they're interested in playing with sex toys. Overcome your shyness and you may discover something new about yourself. Enjoy, but beware of using sex aids as "cures" for problems—for example, relying on videos to create arousal or vibrators for orgasm every time. In those situations, they become a means of distancing yourself from your partner and your feelings. Also, don't use sex aids that cause pain or that aren't manufactured by a reliable company for specific use as a love toy.

➤ **Settings.** Sex does not always have to take place in the bedroom. Couples who occasionally make love in the bathroom, living room, office, or outdoor pool know how to make the same old steps seem new again. Like transforming a basic dress by adding accessories, making love in an unexpected setting can be a reviving experience.

Dr. Judy's Rx

Sex shouldn't follow a time-table, any more than it has to take place only in bed or only when you're naked. You can add variety to sex by making love without having intercourse or by having an occasional "quickie," a brief but urgent episode of love-making that's centered on intercourse. Try new times, new places, or making love with most of your clothes on for a change.

Sex Fantasies

Men and women alike have sex fantasies, romantic and erotic daydreams that are food for the libido. A fleeting thought about sex, a romantic image, or a memory of a wonderful time is just as legitimate as an extended story that's much like a novel or a film. These fantasies can charge your sexual energy, spice up your private pleasure, and enrich your relationship when occasionally shared. Some people say, "No, I don't fantasize." Perhaps they think only elaborate or unrealistic sex daydreams qualify. Not so. A pleasurable thought is a fantasy.

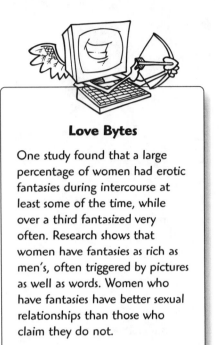

Love Bytes

One study found that a large percentage of women had erotic fantasies during intercourse at least some of the time, while over a third fantasized very often. Research shows that women have fantasies as rich as men's, often triggered by pictures as well as words. Women who have fantasies have better sexual relationships than those who claim they do not.

Often a fantasy is a mental sexual script of how we'd like lovemaking to be played out. Not every fantasy is an expression of a real desire. Most people have had the occasional homosexual or S/M (sadomasochistic) fantasy though they are not really attracted to people of the same sex or don't actually want to experiment with instruments of torture.

Sharing fantasies is a good way to find out what you both like and need, emotionally and sexually. Relating fantasies can help men and women pace their love-making, too. Generally since men get excited faster, a woman can catch up by talking about her fantasies. Imagined sex can work on the body and mind much like a real touch.

By telling each other your sex dreams, you and your partner can put variety into your love life without investing in new lingerie or a weekend getaway. Thinking and talking about a kind of sex doesn't mean you have to do it. If you have a good and trusting relationship, you can share these thoughts without feeling pressured to perform or events act them out.

Five Common Fantasies and What They Really Mean

Many people worry unnecessarily about whether their fantasies are healthy. Here are some of those common fantasies:

Love Lookout

Fantasies can hurt a partner if he feels left out, insecure, or unloved. Also, never force a partner to act out a fantasy.

1. **Another partner.** Making love with someone else, either a stranger, celebrity, or someone you know, is an extremely common fantasy for both men and women. This is not necessarily an expression of unhappiness with the relationship (unless you are really having problems), but a way to learn about what turns you on. Treat your real partner as you do this fantasy person.

2. **Multiple partners.** For men, the two-women fantasy is a classic favorite. In it, they always please, and are pleased by, both women beyond their wildest expectations. Women also imagine having sex with two other people. See this as a wish to be avidly desired and admired for one's skills as a lover.

3. **The romantic fantasy.** Sex in idyllic surroundings (such as the beach at sunset) has been traditionally more common for women, but recent surveys show that men enjoy these romantic fantasies as well. Straightforward fantasies indicate that you enjoy indulging your sensual and romantic side.

4. **"Taboo" sex acts.** Making love in public, spanking or being spanked, or behaving as an exhibitionist or voyeur are all examples of traditionally "forbidden" fantasies. These acts typically have power to excite because they are taboo. Of course, they don't have to be acted out, but can function more like private X-rated videos in your mind.

5. **Forced sex.** Previously (but no longer) called "the rape fantasy," the domination fantasy can appeal to both men and women. Imagining she or he "made me do it" relieves the fantasizer of guilt about pleasure or responsibility for sexual performance.

Five Guidelines for Sharing and Acting Out Fantasies

Sharing a fantasy is a legitimate way to enhance lovemaking. Imagining your partner will react negatively may be a reflection of your own fear of sharing these private thoughts. If you are still concerned that your partner will react in a negative way, start out slowly. Begin with a fantasy such as making love in the back seat of a car or at sunset on the beach. Then follow these five guidelines:

1. Expect differences in your fantasies. Men have been brought up to focus on quantity of sex and quickness, while women dream of quality and slow build-up.

2. Don't judge. Don't pass judgment on your partner's fantasies, calling them weird, sick, silly, or disgusting. You don't have to like it or find it arousing. Just listen to, support, and understand your partner's thoughts.

3. Learn to tell a good story. Draw it out. Weave in sensual and erotic details. Describe each element of the fantasy and how it makes you feel.

4. Verbalize fantasies more often than you act them out. Talking is preferable to acting much of the time. If a man wants sex in a particular position that his partner does not like or finds painful, have sex another way while he fantasizes about it.

5. If you decide to act out a fantasy, remember that it may have to be scaled down from the script in your head. Plan the details. Make sure that both of you are comfortable with an activity that is safe and pleasurable.

How to Negotiate for Better Sex

Love partners don't always match each other's every mood and changing feeling. One person can't possibly satisfy all your needs, nor you theirs. It's unfair to expect that of a lover. Sometimes you and your partner will want different things. Sexual decisions will have to be made with some compromises. Learn to negotiate.

Keep these six points in mind while you are negotiating when, how often, where, how, and other sexual issues:

1. Appreciate and love yourself first. Only then can you share openly and fearlessly with your lover.

2. Lower your expectations. Maybe your needs are not reasonable given the current conditions in your partner's life.

3. Make love in a nondemanding way. Consider your partner's needs and desires as well as your own.

4. Replay pleasurable scenes from your past together. Recreate some of those scenes when you can.

5. Show and tell your partner what you like. Use positive "I sentences"—"I'd like you to do this for me," rather than critical negatives like "You're not satisfying me."

6. Treat each lovemaking session as though it were your first time; seduce each other.

Getting over Inhibitions

What good is sharing fantasies and adding variety to your sex life, if you still feel uptight about letting yourself go? Try filling your mind with affirmations ("I can enjoy this" or "I deserve this") rather than thoughts of failure or embarrassment. Separate your desires from what you were taught was not okay while growing up. Relax in a comfortable place (in the bath or bed), play soft music, close your eyes, breathe slowly and deeply, and allow any sexual thoughts or fantasies to cross your mind. Share these with your partner, without fear. Review past evenings together and imagine one new thing that you will risk doing next time. Be—both in and out of bed—the lover you would most like to be. Teach your partner new ways to please you, not just in lovemaking, but in daily living as well.

The Least You Need to Know

➤ Frequency of lovemaking is the most common source of disagreement when it comes to sex. Avoid this by recognizing and accepting the changes in desire that affect you both and making compromises.

➤ Variety is essential in lovemaking to avoid boredom. Create mutually exciting ways of adding spice to your love life.

➤ Both men and women have sexual fantasies that can enrich and recharge a love relationship when shared. Act out only the mutually pleasurable and safe fantasies.

➤ It is possible to resolve differences in your sexual preferences by respecting each other's needs and making compromises.

➤ Consider your lovemaking life together as an adventure.

Part 4

Obstacles to a Lasting Relationship

Are you and your partner fighting a lot? Are either of you stressed out? Are work problems destroying your love? Every road to lasting love has bumps and even some roadblocks. If left unchecked, they can prove disastrous to your pursuit of a healthy relationship.

In this part, we'll explore the most common challenges couples face over the course of their relationship. Learn the signs of love burnout so you can avoid them! You'll find that many problems are rooted in feelings and events of past relationships—what I call "love ghosts"—that are explored in Chapter 19. Life is not just about love and the two of you. You have family, careers, friends, daily life, crises, and money to manage. Identify the problems in these areas that could be interfering with your relationship happiness, and I'll show you how you can overcome any obstacles to a healthy relationship.

Chapter 18

Preventing Love Burnout

In This Chapter

➤ A quiz to test your Love Burnout factor

➤ The top 10 love turn-offs

➤ Ways to overcome boredom in a relationship

➤ How to find more time for love

He used to tell you how pretty you are and bring you little gifts. You laughed at his jokes and found the details of his job or workout routine fascinating. You finished each other's sentences, caught each other's eye at dinner parties, and just "knew" what each other was thinking. When you were apart, you longed to be together. No matter how busy your individual schedules were, you made time for each other.

Now he's too tired for sex. He knows you're taking a class in something, but he can't remember what. You can't remember if his favorite team made the playoffs. You're both often too busy to talk, much less make love. Time together is rushed or filled with routines and chores.

Where has that excitement you once had gone? Is love over? Not quite. You're suffering from Love Burnout, a condition that plagues almost every couple at some point in their lives together.

What Is Love Burnout?

Love Burnout is a case of the relationship "blahs." Nothing may be seriously wrong, but nothing is not really right, either. You may bicker about silly little things. More often you're simply too busy, too tired, or too stressed to relate. You have a lingering sense that nothing, including talking together, is worth the effort anymore.

Dr. Judy's Rx

Boosting your physical energy can take the edge off burnout. Get regular exercise and adequate rest. Eat a healthy diet. Avoid heavy foods and too much alcohol when you're with your partner, as they'll dull your senses.

These feelings can stem from physiological causes, including illnesses (everything from a prolonged bout of colds or flu to recovery from an accident or surgery), chronic fatigue, or the effects of prescription medicines such as antihistamines or certain antidepressants. Love Burnout can be the result of one person's anger or depression. Outside forces can figure into it as well. Career crisis or job loss (particularly if one of you is doing well), family problems, and many other external issues can cause stress or drain the time and energy that you want to devote to love. Even seasonal factors, like harsh winter weather, can play a role.

Healthy or Unhealthy?

Is it healthy to be together all the time? An interesting variation of burnout happens if you loved at such an intense level it seemed unsustainable. Like workaholics, even the lovers who seemingly can't get enough of each other might reach the point where they have had enough, at least for a while. Constant togetherness, especially if it excludes other people, can be ripe for Love Burnout. It is sometimes far healthier to make some space for others and for some individual time alone.

In some instances, Love Burnout is nothing more than a serious case of boredom. The excitement that accompanies discovering a new person has subsided. The thrill may seem like it's gone. At this point, some people look for a new love, for a new thrill. But it's important to realize that feeling bored is not cause for ending a good relationship, just a signal to take the one you have to a higher level.

The Top Ten Love Turn-Offs

What do men and women do in relationships that sets the stage for Love Burnout? Here are 10 behaviors that almost certainly will induce that effect.

1. **Insecurity.** The man or woman who constantly needs reassurance of self-worth from a partner can wear out even the most devoted lover. We all have moments of insecurity, but they shouldn't be lasting and recurrent.

2. **Possessiveness.** A little jealousy now and then might be perceived as flattering. But the partner who is persistently possessive and jealous makes the other feel imprisoned, not loved.

3. **Excessive nurturing.** This has traditionally been a female flaw because of social conditioning. Excessive nurturing makes a man feel "mothered" and "smothered." When he has the flu, he might appreciate this; otherwise, he might tire of it. The same goes for a woman who is being smothered by an overly attentive man.

4. **Spying.** He unexpectedly shows up at the restaurant where she's meeting a group of women friends. She routinely searches his pockets after he falls asleep, suspicious over the meaning behind unfamiliar matchbook covers and credit card receipts. Like smothering, spying is a big love turn-off.

5. **Moping.** Who wants to be around the man or woman who's always down? If you hate your boss, the political system, health care, and everything else, blaming the world for your sorry life, don't look now, but your partner's love is burning out.

6. **Controlling.** If you have to have your way all the time, your partner probably feels limited to two response choices: struggle for power or give up the struggle and acquiesce. Either option is unsatisfactory.

7. **Lying.** Inevitably you will get caught in your lies. Once your partner no longer trusts you, the relationship is headed for burnout fast.

8. **Disregard.** He's always late, forgets to call, neglects to pick up the video, the steaks, and the wine. She won't put herself out to be nice to his mother, boss, or best friend. It's hard to sustain love under these circumstances.

9. **Manipulation.** She's read the singles books and is going for "the ring." He's read The Code, and he's going for the score. No one likes to be used just to satisfy someone else's needs. Manipulating a partner's feelings through your own behavior always guarantees trouble.

10. **Space invasion.** Even the closest of lovers need private space. The invasion can be physical or intellectual. Insisting someone talk when she or he doesn't want to is an invasive behavior; leave the probing to doctors and investigators. The more you give a partner the space he needs, the more he will want to be with you—by choice.

The Love Burnout Quiz for Couples

Both you and your partner should take the following quiz to see if you both suffer from Love Burnout. If you answer "Yes" to more than two of the following 10 questions, the bad news is that you are on your way to suffering from Love Burnout. If you answer "Yes" to five or more questions, you're in the danger zone. But the good news is that it's totally curable. You can bring back the thrill!

The Love Burnout Quiz

1. Has it been more than a week since you said "I love you," or showed your love in a special romantic way?

2. Have you stopped looking forward to those quiet evenings together, like spending time watching a video or listening to music?

3. Have you lost track of what's happening in your partner's life (at work or with family or friends)?

4. Are you always too tired for lovemaking?

5. Do you no longer tell important news, good or bad, to your partner first?

6. Are your dinners together eaten in front of the TV, always with friends and family, or consumed in a hurry with a minimum of conversation?

7. Are you calling each other less often at work to say "Hi, how's your day going?"

8. Do you touch each other less frequently now than you did?

9. Have you stopped falling asleep in each other's arms or curling up spoon fashion?

10. Is it just too much trouble to tell your partner how you feel most of the time?

Now, go back over the quiz questions. They each describe an activity that new lovers enjoy: looking forward to time alone, enjoying being curled up in each other's arms, asking each other questions, and sharing experiences. To get back the thrill of your young love, resolve to do each one of the activities described.

Overcoming Boredom

The most basic cause of Love Burnout is plain boredom. It's almost as common as the head cold and household dust. But fortunately, it's also an easy problem to overcome. Is boredom inevitable as a relationship progresses? No. As long as you grow and change as individuals, the relationship can also grow and change. You can continue to delight and surprise each other, even after you're long past the initial stage of learning about each other through long conversations that last into the night. There's always more to learn!

The following five tips will help you and your partner overcome routine boredom in your relationship:

1. Face it instead of pretending it's not happenings. Realize it's *both* your responsibility: *You* can be boring, too. Tell your partner the truth: Your relationship has a case of the "blahs." Don't get angry when you hear, "I'm bored, too." It's not your partner's responsibility to excite you again. You both have an obligation to yourselves as well as to each other to be the most fully evolved and interesting people you can be. You both have to acknowledge the problem and agree to help each other do something about it.

2. Add variety to your life together. Change your weekend routine. Do something together that you don't normally do, such as visit a museum. Play tourist in your own city or take up a new hobby or sport together.

3. Find a new activity independent of your partner that will help you grow as a person. Take an adult-education class or work as a volunteer. Take the piano lessons your parents couldn't afford to give you when you were growing up.

Love Bytes

Numerous studies have shown the link between happiness in love and satisfaction with life in general. If you're expecting a relationship to make up for job dissatisfaction, family turmoil, or low self-esteem, you're expecting too much. It may seem in the beginning that your partner's love can compensate for everything else you don't like about your life; over the long haul, though, it can't.

4. Get a makeover, either alone or with your partner. A different hair style can make anyone feel like a new person. Change your lipstick. Buy a new outfit. If you live in black and neutrals, add a note of color with an exuberant scarf or tie. Spend a day or weekend together at a health and beauty spa.

5. Make a few adaptations to your love style. Now that you understand your partner's love style better than you did, target your loving words, gestures, and actions more surely to your lover's often unspoken needs and desires. (Go back to Part 3, "How to Keep Passion Alive," for ideas on putting the sizzle back in romance and sex.)

Make More Time for Love

For many couples, Love Burnout happens because they have stopped making sufficient time for each other. As in parenting, people can debate "quality" over "quantity" time without achieving a consensus that feels right for everyone. Every couple has different time requirements for a rich and satisfying love relationship. Like minimal requirements for food, water, and sleep, they must be met or we don't thrive. If you and your partner aren't spending as much time together as you need to in order to sustain your emotional connection, what can you do about it?

➤ Set aside 15 minutes every day to talk. If you aren't together, talk on the phone. Use this time to discuss things that matter to you. Ask about each other's feelings and private thoughts.

➤ Keep in touch with your memories. Maybe work and family or other responsibilities have prevented you from having as many good times together as you had in the past. Hold on to those good times. Remember them when you're feeling lonely. Remind your partner of them, too.

➤ Make dates with each other. Often couples who are engaged, living together, or married stop setting aside special time to go out to dinner or the movies just as a couple. They socialize with family and friends, or they stay home and juggle chores and take-home work with their relationship.

➤ Create private space. If you're never alone, it can be hard to be truly together. Set aside time and create a space, even if it's only a chair in the corner of the living room, that is yours. Recharge your emotional batteries and you'll be better able to connect with your partner.

➤ Be sure that you are meeting your partner's need for time spent together as well as your own. If one of you needs more togetherness than the other, some compromises obviously have to be made. Don't leave your mate feeling neglected.

Ask Dr. Judy

Brian and Joleen called my *LovePhones* radio show complaining that they were once madly in love, but now felt estranged and more like distant roommates, passing each other in the night. I helped them reexamine their daily schedules, insisting they make time to be together at least an hour every day, doing anything together (even if it was going grocery shopping after work). This would get them back in touch with each other. I told them that one of those hours a week would be devoted to time in bed, not intentionally being sexual at first, but just talking and touching. This would—and did, as I learned when they called back—revive their passion for each other.

The Least You Need to Know

➤ Love Burnout, a case of the relationship "blahs," does not signal the end, but rather the need for a new beginning.

➤ The causes of Love Burnout can be physical or psychological. Lack of time and simple boredom are leading culprits, both of which can be solved.

➤ Brainstorm about things you can do today to bring variety and excitement back into your love life.

➤ Making time for each other is one of the most important ways to avoid love burnout.

Chapter 19

Ghost-Busting Your Relationship

In This Chapter

➤ Recognizing love ghosts in your current relationship

➤ Playing out family love scripts

➤ Ghost-busting your love life

➤ Completing unfinished business in love

Love ghosts of the past are specters of past relationships that interfere with your present love match. We bring ghosts of our past into our present love. It's like the common statement made these days about the necessity for safe sex: When you have sex with someone, you are having sex with everyone else that person has ever had sex with. The same is generally true of your current relationship: When you are in a relationship with someone, you both bring to the table your entire past—all the residues and memories of past experiences with other important people in your life.

I'm proud of having identified this concept of "Love Ghosts" because I know how valid it is and how important a role it plays in people's relationships.

These important people who define your love ghosts always include your parents or any other major caretakers throughout your childhood. The next greatest impact comes from important early love experiences—your first love, your first break-up, or some other love that mattered a great deal to you. Then there are a host of other people to whom you relate who affect you and condition how you feel about relationships. These include extended family members, children, friends, teachers, bosses, and co-workers.

Knowing how these ghosts affect your present relationship—and preventing them from interfering with it—is important for long-lasting, healthy love.

Uncovering Your Love Ghosts

Doing the following exercise will help you identify—and bust—your love ghosts.

Quickly think now of all the people who have mattered to you in your life. Start from your childhood and work your way through your major life stages. Allow whoever comes to mind, without censoring yourself. Write down these people's names in the "Past Love Influences" column on the following chart.

Now, in the "What Happened" column, write down a major experience that happened between you and this person that conditioned your experience of love. In the "How It Affects Me Now" column, write down what impact or decision that had on how you view love or relate to lovers, including your current partner. Use a separate sheet of paper if necessary.

Here's an example you can follow: The first person who popped into Jerilyn's mind was Lee, her first boyfriend from high school. He was the captain of the swim team and a real catch for her, but he cheated on her with her best friend. She wrote this down in the "What Happened" column. "I distrust men now," she then wrote in the "How It Affects Me Now" column. The next person she thought of was her father. In the "What Happened" column, she wrote that he had an affair when she was young, which sent her mother into a depression. Now, it affects her in that she feels angry and disappointed in men. When she next wrote down her current boyfriend's name, she realized that, once again, she was picking a man whom she might not be able to trust. Reviewing these ghosts allowed her to see how her present love relationship is being controlled by these ghosts of the past.

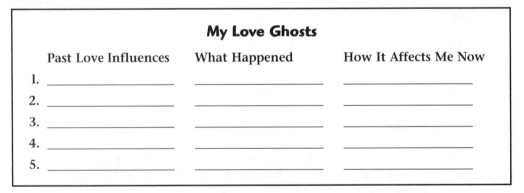

Once you realize these love ghosts exist, you can learn how to stop letting them control you.

Family Love Ghost Scripts

Ghosts from your past can be revealed in what I call your "family love ghost scripts." When you end up behaving toward your mate in ways that recall the relationships in your family when you were growing up, you are acting out a family love ghost script. I find so often that people pick mates to repeat, or run away from, a similar type of relationship they saw or experienced with a parent. For example, a woman whose father neglected her and her mother may stick with a similarly neglectful boyfriend. Or if her father adored her, she may never be satisfied with any man who cannot adore her as much.

Of course, there are healthy outcomes of these matches too, when you pick a partner with good qualities like your parent and avoid the negative or hurtful qualities.

To determine your family love ghost scripts, do the following exercise. Answer the questions as they apply to your parents' relationship, and then your own. (Consider any two people who were in a major parenting role for you, whether grandparents, step-parents, or others.) Use a separate sheet of paper if necessary.

My Family Love Script

Situation	For My Parents	For Me and My Mate
What happened when they met		
How he felt about her		
How she felt about him		
How they got along		
What problems they had		
What happened when they got married		
What happened when they had children		
What happened later in life		
How are they now (specify):		

Review your answers as they apply to your parents and to your own relationship. Observe the similarities and differences. If there are a lot of similarities, and these are positive experiences, you could simply have had a good example in your past that set you on a good path. If the situations are negative, you might be sadly repeating past negative experiences, either because you are more comfortable that way or because you secretly hope that by repeating the past you can magically change it.

You and Your Shadows: Ghost-Busting Your Love Life

To separate your own decisions about your love relationship from other influences (parents, friends, media, other), and ensure that you are making independent decisions, do the following exercise. Review the various actions described below and circle the appropriate choice.

Influences on My Love Decisions

Regarding:

My choice of mate:

I choose	My Parents	My Friends
Yes/no	Approve/disapprove	Approve/disapprove

Where we live:

I choose	My Parents	My Friends
Yes/no	Approve/disapprove	Approve/disapprove

Our choice of jobs:

I choose	My Parents	My Friends
Yes/no	Approve/disapprove	Approve/disapprove

What we do with our money:

I choose	My Parents	My Friends
Yes/no	Approve/disapprove	Approve/disapprove

Where we go:

I choose	My Parents	My Friends
Yes/no	Approve/disapprove	Approve/disapprove

How we lead our daily life:

I choose	My Parents	My Friends
Yes/no	Approve/disapprove	Approve/disapprove

Whether we have children:

I choose	My Parents	My Friends
Yes/no	Approve/disapprove	Approve/disapprove

Other (specify) _____:

I choose	My Parents	My Friends
Yes/no	Approve/disapprove	Approve/disapprove

Review your answers to determine whether you make choices (checked "yes") about your life and your relationship, or whether you might be conforming, rebelling, or blaming others. For example, you may be conforming if you checked "no" for your own choice, but "approve" by family or friends. Or you may be rebelling if you checked "yes" for your own choice but "disapprove" for family and friends.

If your decisions are mostly yours, without being either accepted or rejected by others, you are the captain of your own ship. If your decisions clash with others, you might be rebellious, and should consider what others have to say. If your decisions mostly comply with others, you may have made good choices that important people in your life also see the value of. Or, you may need to question whether you are going along with others, and need to focus more on what you want.

Completing "Unfinished Business"

When an experience from a past love lingers with you—when you constantly obsess about that person—you have what's called "unfinished business" with that person. You need to say what's burning in your heart in order to free yourself from thinking about that person.

My favorite technique to complete unfinished business is the "empty chair exercise," from Gestalt psychology. I am indebted to Marilyn Resanes-Barrett, a Fritz Perls protégé, for my excellent training in that field. The principle is that you need to tell important people in your life (present or past) certain things, and that one statement may trigger memories of other experiences and people who also need to be addressed. You do not talk to the people in real life at first, as that is not as therapeutic as working through the experience by yourself.

Love Bytes

In an advanced version of the empty chair technique, you would switch roles and imagine being the other person as he listens to you, and respond as if you were him.

Try this exercise: Sit comfortably in a chair in a quiet room. Place another chair opposite you. Now imagine someone you are angry with. Picture this person in the chair opposite you. Really "see" him or her there. Picture the hair, eyes, clothes, mouth, and posture of the object of your anger. Again without censoring yourself, say aloud what you really want to say to this person, but would be afraid to say in real life (out of fear, guilt, or embarrassment).

By actually vocalizing what you feel, you purge yourself of some unpleasant feelings and clarify both the source and extent of others. Then you can more constructively decide what to do about these feelings (how to handle them and whether to share them).

Staying Together by Moving On

It is common to keep alive the spirit of a loved one, even to the point of resisting fully committing to a new love, or your own life. Phoenicia's ex-boyfriend died of

AIDS, and now when she has sex with her new boyfriend, she has dreaded feelings that she, too, should die. Paulette cannot have sex with the man she has been dating for six months because she still feels connected to her ex. While undying love is romantic and applaudable, it can also represent fears, dysfunctional dependence, depression, and survivor guilt that keep you from being fully present in a new relationship. Affirm that you deserve love in this all-too-fleeting life.

The Least You Need to Know

➤ Patterns of your past affect your present choices in love. To achieve a healthy relationship, you and your mate need to confront past experiences and ghosts from your past and from earlier love life.

➤ Recognizing echoes of your parents' love life frees you to pick your own path.

➤ Completing unfinished love business allows your current love to flourish.

Chapter 20

Dollars and Sense: A Healthy Couple's Guide to Handling Money Issues

> ### In This Chapter
>
> ➤ The "Principal Priorities" Quiz
>
> ➤ The "Is It Healthy?" Money Quiz
>
> ➤ The effect of money on love and sex
>
> ➤ How to avoid money matters from destroying your relationship
>
> ➤ The "Dozen Dollar Decisions"

Money is an inextricable part of our daily life and relationships. It certainly provides for physical security and momentary pleasures, but it cannot buy lasting love. Nor can it lift you to the highest, "spiritual" or fifth dimension of a healthy relationship.

In fact, it's something that requires you to be wary. Surveys show that money is the one of the three top sources of tension between couples (besides sex and raising kids). For many, it's the leading cause of trouble.

In the new millennium, money plays an increasingly important role in relationships, as more women increase their earning power, as more couples face the threat of company downsizing, job loss and decreased income, and as more women as well as men become of new ways to enterprise income, with at-home businesses, playing the stock market, and investing. I mentioned this at the beginning of this book, as an important dimension of a healthy relationship. In this chapter, we'll go through ways to prevent money from breaking your emotional bonds.

The priority you place on money in your life, the symbolism you attach to it, and the way you use it, greatly affect how you approach life in general. As a result, it will greatly affect how efficient the practicalities of your partnership can be, as well as how emotionally satisfying and long-lasting your relationship can be.

Sex, Love, and Calculator Tape

Attitudes and behavior surrounding money are intimately intertwined with other aspects of life. Your answers to the questions in this chapter about handling money can reflect your personality style in general and reveal clues about you and your partner's compatibility. Once you know your and your mate's money style, and how it relates to your approach to other aspects of life, including sex, you will be better prepared to avoid problems and to enhance your pleasure together.

Ruled by Rubles

Some people approach life with the attitude that money talks: If they're getting paid, you've got their attention. People from a contrasting perspective listen with their hearts instead of their pocketbooks. Hardly any of us can afford not to think about where our money is coming from and how much we have. But you can have different priorities on how important money is to you and how much you need to be happy. A difference in your priorities can make for an unhealthy relationship. Francine could not forgive Stephen for taking a job he loved when he was also offered another one at twice the salary. To her, money was of utmost importance. But Stephen chose to work for a nonprofit organization rather than a big corporation because what mattered to him was not his paycheck, but the payoffs of enjoying what he did and doing good for the world.

In the following exercise, read each statement and decide if it is true of you (if so, circle "Me") or not true of you (if so, circle "Not Me"). Choose whichever one seems to most apply to you most often, even if it only describes you sometimes or somewhat. Then have your mate answer the same questions, marking his answers in the column indicated.

The Principal Priorities Quiz

	My Answer	My Mate's Answer
1. I judge my personal worth by my net worth.	Me Not Me	Me Not Me
2. I'm more interested in people who have money.	Me Not Me	Me Not Me

---

3. In picking friends, I'm swayed by how rich they are.	Me	Not Me	Me	Not Me
4. I think being poor is a sign of failure in life.	Me	Not Me	Me	Not Me
5. I've turned down work that didn't pay me enough.	Me	Not Me	Me	Not Me
6. I'm always worried about money.	Me	Not Me	Me	Not Me
7. I pay strict attention to price tags.	Me	Not Me	Me	Not Me
8. I like to buy designer items no matter what the cost.	Me	Not Me	Me	Not Me
9. I'd rather be rich than smart or beautiful.	Me	Not Me	Me	Not Me
10. I have a fear of ending up penniless.	Me	Not Me	Me	Not Me

The more items you have checked in the "Me" column, the higher priority money is to you. If you have seven or more checks in the "Me" column, others may accuse you of being obsessed over money or "money hungry." You may in fact be so concerned about greenbacks that you miss (or avoid) emotional interchanges or deep feelings. If you checked between four and six questions in the "Me" column, then money matters to you, but so do other things in life—your feelings about people, your enjoyment of experiences, and your spiritual growth, for example. If you agreed with three or fewer statements, money does not rule your life and is not a big consideration in who you relate to and what you spend your time doing.

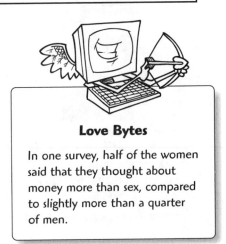

Love Bytes

In one survey, half of the women said that they thought about money more than sex, compared to slightly more than a quarter of men.

No score is "good" or "bad," "right" or "wrong." It simply refers to your approach to money in your life. Your particular approach does not automatically spell trouble in your relationship. But a discrepancy in your scores could signal trouble. For example, if one of you scored more than six marks in the "Me" column, and the other scored fewer than four in the "Me" column, there could be trouble. More financially focused mates may become impatient with those who could care less about accounts. Mates who value people and experiences based on their emotional and spiritual payoff can become disillusioned with mates devoted to dollars.

> ### Healthy or Unhealthy?
>
> So you and your mate don't see eye to eye when it comes to money? That's okay. Remember the three A's of a healthy relationship: acceptance, appreciation, and agreements. You can disagree, but you have to come to agreements. It's easier to make agreements if you accept and appreciate each other.

Tracing the Roots of Money Matters

Each of you developed your attitudes about money from a combination of your experiences, cultural and religious background, the realities of the economy, personality traits, and certainly from what you learned while growing up. Reflect on what you learned about money from your parents. What did your mother teach you about money? What did your father teach you? How did you see your mother handle money? How did your father handle money? In what way did what you observed or heard from your parents affect your own attitudes about money (did you resolve to be like or unlike them)? Realize that you can make your own new choices about money if you desire. Discuss your money influences with your partner to get a better understanding of your present behavior. Did you grow up rich or poor? How did you feel about that? How did that influence your decisions about how to behave now?

Dr. Judy's Rx

Remember, the best possibilities for a healthy relationship exist in moderation and combination. In money matters, value planning and security, but also be able to take a risk occasionally.

A Money Quiz

Answer the following questions as they apply to you by choosing **a**, **b**, or **c**. Then ask your mate to write his answer in the appropriate place. Don't worry about which answer is right or wrong. Pick the one answer that most applies, even if several may be true, or apply under different circumstances.

The "Is It Healthy?" Money Quiz

1. What do you prefer to do with money?

    a. Invest it

    b. Spend it when I'm in the mood

    c. Splurge

    My Answer _____   Mate's Answer _____

Lavish spenders who answered **c** can be exciting since they have a devil-may-care attitude toward life and love. But they also may use money as a sign of status, a way to impress others, and to feel important. They may be happy only when they're admired and desired. Those who answered **b** are more like moody spenders, who tend to be emotional people who make decisions about money or sex based on what they feel at the moment, rather than what's wise or practical. They'll be very happy in love if you talk about your relationship, promise to take care of them, and share a lot. In contrast, answering **a** suggests you prefer practical more than passionate choices in money matters and likely in love as well. You likely need to be in control and reassured that you made the right move.

2. How do you like to keep money?

   a. Loose in pockets or drawers

   b. In safe or hidden places (locked boxes, safes)

   c. Easily accessible, always carrying a lot, or where others can see the wad of bills you have

My Answer _____   Mate's Answer _____

Your answer to this question suggests how much security you require, and how free you allow yourself to be. If you answered **a**, you likely need reminders wherever you look that you are financially secure—and symbolically secure in general. Remind such partners constantly that they are taken care of, loved, and desired. If you answered **b**, you may also be likely to prefer playing it safe in bed. If this is your mate, don't demand that he be experimental or wild in love, but appreciate the safety and stability he offers. People who answered **c** are the opposite: Players in the market, they often also play love games. Drawn to risk, they like the thrill of the chase and hunt, putting themselves on the edge. If you're with a high-roller, go along for the ride. Keep her on her toes with sexual surprises.

3. How much do you spend on others?

   a. Hardly any

   b. About as much as on myself

   c. A lot

My Answer _____   Mate's Answer _____

Stingy people who answered **a** are often equally selfish lovers, fearful that giving leaves them depleted. But people who splurge excessively on others, those who answered **c**, may equally have a problem: depriving themselves, giving out of low self-esteem, co-dependency, fear of being obligated, and needing to buy love. The healthiest love partner, who answered **b**, can treat as well as be treated, give as well as receive, please as well as be pleased.

4. Who takes care of the finances?

  a. Me alone; I couldn't trust anyone else

  b. Myself as well as my partner or trusted other

  c. Others; I hardly know what's going on

My Answer _____ Mate's Answer _____

Those who are too vigilant about controlling finances by themselves and who answer **a**, may need to be in control in love as well. But deferring all money management to others, answer **c**, can signal that you're too dependent, expecting others to always take care of you. Making mutual decisions, as would be suggested by a **b** answer, is a good indication of sharing sexual responsibilities as well.

5. What does money represent to you?

  a. Self-worth

  b. Power

  c. Freedom

My Answer _____ Mate's Answer _____

If you answered **a**, that money is a sign of your self-worth, you may see having a lasting relationship as a sign of your value as well. If so, beware that you might be prone to insecurity. A mate would be wise to always reassure you of how important you are to him. If money equals power for you, as in answer **b**, you may see your relationship in terms of power while being concerned with who is in control. Sex might also trigger power issues for you, including concern over who is submissive or assertive, who takes initiative, and even in the type of lovemaking positions you prefer. Those who picked the **c** answer and who value freedom may be hard to pin down but may also be creative, fun, imaginative, and playful in love and sex.

For Love or Money?

The reality is that couples do break up over money troubles. Statistics from the U.S. Census Bureau even show that rich couples are twice as likely to stay married as those without money.

I find that men and women alike are still idealistic—they would like to deny the importance of money in love. Whenever I lecture about finding Mr./Ms. Right and ask about the three top criteria for attraction, someone invariably jokes, "cash, cash, cash." But when it comes to writing down what you look for in a partner, money doesn't even show up in the top three. In my surveys of thousands of men and women, personality ranks higher than portfolio in choosing a lifetime partner. The most common answer to my Internet chat show question about "How do you know it's true love?" was: "You can live in a cardboard box/have no money/lose your shirt and still care only about being together." My conclusion: Where idealism and romanticism thrive, nonmaterialism has a chance.

Twelve Routes to Derailing on the Money Track

Certain experiences related to money matters test the strength of your relationship. Being alert to them can prevent you from deteriorating into arguments that could create a dangerous strain between you. Think of your relationship as a train going down a track. At certain key stations you can run into roadblocks. Whether or not you heed the caution lights can mean either a safe journey ahead or a tragic crash. Here are 12 key switching points along that train track:

1. **When you have some extra cash and disagree on how to spend it.** If one of you wants to buy a new stereo but the other wants to save for a new couch, you could be headed for a fight. On a deeper level, you might end up resenting each other's values in life, accusing one of being a spendthrift and the other of being a tightwad. Disagreeing over small-ticket items could mean you're making mountains out of molehills, or the discrepancy is just the tip of the iceberg of bigger incompatibilities in how you will approach the bigger picture.

2. **Making a big purchase.** When it's time in your relationship for the two of you to undertake a "big ticket" item—like a house or car—make sure you discuss not just the practical details, but the emotional implications. Large expenditures tend to imply long-lasting involvement that can stir up feelings about the solidity and longevity of your commitment to each other.

3. **Christmas and other holidays.** With pressures to spend—on everything from gifts to parties—it's easy to let expenditures and emotions get out of control. Wanting to please others and getting in the holiday spirit can cloud judgment and cause long-lasting debts. Make agreements on limits ahead of time on gifts and other purchases for these occasions, and come up with noncommercial ideas for enjoying these times of year.

Dr. Judy's Rx

Since money is one of the top sources of discord with couples, identify how your styles in handling money may be affecting your love life. The next time you open your wallet, consider what it reflects about opening your heart.

4. **Birthdays, anniversaries, and other personal celebrations.** Special occasions between the two of you also cause pressures to please that can strain your pocketbook. As with holidays, find ways to celebrate that are within your means and value nonmaterial displays of thoughtfulness.

5. **Time off.** Every couple needs and deserves refreshers for their romance. Building these into your relationship at various intervals can be healthy for your personal as well as interpersonal health. But attitudes on how to apportion your resources for time off, what to do, and how much to spend can make what should be a dream vacation turn into a nightmare. Resolve your differing attitudes ahead of time, like going economy or first class.

6. **Having a child.** The big expense of having a child demands budgeting. This starts from pregnancy and escalates at every stage from birth to childhood, teenagehood, and even when children become adults. Expenses include food, doctor's bills, clothes, furniture, schooling, and entertainment.

7. **Children's schooling.** With the problems of school systems today, parents often feel pressured to send kids to private school starting in elementary grades. This presents a financial strain early on. College costs have also skyrocketed, making a four-year education cost up to $100,000. Few couples can afford to pay that without scholarships or financial aid.

8. **Stepfamily expenditures.** If one of you had a previous marriage, you may have alimony and/or child support payments that require you to support two households. Be especially careful about emotions that can be triggered by those responsibilities (feeling resentful, deprived, or competitive). Be clear about exact responsibilities, plan accordingly, and accept the realities. This requires financial planning and emotional acceptance.

9. **Tax-time traumas.** The annual springtime strain of tax time brings deadlines, panicking over paperwork, and losing sleep that can lead to arguments and even make you too tired and distracted for sex. This can pass, unless evaluating your "worth" triggers feelings of inadequacy, frustration, and disappointment with yourself or each other. Trust might also be destroyed if one of you suspects the other of hiding assets or being dishonest. It is crucial to be honest, prepared, share tasks, and be supportive of each other.

10. **Demotions, layoffs, unemployment.** Losing income affects practical decisions about lifestyle, as well as triggers emotional traumas that can destroy your relationship. Be alert and tolerant of potentially tumbling self-esteem and confidence. Have regular discussions about planning your expenses and adjusting your lifestyle according to new income levels.

11. **Promotions and other income increases.** Weathering windfalls can be just as much a source of stress as tumbling finances, as you face practical decisions

about what to do with the money. Discuss the changes in your feelings and lifestyles triggered by escalation in your income bracket.

12. **Retirement.** If you've planned ahead, the money you have for your later years can accommodate your needs. But if you end your work life without sufficient resources, the golden years will have no glitter and can tarnish your love.

Love Lookout

Many couples live on credit these days, both out of necessity and convenience. They may have several credit accounts, juggling monies. This can lead to credit problems, racking up interest charges that lead to a vicious cycle of debt. Statistics reveal shocking numbers of men and women who get themselves into serious debt every year. Take care not to fall into this trap—call a credit counseling service (look in the Yellow Pages).

Be prepared for the stages in life that you expect will challenge your finances, and highlight the differences or similarities in the way you both handle money. Being forewarned is forearmed when it comes to resentments, distrust, or arguments that can ruin your love—and can be more detrimental than any financial ruin.

What to Say When Money Talks

Following the familiar saying, "money talks," you have to talk about money together. There's no place for embarrassment, shame, fear, or guilt in these discussions. Since many decisions regarding money are made at every step of your relationship, questions and curiosity will constantly be in the air. For a healthy relationship, you have to become comfortable talking about what you earn, owe, and own. And you have to talk more, not less, as your relationship progresses.

Dr. Judy's Rx

The sooner you begin to discuss money matters as a couple, the easier it will be. Don't be afraid to broach the subject. Realize that you deserve to know. Disclose facts to each other honestly. Be aware of how your attitudes affect your sharing.

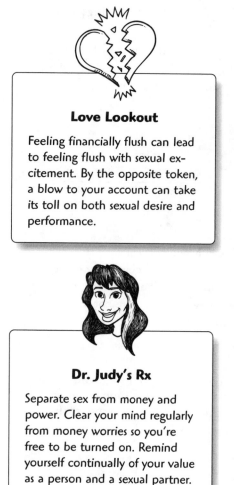

Love Lookout

Feeling financially flush can lead to feeling flush with sexual excitement. By the opposite token, a blow to your account can take its toll on both sexual desire and performance.

Dr. Judy's Rx

Separate sex from money and power. Clear your mind regularly from money worries so you're free to be turned on. Remind yourself continually of your value as a person and a sexual partner.

Money talk is necessary. First, for practicality. You will always be confronted with deciding who pays for what. Second, money talk is necessary for compatibility. Working out money issues proves whether you can get along on the most sensitive issues for couples. Third, for protection. Protection is necessary if you separate or divorce. No one likes to think of this, but neither of you wants to be left insecure or cheated. You have only to read about celebrity divorce scandals with highly contested claims and settlements to be frightened into protecting yourself. You also need protection in case of a spouse's illness or death. No one likes to think of that either, but insurance policies and wills are a must, or you could end up financially unstable.

When you are first dating, the most common issues concern who takes care of which expenses (do you take turns paying or go Dutch?). This decision is affected by how much each of you earns, your experience, sex role stereotypes (that men should pay or that women should share equally), and underlying psychological needs or conflicts.

In an ongoing relationship, the conversations about money can go deeper. Many couples will want to know what their future will be like together, so they try to get as much information as possible about each other's financial resources (present salary, overall personal worth, earning potential for the future, parents' worth, potential inheritance).

When you decide to make a serious commitment (especially marriage), you should step up the disclosures, finding out the famous trio: what each of you earns, owns, or owes. Here are what I call the "Dozen Dollar Decisions" for a healthy relationship—12 key points of money talk that are necessary.

The Dozen Dollar Decisions

When you commit to each other:

1. How are each of you going to organize your expenses, savings, and investments?

2. How will you make joint decisions about money management?

---

3. Will one of you require a prenuptial agreement? What are the laws in your state regarding financial settlements in divorce?

4. How will you individually and jointly pay bills and keep records?

5. What type of checking and savings accounts will you have?

6. Will you merge all your money or keep some separate accounts?

7. How will you decide about discretionary income (in other words, who will spend what on luxury items such as a stereo, clothes, or a car)?

8. What type of credit card accounts will you have? Will they be in both of your names?

9. How will you set short-term and long-term plans for money management or important life results that you are preparing for (vacation/buying a house/kids education/retirement)?

10. Do each of you have a will? Are you each other's beneficiaries?

11. What insurance (medical/life) will you each get and who will be the beneficiary?

12. Will your parents or other sources contribute to your expenses?

Discuss each of your answers to the above questions. Come to agreements about how to handle each of these important issues.

Deciding together on how you are going to handle your money matters is crucial. Set aside time together at regular intervals (weekly) when you will go over your finances and reevaluate your plans. Constant attention prevents storing up problems that could lead to unexpected explosions. Recognize when you're stressed, so you don't take it out on each other.

Dr. Judy's Rx

Keep track of spending on small- as well as big-ticket items. But always keep pleasure reserves for the two of you, even if it's just for pizza and a movie.

Money talks should follow the same rules as outlined in Chapter 10, "Communication—Can We Talk?" That includes not blaming ("You're driving us into the poorhouse"), name-calling ("tightwad" or "spendthrift"), generalizing ("You're always spending too much"), or comparing ("Why don't we have as much money as …"). Discuss mutual goals for your common good.

Love Bytes

A number of experts recommend that it's healthy for couples to maintain three pools of money: a joint pool and a personal pool for each of them. This allows for a feeling of teamwork, but also independence.

A Wise Investment in Your Future

Learning about money is a great project to undertake with your partner. Read books, take courses, and attend seminars together on money management and financial planning.

Terry Kassel, a friend of mine and a former account executive at the Dean Witter Reynolds financial firm, tells the story of a couple whose money she had been managing and whose marriage was on the rocks when they came to her to find out about their assets. Although they started out the discussion somewhat hostile toward each other, over the course of the discussion, Kassel kept pointing out how well they had been doing together, focusing them on their effectiveness as a team. By the time they left, they were so much more positive about each other and their future together, that they decided not to divorce but rather work things out.

Love Bytes

As more women have careers, marry later, and spend more years being single, they have to take responsibility for their financial matters. Statistics show that approximately 35 percent of the country's 51 million common stockholders are women. Unfortunately, a large number of women still need to learn more about investing and other financial planning.

The Least You Need to Know

➤ Attitudes about money stem from your experiences, cultural and religious backgrounds, personality traits, and what you learned from your parents.

➤ Accept, appreciate, and make agreements about your individual style of handling money.

➤ Having ongoing discussions about money is essential to a healthy relationship and will prevent problems down the road.

➤ Whether you come across a shortfall or a windfall in your finances, keep level-headed and even-tempered with each other.

➤ Count your blessings more than the balance in your bank account.

Chapter 21

Working Nine to ... with Time Off for Love

> **In This Chapter**
>
> ➤ How your attitude toward your job can affect your love life
>
> ➤ Pitfalls to working too much—or too little
>
> ➤ Balancing your career and your relationship
>
> ➤ The pros and cons of romance in the workplace
>
> ➤ Making love work when there's trouble at work

Unless you're a trust fund baby (or you've got a sugar daddy or mommy), you and your partner are likely working to pay the rent (and the phone bills, car payments, student loans, and so on). And, if you're like most working people today, you probably don't get to enjoy a consistent 9-to-5, eight-hour day. It's more like 8 A.M. to whenever the work gets done, or double shifts. So, considering that you spend most of your life at your job, it makes sense that your feelings and experiences at work will impact the rest of your life, including your love relationship.

Do What You Love

Do you really have to love your work in order to have a happy and healthy love life? It certainly helps. Your job not only determines your mood during most of the day, but it's an important part of your life (at least in terms of time commitment), so it influences how you feel about yourself in general—and you bring all of this home to your relationship. The happier you are during the workday, then, the more satisfied and fulfilled you will feel as a person, and the better the attitude you will bring to your love life.

What If You Hate Your Job?

Let's assess how you feel about your job. For starters, take the following quiz. Check "Yes" or "No" in the columns on the right. Have your partner also take the quiz.

The Job Satisfaction Quiz

	Yes	No
1. Do you go to sleep at night dreading going to work the following day?	____	____
2. Are you in a bad mood first thing in the morning because you have to face your job?	____	____
3. Do you spend the day silently hoping the clock will speed up?	____	____
4. When you're at work, do you wish you could be doing anything other than what you're doing?	____	____
5. Do you count down the workdays until your next days off or vacation?	____	____
6. Do you feel that your job is basically the worst part of your life?	____	____

Clearly, if you answered "yes" to most (or even one) of these questions, you're probably not a very happy camper. (The only "yes" answer that excuses you from this source of unhappiness is No. 5, since everyone welcomes some free time.) Sadly, about 80 percent of working people in this country do not love what they do. If you're one of the 80 percent, I hope you'll rethink your job and your career and make some changes.

You could probably come up with many different reasons for feeling stuck in your current job or unable to make a change. But, you *can* make a change—as long as you realize that *you* are the one who has to take responsibility to make a real difference in your career, and that you can make a living doing something you enjoy? Every year, more and more people are becoming entrepreneurs, starting their own business based on their hobbies or passions. Think of the mail-order catalog queen, Lillian Vernon—her multimillion-dollar business began nearly 50 years ago with just a few ads placed in the back of a women's magazine. Or how about Tumina Camark, who invented a simple plastic device that lets you create inverted ponytails in your hair? She then marketed her invention—the Topsy Tail—through infomercials and also enjoyed multimillion-dollar results. Even if you're not the entrepreneurial type, you can still make a change: Scan the classifieds section of the newspaper, go to a headhunter, or network to find a job that excites you.

Appreciate Each Other's Work

Since work is so much a part of a couple's life, it's important that each person knows about and appreciates what the other does. Ideally, when you come home to each other, you share the events of your day and each get support from the other. But sometimes this scenario is just that, an ideal. Too many people don't have a clue about what their partner does all day. Be interested in your lover's career. Listening to and supporting her efforts will make her feel loved, and you more loving.

Do you remember how good it felt when you came home from your first day of kindergarten and your mother was waiting for you with a smile, milk and cookies, and a "How was your day, sweetheart?" Couples should do the same for each other. Reserve at least 10 minutes every evening for a recap session. Share the events of your day with each other; talk about your successes as well as the frustrations. Doing so not only makes you feel cared for, but clears the air for more intimate encounters.

Married to the Job

Loving what you do so you can better love your mate is a wonderful equation—just be careful not to take it too far. In other words, don't fall so deeply in love with your job that you end up neglecting your love life. Becoming obsessed with work is called "workaholism," and like any overindulgence—in food, sex, exercise, or drugs—work can become an addiction.

To find out whether you've crossed that line to loving your work a little too much, take the following quiz.

The Workaholism Quiz

	Yes	No
1. Do you always make work your top priority?	____	____
2. Do you constantly work late, overtime, and on weekends?	____	____
3. Do you rarely take time off to relax or do nothing?	____	____
4. Are you anxious, antsy, or unhappy, when you are *not* working?	____	____
5. Do you throw yourself into work when you feel depressed, angry, or otherwise bad?	____	____
6. Do you pass up social engagements, family gatherings, or even eating because of work?	____	____
7. Do you take work with you wherever you go (family visits, train rides, to the beach, on vacations)?	____	____

	Yes	No
8. Do you avoid taking time off and have you racked up loads of unused vacation time?	___	___
9. Does your lover complain about being neglected?	___	___
10. Do you prefer work to sex?	___	___

Ask Dr. Judy

Danielle had a history of bad relationships with men. First she'd let herself be taken care of by men, then she'd let herself get dumped and hurt by the same guys. Finally, Danielle decided to break out of this pattern and made the wise choice to build her own independence. Danielle set off to start her own job-lot business and spent countless hours cultivating contacts and hunting down products. She also met a really nice guy, Keith, and even moved in with him. By this time, however, Danielle was so immersed in her work that she barely had any time for her relationship. She'd work at her computer until the wee hours of the morning and stopped joining Keith in bed and having sex. When he threatened to leave her, Danielle came to me for help.

I congratulated Danielle on her business enterprise, and I applauded her healthy choice to develop her own life and stop being so dependent on relationships. But I pointed out that, although I don't think there's anything wrong with pouring your mental and sexual energy into your work, I do think you can take it too far, as Danielle had. Certainly, working excessively hard for some period of time doesn't automatically equal a problem. In fact, it could be necessary for securing your future and as a positive channel for your energy (especially if you love your work so much that it's hardly work at all). But even if succeeding at work seems as fulfilling as sex, it should never become a substitute or escape from real love and lovemaking with your partner.

If you answered "Yes" to four or more of these questions, you're in danger of letting work squeeze out your real love for the No.1 spot in your heart. You need to force yourself to make time not just for your partner (see Chapter 12, "Making the Honeymoon Last," for some helpful hints), but also for yourself. Hang out together just relaxing or doing nothing and overcome that compulsion to "be productive."

Think about why you're such a workaholic—some people fear that they are nothing if they do nothing. If this is how you feel, you need to understand that you can be loved just for you, rather than for your achievements. And no matter how much you truly love your work, you still need balance in your life. Trust that you'll actually be more productive if you play more.

Healthy or Unhealthy?

Do you and your mate constantly miss each other? Do you feel as if you never spend enough time together? Working too hard can be unhealthy for love. If so, change the way you manage your time and arrange your priorities—maybe you're letting everything else in your busy schedule take precedence over your relationship. One good practice is to schedule time together and actually write your meetings into your daily planners.

All Play and No Work

All work and no play can certainly make you dull, but the opposite (you're too lazy or unmotivated to work at all, can't find a job, or keep getting fired) can also be a problem. The effects that not working can have on a relationship can be just as detrimental as those of working too much. After all, balance is key. Not to mention the fact that career success is sexy and ambition is an aphrodisiac. If you're lackadaisical, your mate's passion could also smolder.

Ask Dr. Judy

Keisha called my radio show complaining that her man didn't have a job and would lie around the house all day while she was off working. To make matters worse, he wouldn't even pay attention to her when she came home in the evening. Needless to say, when he wanted sex, she found it nearly impossible to get turned on by him anymore.

In relationships like Keisha's in which friction arises because of one partner's ongoing un-employment, you have to look at the personalities, backgrounds, and deeper issues of both partners (not just of the unemployed person) to solve the problem. Keisha herself was fulfilling her mother's threat that all men are no good, while her boyfriend was re-peating his father's pattern of letting his mother do all the work.

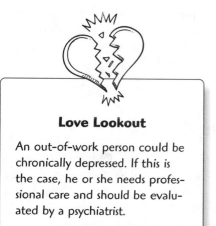

Love Lookout

An out-of-work person could be chronically depressed. If this is the case, he or she needs professional care and should be evaluated by a psychiatrist.

To understand where the problem lies in relationships with one unemployed partner, first consider the character of the unemployed partner. If the partner is basically lazy, all the complaining or encouraging in the world isn't going to motivate him. He probably has some deep-seated resistance to facing the world and doesn't want to try to achieve his goals for fear of failure. This fear paralyzes him and he ends up hiding out all day at home. To change this pattern, the unemployed partner needs to dissect his own personality and understand where his behavior is coming from. Like many other fear-of-failure types, he is probably repeating the patterns of his parents—perhaps his father was a ne'er-do-well or could never live up to his own potential.

Now let's look at the employed partner. Why is she with this freeloader in the first place? There are actually many women who are attracted to losers—unambitious men who work below their standards or don't work at all. A woman like this needs to explore the roots of her behavior. Perhaps she needs to prove her belief that men are no good and that women are the stronger sex. Or maybe she is repeating the patterns of her own family in which the woman was the mainstay of the house and the man was a "good for nothing." Or she could be acting to alleviate her own feelings of insecurity. By working and being financially independent, then finding herself a less-accomplished man, she may be protecting herself from some unconscious fear that no truly successful man would want her. Or it could be that she has a fear of abandonment. By staying with a less-successful man, she feels that she wouldn't be so devastated if he left her. Recognizing these patterns can help her decide whether her problems with the relationship are stemming solely from his unemployment or from her own unhealthy behavior.

Nowadays, when more dual-career couples are the rule rather than the exception, I hear more complaints from men about female partners who do not work. As one man put it, "I want her to get a job and to pull her weight." Another said, "I wish she wouldn't sit around all day and watch TV. I can't stand the pressure of being the only one bringing home the bacon." The same issues described earlier also apply when he wants her to work.

Mixing Business and Love

Although the success and happiness of your love relationship are tied to your success and happiness at work, it's important to keep these two areas of your lives separate, to an extent. More specifically, you must be careful not to let the demands of your relationship interfere so much with your professional life that your work suffers—and vice versa. Remember, balance is key.

Working Around Your Ball and Chain

You probably know someone who's like this, or maybe you've been this way yourself: Things are such a mess with your partner that you get to work and just can't concentrate on what you're doing; you stop caring about your work, make mistakes, or daydream when you should be tending to your responsibilities. Or maybe things are so blissful in your relationship that you're too happy to think about anything else, least of all work. In either case, you've become so consumed by your relationship that you're failing to see the rest of your life from a healthy perspective. You need to reorganize your priorities and stop letting your relationship ruin everything else in your life.

Healthy or Unhealthy?

Danny is at risk of losing his position as a manager because his possessive and jealous fiancée deliberately prevents him from getting his work done. She calls him at the office every day and demands irrationally, "I want you to come home right now." And Danny, fearing the loss of his love, always complies.

Any lover who makes you choose between your relationship and your work—to the point where your work is being sabotaged—is selfish and unreasonable. A lover whose importance you're forced to prove so excessively is insecure and unhealthy. If you acquiesce as Danny does to such a person's demands, you're equally unhealthy. Your behavior is "co-dependent" and reflects your need to be dominated and your fear of standing up to your mate. A love relationship is healthy when both partners feel secure about being loved by the other—without needing excessive proof—and can strive for a reasonable balance of work and love.

Here are four steps to finding a healthy balance between work and love:

1. Figure out how much time you can reasonably spend with each other to meet your individual needs for togetherness and also to satisfy reasonable responsibilities at your job.

2. Determine whether one (or both) of you has an overwhelming attachment need—that is, one of you smothers the other person and gets possessive or jealous when he or she spends time with other people or doing other activities, such as work.

259

3. If you discover that you are the smothering type, retrain your brain to understand that paying attention to other parts of your life is exactly what:

   ➤ Allows you to put your relationship in perspective, so that it doesn't get out of hand

   ➤ Lets you get involved in something else and take a step back from any problems you're having in the relationship

   ➤ Gives you a different opportunity to succeed, so that you can raise your self-esteem enough to cope with any problems in your relationship

4. Examine your family script to see whether it was your family who taught you that one person should sacrifice parts of his or her life to sate the other's neediness. Perhaps your mother was co-dependent and demanding of your father, always complaining that he spent too much time at work and ignored the family. Understand that you do not have to repeat these patterns.

Love on the Job

With people spending so much time at work, it is inevitable that more couples will meet on the job. Many people call me on the radio with problems that emerge from this arrangement, or questions about whether office romance is a good idea.

Love Lookout

For all its benefits, working together could also incite competition between lovers. One person's success could be inspiring, but also lead to the other feeling inadequate. You should never consider your partner's success as a sign of your own failure. It's far healthier to redirect that competitive energy inward and work to top your own performance and outdo yourself.

One perk of working with your partner—or finding love on the job—is that you're both knowledgeable and appreciative of what the other does for a living. Working together could also improve your love life. Experts who have studied co-worker relationships have corroborated the fact that sharing your work life spawns eroticism. This is not surprising considering that 1) most of us find successful, ambitious people attractive; 2) most of us have greater self-esteem when we, too, succeed at work; and 3) most of us spend a good part of our lives at work.

The benefits to love on the job include spending time together, sharing experiences, and understanding and appreciating each other's efforts and schedules. But there are also drawbacks: Working together could create tensions both in the workplace and at home (if you have differing views about an issue at work, for example); limit your independence; or leave you with no "me" time (some of which you might have spent missing and fantasizing about your mate, which would have made your time at home that much more meaningful). Also, let's say you're going out with your boss—such a relationship would be further complicated by reactions of colleagues who might develop resentments or fears of unfair favoritism. And what if you end up breaking up? Seeing each other every day might then not be quite so fun.

The importance of these pros and cons is heightened if you and your mate actually start a business together. Such an endeavor could either strengthen your relationship dramatically or tear it apart altogether. To make it work, be aware of each other's strengths and limitations without blame, consider yourselves a team, appreciate what you each bring to the table, and always make time for play.

Bringing a Bad Day Home

Any blow you suffer in business can be a blow to your self-esteem. If you're pink-slipped at work, for example, you could get so depressed that you let your love life slip, too. During those troubling times, it's important to remember that your personal value is not tied inextricably to what you do for a living. Acknowledge the frustration, anger, and fears that you feel after being laid off or fired, but resist the urge to withdraw into yourself, pick fights with your partner, or otherwise take your feelings out on your relationship. Instead, allow your partner to help you get through the difficulties.

You should also be careful of placing too much importance on your partner's success at work. Take Jeffrey and Courtney's relationship, for example: Jeffrey noticed that Courtney was buying racy lingerie when he was on the fast track at his job, but years later when his work stalled, she was suddenly too tired for sex. He found out that Courtney was a lot more materialistic than he thought, and that her passion for him was fueled by his success and cooled during his less prosperous times.

In the healthiest relationships, couples come close to achieving the ideal of unconditional love. Ask yourselves: Would you love each other regardless of how you were both performing at work? Would you love each other regardless of what you did for a living?

Love Lookout

Relationships with inherent power imbalances—between employees and bosses, students and teachers, or doctors and patients—can be particularly seductive, but also lead to emotional distress, abuses, and even legal actions. Be aware of these. Think about whether you're really attracted to this person or just to a relationship based on authority, power, or care-taking.

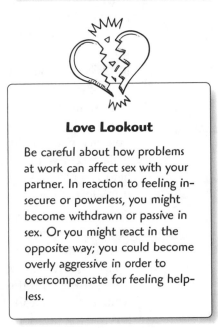

Love Lookout

Be careful about how problems at work can affect sex with your partner. In reaction to feeling insecure or powerless, you might become withdrawn or passive in sex. Or you might react in the opposite way; you could become overly aggressive in order to overcompensate for feeling helpless.

What Works in the Boardroom May or May Not Work in the Bedroom

When you're caught up in advancing your career and making the right impression at work, you learn certain behavior patterns—those that work for you at the office. It's easy to get so comfortable with how you act and interact at work that you begin dealing with your mate in the same way. Not every tactic you use at work, however, can be applied successfully to love. In fact, sometimes it backfires.

Five Steps to Better Business (but Not Better Sex)

Read on to find out which strategies will work wonders at the office but won't bowl your mate over in the bedroom.

1. **Plan ahead.** The most successful businesspeople set specific goals and plan steps to get to where they want to go. Yet striving for a particular goal is the worst thing you can do in the bedroom. Setting such firm expectations leads to performance anxiety (both for you and your mate) that sabotages your very goals for pleasure. Instead of worrying about the end result, focus on and fully enjoy what is happening between the two of you at the moment.

2. **Always please others first.** In business, the customer, the boss, or the company always come first. If you're looking for career advancement, this is a fail-safe tenet. But in the bedroom, you need to concentrate on your needs as well as those of your partner. If you're either too selfish or too giving in bed, the sex just won't be as good as it could be. Remember, your partner will be as turned on by your own pleasure as you are.

3. **Put on an image.** Presenting a confident and capable front is crucial in business. You've probably heard the warning: "Never let 'em see you sweat." In sex, however, vulnerability is not only acceptable, it also facilitates intimacy. As one male executive told me, "I'm so busy putting on a face all day at work, it's a relief to be able to say to my wife, 'I can't' or 'I'm afraid' without any fear she'll think less of me."

4. **Stay in control.** Losing control of yourself would not be beneficial at the office. You can't scream in frustration or jump for joy in the middle of a serious business negotiation. But holding back or being a control freak during sex reveals insecurity and fear (of rejection or embarrassment) and only inhibits satisfaction. Letting go is the name of the lovemaking game. In fact, most men and women need to learn to be freer in bed—be it with noises, words, attitudes, or lovemaking positions.

5. **Be single-minded.** To get to the top of the corporate ladder, you have to be prepared to put your career first, often making personal sacrifices along the way. In one national survey, career-committed single people reported that they believed partners and children would get in the way of their career success. By contrast, to have a good sex life, you should be anything but single-minded. If you are successful, secure, and fulfilled in all other aspects of your life and relationship, your sex life will reflect that happiness. In addition, having a good sex life does not take away but rather facilitates success in the rest of your life by giving you security, energy, and support.

Love Bytes

During one particular study I conducted, I found that the majority of women who learned to have orgasms also made positive progress in their careers. Remember that a balanced life is healthiest.

Five Steps to Better Business AND Better Sex

Sometimes mixing business and pleasure can produce some spectacular results. The following five steps show you how:

1. **Take responsibility.** When you make it in business, you shouldn't think passively "It just happened" or "I got lucky"). Rather, you should take credit for your ability, determination, and talent. Likewise, your pleasure in sex isn't just up to your mate—it's also dependent on your efforts. A partner helps you reach a peak of pleasure, but isn't solely responsible for your satisfaction.

2. **Be assertive.** Successful people don't wait for opportunities to fall in their laps. They make things happen. Instead of waiting around passively for a shot at covering the top stories, an assertive reporter I know went to the editor and said, "I know I can cover the big stories and I want a chance to prove it." In sex, too, you have to ask for what you want instead of expecting or hoping your partner will read your mind.

3. **Say "no."** Setting limits is very important at work. If you become too much of a "yes person," you'll end up taking on too many duties and overextending yourself—then both you and your work will suffer. Likewise, if you're so concerned about being liked that you become too agreeable in bed, you'll end up being asked to perform in ways that you're not willing or able to handle. Tell your manager and your mate what you're really willing to do.

4. **Let yourself be "on top."** Some people are afraid to express dominance at the office. They fear that they'll be making themselves vulnerable to opposition or that they'll be criticized as "too aggressive." Others suffer from "fear of success." Remind yourself that you deserve to have what you desire. In sex, you—women in particular—also need to learn to be comfortable being "on top" (literally and figuratively). And loving couples need to allow each other to express their power in sex without being threatening or feeling threatened by each other.

5. **Free yourself from gender-based stereotypes.** Just as you need to be more accepting of gender equality in the workplace, you also need to dispel any stereotypical notions of what is masculine or feminine in the bedroom. Men should be able to feel vulnerable and express emotions during sex without judging themselves as "unmanly." Women should feel comfortable initiating sex without considering themselves "unfeminine."

The Least You Need to Know

➤ Find a job that you love and your love life will be better.

➤ Appreciate and support each other's work and you will strengthen your love bond.

➤ Strive for a healthy balance between work and love—don't let love problems interfere with your career, and vice versa.

➤ Work can be just as addictive as food, alcohol, or sex—moderation and balance are key. Make sure you don't fall prey to workaholism—an addiction to work as an escape from other aspects of life.

➤ Before cultivating an office romance, be aware of the potential repercussions.

➤ Value your love relationship regardless of what happens in your career.

➤ Some behaviors that work in the boardroom (like keeping up an image and staying in control) won't necessarily work in the bedroom.

Chapter 22

Offering Constructive Criticism

> ### In This Chapter
>
> ➤ The "do's" and "don'ts" of giving criticism
>
> ➤ How complaints about sex affect your relationship
>
> ➤ How an inner critic can damage a healthy relationship

"My boyfriend doesn't touch me in the right place when we make love, but I'm afraid to say anything that might hurt his feelings."

"I'm always fighting with my wife because she picks on me all the time."

Criticism bites. Few of us can give or take criticism well in any context, much less from a lover. The criticism of a lover hurts more than that from a stranger; you can rationalize the latter doesn't really know you. However, when criticism comes from someone you know intimately, you feel especially attacked, inadequate, or frightened of not being able to please someone whose love you value or need.

Criticism from loved ones, though, can be constructive. Since they know you best, loved ones are able to offer helpful hints about how to change and grow. Of course, how helpful such criticism is depends on how your partner delivers it. Mean-spirited criticism is unacceptable under any circumstances, and only causes defensiveness. Sometimes, however, even "constructive criticism" can't be heard—your own inner critic is so busy, you can't "hear" something valid that your partner has to say.

"I'm Saying This for Your Own Good ..."

Who hasn't heard this phrase, "I'm telling you this for your own good," followed by criticism that sounds anything but well-intended? Parents, bosses, friends, spouses, and lovers can give us valuable suggestions about how to improve ourselves—and in many cases, we can return the favor. But, if criticism isn't constructive, though, it causes pain with no gain. Some people seem to relish dishing out that kind of mean-spirited critical commentary, but no one enjoys being on the receiving end.

Criticism doesn't have to be a source of friction. When both partners are striving to learn, refine, and improve upon their relationship and themselves, it's a valid tool for achieving those goals. Constructive criticism takes place in an atmosphere of love and security. When the criticism is destructive, there is no sense of safety.

To deliver or receive constructive criticism:

❏ **Determine the motive for the criticism.** Are you angry about other things and using this argument as a smokescreen? For example, do you criticize your mate for dropping his clothes on the floor when really you feel deep down he or she doesn't listen to you? Or, are you disappointed about yourself and projecting it onto your partner? For example, you might not say what you want in sex so you get angry when your mate does the wrong thing. Is this a carryover from unexpressed disappointments with other people in your past who have upset you similarly?

❏ **Determine any difficulties you may have in hearing criticism from your partner.** What are your past childhood patterns? Perfectionism is a common one. Are you slavishly concerned about pleasing others, so any slip makes you dismiss yourself? For example, your lover might say, "You didn't ..." but you hear, "You're a bad person, a total failure, and I may not want you."

Dr. Judy's Rx

A complaint is most effective, both in personal and professional relationships, if it's made in a civilized tone of voice. Delivery is key. Don't condescend, snarl, yell, or whine. A lack of courtesy puts the other person on the defensive before you've even finished speaking.

Love Lookout

Don't take criticism as a dismissal of your self-worth. Review what was said and separate your distortions. Place what was said in context of what's going on with your mate. Does he or she have a valid complaint?

Giving Criticism

Here are two examples of criticism in the relationship of a couple, Anne and Ted. Ted was spending a lot of money and Anne panicked over their finances. The first example is a destructive exchange between them; the second is more constructive:

➤ "You never pay attention when I tell you what I want for my birthday," Anne accused Ted. "This watch must have cost too much money. All I really wanted was the *Evita* soundtrack. We agreed we can't afford expensive gifts and you buy this. You never listen. You always spend too much on gifts, especially for people who don't really matter. Our budget is blown again."

➤ Several days after she'd thought about her impulsive, critical reaction, Anne changed her tune. She graciously thanked Ted for the expensive watch and acknowledged his thoughtfulness. Then Anne suggested they go over the budget together. "I worry that we're spending too much money and not meeting our savings goals," she said. "What can we do to get back on track?" Then she proposed a few areas where they could cut back, such as on gifts.

It's obvious Anne came across as ungrateful in the first example, even if she had a valid concern. It's important to know how she—and you—could handle these types of situations differently and effectively.

Before delivering criticism, identify the issue and allow only one issue per conversation. Dumping all your frustrations and complaints on your partner at once will make him angry and defensive. Blame marathons are nonproductive, so stay on the subject. For a more productive session, pay attention to the following "do's" and "don'ts":

Do:

➤ Pick an appropriate time—when your partner is receptive, relaxed, and reassured.

➤ Be specific about the exact behavior—talk about one thing.

➤ Focus on the behavior, not the personality.

➤ Mention positives.

➤ Stay in the present—don't dig up the past.

➤ Understand why you feel the way you do.

➤ Invite an explanation.

➤ Stay in control—don't be overly emotional.

➤ Separate the facts from feelings—don't stretch facts to support your view.

➤ Know when to stop—don't beat a dead horse or nag.

➤ Offer forgiveness and offer options for how you would like it to be.

Don't:

➤ Generalize—"You always …" or "You never …"

➤ Personalize—"You are a bad person."

➤ Awfulize—don't make it worse than it really is.

➤ Futurize—"You'll always do this."

➤ Blame—instead, take responsibility. "I get upset when you …"

➤ Play psychologist—"I know what you really mean."

➤ Call names.

➤ Attack family members—"You're just like your father."

➤ Curse.

➤ Insist on an immediate discussion—some people need a cooling-off period.

How to Receive Criticism

If you're on the receiving end of criticism, remain open and nondefensive. To be sure you "hear" the message, follow these "do's" and "don'ts":

Do:

➤ Ask for specifics so you know what you did to upset your partner.

➤ Quiet your inner critic so you can hear your partner.

➤ Lower your defenses.

➤ Listen.

➤ Reflect on what you hear instead of reacting instantly.

➤ Understand the statement in context of the other person.

➤ Ask for clarification. Probing helps get to deeper reasons for your mate's upset. Ironically, getting to the deeper issue lessens rather than intensifies the hurt because the person feels understood.

➤ Respond constructively. If your partner's point is valid, admit it and apologize. Face up to it. Even if all of it is not true, find something you can admit. Surprise your partner by saying, "Maybe you're right. I'll think about it and work on it." It shows you have an open mind and that you care about your mate.

➤ Discuss solutions. Set up a way to monitor progress. Show your partner that you heard what was said and are doing something about it.

Don't:

➤ Get defensive or make excuses.

➤ Deny. Don't negate what your partner said, even if you disagree. After all, it was important enough to make an impact on him or her.

➤ Countercriticize. Don't instantly hurl a return insult or remind your partner that she did the same thing herself. Give each other a chance to be heard.

➤ Deal with too many things at a time. Focus on one issue.

➤ Withdraw. Don't shut out your partner when it's clear he really needs to communicate a problem.

➤ Wallow in guilt.

➤ Get passive-aggressive. Don't pretend to hear or go along with what's being said and then later do something designed to upset or discount the critic without directly saying so. ("That dress looked better on you when you were thinner.")

➤ Use physical violence. Words may hurt but they can also heal. Physical reactions are unacceptable, abusive, and unconstructive.

➤ Take it too personally. Think of it as feedback, not an attack. Think, "I want to be a better mate."

Love Bytes

Practice the "cinematic approach to criticism," to align your emotion so you can receive criticism without being defensive. As described by gender expert Warren Farrell in *Women Can't Hear What Men Don't Say* (Tarcher, 2000), visualize yourselves on a movie screen and immerse yourself in the criticizer's storyline. This gives you distance and empathy so you can appreciate what is being said and overcome what Farrell called "the genetic response to kill the criticizer that is good for survival but bad for love."

Sometimes the problem is that you are not giving some criticism to your mate out of fear that, if you said anything negative, you would lose her love, or hurt his ego. While I certainly endorse being considerate, storing upsets can lead to blowing up, and prevents constructive changes that could help keep your relationship healthy. For example, Sonya was afraid to tell her boyfriend, who worked in a garage, that it was offensive to her that he came home reeking of unpleasant odors. She couldn't understand why he would shower before going off to work, but not when he came home to her. Afraid to hurt his feelings, she couldn't say anything. Yet holding them in, she was feeding her upset. It's important for her to let him know how she feels and what she needs him to do to please her.

Sexual Criticism

Is it unhealthy to criticize a partner's sexual behavior?

It depends—not on what you say, but how you say it. Registering complaints can lead to trouble, while requesting changes can lead to improvements. It's inevitable in an intimate relationship that partners will sometimes need to request changes. This doesn't mean you don't love each other but rather gives you the opportunity to grow yourself, and to learn more about each other and how to please one another.

Being criticized for your sexual performance, reactions, or attributes (or lack thereof) is devastating to both men as well as women. Criticism really "hits below the belt" when it's geared in that direction.

I've heard nearly everything, but I get upset when I hear the hurtful things people say to their lovers. It is not uncommon that a man calls me on the radio and tells me a girlfriend admitted to him that she wasn't satisfied sexually because his penis was too small. While a woman may not like a man's size, saying that outright to him damages his confidence forever. Instead of pointing out his inadequacy, she should simply find and point out the way to better satisfaction, and concentrate on that.

Some partners deliver insensitive sexual criticism as a way to take out their frustration about sex in general, their own sexual inadequacies, insecurities in general, or their past rejections from other partners. Such projection is unacceptable, and destructive, in a relationship. People who do this need therapy to resolve their inner problems in order to be able to relate to others in a healthier way.

It is essential, however, not to let your partner continue to do things that displease you sexually. As Patty said to me, "My boyfriend pinches my chest so hard it hurts and leaves marks that I don't like, even though I pretend I do. He seems to enjoy doing it and likes me to do it to him, so I'm afraid to tell him otherwise because it might hurt his feelings. How can I get him to stop?"

Dr. Judy's Rx

Speak up soon—the longer unwanted behavior or sexual advances persist, the harder they are to change, and the more resentment brews.

I told Patty she has to first stop faking and holding back what she prefers as well as what she dislikes. When you pretend to like some sexual act your partner does that actually hurts or displeases you, you're not protecting him from being hurt, as you think, but actually hurting him more by making him think he's being a good lover for that act, when he's not. You wouldn't want him to let you keep doing what he doesn't like, would you? You're also doing a disservice to yourself, depriving yourself of pleasure and letting yourself be hurt. Do both of you a favor by correcting your partner's behavior (setting the record straight like this is called "leveling"). Accept that it's okay for you not to like a certain kind of stimulation your partner likes.

Some lovers, such as Patty's boyfriend, follow the rule in sex, "Do unto others as you would have others do unto you." This can work if you genuinely have similar fancies or until proven otherwise. A better rule: "Do unto others as they would have done unto them." That requires "show and tell." Let your partner know what you prefer. You're probably afraid that criticizing your partner's lovemaking would not only make her hurt or angry, but also dampen his sexual ardor. Rest assured that it's not what you say but how you say it that counts. Negative sexual criticism or cold complaints such as "Don't touch me there (or like that)" or "That doesn't feel good," indeed leave the lover discouraged, defensive, and unsure what to do. Instead, start with praise, use a loving and encouraging tone, and say what you do like. For example, "I love how you make love to me and I especially love it when you touch me here softly" or even, "I prefer a soft touch to a harder one."

Ask Dr. Judy

Valerie complained to me that her boyfriend gets upset with her every little movement every time they have sex. "When my hips move almost involuntarily," she said, "he asks why am I pushing him out, and if I take a breath he asks if that was me making noise." Since her past lovers seemed to like such movements, Valerie was confused. Like many partners, Valerie was taking her lover's sexual criticism seriously, and to heart. But she was also blaming herself inappropriately. Valerie was demonstrating all the normal, appropriate, and even highly desirable signs of heightened orgasmic sexual response cycle, including involuntary muscular movements in other body parts, heavy breathing, and vocalizations. Many women would be delighted to be able to express themselves as openly in sex. Since many women are self-conscious about sex (which ruins their ability to respond freely), it is to Valerie's credit that, despite her boyfriend's criticisms, she still let herself go.

It would be a shame for Valerie to judge or inhibit herself because of her lover's reactions. A man such as her lover, who intimidates a woman sexually, is sexually intimidated himself, likely inexperienced, insecure, jealous, controlling, and fearful of his own inability to perform. An emotionally secure and sexually confident man would not criticize, but rather compliment his female partner's sexual expression. An emotionally secure and sexually confident woman would also do that for herself.

Toxic Criticism

Sadly, some lovers criticize to hurt their partners or because of their own excessive anger. This has been called toxic criticism. Deep down, lovers who constantly deliver toxic criticism aren't really committed to having a healthy relationship, or can't have a healthy relationship because they have too many emotional problems. If you are the one delivering toxic criticism, you need help. If your partner is being consistently destructive, it's time to reevaluate, get marriage therapy, and possibly get out. Stay out of the other's way and don't take the criticism to heart.

Criticizing Yourself

Self-criticism can be just as damaging to a healthy relationship as downgrading your mate.

I get so upset when I hear so many men as well as women "dumping" on themselves. Their self-criticisms can cover any aspects of their personality, looks, body, or behavior.

In any case, self-criticisms can be extremely damaging, especially when they involve sensitive areas such as sex. Pauline told me, "I never got fully undressed in front of my husband until we got married a year ago, but even now, I'm very self-conscious about my body. When we have sex, I'm always telling him not to touch my stomach because it's so fat, and hiding my thighs or butt because they have clumps of cellulite on them. He started out telling me it wasn't true and now he just yells that he hates when I do that and tells me it's turning him off more and more. I can't seem to stop, so what do I do?"

Pauline's husband is right. Her constant self-criticism erodes not only her own self-esteem, but eventually his view of her. If you persistently point out your inadequacies, even the most positive partner can eventually be worn down and finally be swayed over to your negative assessment. Ask yourself, "Why am I sabotaging myself?" Do you feel so undeserving of appreciation and happiness? Give yourself permission to enjoy your body and feel good about it—and yourself.

Even though innumerable surveys show that the majority of women feel dissatisfied about their bodies and looks and victimized by the media and the diet and beauty industries, you do not have to continue feeling this way. Examine yourself in a full-length mirror and change criticisms to neutral or positive observations (for example, note smooth skin rather than fat rolls). Give up self-criticism like a bad habit: firmly resist indulging in it, and instead re-focus on body parts or movements you appreciate. Point these out proudly to your partner. Even if this feels unnatural at first, continued practice will make your more positive attitudes feel more real, and will also rebuild your partner's confidence in you.

The Least You Need to Know

➤ Criticism that is not constructive ends up causing hurt and pain, especially if it comes from a loved one.

➤ When giving criticism, make sure it's not a smokescreen for a deeper issue. Often criticism is used as an excuse to start an argument. Criticize the specific behavior, but never the person.

➤ Don't get defensive when receiving constructive criticism. Recognize the specific behavior that is troubling your mate and be open to solutions. Don't take it personally and respond constructively.

➤ Give up self-criticism as you would any bad habit. Learn to appreciate and be good to yourself.

Chapter 23

Time Out on Fighting

In This Chapter

➤ How to prevent arguments

➤ Rules for fighting fair

➤ How to recognize hidden agendas in arguments

➤ What to do if fights fuel sexual desire

➤ Twelve ways to stop fights before they start

"Never go to bed mad. Stay up and fight."

—Comedienne Phyllis Diller

Do couples in healthy relationships fight?

Yes. But when they do, it's not vicious. As my mother used to say about arguments with my dad, "We're not fighting, we're having a *discussion*." Ah, but a loud and animated discussion!

What distinguishes heated discussions from a fight is the intention—not to hurt but to air feelings and frustrations, not to end with a winner or loser but for both to feel they gained something, and more importantly, not to divide you and your partner but to give you a chance to resolve differences, solve problems, and work together toward mutually satisfying solutions.

Preventing Blow-Ups

Like dust that piles up until you sneeze and the proverbial molehills than turn into mountains, little upsets grow until you explode. To avoid this build-up, deal with small issues before they explode. Keep track of them. I even ask some couples to have regular "gripe sessions" to discuss all their concerns before they escalate.

Love Lookout

Holding in anger leads to physical symptoms that can be damaging to your health, or to habits such as smoking, overeating, excessive alcohol consumption, and other addictions.

Dr. Judy's Rx

One of the best predictors of marital success is a couple's ability to handle conflict constructively. Therefore, rather than fretting over disagreements, welcome them as opportunities to heal individually and to bring you closer together.

Learn how to deal with stress to avoid arguments. Distract yourself with activity, or purposefully change thoughts that are going in a negative cycle. Visit a health club, take a walk in the park, write in your journal, browse in a bookstore, or pound pillows. Switch your mind to something positive.

Recognize your needs instead of focusing on superficial issues. Hank complained, "My girlfriend and I break up frequently over fights. What do we do?" Figure out what you're fighting about and address that. People keep arguing over the same things when they never get to the real issue. Peel away the layers of the onion and get to what you really need that the other person is not giving you. I suspect Hank and his girlfriend both really need reassurance they are cared about. They need to use all the techniques described in this chapter!

Learn to really listen to what the other person needs. Paul does it the wrong way. When Trish comes home and says, "What a horrible day, I feel rotten," Paul, who has been expecting to have sex, says, "Stop worrying about it," and grabs her. Trish is irritated, and says, "I told you I feel bad, how can I think of that now?" Paul walks off in a huff thinking she's a drag and that he should find another girlfriend.

Instead, when Trish comes home upset, Paul should empathize and repeat what she said, to show that he heard her, saying something like, "It sounds like an awful day, no wonder you're in a huff." Then he can start talking slower, to demonstrate a more relaxed state of mind that Trish could copy. If she feels understood, and begins to relax, she can be more responsive to Paul's mood or advances.

Lessons in Love from Fighting

Arguments and anger are inevitable. Learning how to have a healthy relationship, learning how to love, also involves learning how to fight right.

As I suggested earlier, the first step is learning how to redefine fighting. Don't see it as a tragedy, but as an opportunity for some new direction. Don't view arguments as a sign that the relationship is on the rocks, but that it is being refined. Remember the saying: "A gem cannot be polished without friction."

Fair Fighting Rules

Okay, so every relationship has its moments of disagreements and arguments. But can you have a fight where both people come out winners?

Dr. Judy's Rx

Pay attention to the words you use during an argument with your mate. Eliminate those portending bad outcomes ("I'm going to have a nervous break-down") and rephrase others (instead of "You're breaking my back," say "That really hurts me").

Yes! For as long as I've been treating couples, there have been rules on fighting and arguing that ensure a "fair fight." Certain principles apply. As the following table shows, there are fouls and "hitting below the belt," and there are fair ways of arguing. Circle the ones you do often and underline the ones your mate does. Then talk about the impact of those behaviors.

Rules for Having a Fair Fight	
Foul	**Fair**
Generalizing ("You always/never ...")	Sticking to the present ("This time you ...")
Blackmailing ("If you don't ...")	Making agreements ("What can we resolve?")
Stereotyping ("All men/women ...")	Pointing out specific behavior ("When you interrupt me, I get upset.")
Using negatives ("Don't ...," "You're not ...")	Being positive ("Next time, please do ..."
Personal attacks ("slob," "ingrate," "bore")	Concentrating on the act
Testing ("If you loved me ...")	Describing feelings ("I feel unloved when ...")

Foul	Fair
Judging ("You're wrong")	Seeing each other's point of view ("I can understand …")
Put-downs ("You're worthless")	Respect
Sulking or withdrawing	Facing the issue
Blaming parents ("Just like your father!")	Sticking to individual behavior
Blaming ("You made me …")	Using "I" statements ("I was upset when you …")
Being vague	Giving details
Interrupting	Being fully attentive
Closed-minded	Open-minded
Speaking for the other person	Allowing self-expression
Trivializing ideas	Taking points seriously
Dismissing points	Considering everything
Making threats	Requesting change
Using profanity	Choosing gracious wording
Getting verbally or physically abusive	Staying in control

Love Bytes

Couples who learn to argue "fairly and effectively" are at a lower risk of splitting up or becoming violent. In a study of 150 couples studied over 10 years, researchers found those who handled conflict well had a 50 percent lower divorce rate than those who did not.

If you argue, start with an open mind and an affirmation that you care. That sets the proper stage, showing that you desire to work things out, thereby preventing deeper fears of abandonment from arising and interfering. Refer to Chapter 10, "Communication—Can We Talk?" The same rules and steps for fighting apply: listen, empathize, and come to agreements.

Fightis Interruptis

When couples fight repetitively about the same things without making progress, a deeper issue is not being addressed. You need to find out what that issue is. But before you can do that, you need to stop the fight. Develop a strategy to stop escalation. One effective technique is called a "pattern interrupt": something that shifts the energy between you. It should be something surprising or funny.

Healthy or Unhealthy?

If your children see you fight, are you being a bad example? You should avoid purposeful-ly arguing in front of children. Using them is not fair, and is hurtful to them. Constant tension between parents creates insecurities and negative role models. However, if fights happen, showing children how loving parents can argue and resolve differences provides a healthy example.

Decide on a word or phrase, like, "code blue" or even "spaghetti." When one of you says that word, it means, "I feel this is escalating; let's stop now before we regret it. We can talk later." You both have to agree to respect the message. You'll be surprised, when you return to the conversation, that the anger will be diffused.

When fights get repetitive, nasty, or non-constructive, you must put a stop to them. Here are four ways to interrupt fights that are going nowhere:

Dr. Judy's Rx

Call "time out" for an hour when a heated discussion is going no-where. Set an alarm to let you know when the hour is up. During the break time, reduce tension by jogging, watching TV, calling a friend, or baking a cake.

1. Use that predetermined word or phrase you both agree stops the fight the way you are going and makes you hesitate, and go back in your corners to figure out a new approach.

2. Put aside who's "right" or "wrong" and try a sudden apology. This may stimulate an apology from your mate as well, and make you both feel calmer—and closer.

3. Employ a sudden change in tone and attention. Change the topic (say something complimentary, like "We're yelling, but you know, I just noticed how your eyes sparkle. What beautiful eyes you have.").

4. Shift feelings with an affirmation of the opposite emotion (love instead of anger). For example, instead of screaming, drop your voice, and say "I love you so much."

"I Gotcha!": Using Smokescreens to Win Control Battles

When you constantly argue about the same thing and seem to get nowhere, you are likely using the present argument as a "smokescreen" to deflect you from revealing the real—more threatening or scary—issue of contention. You must get to this deeper level. Say to your mate, "Let's stop arguing about this superficial issue and get to the deeper problem, if we both have courage."

Ask Dr. Judy

Eric did not want a vasectomy but his wife was pressuring him, complaining about spending $30 a month on birth control pills. "This is a typical example of a superficial argument with a smokescreen that deflects from the real issue," I explained to them. We found out what that deeper, real issue was as soon as I asked, "Why do you *not* want the vasectomy?" Eric replied, "In case I have to get married again, because every time we fight, she threatens divorce." Aha! No wonder Eric did not want a vasectomy. He feared that the resulting infertility would make him undesirable to other women, and leave his wife in control of him. He would be fearful of ever leaving her when she threatened divorce. This revelation gave them courage to discuss the real issue of their arguments: his wife's need to control, and both of them feeling anger and fear. Ultimately, they discovered that they both were really committed to their marriage.

Many couples suffer from control battles that can show up in subtle ways but make one person feel the other is pulling all the strings. In reality, a person has power over you only if you allow him or her to have it. If your partner withdraws when you want to approach, it can *feel* like he is in control, but you *can* maintain your own sense of control over your own life by your reaction and by making *your* choices.

Preventing Mountains from Growing Out of Molehills

Arguing over petty things is a common problem for couples. "She's always picking on me for little things, and I get annoyed," said Lavar. "He's got a trigger temper," Angela argued back.

It's essential for people with tempers to tune in to their body and notice how they react to stress, so they can react in a calmer way. Lavar noticed that as soon as something happens that irritates him, he gets a rush through his chest and arms, and he explodes. I asked him to pay attention following the rush, instead of blowing up at Angela, and then to sit down and breathe evenly and deeply until the rush passes. By that time, his temper would have cooled, and he would be more civil and able to talk.

Ask Dr. Judy

Bonnie and Derek are always arguing about silly little things. "We can't seem to stop it," she said. "But it's ruining our relationship, because now we argue in bed. What should we do?"

The best way to avoid constant senseless bickering that erodes trust and closeness is with the techniques used in this chapter. Use the "Interrupt" technique and force yourself to hesitate when you feel about to erupt. Walk away from each other for a "cool-down" period, during which time you can unleash explosive and unreasonable emotions. Reflect rationally about the issue, and remind yourself about your commitment to get along.

Examine the source of your tension. If the persistent arguing is a result of tension in your individual life, taken out on each other, share what is bothering you. If smaller spats reflect the tip of the iceberg of more serious compatibility problems, admit and confront those calmly, even if you fear that it could lead to ending the relationship. If arguing is a style you learned from copying family interactions, resolve to resist repeating that.

Reconvene to discuss your upset calmly and express your needs. Or write your complaints in a notebook and share them during weekly "gripe sessions," where each person takes turns quietly listening to the other and then responding. Hold these in any room other than the bedroom (that should be a sanctuary from strife) as I explained earlier in the chapter about sexual criticism. Always end with doing something enjoyable or intimate together to reestablish positive rapport.

Love Bytes

A unique technique encourages couples to purposefully yell at each other for a minute, timing themselves (to contain the anger) and escalating the intensity of the fight. This ironically dissipates the force of the feelings and reveals the senselessness of the argument.

Using Truth as a Weapon

Some things are better left unsaid, as in this situation that one woman, Sherri, described to me:

"My husband and I have been together 13 years and have four children. We used to enjoy sex, but over the years, I've put on 40 pounds, and he's gained about 30 pounds. When we first met I pointed out a fat woman and told him that if I ever look like that he should let me know and I wouldn't blame him for not being turned on to me. Last week he told me and now I'm furious and turned off. Should I be, since I told him to tell me?"

When a woman feels in shape, it's easy to teasingly tell her man to remind her if she ever puts on weight. But if he actually takes her up on it, she never welcomes the news, and instead feels resentful and unappreciated. The criticism and resulting lowered self-esteem surely douses her sexual desire.

While some men might be spiteful, Sherri's husband does not sound deliberately hurtful. Rather than festering over or retaliating against a perceived insult, turn it into inspiration for you both to do something about getting more fit. Start an exercise routine and healthy eating program together so you can inspire each other. Embarking on such a project together will bring you closer emotionally by helping and supporting each other, and may even spark some romantic flames between you, as you focus more on your bodies as well as on pleasures other than through food.

Can Fights Fuel Sex?

"Over the 25 years of our marriage, my husband has always picked fights with me before we have sex. He can't seem to do it when we're pleasant to one another. For years I went along with it, but now it's getting tiresome. I'd like some peace and quiet but if I don't fight back, he's turned off, so now we're not having sex. Is there something wrong with him and how can I put a stop to this?"

This woman's response is common to about 35 percent of men and 23 percent of women in a major sex survey who agree that making love is the best way to make up after an argument. Granted, flare-ups can be emotional fuel for any couple's sexual fires, as you "prove" your love by resolving your differences. Making up can also be an excuse for a more romantic or raunchy make-out than you would normally feel comfortable with. While these resolutions can certainly work, beware of purposefully arguing to get to the pleasure afterward.

If one of you has to get mad to get turned on, you're likely scared of really being close, vulnerable, and intimate. Seek marriage counseling to support your own transformation and to explore why you need to be angry, what you're afraid of, and how you can learn to

Dr. Judy's Rx

Just as with communication or criticism about sex, remember, never argue in the bedroom, bed, or any other space where you ordinarily make love. Always keep those areas sacred for loving energy, not infused with anger. If you feel an argument arising, immediately go into another room of the house.

tolerate tenderness. Some men are afraid that if they temper their temper they'll lose their sexual desire or their erection. Reassure such a man that you'd love a lamb as you have loved a lion. Warn him that disagreements can erode health. At every opportunity of harmonious times together, tell him you find him sexually attractive, so he begins to link peace with passion. Ask him to try—even if it's as a favor to you—one night of quiet massage. Don't fall back into your old pattern now that you've learned that you deserve ardor instead of arguments.

Twelve Ways to Stop Fights Before They Start

The goal here is not just to interrupt a fight, but to stop it from recurring. To do this, you can sue the following twelve techniques:

1. **Try my favorite Indian Trick:** Walk a mile in your mate's moccasins. Always imagine yourself in the other person's shoes before you blow up. Switch places, actually saying, "I'll be you and you be me. How would you feel? What would you do?"

2. **Try my favorite Onion Trick:** Peel away the layers of the onion of your upset. Instead of being lost in the specific superficial issue, get to the bottom of it. Once you recognize, acknowledge, and even satisfy the deeper need (to be loved, appreciated, respected, independent), you can listen to the specific complaint more easily.

3. **Try my favorite Hesitation Trick:** Hesitate a moment before you indulge yourself. Stopping gives you a chance to choose another way to cope, rather than having a knee-jerk reaction.

4. **Try my favorite Ghost-Busting Trick:** Recognize the issues from the past that are being brought forth into the present-day argument. If she is disappointed and angry, "You didn't get me a birthday present," she may really mean, "You don't care about me." Perhaps she is remembering all the people in her life who "forgot" her birthday or more accurately, "forgot" her.

5. **Correct false assumptions.** Determine whether anger is the result of anticipated rejection, jumping to conclusions, or distorted thinking. Let's say he talks to another girl at a party, and you immediately assume he's making a pass at that girl, and then go on to decide you're not pretty enough. You really get furious at him, when the upset is actually fueled by your own insecurity, and you weren't reading his intentions right at all.

Dr. Judy's Rx

Take out your aggressions on a pillow. Doing so lets off steam safely, so you can clarify your feelings and calm down enough to have a nonviolent and more constructive interaction.

6. **Call a truce.** Moods escalate as mutual tempers rise. Hold off arguing. Someone has to start calming down. Agree to disagree for the time being.

7. **Use self-disclosure.** Admit outright that you're angry instead of acting or talking angrily. Taking responsibility reduces blame.

8. **Instruct.** Spell out exactly what made you upset.

9. **Make requests.** Explain what your mate can say or do to make you happier: "In the future, I'd be really happy if you ...."

10. **Make it safe to tell complaints.** Write them down. Tell each other you can take it. Gently present your hurts. Make sure you don't frame them in an attacking or hurtful way.

11. **Accept instead of attack.** Recognize differences in your styles of handling stress or disappointments so you are not attacking each other.

12. **Make time to talk about your needs** and your "hot buttons" so your partner is prepared, knowing what sets your off and what calms you down.

The Least You Need to Know

➤ Use fighting productively to learn how to resolve your differences.

➤ Call foul if the fight is not fair.

➤ Look deeper beneath the smokescreen of arguments to find the hidden agenda.

➤ Stop a fight with a surprise proclamation of love.

➤ Don't fight to spark passion, but do resume passion after a fight.

➤ Replace arguing with ardor.

Chapter 24

Affairs: How to Stay After One of You Strays

In This Chapter

➤ The difference between harmless and harmful flirting

➤ The "Would My Mate Cheat?" and "Would I Cheat?" Quizzes

➤ Rules for confronting a cheating mate

➤ The six top reasons men and women stray

➤ Cybercheating

➤ The three key questions to understanding and prevent affairs

➤ The steps to relationship recovery: How to forgive, forget, and rebuild trust

➤ The Affair Survival Checklist

"We've been in trouble ever since Eve bit into that apple," a comic quipped at a show I saw recently.

In fact, the statistics on extramarital affairs show that many of us do fall easily into temptation. About 50 percent of all American marriages have suffered an affair, and statistics from some informal surveys soar even higher, placing the number of adulterous men at 80 percent of all married men, and adulterous women at 50 percent.

No one's relationship is immune to infidelity. Stories of scandals and adultery are all over the news—from former President Clinton to Frank Gifford to Bill Cosby. As solid as a relationship may seem, don't wear rose-colored glasses. Staying faithful takes effort and understanding that will improve your chances of success.

Perceived Betrayals: Is Flirting Harmless?

Before we get into a discussion about infidelity, let's talk about that favorite pastime, flirting. While I've described how flirting *with* your partner can enhance your relationship, flirting with someone else—harmless or not—is risky among many couples and can often lead to situations of perceived betrayal.

Dr. Judy's Rx

Sex counselor Dagmar O'Connor teaches couples to think of their sexual relationship as the most exciting affair of their lives. This is one of the many lessons she outlines in her book *How to Stay Married to the Same Person for the Rest of Your Life*. Dr. O'Connor has helped improve the sex lives of 80 percent of her clients.

"Whenever she's around any other guys, my girlfriend is always flirting. I know she's like that because I know what she was like when she first met me."

"The man I've been seeing says he's crazy about me, but I once saw a girl rubbing up against him and he looked like he was really enjoying it."

In some cases, a partner's flirting can excite the mate, who enjoys a challenge—but only if it's really just pretend. However, a mate's flirting can stimulate feelings of insecurity and jealousy in the partner, feelings that can get out of hand. Some people feel that watching their mates flirt is as upsetting and damaging to their relationship as catching their mates cheating. Sometimes flirting is totally harmless: Some partners flirt with others to boost their egos, enjoy their attractiveness, learn about other people, or just have a little fun. Other times, of course, flirting can be dangerous: It can be a sign that your mate wants to date or have sex with the person he or she is flirting with. So, how can you tell the difference? Read on.

Testing Your Suspicions

While most people seem shocked by the discovery of a mate's infidelity, the truth is, many of them missed the warning signs. It's important not to overlook or deny these signs. Take the following quiz to test your mate's monogamy.

The "Would My Mate Cheat?" Quiz

	Yes	No
1. Is your mate really the type of person to have an affair?	_____	_____
2. Has your mate ever cheated before?	_____	_____
3. Is your agreement about sexual exclusivity at all vague?	_____	_____
4. Does your mate have a reputation as a "player"?	_____	_____

	Yes	No
5. Is your mate exceptionally insecure about his or her attractiveness?	___	___
6. Does your mate question whether it's possible to have only one partner forever?	___	___
7. Are all your mate's friends single and running around?	___	___
8. Does your mate always disparage the idea of commitment when it comes up in conversation?	___	___
9. Did your mate grow up with unfaithful parents?	___	___
10. Does your mate believe that all men (or women) cheat?	___	___

As surely as you want to know about any infidelity in your relationship, you also want to avoid false accusations. To find out whether you're being unnecessarily suspicious, examine your own behavior, attitudes, and history. Take the following quiz to see if you may be reading your mate wrongly.

The "Would I Cheat?" Test:
My Own Tendency to Stray or Be Suspicious of My Mate Straying

	Yes	No
1. Do you tend to be overly sensitive to being slighted or rejected?	___	___
2. Have you been cheated on in the past?	___	___
3. Have you cheated on a partner in the past?	___	___
4. Do you tend to jump to conclusions prematurely?	___	___
5. Are you co-dependent (desperate to be in love and panicked if it ever ends)?	___	___
6. Are you having problems with your mate that are still unresolved?	___	___
7. Do you have personal problems that make you feel generally insecure?	___	___
8. In your view, is your agreement about sexual exclusivity unclear?	___	___
9. Do you believe that all men (or women) cheat?	___	___
10. Did your own parents have an adulterous marriage?	___	___

Love Lookout

Alcohol is the culprit in many betrayals. Take responsibility for your actions— being drunk is no excuse. Avoid drinking and temptation.

Dr. Judy's Rx

Make sure that your agreement about sexual exclusivity is clear to both of you. In too many relationships, one partner will claim that the other has been unfaithful even when the two of them have never verbally agreed to a monogamous relationship.

If your answers to the 10 questions in the "Would My Mate Cheat?" Quiz were mostly "Yes," it's possible that your suspicions about your mate's potential infidelity are well founded. Questions 1, 2, 4, and 8 are more serious indicators. Questions 5 and 6 carry less weight. If a majority of your answers to the 10 questions in the "Would I Cheat" Quiz were also "Yes," you have to factor your tendency to be suspicious or insecure in love into the equation. If you feel generally insecure and/or wouldn't trust yourself in similarly questionable situations, you could be overly sensitive to perceived betrayal. You could also be projecting your own temptations onto your partner. Examine whether you are obsessively jealous, defeatist (always expecting that you will be cheated on), or cynical (thinking that all men and women will cheat). If so, you need to get over these attitudes, or you'll either drive your mate away or never achieve a happy, healthy relationship.

Collaring a Flirt

If your mate's flirting upsets you, by all means, confront him. Regardless of what your mate's flirtations signal—harmless fun or real infidelity—you have the right to ask for it to stop if it really makes you uncomfortable. When you confront your mate, however, don't do so in a spirit of scolding—that will only make your partner defensive. Instead, discuss your feelings and describe how you would like to be treated and how your mate's behavior affects you. If you bottle up your feelings, you're denying your partner the chance to please you. And if he or she reacts poorly to your request, it could be a sign that your mate isn't particularly considerate of your feelings. I hope you would not really want to put up with being treated poorly.

Signs of Cheating

"How can I tell if he's cheating?" is a question I'm asked a lot. Will he look different? Can you tell by the way she behaves? Once you've ruled out the possibility that you're being overly suspicious (according to the quiz in this chapter), look for these concrete signs that your partner could be sneaking around:

➤ Unexplained absences. He isn't around at the usual times and seems to be out more than normal.

➤ Vague answers. You ask a question and the answer lacks details. You never feel like you have a complete picture of what your mate is saying.

Ask Dr. Judy

Jessica and her boyfriend, Kyle, were embracing at a party. Over her shoulder, Kyle noticed a woman he wanted to talk to, who was leaving the party, so he abruptly disengaged from Jessica and ran outside. When he returned, Jessica and he got into a big fight over his departure. Kyle spit out that he hated jealous and insecure women and couldn't continue to be with Jessica if she persisted like that.

After thinking about it, Jessica concluded that she wasn't an unusually insecure person and that she shouldn't let Kyle intimidate her out of expressing her feelings. She decided that it was Kyle's problem, not hers. She was right. In any healthy relationship, Kyle would have acknowledged, not demeaned, Jessica's feelings. And he would have acknowledged his own contribution to her reaction. If you're ever in a similar situation, ask your mate to talk it through with you. If he or she won't, be thankful that you're getting to see your partner's limitations now before getting even more involved.

➤ Surprising changes in behavior. Your mate could be *more* pleasant and sexual with you in order to deflect attention or because he or she is more satisfied by the affair. Alternatively, your mate could be less pleasant and less sexual with you. Look for unexplained changes in behavior in either direction.

➤ Strange phone numbers on her beeper, or strange charges on his credit cards.

➤ Changes in your partner's schedule: leaving the house earlier, coming home later, taking longer lunches.

➤ New friends that your partner resists you meeting. These new friends could be linked to a new romance.

➤ Unusually strong reactions to affairs portrayed in the media (movie scenes, news stories). Your mate could become either overly tolerant or overly critical.

➤ Your gut tells you something is wrong.

Love Lookout

Contracting an STD is not an automatic sign that your partner has had an affair. Some viruses (such as the ones that cause herpes and warts) live dormant in the body indefinitely, and an outbreak of symptoms can be triggered years after the initial exposure, regardless of sexual activity.

Cybercheating

Flirting, and cheating, these days have gone technological, with more couples likely to find their partner logging on in secret rather than sneaking off to a secret rendezvous. The issues regarding this new challenge to relationships is discussed in Chapter 5, "So, You're a Couple—but Are You Friends?" But it is important to note here that all the topics in this chapter apply to cheating by computer, as to cheating in person.

Rules for Confronting an Affair

If you strongly suspect or are certain that your mate is having an affair, it's never healthy for you to keep that knowledge under wraps. You should always confront your partner. Remember these rules:

Rule #1: If your relationship is solid, anything you bring up will be accepted and dealt with. If you cannot speak your mind, commitment and unconditional love are lacking.

That said, you should also remember …

Dr. Judy's Rx

Instead of bottling up your hurt or anger, tell a cheating mate exactly how his or her behavior affects you. Confronting your partner without fear helps reclaim your power and self-esteem. The feedback could also be a valid lesson for your mate on how to treat others.

Rule #2: Be wise about how you confront. Impulsive explosions are not a good idea. You'll only reveal your insecurity and stimulate your mate's defensiveness.

No matter how rightfully upset you are (maybe you caught him kissing another girl, or you answered a phone call from a nervous-sounding guy who hung up fast), resist immediate attack, especially if you're already having problems. A full-fledged attack will only escalate anger and denial, and give the potentially "guilty" partner an excuse to withdraw. Exert self-control and invite resolution of your ongoing disputes. On some other calmer occasion, you can discuss your suspicions.

If you've confronted your partner and discovered an affair, there's always an impulse to want to know why the infidelity happened. It can be helpful to take a step back from the situation for a while and let your emotions cool down first. Then you can discuss whether you both want to rebuild your relationship, and begin to understand why the infidelity happened.

Love Lookout

If you have sex with an ex while you're single, the temptation to do it again can carry over into your next relationship. Infidelity isn't excusable just because it was with someone you used to sleep with. In fact, this can be even more threatening to your mate. In cases like this, you need to redefine your beliefs about sex without love or commitment, and put distance between you and your ex to minimize temptation.

Why We Cheat

Here are major reasons people cheat:

➤ **The monotony of daily routine.** Commitment provides the security most of us seek. After a while, however, those comfortable routines we build together seem a little monotonous. Some people have affairs not so much for the sex as to create excitement ripples in the calm lake of togetherness. For many, the risk of discovery adds to the thrill.

➤ **Sexual boredom.** Humans have an need for sexual variety. When things get boring in the bedroom, some people buy books on sex techniques, some wait out the lull, knowing their desire for each other will come alive again, while others have affairs.

➤ **Unexpressed anger.** An affair can be a passive-aggressive act. Rather than confronting anger and difficult issues, one partner may sabotage the other through having sex with someone else. An affair can also be an act of revenge against a partner who isn't paying enough attention or has had a fling of his or her own.

➤ **Increased opportunities.** In our grandparent's day, the men worked and the women stayed home. Today, with more women in the workplace and more women traveling alone on business, the opportunities for affairs are greater than they were in the past.

➤ **Life crises.** Job loss, death or illness in the family, a sudden change of fortune (for the worse or for the better), even a significant birthday (like 30, 40, or 50) can precipitate an affair. These events put stress on individuals and relationships. A person in crisis may feel distant from his or her partner and reach out to someone else. The resulting affair can be an ego boost as well as a way of avoiding problems.

➤ **Cultural expectations.** We expect more from our marriages and our relationships than our parents and grandparents did. Some of our expectations of each other and ourselves are unreasonably high. People who have affairs because "something is missing in my life" often expect more than a partner can provide.

My Three Affair-Proofing Questions

There are three key questions, that I advise you to ask, to help you understand why you or your mate had an affair, and to start putting your relationship back together:

> **Affair-Proofing Question 1:** What happens in the affair that you can't let happen in real life? Let this happen in real life.
>
> **Affair-Proofing Question 2:** How does the lover behave that your real lover doesn't? Let him be that way in real life.
>
> **Affair-Proofing Question 3:** How do you behave with this person that you don't with your real partner? Act that way with your partner.

You can also ask these questions if either of you is repeatedly having fantasies about other people instead of each other. Although fantasies can be a harmless indulgence adding only sizzle to your sex life, they could consume you if you let them get out of hand. Asking the previous three questions and following the corresponding suggestions can prevent your fantasies from leading you to cheat.

Relationship Recovery

Any affair shatters trust. Some people never regain that trust; for others, it takes years. Some walk right out the door when they find out; others (couples who share businesses, homes, children, finances) stay together longer, but might never feel the same again.

Despite the heartbreak that comes with infidelity, couples can still make their love work—as long as both people are willing to put in the effort. Bill Cosby's wife and Kathie Lee Gifford publicly pledged to stand by their respective husbands in the face of evidence or admission of an affair. Both women focused on forgiveness and love, and refused to dismiss the years of history they had built with their husbands. Both husbands expressed remorse and pledged future faithfulness. To rebuild a relationship, you also need to set new agreements and commitments. Marriage or individual counseling always helps.

Kathie Lee Gifford's reported reaction to her husband's dalliance was to make demands: He had to carry a beeper, call her parents to apologize, attend marriage counseling sessions, and join her at a religious retreat for "couples in crisis."

The prognosis for recovery also depends on how strong the relationship was before the affair. Were you compatible? Were you able to communicate? Could you cooperate? If your relationship worked well before, it can survive and get back on track. The partner who strayed feels guilty, the other feels betrayed. Feelings of guilt and betrayal are inevitable, but they don't have to last forever.

Will I Ever Forget?

Whenever I recommend that you put your partner's infidelity behind you, I invariably hear the protest that it's just not possible. That's true only if you want it that way. Otherwise, you *can* forgive and forget—and you absolutely *must,* if you want to rebuild your relationship. Continual obsession about the affair, will only erode your trust, and confidence, permanently.

Catching a partner in the act makes it more difficult to put the affair out of your mind. The visual imprint on your brain can be hard to erase. It certainly takes more effort, but it can be done.

Accept and face your feelings of anger, depression, and distrust. Then you and your partner need to discuss the terms of your commitment and your relationship. You must decide whether you can come to a new agreement about fidelity, or whether a life apart would really be in your best interest. Don't let yourself wallow in disappointment or start thinking that "nothing ever works out" or that "all men (or women) are cheaters."

Dr. Judy's Rx

Advice in a book about recovery from abuse is very appropriate here: You can become "strong at the broken places." This means that the opportunity (however unwelcome) to reevaluate your commitment and fidelity can lead you to a better understanding of what your promises to each other mean and how much they're worth to both of you.

Can Trust Be Rebuilt?

After an affair, one of the most pressing questions is: Can trust be rebuilt? The answer is "yes," but it will take time and effort. If you've been unfaithful, you have to prove through actions—not just words—that your mate comes first, that you would not again do anything to hurt him or her, and that you would never break your agreement of commitment again. You can prove the latter even with small agreements, like coming home at a certain time, or calling when you say you will. Spell out clearly what you expect from each other and how you will behave. You also need to prove you can trust yourself if you are tempted again. If you don't believe in yourself, you can't expect your partner to believe in you either. Over time, trust will return—as long as the commitment is real. Being thoughtful, considerate, and loving (including in sex) is crucial.

If you've been cheated on, trust your feelings of hurt, but don't wallow in them. If you decide to give your love a chance, then do that! Be open to your mate's reassurance and proofs of renewed devotion. Take your time but be positive.

Dr. Judy's Rx

Make requests of your partner to help rebuild trust. Make a list of 10 things—large or small—you would like your partner to do for you. This can include: "Give me a big hug when you come home"; Sleep close to me"; "Come shopping with me." Give your list to your partner. Which does he agree to?

One person e-mailed me a variation of a commonly known belief: "It's better to have *trusted* and lost, then never to have trusted at all." I agree. Even if, sadly, your mate has proven not to be worthy of your trust, you must not generalize that feeling to everyone else. There are people out there who are trustworthy. Trust is a cherished feeling that enriches your heart and soul. Don't miss out.

Can a Leopard Change Its Spots?

Some people can learn from their transgressions. After having an affair, they can be even more certain of their love for their partner, and the couple's bond can strengthen.

Remember, all people can change if they want to. Be aware, however, that you cannot force a person to change. Missy went after, and caught, a real "player." She thought she was giving him everything he could want in love and sex, and she thought she could change him. But despite her efforts, he went back to his old ways, seeing several women at a time. If this happens to you, don't let yourself feel like a loser. Take back your self-esteem, accept the reality of the situation, and find someone who is more likely to be as faithful as you'd like.

The Affair Survival Checklist

Once the affair is uncovered, both partners have to make changes and adjustments. Here's a checklist of steps to get you back on track.

❏ **Identify and accept your feelings without becoming obsessive or losing control** (For example, thinking, "I was such a fool," or "How could I be so blind?" or "I'm so mad I could kill him").

❏ **Take a "time out."** Give each other time and room to begin healing. For some couples, that may mean a separation; for others, it could mean just not arguing, analyzing, or deciding anything together for a few days or weeks.

❏ **Reexamine your attitudes about commitment and monogamy.** Maybe the straying partner wasn't ready to commit. Maybe his or her idea of monogamy doesn't preclude an occasional one-night stand.

❏ **Reevaluate your past agreement.** If you never achieved a consensus on your commitments before, do it now.

❏ **Understand why it happened** (see "Why We Cheat" earlier in this chapter). Stop accusing and start listening. If you're the one who strayed, stop defending and start explaining. To get past an affair, you have to get past the "blame" stage. Listen to each other's points of view.

❏ **Reevaluate your ability and desire to be sexually exclusive.** Avoid cheating and guilt by not making agreements about fidelity that you can't keep.

❏ **Have compassion for each other.** The philanderer must understand a partner's pain and sense of betrayal. But the partner needs to understand that guilt has its own measure of pain. Each should take some responsibility for the situation.

❏ **Get counseling if you need it.** A therapist can help put the relationship back on track. If you can't communicate honestly and openly with each other, you need professional intervention.

❏ **Recommit to each other all over again.** Put the experience in the past and start rebuilding trust.

❏ **Make new agreements.** Just as you would in a legal document, decide on the specific new terms of your commitment and relationship.

❏ **Make changes in your lifestyle** that will increase your confidence, solve other problems, and allow time for each other (take a second honeymoon, start a hobby or project together).

The Least You Need to Know

➤ Always be clear about your agreements and the terms of your commitment.

➤ Never ignore your suspicions about a partner's affair, but temper those if your own insecurities cloud your perceptions.

➤ An affair can be forgiven and forgotten if you both put in the effort.

➤ Go ahead and have an affair—with your partner. Make it an affair to remember.

Chapter 25

Dealing with Crises as a Couple

In This Chapter

➤ Common physical and emotional crises couples face

➤ The stages of reaction to a crisis

➤ The four F's in coping with crises

➤ How to cope with parent's and children's crises

➤ Dealing with his or her mid-life crisis

➤ The test of devotion

Every relationship goes through its share of crises. How you weather them depends on your commitment and maturity.

A crisis can involve real or perceived losses of many kinds, from the loss of a loved one, job, status, or belongings to the loss of youth. There is a truth to the saying: Forewarned is forearmed: There are some predictable crises you may face individually or together, and there are predictable reactions to them. These crises can be transient or chronic. They include medical and emotional illnesses, upsets in your own or your loved one's life, and life stage transitions.

Five Expected Reactions

The reactions to crises or loss follow expected stages. They apply to situations from failing an exam or losing a job to losing a loved one through differences, divorce, or death. The stages can overlap in order and include:

Love Bytes

Research proves that couples who go through counseling together, in private therapy or support groups, cope with crises better than those who do not seek such help. Therapy facilitates necessary understanding and communication. Groups offer essential reassurance that couples are not alone in their problems.

1. Initial shock, numbness, and denial, such as feeling "This can't be happening."

2. Bargaining, or making promises such as, "If the problem goes away, I'll … (spend more time with … /donate money/help others)"

3. Anger (toward a mate, doctors, or God for deserting you, or toward yourself or another for being vulnerable)

4. Depression, guilt, hopelessness, physical symptoms, helplessness, and self-blame (such as wondering "Why couldn't I stop this?")

5. Acceptance, resolution, and constructive action

Be aware of how your own and your mate's styles in reaction to a crisis may differ. One of you might be a "withdrawer" who wants to be alone until the worst is over, who pushes even loved ones away, out of fear of exposing vulnerability or experiencing more loss. In contrast, the other might be a "support-seeker" who needs increased intimacy or closeness for comfort and insulation from further loss. Although a generalization in the face of a crisis, men are more likely to immerse themselves in activities (work, sports) to restore a sense of power and control, while women indulge their feelings. Give each other the space or support needed.

When Sickness Strikes

Innumerable challenges to health plague us all, from simple colds to chronic illness. They affect your relationship when they happen to you, your mate, or other loved ones. Be prepared for what these illnesses might be. Check back over the list of expected reactions previously listed. The impact of these problems on your relationship will depend not only on the problem and treatment, but on your attitudes and love. Many studies have proven that love heals, by renewing hope and boosting the immune system.

While illness can strain couples, consider inspirational cases. For Christopher Reeve, breaking his neck did not break up his marriage. His wife stood by his hospital bed, and now his wheelchair. And actor Pierce Brosnan reportedly stayed loyally by his wife's side through her cancer until her death, even going so far as to proclaim at the time that he would never remarry.

A partner's ability to cope with the other's potential illness can be predicted from strength of character, support during past disappointments and illnesses, values (about devotion through tribulations), concept of love (as everlasting and steadfast), and capacity for intimacy and commitment. Self-absorbed, narcissistic people may not cope well with another's illness. Likely to feel personally injured, they may be tempted to have affairs, or leave.

Here are the most common health problems a couple may encounter during the course of their relationship:

➤ **Heart problems.** Heart disease is the number one medical illness both men and women face. Hypertension and heart attacks can happen even at a young age. Fortunately, many conditions are monitored today with sophisticated methods. But many couples still worry about the impact of a weak heart on every aspect of their lives, including sex.

➤ **Cancer.** It's a dreaded "C" word that threatens life. But early detection and advanced treatments are offering higher hope for survival. Over the years that her husband was being treated for colon cancer, Diane was on an emotional rollercoaster ride. She couldn't concentrate at work and feared getting fired. Diane had to realize that her own life had to go on, despite David's illness. Making herself sick, too, would not help either of them. Things might never be as they were, but they must make the best of it, and create inner peace for the best possibility of health.

➤ **Prostate problems.** These affect more than half of men over 50 years old. The gland at the base of the bladder becomes inflamed, causing urinary pain, extending to back pain and trouble with erections and ejaculation. With certain treatments, sexual functioning can be affected, but sexual interest, activity, and pleasure can continue. Prevention of prostate cancer is crucial, with a nonfat diet and early detection through yearly exams after age 40.

➤ **Arthritis.** You don't have to be old to have inflamed and painful joints that restrict activity. Curiously, sex and orgasm can help ease pain, because anti-inflammatory chemicals are produced in the body and pain-killing chemicals are released in the brain during sex. Use pillows, heating pads, warm baths, massages, and mild exercise to reduce stress and ease discomfort.

➤ **Diabetes.** Diabetes is another problem that can affect young as well as old people. Fear of being debilitated from related complications can keep a partner from carrying out daily responsibilities of a couple's life. In addition, about half of men with diabetes experience erection problems caused by restricted blood flow, nerve damage, drug side effects, depression, or loss of confidence. Proper diet and exercise are essential.

➤ **Disability.** A condition that results in a physical challenge (stroke, paralysis, loss of hearing or sight) tests love that goes beyond the physical dimension. In any case, life routines can resume with readjustments, and lovemaking can continue in other than traditional forms.

Love Lookout

You should both be aware of the subtle or complicated side effects of any medications that can influence your mood and therefore, your relationship.

Dr. Judy Rx

Reassurance in the face of infertility is essential. One of the most beautiful reassurances I ever heard was one TV drama where the lover told his "barren" girlfriend, "I shall plant seeds there, in your heart."

➤ **Infertility.** One in seven couples suffers from the inability to have a child. The physical cause may be in his or her reproductive functioning, but half of couples break up over the stress. Men are deflated over "shooting blanks" and women blame themselves for not "being a woman." Both can be flooded with conflicts over having a family. Finances become exhausted, as does passion, from scheduling sex and procedures like ejaculating in jars. Fortunately, more medical options are available today (artificial insemination, surrogate mothering). Commitment and reassurance are essential. When Keith's fiancée found out she couldn't have children due to past surgeries, she stopped returning his phone calls. Keith had to reassure her that she would not be dooming his life, and that he loved her enough to face it together.

➤ **Accidents.** Unpredictable circumstances make most people traumatized about being in the wrong place at the wrong time, and trigger particular helplessness. But when a mate is involved in an accident, the blame can be even greater than in the case of other illnesses. When Jillian's boyfriend rear-ended another car when they were on their way home in the rain, she couldn't help blaming him, feeling "unsafe" with him, and losing confidence in his ability to protect her—foundations in any relationship. Allowing him to help her heal her wounds was essential. Forgiveness was necessary, but it took a long time. Dedication, loyalty, and reordering priorities (that life and love are primary) are critical.

➤ **Sexually transmitted diseases (STDs).** Over 50 million men and women currently suffer from an STD, and the numbers are increasing. These diseases range from herpes, warts, chlamydia, and yeast infections to the deadly HIV. As I've mentioned in an earlier chapter, that bears repeating, couples can unknowingly pass a disease between each other ("ping-ponging") because symptoms can be masked or go unnoticed. Facing feelings (blame, distrust) and getting medical treatment for both people is essential.

Love Bytes

Some STDs, if untreated, can cause severe emotional and physical problems and even infertility. In one study, over two thirds of sufferers reported a decrease in sexual pleasure from depression and fear of transmission to a partner. If treated, however, you can continue loving interactions with a mate, and even have healthy children. Depending on the STD, condoms, stress reduction, or medications can help. For information on STDs, see the Web site for the American Social Health Association at www.ashastds.org.

The Four F's to Deal with Health Crises

A health concern for either one of you will test the strength of your commitment. This is especially true if the health crisis requires ongoing rehabilitation and treatment. Of course, there are ways to deal with sudden health problems that allow you to offer support and still maintain your separate identity in the relationship.

Follow my four F's in dealing with a health crisis:

➤ **Get the Facts.** Surveys show three-quarters of people have unanswered questions about their health. Overcome embarrassment, shame, or fear about asking your doctor to clarify any issues you have. Expect that you deserve your doctor's time and attention. Contact national organizations and associations for particular problems.

➤ **Face your Fears.** These range from fear of loss of love to disability, death, and sexual dysfunction.

➤ **Express your Feelings.** Emotions are triggered that, if expressed, can increase the quality of your communication. The most pressing emotion is a sense of powerlessness or helplessness that comes from limitations, and having to depend on others. These emotions must be expressed in order to get to the positive attitude that is essential for good health.

Love Lookout

Loved ones often suffer from "survivor guilt," wondering why they are healthy while their mate suffers, expecting they will be punished (with bad luck, loss, or illness). If you are not the stricken one, give yourself permission to enjoy life.

➤ **Continue aFFection.** Withdrawal leads to feeling rejected, insecure, and iso-lated. Loving support boosts your mood and a strong immune system necessary for healing. Even if certain intimate activities have to be curtailed, cuddling and kissing can keep the loving going and boost both your spirits. If you go through the crisis with mutual support, your relationship can emerge stronger.

Ups and Downs: Handling Emotional Problems Together

With millions of men and women suffering from stress, the probability of one or both of you suffering from some sort of emotional problem at some point in your re-lationship is high. Let's look at some familiar psychological concerns that many cou-ples may have to confront during their time together:

Love Lookout

Sexual problems may result from fears and feelings of impotency, insecurity, and inadequacy. These must be addressed to prevent a vicious cycle of inhibited desire and avoidance of sex.

➤ **Anxiety.** Fears and worries are a normal part of everyday life and can motivate you to action. But dread and discomfort gets so severe for 1 out of 10 men and women that they suffer physical symptoms (such as shaking, palpitations, or dizziness) and cannot go in elevators, to parties, or even out of the house. In extreme cases of panic attacks or "social phobia," a person won't even leave home.

Fortunately, in 9 out of 10 cases, a combination of medications and therapy helps.

➤ **Depression.** Almost everyone gets blue occasion-ally, but severe depression can strike up to one in four people. There are many biological, social, and psychological causes (such as oversensitivity, hormonal changes, abuses, or unresolved anger in relationships).

Combat minor blues by getting active (take a walk, play a game), becoming in-terested (read a book, start a new hobby), or intensifying intimacy (with friends or mate). Avoid blame, guilt, shame, and self-doubts. Confront frustrations in your life or marriage. Serious depression requires professional help.

➤ **Being "hyper."** Paul can't sit still. Barbara constantly checks on the children, writes dozens of reminders, and chatters incessantly. If you're driven to distrac-tion or driving yourself and your mate crazy, you could have Attention Deficit Disorder (ADD). With life so fast paced, ADD is one of the most undiagnosed disorders, and it can affect up to 15 million adults. The impatience and impul-siveness resulting from ADD can provoke arguments.

Develop mutually recognized signals for your behavior and enlist your mate's help in becoming organized so you don't get overwhelmed. Keep your self-esteem high by thinking of yourself as "energetic" instead of "hyper."

➤ **Addictions.** Addictions cause emotional havoc in relationships, as the addict compulsively indulges in behaviors that are destructive to himself and his loved ones. Uncontrollable activity—eating, drinking, using drugs, gambling, shopping, having sex—is an escape from feelings and intimacy. Recovery programs are helpful and often essential. When Nancy started drinking heavily, her husband tried to make her stop by hiding the bottles, nagging her, and sleeping on the couch.

Love Bytes

Research shows that antidepressant medications can be extremely helpful; but check with your doctor about those (like Remeron) that do not have side effects that interfere with your sexual frustrations. Log on to the Web site, www.matureamerica.com, for information related to depression and how to talk to your doctor and your partner about depression.

Nothing works until the addict admits the problem and seeks help. Kicking the habit requires experiencing life without numbing oneself, meeting others' demands without resentment, and controlling one's behavior. Mates must look out for themselves. Keep in mind that recovery is a lifelong process. Seek help from 12-step programs and support systems.

➤ **Past abuse.** Physical, mental, or sexual abuse occurs in shocking numbers, to women as well as men, children as well as adults, poor as well as rich. The resulting shame, guilt, depression, and rage destroys trust and prevents intimacy and sexual pleasure. So many women who have abused despair of even opening up with a loving partner. Like Marcy, they commonly say, "My boyfriend is so wonderful, but I can't enjoy sex with him. I was abused by my stepfather when I was little. Could this have an effect now?" Sadly, the answer is yes, but happily, recovery is possibly.

Many victims repress memories for years, but can become survivors with supportive therapy and groups. Tell a loving mate about the problem so he will not feel rejected or blame himself. He can help by reminding you that he is not the ghost of your past.

➤ **Eating disorders.** A shocking number of women and men suffer from eating disorders that range from uncontrolled eating to taking extreme measures to control weight (such as bulimia and anorexia). Social standards, emotional conflicts, peer pressures, and relationship problems must be overcome to conquer the problem.

➤ **Post-Traumatic Stress Disorder (PTSD).** The after-effects of a trauma can last for years or reemerge at unexpected times. Such an aftershock includes common symptoms of irritability, guilt, anger, blame, depression, and even suicidal thoughts. PTSD came to light as the result of recognizing the problems of soldiers who have been through war, but also applies to equally shocking experiences such as rape, incest, natural disasters (earthquakes), neighborhood violence, even unrequited love. To deny death and reaffirm life, and to exert control when they feel powerless, PTSD sufferers can overindulge in pleasurable activities, from compulsive spending to sex.

Coping involves tracing the source, talking about fears, exerting control in life (starting a new project or boosting a career), healing past wounds, and asking loved ones to offer love and safety.

Healthy or Unhealthy?

"My girlfriend's job takes her on long trips. Since we spend so much time apart, sometimes I feel we're better off breaking up." "My boyfriend lives in another state. Can it work?" There are men and women who admit, "I can't be alone," and will not tolerate separations. Relationships represent attachment and security for them, not healthy unions of two independent people. You can survive any separation as long as you are individually secure and solid in your commitment.

Dr. Judy's Rx

As your parents age, don't be afraid to face threatening questions in preparation for illness or death. Inform yourselves about your parents' health and life insurance, property, power of attorney, and wills.

Family Illnesses

It is sad but inevitable that parents become ill and eventually die. Be prepared for these problems, particularly the strain on finances and disagreements with siblings that can drain you and your relationship.

Unlike accidents, where the loss is sudden and irrevocable, chronic debilitating and deteriorating illness requires different coping. As disease slowly takes a loved one's life away, you face a constant double challenge: prepare for your loved one's death but also keep affirming your own life.

When there have been conflicts in the relationship with a parent, a common reaction of the child to a parent's illness is withdrawal from his or her mate. When Lori's father was dying, she refused to talk to her lover, Robert. Fortunately, as a psychologist, he understood how her currently being flooded with memories of her father's past abusiveness and addictions made her distrustful of herself and men. Robert's understanding and persistence helped her overcome her unnecessary resistance.

The opposite can also happen. Rodney's wife had been so miserable about his lack of attention to her in the past few years that she was ready to leave him. But when his mother had to go into the hospital, he was suddenly nicer to his wife, even initiating sex for the first time in two years. The threat of losing a parent can allow an adult child to more fully realize the value of love and family, accounting for Rodney's renewed romance toward his wife. These reactions can be temporary (until the crisis passes), or they can trigger a more permanent new approach to life and love.

Love Lookout

The death of a child leads to the end of the marriage for half of the couples who suffer this terrible loss. Facing such a tragedy, couples often do not accept their different mourning styles and start to blame each other. Counseling and support are necessary to prevent this outcome.

Crises with Children

Once you have children, you are always a parent, and any experience your children go through will impact you personally and in your relationship. These crises include kids' traumas with health, peers, teachers, and eventually mates and their own children. Spouses need to band together to present a unified front to their children, despite any differences. Single parents have a bigger challenge: to endure their upset over their children's upsets and help however they can without the luxury of dividing the responsibilities with another adult, or having someone else to share the joys with, as they would if they were still together.

Love Bytes

Women do not have to lose their sexual desire during menopause. On the contrary, desire can increase with elimination of pregnancy concern, as long as women maintain high self-esteem and self-assurance of being feminine and sexy. Consult medical experts about remedies for lack of lubrication or other physical problems.

The Mid-Life Crisis

The mid-life crisis is notorious. The stereotypic 45-year-old man, traumatized by aging, trades his station wagon for a red sports car, and his wife for a similarly flashier, usually much younger, model. More women, increasingly independent at mid-life, are doing the same. Because life is so stressful, the syndrome is even starting earlier, in men and women only 35 years old. Successful adjustment requires acceptance of change and rededication to enjoying life without fearing that time is running out.

Male Menopause

Do men go through a menopause as women do? More evidence suggests that indeed they do. One woman described this condition in her husband: "He used to be very active, but in the past year he seems exhausted all the time, moody, and disinterested in sex. Sometimes he jokes he's getting too old to "do it." He's 49 and in good health, so could this be the dreaded mid-life crisis, and what can I do for him?"

Rather than a mid-life crisis that connotes passing panic, this man is more likely experiencing the male transition into aging called andropause or viropause (the Greek and Latin prefixes for "man"). Compared to the equivalent stage in women (ironically called "men"opause), where changes in hormones and the reproductive system ending menstruation are uniform and easily identifiable, hormonal changes in viropausal men are more gradual and erratic. Also, the syndrome does not lead inevitably to infertility and can occur without distinct medical changes or problems.

Physically, men may notice decreased muscle mass and strength, but as Oregon physician Aubrey Hill describes in his book, Viropause/Andropause, The Male Menopause, the signs are more psychological. Expected to be severe in 15 percent of men, common complaints include insomnia, fatigue, disinterest in any or all aspects of life, low self-worth, mood alterations, and generalized anxiety. Fears about waning virility lead to depression, decreased desire, and problems in sexual performance, such as gaining and maintaining erections.

Desperate (usually unsuccessful) attempts to reverse this downward cycle lead to reverting to a "second childhood" or those familiar quick-fix clichés about mid-life crisis, such as buying a new sports car or taking a young lover. A successful transition requires combating feelings of worthlessness with reminders about achievements and setting new goals. The man must accept the physical changes of his age, including changes in sexual function (less-firm erections, less ejaculate), and still feeling manly.

Growing Old Gracefully and Together

"I can see us in rocking chairs together," 22-year-old Dina announced, as proof of her love for Andrew. I hope that 40 years from now, she'd still embrace that romantic image.

Growing older happens to all of us. Mental and physical changes are inevitable. What matters is whether you greet them gracefully. Expect and accept the transitions that come with each passing decade, including questions such as, "What have I accomplished?" "Where am I going?" and the more philosophical, "What does it all mean?" Instead of obsessing, "I'm getting really old" (people do that even at 30), embrace changes, focusing on the positives of increasing wisdom and confidence. Stay as fit as you can, mentally and physically. Start new hobbies and challenges. Instead of thinking you can escape aging by exchanging your partner, look to each other for support in your turning points.

Posing the "Hypothetical Test of Devotion"

"Would you still love me if ... (I were old and gray/lost my hair or a limb/got cancer)?" It's a parlor-game question I've suggested earlier in this book that you ask, and bears mentioning again here, as it is highly relevant to dealing with crises. It's a question that can seem scary to ask, but may also yield startling revelations about personal character and commitment to love. Dare to ask it. The answer can be telling. Avoiding it can presage denial of a problem. Reassurance that you are loved unconditionally is a relief and the most ideal answer. That knowledge that you can survive a crisis together is a sure sign that your relationship is a healthy one.

The Least You Need to Know

➤ Expect emotional reactions to crises to follow stages from denial and anger to acceptance.

➤ Accept that you and your mate can react differently to the same situation so that you don't break up because of these differences.

➤ Consider traumas as turning points to strengthen your commitment. Withdrawal can not only hurt emotionally, but hinder recovery. Let crises bind, not break, your bond.

➤ Couples are inevitably drawn into experiences of other loved ones. How you deal with their traumas reflects your ability to handle problems in your own lives.

➤ Stand by your man or woman. It's a cliché that is worth repeating, because unconditional love in spite of health and emotional problems is reassuring to each other and strengthens your physical, emotional, and spiritual health and union.

Chapter 26

It's Not Just the Two of Us

In This Chapter

➤ How healthy are your other relationships?

➤ Do's and don'ts when dealing with parents

➤ Five tips to prevent kids from ruining your relationship

➤ Preventing the Hansel and Gretel syndrome from extinguishing your sexual fires

➤ Seven ways to avoid friends becoming foes

➤ Preventing an ex from x'ing out your love

➤ Pet-proofing your partnership

If you have mastered the art of a healthy self and a healthy love relationship, you can apply these skills to any other relationship in your life—with co-workers, employers, family members, children, and friends.

Since isolation is a problem in our increasingly technological society, the importance of family in the new century will be even more apparent. At the beginning of this book, I discussed the new trend toward extended family affiliations as a dimension of a healthy relationship while couples have despaired of family togetherness in the past decade, the coming decades will demand working through potential problems, with blood relatives and those in one's "extended family." This chapter addresses how to do that.

Feelings of closeness, commitment, caring, and being cared for can, be similar in all your interactions. My relationship with my cherished assistant Alissa meets those criteria. I pass the thoughtfulness test regarding her, as thoughts of her needs or interests pop up spontaneously in my head. For instance, I knew she adored her truck, so I was always on the lookout for interesting paraphernalia (antennae, trunk gear, note pads) in stores or catalogues. Remember the following qualities of a healthy relationship:

➤ The quality of comfort—you feel so comfortable together, that you can say or do anything and accept one another.

➤ Sharing dreams. In her birthday card to me, my assistant Alissa wrote, "My dreams are your dreams. I will always do everything to help you achieve the dreams you so richly deserve."

➤ Appreciating each other's qualities. When I used the word "perspicacity" during a lunch with my online chat show producer, Alissa joked joyfully, "Judy's always doing that, coming up with words no one else would use, that you need spell check for!" It reminded me fondly of my childhood, when my father always tested me on fancy words, and I grew to pride myself on a big vocabulary. A beloved friend, like a lover, senses and touts what you like about yourself, making you feel appreciated and adored.

Once you become aware of the love that you share with everyone in your life, you will be able to deliberately behave in ways that will maintain and escalate that love. The more love that you generate with people, the less alone and depressed you will feel. Your immune system will be stronger. Your mood will be brighter. All this brings you to a state of mind that feels both peaceful and exciting at the same time, that makes you further want to share your love with others.

The Importance of Family

The family is the nest that first teaches you about security and comfort. When you join with a mate, you double your opportunity to feel the warmth and love that an extended family can offer. It is wise to be alert to your mate's history with his or her own family. Find out how important family is to your mate. If being together matters to one of you but not the other, tension results. Reportedly one of the sticking points in actress Julia Roberts' marriage to country crooner Lyle Lovett was Julia being too busy to travel to his Texas hometown for family occasions.

Who Comes First?

When you get seriously involved, you become part of each other's family. In every family, there are patterns of interaction and expectations. Recognize what these are, so that you are not derailed in your love for each other because of conflicting loyalties.

While positive family relations can increase your bond and love, family interference can be damaging and unhealthy to your relationship. Read on to help you recognize and remedy these potentially unhealthy interactions.

When Parents Love or Hate Your Love

Parents are always going to have some reaction to your love choices. They may approve enthusiastically or disapprove disappointedly. When they are pleased with your choice, things seem to go swimmingly. But their disapproval can throw you off course.

If parents disapprove of your relationship, assess whether their objections are realistic. You may be blinded (due to your own conflicts or problems) and unable to see valid observations that could be helpful. Insecure Cassandra was so head over heels in love with John, she refused to see the dangers of his repetitive infidelity and abusiveness that her parents kept warning her about. Until one day, when the abuse reached the point where neighbors had to call the police and Cassandra landed in the hospital. Wealthy Matthew was so impressed that a beautiful woman would want him that he dismissed his parents' warnings that she was really a gold-digger. He finally agreed with them when a year later she divorced him and contested their prenuptial agreement.

On the other hand, parents' objections might indeed be based on their own expectations and needs, and, therefore, you are wise to doubt them and rely more on your own decision. As Janice told me, "My father-in-law always makes snide comments to my husband that he should have married a woman who cares more about the house than about her career." In cases like these, disapproving statements from parents are inappropriate, uncalled-for, and hostile. Parents behave like this when their child's life does not fulfill their own dreams. In this situation, your parents need to learn to accept your choice. And you should stop feeling responsible for fulfilling their dreams.

> **Dr. Judy's Rx**
>
> When mates are committed to a lasting relationship as primary companions, they deserve top priority over family and friends, with consideration for emergencies or extenuating circumstances.

The Do's and Don'ts of Dealing with Disapproving Parents

Your response to your parents' reactions will be greatly affected by your inclination to rebel against them or to please them. You are likely to rebel if you intentionally make the opposite choice from theirs. Since reacting like this does not always lead to positive outcomes, it is always best to clear these ghosts as mentioned earlier in this book, and make more mature, clear choices. Here are some do's and don'ts for dealing with disapproving parents:

Love Lookout

Reactions to a lover's family can be positive or negative, depending on your relationship with your own family. Barbara sought warmth and togetherness because her own family was cold and aloof. In contrast, Sandra took all her resentment toward her own mother out on her mother-in-law. Be aware of these transferences of feelings to prevent them from ruining relationships unnecessarily.

Love Bytes

Even if they disagree, teens are obliged to follow parents' rules about love (dating someone much older, curfews, disallowing sleep-overs). Both teens and parents should make efforts to understand and be tolerant of the other, no matter how unreasonable each other seems.

➤ Don't hate your parents.

➤ Don't argue with your mate about your parents.

➤ Do give up needing your parents' approval. If they can't appreciate you, they are losing out as much as you.

➤ Do come to a united plan with your mate about how to deal with parents.

➤ Do recognize deeper conflicts in your parents' lives (their own relationship problems, past experiences, fear of losing you).

➤ Do recognize your own conflicts over growing up and making decisions on your own.

The Enmeshed Family

In this century we've inherited important awarenesses about family dynamics from the past decade. The 1990s became the decade of the "dysfunctional" family—recognizing family dynamics that could be dangerous to the individuals, even if not intentional. One such dynamic is called "enmeshment," where, like "co-dependency," your lives are too inextricably tied together.

Of course you want to please your parents. That's healthy. But the pressure to please can go too far. One woman wrote to me about wanting a divorce but feared disappointing her parents, who had spent more on her wedding than they could afford and who boasted to everyone about their daughter's "perfect" marriage. "He's away for weeks and doesn't notice that I changed my hairstyle or that I am not wearing panties," she cried. "But how can I let my family down?" Putting up a false face just to please others only escalates your pain. Have courage to face any shame or upset and do what you need to do.

Dr. Judy's Rx

No matter how old or mature you are, going back to your parents' house often triggers your own (as well as your parents') regression to old feelings and patterns of interaction. These get further exaggerated during the holidays, when people are especially sensitive to the past. Recognize when repeating the past goes too far. Always respect parents' rules, but realize that you are now an adult, and can react and interact in new ways with your parents.

Another interesting yet potentially destructive dynamic evolves when you are so dedicated to pleasing your parents that you end up unconsciously resenting that your parent (and not you) chose your mate, sabotaging your own relationship. For example, Andrea grew up very close to her mom, sharing every detail of her life and dating experiences. She stopped dating certain men her mother thought were "not good enough for her" (didn't have a good enough job, financial security, social standing) and eventually married a man of means from a respected family. Her mother was overjoyed and relished every detail of their wedding and setting up house. But soon after their storybook beginning, Andrea began an affair with a boy from the "other side of the tracks," whom she knew would horrify her mother. What seemed inconceivable was comprehensible: Although Andrea did love her "perfect" husband, deep down she felt he was her mother's choice, while the boy from the other side of the tracks was her own choice. Once she separated herself psychologically from her mother, she could go back to claiming her marriage as her own.

You are overly enmeshed with your family if …

➤ You grew up extremely close to your parent(s).

➤ The first thought in your mind when something happens between you and your mate is: "What will my parents say about this?"

➤ You feel compelled to report—or want your parents to hear—all the details about your relationship.

➤ Your mother hears your relationship is in trouble and she cries, "How can you do this to me?" or "What will my friends say?"

➤ Your father constantly expresses pride or despair about how your mate reflects on the family or his reputation.

To prevent enmeshment, release the pressing need to merge or please, make independent decisions, and let parents be independent as well.

Intrusive Parents

Of course, parents can offer valuable suggestions from their experience, but they should not insist on you doing it their way. They have to let go and allow you to lead your own life. Since older people can be more set in their ways, adult children often have to change the way they react to them. Here are some do's and don'ts when dealing with parents' opinions:

➤ Do remain calm.

➤ Do listen to your parents' opinion respectfully.

➤ Do explain your own choice.

➤ Do make the conversation impersonal by asking: "How do you think times have changed?"

➤ Do acknowledge how you both come from different perspectives.

➤ Do feel secure about being able to make your own decisions.

➤ Do firmly point out your differences. Say, "I can see how you have one opinion (about our moving, finances, child-rearing), but we feel differently."

➤ Do appreciate parents' higher motives. Say, "Thank you for caring (about our happiness, security)."

➤ Don't criticize your parents as old-fashioned or out of touch.

➤ Don't feel threatened or wronged.

➤ Don't get upset.

➤ Don't say to your parents, "It's none of your business."

Love Bytes

Experts estimate that in-law problems contribute to about two out of five divorces, with those involving the husband's mother being the most difficult.

Love Bytes

Healthy in-laws, Camille Russo and husband Michael Shain point out in their book *How to Be the Perfect Mother-in-Law* (Andrews and McMeel, 1997), generally butt out. But they pitch in to: send food, treat the couple to a day out or dinner out, run errands, buy a present, send flowers, send funny greeting cards, offer compliments, buy books and CDs, and offer restful visits.

Dependent Parents

"My boyfriend's mother is constantly dropping in unannounced," complained Pamela. "So we have no privacy. If I continue to wash the dishes or do chores, she gets insulted." Pamela has a right to her privacy. Parents should respect a grown child's separate life.

Here are some do's and don'ts for dealing with dependent parents:

➤ Do acknowledge their interest and enjoyment of being with you.

➤ Do assure them with statements like, "We love to see you" or "We know how much you care."

➤ Do set limits. Say, "Peter and I are spending Sunday alone, but we would love to have you over on Tuesday."

➤ Do specify your availability. Say, "At five o'clock I must start my work."

➤ Do encourage divorced or widowed parents to develop new interests.

➤ Do give them gifts of memberships to social groups or music series.

➤ Don't build resentment.

➤ Don't allow intrusions to continue.

Love Lookout

Single parents are more likely to interfere in their adult children's relationships than married parents, because they depend more on their children, and because the children feel more responsible for them. They need to make a specific effort to develop independent friends and interests.

An Eight-Step Plan to Avoid Parental Interference in Your Relationship

To prevent family feuds and potential in-laws from becoming "out-laws," here are some suggestions. Following these suggestions will ease tensions between the generations and bond you more together as a couple.

1. Set your priorities. You and your mate come first.

2. Act as a team. If you argue, stop and say, "Let's not let them come between us. Let's solve this together."

3. Insist on direct communication, instead of talking through each other. For example, don't say, "Tell your mother to ..." and resist carrying secondhand information.

4. Avoid attacking your mate with statements such as, "You're just like your father" that only makes him defensive.

5. Share how your childhood experiences affect present feelings and behaviors toward parents.

6. Present a united front as a couple to others. Come to decisions together before others' opinions interfere.

7. Do let yourself occasionally feel like a child even if you are an adult.

8. Do separate parents' problems from your own problems. For example, Laney constantly complained to Ed about his father dominating a conversation, until she realized that Ed didn't listen to her as much as she wanted. She was focusing on her father-in-law instead of her own issue with her husband.

How Kids and Other Family Members Figure Into Your Love Life

While parents set the foundation for your relationships, other family members also affect your perspective about love and your interaction with your mate. Children are an obvious influence. Their needs are always your responsibility. How you act as a team in relating to them will either be harmonious or complicated with conflict. Other family members impact your love life as well, but not as obviously. Recognizing their impact prevents problems.

Dr. Judy's Rx

Write down what you say about you and your mate's parents. Substitute your partner's name to see if the same complaint applies. If so, talk calmly and directly about it.

Let's start with the positives. Children can create a powerful bond between you. This can certainly be the case if you have the child together, but also applies to blended families—where one or both of you have children from a previous relationship. Doing things together as a family can be fun and emotionally fulfilling. Research also shows that parenting can be physically healthy, when emotional satisfaction in this as in other experiences stimulates chemicals to flow in the body that boost the immune system.

But, as in the case of parents, children can interfere with your love relationship if you fall into certain traps. Children's impact on your relationship is vast, regardless of how you get along or whether they live with you or not. You worry about their upbringing, on compatibility, how they get along with friends, how they do in school, whether they'll get into drugs or have sex. All these worries affect your relationship.

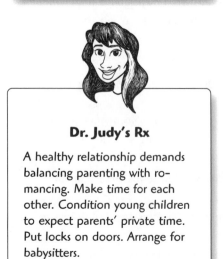

Dr. Judy's Rx

A healthy relationship demands balancing parenting with romancing. Make time for each other. Condition young children to expect parents' private time. Put locks on doors. Arrange for babysitters.

As described in an earlier chapter in this book, agreeing on raising children is essential to a smooth relationship. There are many decisions that you will face. Talking things over and coming to a unified position is critical for a healthy household. As a general rule, always consider the love between the two of you first, but children's presence and needs always have to be taken into account.

Handling decisions about sexual behavior regarding children can be the most challenging. Stephanie allows her five-year-old son to crawl into her bed every night, but her live-in love thinks it's unhealthy, and argues with her over it. When kids are under stress, bedtime comforting can be healthy, but not if it's habitual. Parents must recognize when they may be indulging their own needs like overprotecting kids to vicariously protect themselves, or out of their own fear of rejection, or a subconscious challenge to a mate.

Healthy or Unhealthy?

Pat, a divorced mother of a teenage girl, turned to her daughter as a confidant on dating problems. Pat defends their closeness, but asked me whether it was healthy. While I applaud her sharing (only 2 in 10 families talk openly about sex), I believe turning a teen into too much of a friend is not healthy. You should find your own friends. Be an "askable" parent, but be wary of role reversal (turning a child into your parent).

Here are five tips to prevent kids from coming between you and your partner. They are similar to those given above in the "Eight-Step Plan to Avoid Parental Interference in Your Relationship."

➤ Decide that you deserve to have your own life.

➤ Make time to be lovers instead of just parents.

➤ Train kids to get used to your privacy.

➤ Consider you and your mate a team.

➤ Don't let kids divide your loyalty.

The Hansel and Gretel Syndrome

Good relationships with siblings can be a great foundation for mutual respect, cooperation, and caring in marriage. But if you are too enmeshed with your siblings, you may choose a partner who reminds you of your brother or sister, and later lose interest in sex, because you've triggered an "unconscious incest guilt." You may suffer then from what I call the "Hansel and Gretel Syndrome."

One of my patients, 26-year-old Mandy, married a man whom she loved but had no passion for. After a year of marriage, she became emotionally and sexually frustrated. I pointed out how similar to her brother this man was: overweight, shy, and sweet. Why would Mandy pick a man just like her brother to marry? Because she couldn't change her brother but thought she could change her husband, as if to make up for her disappointment with her brother. In high school she tried to fix her brother up on dates, but her friends were not interested and Mandy was ashamed. She dreamed that he was the captain of the football team and that all the girls wanted him.

Mandy nagged her husband to lose weight and to come out of his shell. But faced with her disapproval, he only got heavier. In therapy, she came to realize that nagging her husband would not make him become what she fantasized, and even if he changed, it would not change the pain she felt in the past for her brother. As she stopped making her husband the object of her unresolved feelings about her brother, she became less angry and demanding toward her husband, and the marriage improved.

Another patient of mine, Holly, had a similar problem, but from a different perspective. Holly adored her younger brother, who was the most popular boy at school. Not surprisingly, Holly picked boyfriends who were just like him—younger than her with similar dark hair, green eyes, and taut muscles. But after dating them for a while, she always ended up sexually turned off. She was confused and miserable about this until she realized in therapy that her lovers were so much like her brother that she ended up behaving like a sister to them rather than a lover.

Same sex siblings can influence your love relationship, too. Rita's sister always called her stupid, making fun of her for reading romance novels instead of Shakespeare. When Rita recalled these experiences, she finally understood why she was always criticizing her husband for not knowing enough about literature, art, or classical music. She was treating him just like her sister had treated her.

Tracing the roots of problems with love partners to relationships with siblings helps minimize distress. Ask yourself, "In what way is my boyfriend like or unlike my brother?" "How do I treat the woman in my life—like (or unlike) I used to treat my sister?" "Do I secretly want my mate to be the perfect brother I never had?" There is nothing wrong with any of these choices. You just have to see the potential pitfalls so you don't ruin your chances for happiness.

Figuring Friends Into Your Relationship

"We know that my friend's boyfriend is cheating on her. Should we tell her?"

"We were out to dinner with another couple and he made a crack about her being fat and she said he should only be so big in bed. I scolded him and now they're both not talking to me. What should I do?"

Friends are important in life. Even with the healthiest love relationship, very few of us can exist without friends. But problems with friends, as with family members, can cause tension between you and your mate.

Here are some common friendship problems with tips on how you can resolve them:

➤ **Getting in the middle of friends' love dramas.** Putting in your two cents shows you care, but risks danger. Stay out as much as possible (except in the cases of abuse, endangerment, or addiction). When they need help, offer: "I want you to know I'm always there for you."

➤ **Revealing secrets in their lives especially about affairs.** Bearing bad news can make you the brunt of others' anger. Examine your motives for telling (revenge, purging your own hurts). Ask general questions or questions that lead to their self-examination ("Where was he last week?" "Do you think men can be fully faithful?").

➤ **Considering friends over your mate.** In a long-lasting relationship, your love partner should take priority.

➤ **Dropping single friends when you become a couple, due to divergent interests or perceived threat.** In one survey, two-thirds of men and women said they neglect single friends when they marry. Friends can react like rejected lovers when you replace closeness with them for a mate. Understand and give them time and attention, but do not let their reactions sabotage your love.

➤ **Friends sabotaging your love.** They might do this out of jealousy, possessiveness, or not wanting to lose your attention.

➤ **Trying to isolate your mate from friends.** Some men, as well as women, become so possessive of their mates that they attempt to cut them off from relationships with others. Refuse to do this or to allow it to be done to you.

➤ **Spreading rumors.** Assess the validity of others' accounts, but view troublemakers unworthy of your friendship.

Healthy or Unhealthy?

Valuing friends but making a mate top priority is healthy. Cutting each other off from friends and using friendships to escape love is unhealthy.

How Past Loves Figure Into Your Present Love

Unless this is your first and only love (a rare circumstance), both of you may have been in a relationship or in love before. Those experiences will condition how you feel and act in this present love. The ex-lovers themselves may also show up in your life. How you deal with the memory or presence of exes will affect how healthy your present love is.

Contact with exes may serve several purposes: to recall the past, clarify your personal history, repair past unresolved issues, reaffirm that you were loved, boost your ego, or maintain freedom.

Here are some common scenarios:

➤ **You can't stop thinking about an ex.** On holidays, Cierra's thoughts drift to old boyfriends. Now she wants to call one, but worries her boyfriend will get mad if he finds out. Memories and curiosities about exes (especially at nostalgic holiday times) are normal, and shouldn't cause guilt. Recognizing needs ("What do I want from this contact?") and imagining the encounter could be satisfying enough. With innocent motives, contact can be harmless and even healing. Use it to discuss your past or present needs with your partner.

Ask Dr. Judy

What should you do if you discover that your friend's mate is cheating on him or her?

This is a situation I'm often asked about. First, examine your own motives. Chandra's girl-friend's boyfriend came on to her. She didn't encourage him, but thinks she should let her friend know. What are her motives in telling? As Chandra said, "If he did it to me, he'll probably do it with other girls, and she should know how he is." Fair enough, but what does his flirtation really mean to Chandra and what are her deeper motives for needing to tell her friend? Even if she thinks she "just wants to be a good friend," it turned out she too had been hurt by men, and protecting her friend was a vicarious way to heal herself. Also, telling her friend is a way for her to get back at him, and men in general.

Assess the value of the information for your friend. If she could be hurt or abused, consider your duty to protect her. Also, assess her character to determine how she'll react. She may be "blind" in love and deny it, get angry at you, or stop seeing you instead of him (like shooting the messenger when you don't like the message). Apologize for causing her any pain, acknowledge that you know she loves him, and gently suggest that she should be alert to any further clues. Hard evidence—such as something he wrote or said documented on paper or tape—can help, but don't go out of your way to trap him. If she re-acts angrily to you, reassure yourself and her that you acted in good faith, pledge your loyalty, and let her be until she comes around.

➤ **Your mate is having constant contact with an ex.** Marshall sees his ex often for dinner, without inviting his fiancée along. No wonder she's upset. Being excluded triggers suspicions. Confront him with your doubts. If you become reassured their friendship is innocent, work toward a compromise: he agrees to limit contact with her, and you work toward decreased insecurity and complaints. Working this through together will hopefully confirm your trust, which is essential for the future of your relationship.

➤ **You ask for all the details about your mate's previous relationships.** Kim wanted reassurance from the man she was seeing, who left his wife for her, so she asked him what their sex life was like. He told her they did the same things in bed as he and Kim. Now Kim can't stop thinking about it when they're in bed together. Kim set herself up, asking for a confession that now tortures her mentally. Do not ask questions the answers to which you cannot handle. Resolve to use answers constructively. Know your motives for asking about the past. Get reassurance (of faithfulness or being special) that you need. Stop obsessive thoughts by switching to another thought or action.

Healthy or Unhealthy?

Healthy relationships can allow for independent activities and friendships, and objections should be curbed if motivated by insecurity or a need to control. However, objections to a mate's persistent contact with an ex are valid if they erode your relationship (which should be top priority) or lead to infidelity.

How Pet Love Affects Your Love Life

About 100 million men and women of all ages across America own pets. Many studies and programs prove that pets are healthy for people, and can even lower blood pressure. But love for a pet can be an escape or an excuse for partner problems. In one study, 8 out of 10 pet owners said they were closer to their animal than to friends or family. On one episode of TV's *The Richard Bey Show* that I appeared on, called "Can This Relationship Be Saved?" the complaint among all the couples on the panel was: "My Mate Loves Our Pet More Than Me." One man was consumed nightly with feeding his pet snake instead of coming to the dinner table with his wife. A woman stroked her poodle more than her husband. Adore your pet, but consider your love priorities. Beware of giving a pet the pampering you or your mate need.

Choosing between a pet and a mate can be tough. Peter had his cats long before he fell in love with Lorraine, but she has a bad allergy to cat hairs. As a result, they can never visit in his apartment and have not moved in together. But Peter refuses to give up his cats. Although Lorraine understands his cats are like his children, she despairs it will break them up unless he asks a friend to provide a "foster home."

The opposite of Peter's and Lorraine's dilemma is also true: A pet can provoke stronger pairing. Childless couples can use a pet as a substitute for having something important over which to share caretaking and strengthen their commitment to each other. One woman who was dating a man twice her age who already had two grown children and didn't want more kids or marriage, found that buying a dog was the key to him being more committed and spending more time with her. Better yet, a pet can patch up a faltering pair. Supposedly, TV *Nanny* Fran Drescher struggled to reunite with her high school sweetheart hubby, whom she left after 18 years, partly because their pet pooch couldn't take its "parents" being apart.

Ask Dr. Judy

Kenny called my *LovePhones* radio show because his dog was whining when he put the pet outside his bedroom while making love to his girlfriend. I explained that pets can react to new competition (a new baby, sleep-over visitors) or losses (children leaving home, divorce, deaths) with behaviors such as sleep or eating disturbances, regression (urinary or other "accidents" in the house), and aggression (chewing furniture, messing up closets). Kenny needs to remember that he is entitled to privacy with his girlfriend, and to resist feeling guilty about his pet, and to retrain the dog to accept the new arrangements.

The Least You Need to Know

➤ The healthier your relationship with others, the healthier your love life.

➤ Consider parents and friends, but make your mate your top priority.

➤ Balance parenting with romancing.

➤ Contact with exes can give clues about needs in your present commitment.

➤ Don't let pets compete with partners.

Part 5

Where Do We Go from Here?

Now you know the signs and secrets of a healthy relationship. You know ways to keep the passion alive, and you know how to deal with problems. You've improved your four C's to relationship happiness: compatibility, cooperation, communication, and commitment. You've learned how to stop fights—or at least to fight fair. You've taken the quizzes, done the exercises, and followed the tips to accomplish all this.

What's next? Well, the fact that you have taken time out of your life to read this book and follow the advice in it means that, at the very least, you're either well on your way to making your relationship all that it can be, or you're at a crossroads that could lead to breaking up. To help you make it work, we'll look at how you and your partner can build a life together, and then I'll go over some exciting techniques for the new millennium you can apply to solve problems and make improvements. If serious trouble strikes, I'll tell you how to get professional help. Remember, keeping a relationship healthy is an ongoing task, filled with ups and downs, but you can make it work if you both want to.

S/He's the One for Me!

In This Chapter

➤ Setting up house together

➤ Marriage proposals to suit every style

➤ Honeymoons to start you off right

➤ Starting a family

So, you recognize the signs of a healthy relationship, and are a master of keeping it vibrant and strong. You're also confident enough about jumping over any hurdles that might threaten a lasting bond. Basically, you've come to the conclusion that your mate is the one for you. What now?

It sounds like you're ready for a long-term commitment. But what exactly is the next step? In the 1950s, couples pledged their love for one another by getting "pinned." He gave her his college ring as a sign to other guys, "She's taken," and as a sign to her, "You're mine." But tokens fell out of popularity over the years. Today some couples are "branding" each other—with tattoos that prove they belong to each other. Actress Pamela Anderson and rocker Tommy Lee set such a trend, for example, had their ring fingers tattooed with each other's names when they got married (even though their tumultuous union didn't last).

How should you show you are ready to take the next step and get "serious" with your partner?

Moving in Together

Deciding to set up a household together is a statement of togetherness. Not long ago, moving in together literally meant that wedding bells were just around the corner. In modern times, however, moving in together is a far more casual event. No doubt it's a test of compatibility, but not necessarily proof of impending marriage.

"I would never marry anyone unless I lived with her first," said Bucky. "I'd have to be sure that we got along, and living in the same house would be the only proof. I'd have to see whether she lets me leave my socks around, watch TV, and not wash the dishes."

Men are not the only ones who want to test home-making compatibility. Women these days also want to see what he's like day to day.

Some still hold onto traditional values, like Kellie. "My boyfriend wants to move in together," she said, "but I want to marry first." Indeed, follow your values.

Setting Up House Together

Deciding where to set up a joint household is based on factors such as availability, convenience, and finances. Because of finances, not everyone can afford a new place. You might have to move into his or hers. But as much as possible, make it yours together.

If your partner lived with someone else, you can respect his or her memories by not throwing things out, but collecting them and putting them away. When Courtney moved in with Burke, she had the house completely redecorated and removed anything that remotely had to do with his former live-in love. Because Tamara didn't have the money to do that, she merely collected all the trinkets of Billy's ex and put them in a box in the back of his closet. To change things as much as financially feasible, she bought slip-covers for the couches, new throw rugs, and changed the pictures on the walls. Over the coming weeks, she insisted that Billy go shopping with her to pick out new bed coverings.

Dr. Judy's Rx

Your joint home should reflect your love and energy for one another. American Indians and other cultures believe every item in life—animate or inanimate—has an energy of its own, so make sure each piece of furniture and every plant have the kind of energy you want to exude on your lives together.

Love Lookout

Be sure that the partner whose home you move into does not maintain more power in the relationship. It is usually more advisable to find a place that is new to both of you. Be alert to the consequences of whose name is on the lease.

Five Important Adjustments to Living Together

There are always adjustments to be made in living with another person. Here is a checklist to keep in mind as you set up your new home together:

❏ Coordinate your awake and sleep time. He likes to stay up into the wee hours of the morning, but she needs to get to bed early.

❏ Create privacy for both of you. This is especially important since tight finances do not allow for large homes.

❏ Divide household chores.

❏ Agree on mealtimes (when, what, where to eat).

❏ Adjust to each other's particular habits.

Getting Engaged

Perhaps you lived with your partner and have decided it's time to take the big step and make the pledge to be together or you haven't set up house yet together, but know you want to. Either way, getting engaged implies you're ready to get married. It's true, though, that more and more couples these days are having longer engagements due to career and money pressures, which force couples to invest more time in organizing their lives and preparing for marriage. Longer engagements, of course, mean more opportunity to get to know the person with whom you will be walking down the aisle.

How to Pop the Question

A proposal can be private between the two of you, or in front of others in a small or big affair. Which you choose depends on your personality—whether you prefer private affairs or a big showing. Here are some cute suggestions:

➤ **Night owls:** Serve her a glass of champagne at night with the ring in it.

➤ **Early birds:** Bring him orange juice in the morning on a silver platter with the ring in it.

Dr. Judy's Rx

If you make one big purchase when moving in together, choose a new bed—it's the most sacred place for your lovemaking and should be personal. If that's not possible, revamp the bed by buying covers for the mattress and box spring, new sheets, pillows, and coverlets. Or perform a cleansing ritual on the bed, thoroughly "airing" it out and surrounding it with sachets.

Love Bytes

Women can take the initiative to propose. Supposedly, *Married ... with Children* star Katey Segal was the one on bended knee, kissing her husband-to-be's hand, and asking for it in marriage.

Love Bytes

Bruce Willis reportedly first gave Demi Moore a five-carat "friendship" ring from Tiffany's, and later threw the dice asking her to marry him at a gambling table in Las Vegas. They got hitched later that night by a minister in their hotel room.

➤ **Teasers:** Tell him a present is hidden in his closet and have him find the ring (among the mess).

➤ **1950s retros:** Go out for ice cream sundaes and instead of the whipped cream, put the ring on top.

➤ **Pet lovers:** Buy her a kitten and tie the ring to a ribbon around the kitten's neck.

➤ **Computer geeks:** Start a Web page called "My Proposal" and log on for him.

➤ **The family man:** On Christmas Eve, propose in front of the family tree.

➤ **Traditionalists:** Take her to dinner and the opera, then when you drop her off at home, drop onto bended knee, offering up a sparkling diamond (since "a diamond is forever").

➤ **Surprise lovers:** Take her to the movies and put the ring in the bottom of a popcorn box.

➤ **Suspense lovers:** Send her on a treasure hunt with a map and at the last destination, be there with the ring.

➤ **Outdoor lovers:** Take her to the beach and have a biplane write your proposal in skywriting.

➤ **Sports nuts:** Take him to a baseball game and arrange to have "Marry Me Bob" written on the scoreboard.

➤ **Romantics:** Take her to a fancy restaurant and have the waiter bring out a platter with the ring on it.

Saying "I Do"

Even though everybody knows that half of all marriages end in divorce, it doesn't stop millions of men and women every year from taking that step. However, the number of couples marrying each year has declined in recent years. From 1990 to 1993, 100,000 fewer couples made the sacred vows. The graph on the next page shows what's happened to the number of marriages over the last half century. There was a dramatic peak after World War II, and then an equally dramatic drop. During the 1960s era of free love, marriage increased again, and then again in the early 1980s. However, we saw a slow trend downward in the 1990s, so that by 1999 there were 8.6 marriages per 1,000 people, down from 9.7 10 years earlier.

However, don't let these statistics get you down. Hope springs eternal, as the popular saying goes, and rightfully so. Note that there were 8.6 marriages per 1,000 people *despite* the fact that the divorce rate was 4.1 per 1,000 people by the beginning of this new century. Some good news is that this divorce rate declined steadily, from 4.7 to 4.1 over the last decade. So be an optimist. Even if, according to statistics, half of all marriages end in divorce, you can be among the 50 percent who stay together, and the smaller percentage of those who are actually happy. That's the point: As in dating, never let statistics scare you away. The good news can happen to you. As one of my favorite sayings goes: If you can believe it, you can achieve it.

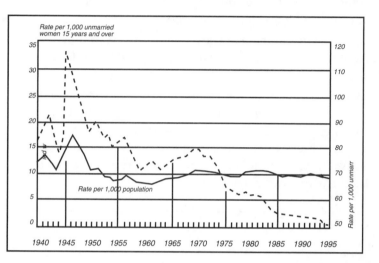

Marriage rates in the United States, 1940 to 1993.

(National Center for Health Statistics)

Apparently, cold feet applies more to those who haven't taken the plunge than those who already got their feet wet even though they nearly drowned. That means that statistically both men and women who had been married before and were divorced were more likely to get remarried than those who were single and never married. According to the National Center for Health Statistics, in the last decade the marriage rate for single women was 24 percent less than the marriage rate for divorced women (57.7 percent compared to 76.2 percent), and for divorced men it was less than half the rate for single men (105.9 percent compared to 47.0 percent). So don't get discouraged!

Love Bytes

Ex–*Entertainment Tonight* host, my friend John Tesh, hired a string quartet to play a song he wrote for love (now wife) Connie Selleca over dinner in a restaurant he rented out for the two of them, with fireworks set outside.

329

Where People Marry and Divorce

Did you know that some states are better for romance than others?

➤ The largest number of marriages take place in New York (before 1997, California was number one).

➤ The next most common places to take your vows are in Florida (also on the rise) and California (with Nevada increasing in past years).

➤ The states fewest people marry in include Washington D.C., Wyoming, Delaware, Montana, Rhode Island, Alaska, Maine, North and South Dakota, Vermont, and Arkansas.

➤ Divorce rates are highest in New York and Florida but have less than half the number of marriages. States with higher rates of divorce than marriage include Pennsylvania, Connecticut, and New Jersey. The lowest rate of divorce compared to marriage is for Hawaii, where more than five times the number of people get hitched versus unhitched (I definitely agree those azure skies, white sands, and hula dancing work love magic).

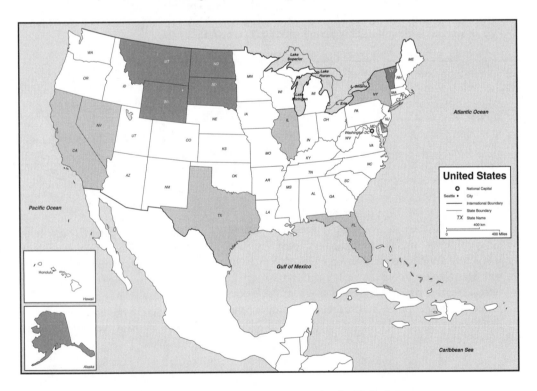

States with the highest and lowest occurrences of marriage in the United States.

This figure, reflecting findings reported by the U.S. Department of Health and Human Services, shows the states with the most marriages (shaded light gray) and those with the fewest marriages (shaded dark gray).

When People Marry

Romance seems to follow seasonal swings. According to the U.S. Department of Health and Human Services, summer is the most popular season to marry. June is the most popular month to marry, with May and August nuptials next in line. January is the least popular month by far, followed by March and then February. By the way, the divorce rates are fairly equal throughout the year, but highest the same months as marriage highs (June, May, and August). This makes sense: People are reevaluating love in springtime and by summer's end before fall.

Saturday is the most popular day to marry. Of course, that makes sense. You get Saturday night for your honeymoon night and Sunday to either recuperate or fly off to your vacation fantasy. It's also easier for people to come to the wedding—they may not have to take time off, and they have more time to travel to your affair.

Love Bytes

People are also waiting longer to marry. In 1990 compared to 1970, fewer brides and grooms were under 25 years old, and more were between 25 and 39 years old.

When Should You Get Married?

Although June may be the most popular month to get married, individual timing is crucial. Whenever anyone makes a big decision, I always ask "Why now?" There is usually something that has precipitated taking a big step. Josh and Lila were together for four years and engaged for three. Why didn't they marry? "Procrastination and lack of funds," Josh admitted. So when he finally got a job that paid well, he felt more secure. For Doug and Alexis, the decisive moment was when she was offered a job in another city; getting married was a way to cement their commitment through their separation. Keep in mind that there are other common triggers: her ticking "biological clock," his realization that all his friends are married. Make sure that you are getting married because you have decided that you have found the right person for you, and are ready to commit now—not because of outside pressures that say "It's time to get married."

Love Bytes

Remember, the biggest factor in your taking that major step and making it work is your intention to stay together and make it work with dedication. All hurdles can be overcome.

Dr. Judy's Rx

Welcome wedding jitters as proof of the seriousness of your decision, of considering a choice that you mean to stay together for a long time. See your fears as a chance to focus and reconfirm your commitment.

Jitters

Everyone gets them—marriage jitters. Nervousness before saying "I do" and pledging to love and honor as long as you both shall live is perfectly normal. You can have those second thoughts even if you are madly in love with each other.

Jitters commonly manifest themselves as an undefined, vague anxiety and finding fault with small things (wedding date, dress) as well as bigger things (shaky self-confidence, choice of mate, confusion over plans for the future). Panic can show up in emotional irritability, arguing, or actual physical symptoms (panic attacks, sleeplessness, eating disorders). Some brides don't fit into their wedding gowns as the wedding date approaches, as anxieties have led to either appetite loss or gain. Some men joke that a bachelor party with strippers (controversial as this is, given many brides' objections) is their last fling at bachelorhood—it's no doubt also a symbol of last-minute commitment fears. (See Chapter 11, "Commitment—Warming Up Cold Feet.")

However, it is not inconceivable that serious or persistent jitters signal that you could be making a mistake and need to reconsider. Here are some ways to tell if those uneasy feelings are telling you that something is not right:

❑ You were pressured into deciding to get married.

❑ You find many areas where you aren't compatible. Review the chapter on Compatibility in this book.

❑ You think you would like to settle down with one person, someone you love exclusively, but honestly, you're not willing to give up your other boyfriends or an ex.

❑ You would like to commit to someone and forge a life together, but you are really not ready for that and need your space.

Why did you not know before? Sometimes you only realize how you feel about something when you make a decision and then see how it feels. You can be very sad if you disappoint a fiancé(e), especially if announcements are made, invitations mailed, and deposits lost, but better to endure that than to go through with walking down the aisle, not smiling, wondering why you're there, or waking up shortly afterward feeling in your gut that you made a mistake.

Although Aimee was anxious to marry her "dream man," a long engagement turned out to be a gift in disguise, as it revealed ultimately that they should not marry.

Incompatibility in lifestyle ended her happy dream of love. By age 38, Aimee had been divorced for eight years from an abusive man and had had several failed long-term relationships. These relationships were with highly successful men in high-powered careers, none of whom could accept her own busy career that required her to travel. At a friend's cookout, she met a retired naval officer who owned a ranch hours from her home and office. He had free time on his hands, and spent a lot of it at Aimee's house and by her side at her business parties and trips. Soon after their engagement, however, he demanded she work on the ranch with him and give up traveling. As the wedding date approached, Aimee became increasingly anxious. Although relieved to finally feel loved by a man, she could not foresee sacrificing her career. "I must face the truth," she said, tears streaming down her face. "I couldn't live just for his love and abandon everything I've worked for all my life. And if he left in the end, I would have nothing." She broke off the wedding, resolving, "I lost this love, but I have myself."

Aimee had to realize that there is no shame in breaking her engagement and canceling their wedding plans. She had to realize that it was better for her to discover these problems before taking that more serious step.

Ask Dr. Judy

Sometimes you break up before the wedding and only then realize you really cared about the person. The pain can be greater when your ex finds someone else.

Joe broke up with his girlfriend when he found out through a friend that she had gotten pregnant and miscarried without telling him. Only when she got engaged to someone else did he realize how much he loved and wanted her.

Joe pined for his ex endlessly. Soon it became evident he had to talk to her to get his feelings off his chest. In Joe's situation, as for many, it's emotionally satisfying to confront "the one that got away"—at least to say your piece and feel you have no regrets, and complete your "unfinished business." Then you are more able to let go of the past.

Going Ahead with the Wedding Bells

Your wedding is a special day. Recognizing this, more and more couples are designing customized wedding events and ceremonies to reflect their personalities. They write their own vows and take them in airplanes or even scuba diving. When my friend Michael Young, a TV host and producer, married a former Miss Universe, Cecilia Bolocco, the wedding guests all flew to her native Chile for the week-long festivities.

Stress over wedding plans, costs, and guest lists can still cause problems for couples. Assign various rights to make decisions (to yourselves or parents), and resolve not to argue.

Wedding Vows

A touching trend is that more and more couples are writing their own wedding vows—solemn words that solidify the sanctity of your pledges to one another.

Here's an example of a wedding vow delivered for couples by California Reverend and hypnotist, counselor, and author, Shelley Lessin Stockwell. Stockwell wrote the following vow for marriage ceremonies she performs.

From Sex and Other Touchy Subjects, *by Shelley Lessin Stockwell (Creativity Unlimited Press, Rancho Palos Verdes, California, 1990).*

(Photo by Jon Nicholas)

Wedding Vow

Today, we are planting a seed in our garden.
We are honored to have family and friends,
standing at the border of that garden and
witnessing its unique beauty.

It took a long time in coming, this garden of ours.
With love and patience we carefully tilled the soil
by taking time to really talk to one another.
And listen. And hear.

Bravely, we removed, one by one,
the weeds of fear, self-deceptions, competition,
old hurts and loneliness;
and lovingly replaced them with understanding,
vulnerability, empathy, compromise and yielding.

And the sun came
and the rain,
and small miracle rainbows!
Our garden dazzles my eyes
with its sparkling energy
and giddy colors!

So, today,
because we have both agreed
to care enough to act with
each other's best interests at heart
we are planting a new seed.

I love me,
I love you,
I love us.

It will grow to be the most beautiful
and precious flower of all
and will reign over all the rest.

The seed is trust
and we have lovingly planted it on this day

The Honeymoon

The traditional trip for lovers after the wedding still carries the mystique of romanticism—a time to be together to affirm love and commitment. Despite reports that one of the most difficult times for couples is when they return from this idyllic experience, couples still embrace the fantasy of such a romantic getaway.

While most couples know each other well enough to prevent surprises on a honeymoon, there can still be unmet expectations, sexual tensions from performance anxieties, and stress over beginning a new phase of your relationship. Anticipating these will help ease the pressures.

Janice and Bob went on a cruise for their honeymoon that turned out to be a disaster. She got seasick and stayed alone in the cabin, while he went gambling each night. Her resentment and distress built to the point where she wanted to end the trip prematurely. Only when she was able to express her need for him to take care of her, and he to realize his mistake in partying without her, were Janice and Bob able to get back on track to make their marriage work.

Honeymoons are a good "marker" experience to be recalled later to refresh your love. Carolyn and Jeff spent a romantic week at the honeymoon haven, Pocono Mountains' Mt. Airy Lodge in a honeymoon suite complete with heart-shaped bed and indoor pool. In the years afterward, they would review their photos and memories whenever they felt distant or disconnected from each other, or when they hadn't made love in a long time. The pleasure of that time retriggered their passion for one another.

Love Lookout

Prenuptial agreements have become more popular in the last decade. However, be prepared the underlying feelings over money can cause tension between you.

Dr. Judy Rx

Consider every day you stay together as a form of renewal of your vows. This will make your relationship more solid and your commitment more conscious.

Starting a Family

When do you want to start a family? How many children do you want, if at all? These decisions are important ones, as pointed out in Chapters 8, "Are We Compatible?" and 25, "Dealing with Crises as a Couple." You'll need to discuss this issue before you reach the stage of commitment, but talking together about children should continue even afterward. Nothing can break up a couple more bitterly or insidiously than disagreeing about family issues.

Remarrying an Ex

It's not so common, but worth mentioning because it's happening more often: divorcing and then remarrying the same person. Perhaps the most celebrated case of

this is Elizabeth Taylor and Richard Burton. The tempestuous two were apparently as locked in love-hate as the characters they played in *Who's Afraid of Virginia Woolf?* Yet Liz is often quoted as saying that Burton was the love of her life.

It also happens in everyday people's lives. Jocelyn and Stephen were married while still in school. "We were way too young," she admits, "and needed to grow up on our own, so we had to split." But 15 years later, neither had remarried, and when they met again at a friend's birthday party, they started dating again. "This time when we decided to get married, we knew who we each were," Jocelyn explains. "I was ready to follow him across the country where he lived, and he was ready to let me be who I am." Ten years later, Jocelyn and Stephen are still married, living independent lives, but still partners.

Dr. Judy's Rx

Be sure to agree on contraception choices. Never trick a partner into becoming a parent; the resentment can last forever. Make a conscious decision about becoming pregnant, not acting out a vicarious need for nurturing.

The Least You Need to Know

➤ Every step toward more commitment is a stage to reevaluate and reconfirm your devotion.

➤ Anxieties at every stage of commitment are common and not an automatic red flag.

➤ There are as many ways to pop the question as there are personalities.

➤ Put your personal stamp on your commitment ceremonies just as you do on your love in general.

Chapter 28

Keeping Your Love Exciting with New-Millennium Body and Mind Techniques

---

In This Chapter

➤ Mutual meditation that increases your connection

➤ Eight ways to make workouts tone your sex life

➤ The healing power of touch between you

➤ Decorating your house for love

➤ Taking a look at your past lives

In the beginning of this book, I mentioned the importance of a spiritual connection between you, as the seventh dimension cementing your relationship.

All the exercises described in this chapter are intended to harmonize the two of you together, tuning yourselves like instruments in an orchestra. You don't have to play the same note, you just have to blend well together. The techniques described in this chapter may be new to some of you; however, remember that these exercises are also meant to be fun. So go ahead, align your energy, your body centers, and your mental state to reach a higher state of consciousness and connectedness with your lover.

Starting with the Basics—the Joy of Exercise

Before we get into topics such as meditation, reflexology, and other holistic techniques that may be new to you, I thought it might be wise to start you into this

Love Bytes

A California study showed that couples who jogged together had fewer problems in their relationship than those where either partner exercised alone.

Love Bytes

A Harvard study of swimmers found that those in the pool over 18 hours a week had little time or energy left for their partners. Running to the gym should not be an escape from relationship troubles.

chapter with something you are familiar with and that I mentioned earlier in this book with regard to "Making the Honeymoon Last"—the importance of working out together.

Most people think of exercising as a solo activity, but actually there are many ways to exercise with your partner. Doing so gives you an opportunity to spend time together. It also gives you something to do together that benefits you both—important for your bonding. Your connection to each other grows as you engage in a mutual interest, in this case, talking about workout routines, proper diets, vitamin supplements, and general health issues.

Choose a Workout Routine

Internationally known fitness guru and personal trainer High Voltage, whom I mentioned earlier, tells of how one of her celebrity clients, a model, had just given birth and as is typical, her sex life with her husband dwindled. The stresses of a new baby, added to her traveling and work, were heading them for divorce. Voltage designed a workout routine they could do together that suited their diverging needs, abilities, and body types. The new-found time and shared interest fired up their interest and passion for one another.

Figure out a mutual workout plan that works for you, from hiring a personal trainer for both of you, to taking classes together at a club, to simply following along at home with a workout video. These mutual routines can vary from aerobics to weight-lifting to combinations of activities.

Simple Stretching Exercises

Here are a few stretches that you could do on your own, but having a partner aid in the movements helps you get maximum benefits. Go through the motions slowly and gently, being sensitive to each other's comfort with the activity, stopping if one of you feels a strain. Notice the position in the following figures.

➤ **Leg pull:** One of you lies on the floor while the other stands at your feet (knees slightly bent), reaches down and grasps your feet, lifts, and pulls.

➤ **Inner thigh and back stretch:** Partners sit with legs spread apart, feet touching wherever comfortable (if your legs are disproportionately long), and hands clasped. Alternate one of you pulling backward, leaning back (as if rowing) as far as comfortable, and holding for 30 seconds. Feel the stretch. Then the other pulls you both to an upright sitting position, and then leans backward similarly. Pull each other back and forth in as flowing a motion as possible. (Vary this exercise by making circles, by leaning to the right and rolling each other around. Then reverse direction.)

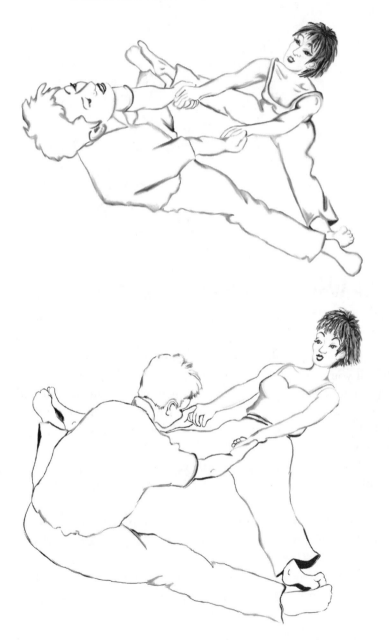

Leaning out.

Leaning in.

➤ **Squats:** Squat facing each other and while holding hands, lift yourselves up to a standing position. Lower down and raise up again. Concentrate on your breathing, inhaling and exhaling at the same time. Note: This exercise is more advanced, requiring balance and muscle control, but the benefits are worth it!

Couple squats.

Eight Ways to Make Workouts Also Work in Sex

Several approaches that you should apply when you are working out together will also improve your lovemaking:

➤ **Practice positive self-talk.** After only one set of leg lifts or six laps in a pool, your mind might tell you, "I can't do this right" or "I can't go on." Partners should cheer each other on, saying, "You *can*," and you will prevail. Similarly in sex, to prevent worrying, "I'm taking too long" or "This won't work," partners should cheer each other on with equally positive statements, "I'm enjoying this," "This feels good."

➤ **Picture your goals.** Instead of giving up a sport, exercise, or sex when you don't see immediate results, reassure each other that you know sex can get increasingly better and better over time.

➤ **Stay in the present and don't focus on the past.** Instead of looking back (to your past shape or sexual relationships), focus on what's happening now and approach each time as the first.

➤ **Avoid comparisons.** When you're busy comparing yourself to others in workouts or sex, you can't do your best. Keep reminding each other how unique you are.

➤ **Breathe.** Holding your breath while doing a sport or having sex can give you a headache and sap your energy. Steady breathing increases stamina and pleasure. Working out together trains you to breathe together, which puts you in tune for good sex.

➤ **Take responsibility for yourself.** Although you are working out together, no one can do an exercise for you. Similarly in sex, you add to each other's excitement by what you do, but each of you is responsible for allowing yourselves to get turned on.

➤ **Remember that more is not better.** Instead of reaching for a goal in sports or sex, focus on and enjoy where you are at the moment. Enjoy tiny sensations and they will build.

➤ **Smile and enjoy.** Research proves that physical expression affects mood, so instead of frowning in sports or sex, smile. Smiling at your partner makes you both happier.

Inner Guidance on Sex

In a technique for satisfying relationships and better sex, developed by personal coach Greg Ehmka, actions come from within rather than being automatic or controlled. As outlined in his book, *Money, Sex, Power and You: Transforming Your Ego,* you only move when you get the impulse from within to move (called Latihan and Sexyhan when in an erotic interaction). Do this inner guidance for 20 minutes on your own, then with a partner. As you each do nothing but wait for inner impulses, you connect with each other in more genuine and intense ways.

Sit quietly with your partner with your eyes closed until an impulse comes through you to move. Then move in slow motion (like t'ai chi), allowing yourself to curl up, stretch, roll over, or become more vigorous moving against each other. Do not plan an action, like kissing, but let whatever happens come up. If thoughts or worries (about performing, pleasing your partner, lasting long) come up, force your mind back to the present by focusing on a body sensation (pressure on your thigh, softness of her lips). Allow yourself to make sounds. Ask yourself (silently or aloud), "What's up now?" You'll know you're doing it right when your every move feels smooth, time seems to stand still, and you feel connected to your partner.

Magnetic Love

In Chapter 2, "The Seventh Dimension of a Healthy Relationship: Spiritual Love," I described how new millennium love creates an "energetic" between you. Some healers recommend using magnets to balance your energy individually and in your relationship, because magnets expand on the principle of energy exchange. Magnets are commonly sold as pocket amulets or jewelry for personal use. Because differing sleep positions and timing can interfere with harmony, magnets placed in pillows and bed pads supposedly balance a couple's sleep patterns, creating more compatibility.

341

All magnets have two poles. The negative pole generally has a calming effect and helps to normalize metabolic functioning, while the positive pole can cause stress, interfering with metabolic functioning and, therefore, lead to disease. A magnetometer is helpful to identify the poles and intensity of the field.

Laying on of Love Hands

Years ago when I was hosting my own show on CNBC-TV, *Money and Emotions,* the topic of one show was "alternative healing." I tracked down a nurse I had heard about who was the premiere practitioner of what was then called "healing hands." The producers were skeptical, asking, "How can someone heal people by just laying her hands on them?" The practice—and the skepticism—date back to the beginning of time, where in "laying on of hands," special people were thought to be able to heal ills from insect bites to more serious illnesses like influenza just by spreading their hands over the person, not even touching them. The practice seemed mystical, and those doing it were often considered witches or the devil rather than angels of mercy having special powers.

Love Lookout

Many health fairs have purveyors of personal-use magnet devices, including wristbands, earrings, and bed magnets. Be sure to check the validity of these vendors, since some products could cause the opposite of the desired effects. And only use magnets under supervision of a qualified professional.

The practice has been revived in the past two decades. Credit goes to Bernie Siegel, who as a cancer surgeon from traditional schooling, managed to incorporate these more untraditional practices of healing, including imagery and positive thinking, into treatments with his cancer patients and publicly promoted their effectiveness. His respectability gave these practices more public acceptance.

In this new century, there is even more interest in the powers of such touch. Certain people can emanate auras (visual patterns), heat, or even electrical sparks through their hands that can be felt by another sensitive person. These electrical fields can transmit healing energy to others. The transmission works best when the transmitter has a specific intention in mind to heal the other.

How is this relevant to this book on healthy relationships? Directly so. Each one of us might have this power but be unaware of it. Some individuals have it to a stronger degree, where they and others can recognize the strength or energies emanating from their hands. Others may have the powers dormant because their consciousness refuses to recognize it. Regardless, the potential can be there. Despite the degree of energy transmitted through the hands, a crucial ingredient is the intention to heal. Do you believe that lovers can transmit their loving and healing spirit to their beloved just by the laying on of hands?

Less formally put, each one of us knows how wonderful, safe, and secure you feel when you collapse into a lover's arms or lap after a stressful day. Perhaps your lover strokes your head, hair, arm, or back. Several benefits occur: You feel safe from the outside world attacks by being enveloped. But you are also receiving the warmth of your beloved's body and his heartbeat calms your own pulse, as you synchronize your more anxious, quick breathing to his more calm rhythm. And the stroking of his hand not only adds to the calming but also transmits the spiritual energy I described earlier.

Love Bytes

Research has proven that stroking helps the doer as well as the receiver. When tested, older people who stroke cats show lower blood pressure.

Everyone is capable of sending love to their partner through spiritual connection and techniques such as laying on of hands. Bill Stratton, now head of the Radiant Health Research center in Encinitas, California, discovered that he was a "Medical Intuitive" capable of "spiritual healing" and "energy balancing" and says anyone can do what he does. He started by doing acupressure (pressure on certain key points on the body) to relieve his wife's allergies, a dentist's back pain, and a woman's spider bite sting. Then he realized every mother has this same power: Put your left hand on top of your child's head and your right hand over the child's heart, letting them feel your love through the warmth of your hand. Gently rub the chest while putting your attention on the highest Source of Energy you relate to (God, Jesus, or Abraham Lincoln). You don't even have to be touching the child, as long as you have a heart connection to the child. All that's required is a few moments thinking and feeling love for the child and intending perfect health for them after connecting to your highest Source. Do it every day even if nothing much seems to happen at first.

Try this exercise: When your beloved comes home exhausted from a stressed day, have him lay on the couch in a relaxed pose. Put on soft music. Breathe deeply and mentally imagine your consciousness connecting with unconditional love of your beloved (caring for him beyond his looks, money, job). Measure your consciousness subjectively on a scale from 1 to 100. Notice if you see any colors around your lovers' body or feel any heat or electrical sparks in your hands as you hold them over him. These are signs of strong energy transmissions that happen even if you feel "nothing" but if your partner is open to receiving your energy.

Mutual Meditation

Meditation has become so accepted in the mainstream that the National Institute of Health has recommended its practice as a treatment for hypertension. Most important, meditation has shown to be effective in reducing stress and in strengthening the body's immune system. Practiced for thousands of years, meditation can be considered any activity that keeps attention focused in the present. The simplest method is

Love Bytes

Four million people currently meditate regularly. Scientific studies have shown that meditation slows the heart rate and changes brain waves, resulting in many health benefits, ranging from increased creativity to reduction in stress, high blood pressure, and drug and alcohol abuse.

Dr. Judy's Rx

The same principles of meditation can be applied to walking together. You and your mate fall in synch with your pacing, and then focus on your internal process and sensations in each body part.

to sit quietly and focus first on your abdomen and chest rising and falling in conjunction with your breath. Inhale and exhale. When thoughts, memories, images, and fears intrude on your mind, attend to them like a witness—observing them but letting them pass—without dwelling on them, bringing your attention back to your breath. Do this for 15 minutes each day.

Although most people consider meditation to be an individual practice, it can also be used to bring couples to unimaginable states of pleasure and harmony.

Consider the "Lovers' Spooning Meditation," which involves lying in a spoon position, with one person's back nestled into the other's chest. Let's say your partner is behind you. He wraps his arms around your chest and rests his hands on your heart. You put your hands over his. Then you and your partner breathe in and out at the same time. Lie still without talking. When thoughts, memories, images, and fears intrude on your mind, observe them but let them pass without dwelling on them, bringing your attention back to your breathing. You can also do this in a sitting position, with one person sitting behind the other, legs wrapped on the outside of the partner's legs.

Many beautiful exercises of this kind to enhance spiritual sexual exchange between couples are described and illustrated in The Art of Sexual Magic by Margo Anand, creator of many seminars to create bliss in everyday life.

Massage

The pleasure in touch and being touched is indisputable. The simple act is psychologically as well as physically rewarding, communicating caring, warmth, and love. Research proves that being deprived of touch can stunt both mental and physical growth, while receiving a loving touch can even help cure mental and physical illnesses.

Massage is the deliberate act of manipulating the body in certain ways to cause certain healthful effects. Of course, going to a skilled masseuse is a treat. But couples can give each other lots of pleasure, and help each other relax, by working magic with their hands on each other's bodies. You can massage the whole body or just body parts (the feet, hands, back, or head).

Use your creativity for where and how you rub your partner's body. Confidence and desire to please are the most important factors. Tune in to your partner's feelings, to gauge what pleases him or her most. But always ask for, and follow, feedback about what feels best, or what is undesirable. Avoid pressing directly on the spine.

To give a back massage, try this: Slightly raise the temperature in your room and dim the lights. Use a light, nongreasy lotion (warm it first). Kneel by your partner's side, sit on your buttocks, or stand. Lean in for more pressure. Place one hand on either side of the spine at the lower back and slide up to the neck and back, warming the spine. Then slide up and outward to the shoulders. Wrap your fingers around the shoulders, thumbs pressing into the muscles, and work your way back up to the neck. Now start at the lower back and make circles outward to the sides of the body, as if spreading the back muscles wider, as you work your way up the back. For another variation, start from the spine and trace your thumbs outward, as if you were tracing the rib cage. Then do similar motions going downward into the buttocks. Establish a rhythm, and then vary the stroke (knead, roll, squeeze, or tap).

Different massage techniques help to relax or open up various parts of the body, which allow the person to breath easier. An excellent technique, taught by counselor Lori Starr at California-based Celebrations of Love's "Breath, Love and Passion" workshop, "opens up" specific body regions.

There are three stages to Starr's exercise. The receiving partner lies comfortably on the floor, arms at her side, while breathing slowly and regularly from the abdomen. This should cause a rise of the abdominal area on the inhale. The chest does not move. The partner giving the massage kneels at her side, or may move to stand or kneel over the receiver. After the sequence, the partners switch places.

Dr. Judy Rx

Prepare your room—and yourselves—for your massage. Use soft lighting, clean sheets and pillows to prop body parts for comfort.

Love Lookout

Pay careful attention to your partner's feedback, as improper massages can cause damage. Also, be aware that certain kinds of touches in certain places may trigger emotions other than pleasure, like shame, anger, or hurt. In fact, certain massage therapies bank on this. Without training, either ease up, or allow these feelings to come up and help your partner work them through as best you can.

> **Stage 1:** Open up the abdomen. Rub the receiver's abdomen gently, with circular motions.

Stage 2: Open up the spine. Stand at the receiver's feet and pull on her legs, and then press forward, so she can feel the full range of her spine.

Stage 3: Open up the chest. Massage the chest starting at the lowest rib. Place your hands at the center of the rib cage and trace your hands outward, massaging on either side of each rib (not on the bone) with your thumb and forefingers. Use the pads of your fingers, with four fingers above the rib and the thumb below. Do one rib at a time. Come back to the center to do the next rib up. Work your way up all the ribs. Then ask the receiver to turn over, and repeat the same pattern on the back. Allow the receiver to rest after you are done.

Acupressure for Lovers

If you've ever been tense and instinctively put your fingers to your temples and pressed hard, you know the principle of acupressure—pressing on certain energy points of the body in order to effect a desired change toward more well-being. Remember the last time your lover gave you a big bear hug? Besides just feeling good, certain points in your energy system might have been similarly contacted to release positive feelings. Touching these points purposefully can either relax or arouse you.

Love Bytes

Acupressure uses the same principles and points of contact as acupuncture, a practice that involves inserting hair-thin needles into the skin at strategic points. Although popular in the Orient, acupressure was largely ignored in America until about 25 years ago. By the 1970s, dozens of professional organizations and publications were reporting the value of this technique for increased health, particularly in reducing pain.

The practice of acupressure originated in China over five thousand years ago and is based on the principles of releasing and balancing life energy—qi or chi—that flows through the body. The energy flows along certain meridians linked to various body organs. The energy is affected by pressing, rubbing, kneading, or vibrating points in the body with the fingers, hands, or other body parts (including elbows or feet).

Couples can perform acupressure on each other, using the power of touch to relax and awaken sensations in their bodies. California acupressure expert Michael Reed Gach, Director of the Acupressure Institute in Berkeley, California, offers seminars, books, and videos to teach the technique. Basically, you press and hold special points on each other's body to open spiritual intimacy and intensify pleasure through embraces, stretches, and movements. Couples who do it have found that the practice deepens their trust and passion.

Gach tells of his close friends, Gail and Scott, who, after 10 years together, felt sex had become "sort of mechanical." Often, they skipped foreplay, or Scott would perfunctorily stimulate Gail manually, leaving her feeling unsatisfied. After six weeks of the acupressure exercises, they felt a renewal of their initial magnetic attraction. As Gail sat in Scott's lap, rocking and pressing her hands into his back, she felt a tremendous flow throughout her body, inspiring her to writhe and slide joyfully against him as she had not done in years. Scott had changed too, breaking out of his habit of touching Gail in only one spot on her body, discovering new places on her that he had ignored for so many years.

Try this exercise: Sit opposite each other and cradle yourself in your partner's lap with your legs either folded under you or outstretched behind your partner. Wrap your arms around each other's back. Start at the neck and press the pads of your fingers alongside each side of the spine (not on the bone itself). Work your way down the spine to the lower back. Move your hands in unison with each other.

Reflexology

Few people are open about foot worship. I'm sure you know some men and women who are so self-conscious about their feet that they won't allow a lover to see their tootsies, much less touch them.

However, massage of the feet (or the hands, or the fingers) can be extremely pleasurable as well as healthy. The effects can be relaxing or stimulating. It was one of the things my stepfather did for my mother that she loved most—and they had a wonderful love life for all the years he was alive.

No wonder. The feet have over 7,000 nerve endings that are interconnected through the spinal cord and brain to all areas of the body. These connections account for the startling health benefits of foot massage. The following diagram, from leading New York reflexologist, Laura Norman, depicts how the feet are a "mini map" of the body from head to trunk, with every section of the foot corresponding to an organ or gland.

Love Lookout

Always do these exercises in the spirit of fun and play. But be alert to your partner's reactions, and ask for feedback about what touches are more or less pleasurable. While it's unlikely that you would ever hurt one another, some people may have injuries or sensitive spots that require caution in positions, movements, and intensity of touch.

Dr. Judy's Rx

Become "sole mates": Spend time pampering your own feet for lovemaking, so you are more proud of them. Wash and apply cream to each other's feet. She can cut his toenails; he can apply toenail polish for her.

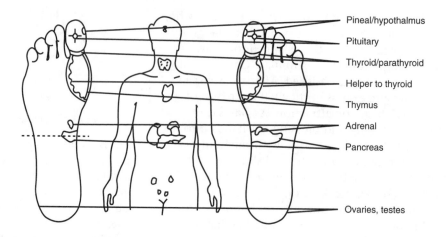

Pineal/hypothalmus

Pituitary

Thyroid/parathyroid

Helper to thyroid

Thymus

Adrenal

Pancreas

Ovaries, testes

Imagine your trunk reduced and superimposed on the bottom of your foot. When you touch a spot on the foot, you are actually touching the corresponding organ or gland elsewhere in the body. Your toes refer to your head and the middle of your foot is your waistline.

(From Feet First: A Guide to Foot Reflexology [Simon & Schuster, 1988] by Laura Norman)

In addition, as shown in following diagram, the outer ankles correspond to the ovaries and testes. The top of the inner ankle refers to the prostate and uterus, the bottom to the penis and vagina. The arc across the top of the foot refers to the woman's Fallopian tubes (wherein the sperm unites with the egg) and the man's vas deferens (the tube that carries the sperm into the penis). The mammary glands are related to the top of the foot at the base of the toes. Pressing on these spots connects with those organs.

To give your partner a good foot massage to enhance sexual functioning, Norman advises that you stroke the feet gently, using a light, greaseless lotion, first together and then individually. (Varying motions can be used later, including pressing, squeezing, and kneading.) Press gently on the solar plexus point—the hollow under the ball of the foot, beneath the second and third toe. Then start at the bottom of each foot with the "thumb walk" (inching both thumbs up to the toes and back again). Give extra attention to tender spots, and spots corresponding to the heart and reproductive organs. Make small circular rotational movements on these spots, and rotate the ankle. End with breezy strokes of both feet. Norman recommends two or three sessions a week, lasting 30 minutes each.

Dr. Judy's Rx

Ease a headache that can interfere with sex by pressing on the toe.

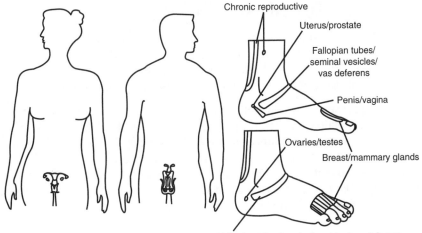

The outer ankles correspond to the ovaries and testes.

(*From* Feet First: A Guide to Foot Reflexology *[Simon & Schuster, 1988]*)

Aromatherapy

Scent is an important way to spice up your love life. Aromatherapy applies this principle by using scented oils to stimulate the brain in ways that sharpen the senses and trigger emotional states, from relaxation to arousal.

Using fragrant oils to heal—or to arouse—lovers is a practice that has been around for centuries in Egypt, India, and China. The chemicals present in extracts from various plants, shrubs, trees, and flowers penetrate body tissues to interact with the nervous system to affect physical conditions, modify immune response, balance emotions, and act as aphrodisiacs.

Each oil, or combination of oils, has specific properties that actually affect brain wave patterns that result in various states. Mixtures relevant to sex depend on the mood you want to create. Some mixtures include relaxation (lavender, chamomile, persephone, and orange); stimulation (rosemary, basil, black pepper, and cardamom); and sensuality (rose, jasmine, ylang-ylang, patchouli, sandalwood, clary sage, and myrtle). Jasmine and rose achieve both calming and sensual effects.

Oils are diluted or applied directly on the skin or in the hair, in baths, in massage oil blends, on light bulbs, or on sheets or clothing. They can be dropped or dabbed from vials or misted from spray containers. You can get premixed combinations of oils, or starter kits (with vials you mix) from various health food stores.

349

Making Beautiful Music Together

Music wouldn't be such a multimillion-dollar business if it didn't have such a powerful effect on our psyche. In fact, sounds have been scientifically proven to affect our mood, change brain waves, and reduce or increase stress, blood pressure, and/or heart rate. Therefore, music affects our overall mood, balance, and strength.

You and your partner can make beautiful music together. Sounds can be made with your own voice, or all kinds of household items that are readily accessible. The easiest, of course, is percussion sounds, made by banging spoons on pots. Look around and see things in your home on which you can make sounds. Or go to a music store and purchase various items (drums, bells, tambourines) that make sound. Use the instruments to "talk" to one another instead of using words. Try "talking" one at a time, and then together, as if the two of you were in a band.

Toning

Sounds of different tones connect to various energy centers of the body. Toning involves making elongated vowel sounds on various parts of the body. Making the sound on a particular body part awakens that part and the emotions connected to it. For example, toning at the heart area will awaken the feelings of warmth and love. Toning at the belly area will trigger feelings of strength or vulnerability. But the sound also resonates through the body, like an internal massage. I have experienced a master of this process, shamanic and sound healer Karin Schelde, do this. While an experienced master of toning and chanting can accelerate such work, there is no harm, and there can be considerable gain, to couples doing this on their own.

Love Bytes

In general, lower sounds are earth tones and evoke feelings related to power, while higher tones tend to break through thought patterns and evoke sensuality. It is not necessary to make any one particular sound. Some experts insist that following your intuition is the best process.

In one exercise I learned at one of Shelde's workshops, the couple gets together on the bed or any special area they have made comfortable with rugs or pillows. Choose one person to be the "sounder" first. That person leans over the partner and chooses a body part. Put your mouth over that body part and be still for a moment, just "listening," and make the sound that seems naturally to come out of your mouth. Don't worry about what it sounds like. The particular sound is not important. The partner listens to the sound, and then either matches the sound, or better yet, harmonizes with it, making a sound that is close but not exactly like it. Again, don't worry about musical ability. As you get more comfortable with this exercise, the sounds will get better. As the sounds meld, you will feel increasingly connected. Sound together for about a minute, or as long as you feel the energy. Then move to another body part and make another sound. As both your sounds harmonize, you'll find yourselves feeling more in harmony with each other.

Love Molding

A favorite movement technique to enhance couples connection, used by my friend, psychotherapist Joan Lessin, is called "love molding." To do this, put on any rhythmic piece of music and move to the music with your partner while being sure to stay connected at one point between your two bodies. Turn, twist, lower down and raise up, while still maintaining one contact point. The purpose of this exercise is to give you a sense of expressing yourself (because you move according to your own style), while still staying aware of, connected to, and cooperative with a partner.

Feng Shui

If you've ever felt that your environment affects your mood, you're right. The ancient Chinese art of feng shui goes even further in emphasizing the importance of bringing your surroundings into harmony with your spirit, and arranging them to maximize positive energies that support your relationship. Simply put, how, what, and where you put things in your house, and especially in your bedroom, can make or break your love life. New York–based feng shui practitioner Alex Stark recommends the following guidelines to enhance your love relationship.

Type of bed:

The bed itself greatly affects the health and politics of a relationship. Here are some things to watch out for:

➤ Consider a bed with rounded corners, as opposed to sharp right angles, to take the edges out of a rocky marriage.

➤ One large mattress is better than two twin ones put together, to eliminate division or barriers between you.

➤ The headboard should be higher than the footboard, to command your position. (A four-poster bed is fine.)

Placement of the bed:

To provide protection so you can enjoy sex freely, place the bed:

➤ Diagonally in the farthest corner of the room, not in direct line with the door, to ensure protection (so you can see who's entering) and also so it's not easily accessible. It you can't do this, hang a mirror so that you can see the door from the bed.

➤ So that there is equal space and access on each side of the bed (to establish equal power for you both). Use similar or identical night tables, with balanced (even if different) items on each. For example, one nightstand can hold a clock and the other a lamp, but one should not be empty while the other is crowded.

➤ So that the head of the bed rests against the wall, instead of setting away from the wall, to stabilize your consciousness and your marriage.

➤ So that the bed avoids heavy, crowded bureaus and armoires on either side that cramp the space of the bed and your love.

➤ In the far-right corner, to maximize the potential of your relationship, as this is the direction of marriage and relationships as shown in the feng shui grid (see the diagram later in this chapter).

Placement in the bedroom:

In addition, follow these do's and don'ts for harmony in the bedroom:

➤ Do decorate with pairs of objects (matching candleholders, sculptures, lamps) to emphasize pairing and the harmony of twosomes.

➤ Do decorate with objects, shapes and pictures with round corners, circles, ovals, and other womb-like images, as symbols of marital harmony.

➤ Do have real roses or peonies (or pictures of them) to represent peace, love, and lasting values.

➤ Do add some large, heavy objects such as stones, sculpture, or furniture to stabilize your love.

➤ Don't have images or symbols of the desert or barren scenery, to avoid similar emptiness in love.

➤ Don't have overhanging beams or knifelike corners (such as a bureau) pointing at the bed, especially across it, since energy collects at corners, and pointed edges imply aggression.

Here are some other guidelines of placements in the home:

Dr. Judy's Rx

Clear clutter in your home to dispel disorder in your relationship. Stark suggests this rule: If you don't love it or don't use it, give it away or recycle it.

➤ If the male is too dominant, decorate with additional symbols of the feminine: seashells; wreaths; round, oval, or crescent shapes such as a round mirror; or the colors yellow, pink, or peach.

➤ If the female is too dominant, decorate with additional symbols of the masculine: square or blunt objects, grandfather clocks, hunting scenes and paraphernalia, metallic objects, and the color white.

➤ Avoid horseshoe-shaped houses with the entrance in the inset of the horseshoe, to ensure the partnership is not compromised.

➤ Avoid having the bedroom or bathroom at the end of a long corridor. Or divide the corridor in sections by using something that hangs (curtains, mobiles, or hanging chimes). The energy can become too intense as you walk, preventing rest (and risking sterility).

➤ Avoid three doors in a row, that pierces your heart energy. Separate them with a hanging chime or crystal.

➤ Close the door to the bathroom if it is adjacent to the bedroom, to close off the energy of elimination.

➤ Clear the space of objects (especially the bed) from former relationships, to eliminate the ex's energy. For example, a divorced woman who remarried and kept her old bed had similar sexual problems with her new husband. Similarly, sitting in an abusive ex-husband's favorite armchair continued a woman's feeling of helplessness. The moment she gave the chair away, her new relationship improved.

➤ Include one heavy object in the house to stabilize the relationship, such as a marble column or a stone table base.

➤ Create an altar of your love—a shelf or table top to display important memorabilia. Place it in the "relationships" corner of your room, as shown in the diagram. You both should contribute to and take care of this altar.

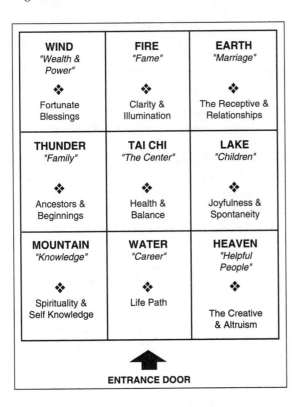

WIND *"Wealth & Power"* ❖ Fortunate Blessings	FIRE *"Fame"* ❖ Clarity & Illumination	EARTH *"Marriage"* ❖ The Receptive & Relationships
THUNDER *"Family"* ❖ Ancestors & Beginnings	TAI CHI *"The Center"* ❖ Health & Balance	LAKE *"Children"* ❖ Joyfulness & Spontaneity
MOUNTAIN *"Knowledge"* ❖ Spirituality & Self Knowledge	WATER *"Career"* ❖ Life Path	HEAVEN *"Helpful People"* ❖ The Creative & Altruism

ENTRANCE DOOR

In feng shui, the different areas in a room relate to the different aspects of life.

Love Lookout

The best way to find a qualified feng shui practitioner is by referral from a friend or other trusted health professional. Stark advises suspicion if large changes are suggested (such as moving), since a legitimate practice would require only minimal changes.

This diagram—called the bagua in the home—shows how areas in a room relate to different aspects of life. Picture the entrance to your room as equivalent to "entrance door" marked on the diagram, and then match up the area in your room to the square area on the diagram, to see what energy or aspect of life is found there.

Feng shui can be used to help overcome specific problems. In the case of sexual boredom, for example, reignite passion by using red colors in the house, bedroom, and on the bed. Keep fresh roses in the house to encourage the feeling of being "beloved." Include green colors or plants as symbols of rebirth and renewal. Display something gold to enhance the worth of your union. Place the bed or altar on the left side of the room to revive your beginnings (if that was a good time), or on the right side, to evoke joy.

Past Lives

Destiny—it's a word we sometimes use in relationships. It describes that feeling that you are inextricably, magically drawn together as if by some force that you cannot control that goes beyond just the "chemical attraction" of the moment. Somehow, you sense that you were "fated" to be together. You might feel that you have known each other before, perhaps, as if you have been together in a past life.

Love Lookout

Because some mediums who claim to do past life regression and rebirthing may allow their own issues and subconscious to affect their statements about you, seek a referral from a trusted friend and research a reader's training and references as much as possible. Experts advise, in most cases, take what is said as possibilities to consider, rather than as absolute truths.

Information about past lives with a mate can emerge from exploring your own past, as characters and issues similar to your present relationship emerge. You can also talk together about what you think may have happened between you. Conjecturing on your own or together, without trained guidance, can give you subjective information that can be useful in deepening your understanding and communication. But it is not always correct.

There are practitioners who offer services and techniques to help people connect with their past lives. A select few of these are able to read what's called the Akashic Records—the records of our souls' journey through time. Those may be opened with only the utmost reverence and respect. They contain detailed information about our past lives. A trained reader of the

Records is Dr. Roberta Herzog, a gifted clairvoyant and student and teacher in the applied metaphysical fields for nearly four decades. I've had the honor and joy of talking with her extensively to report the information in this section.

Practitioners in this area use terminology such as "past life regression," "rebirthing," and "soul traveling." Because of the lack of uniform credentials and controls in this field, there is some controversy about who and what techniques are legitimate. Some practitioners, for example, will give you information about what they "see" in your past. Others put you in a relaxed state, and merely guide you as you imagine yourself and what you have been through. I have been through both experiences and found both interesting. If you suspend disbelief, and trust that what seems meaningful to you is useful, you can gain from the resulting insights.

Dr. Judy's Rx

It's always helpful to tape-record your sessions so you can review the information later. It's difficult and distracting to try to remember everything that transpired during the session, given the uniqueness of the subject matter.

If different information emerges from readings, it doesn't necessarily negate any one piece of information. Rather than insisting on absolute truth, remember that what really matters is what you make of it.

If you accept the principle that any information that comes to you about past lives together is valid food for thought, at least in creating interesting dialogue between the two of you, then happily explore a discussion about your past connections. Start with just talking about whether you believe in past lives. That alone will spark awareness that can lead to ideas coming to you at other points in time, perhaps in the bathtub, driving in the car, or during meditative moments.

The Least You Need to Know

➤ Meditating together puts you on the same wavelength.

➤ Making sounds on each other's bodies keeps you in tune.

➤ Scents can intensify your sensuality.

➤ Massaging each other physically keeps you in touch emotionally and spiritually.

➤ How you decorate your home can boost your love life.

➤ Considering your past lives together can be an interesting and informative way to explore your present life together.

Chapter 29

Helping Each Other Toward a Healthier Relationship

In This Chapter

➤ How dating keeps love alive

➤ The "Getting to Know You" Quiz

➤ Communication techniques

➤ When, where, and to whom to go for professional help

➤ Types of counseling and sex therapy

➤ New sources of advice

In Part 1, "The Signs of a Healthy Relationship in the New Millennium," you learned about what makes a relationship healthy and whether or not your partner is the one for you. Then you learned about the secrets to keeping your relationship loving and lasting, including how to keep the passion alive. You even know how to jump over any love hurdle that may spring up on you. And finally in the previous chapter you learned about fun and slightly offbeat exercises to add spark and freshness so you and your mate can connect on an entirely different level.

Sure, you know the looks, sounds, and feelings of what it's like to be in a healthy relationship ... and an unhealthy one. However, from time to time, the "elements"—stress and time—can chip away at that solid foundation your love was built on. It's then that you may feel that your relationship is less than ideal. There's room for improvement (maybe a lot of it) and you're ready to be proactive and take serious measures. So what can you do?

This chapter begins with simple exercises you and your partner can do together and then offers advice on when and where to seek professional help. More people today accept how therapy can help them realize that it's often helpful to have a third party present to help you communicate together. I'm sure you know what it feels like to be frustrated when you try to get through to each other and can't seem to get anywhere. In these cases, it's clear when a professional guide, facilitator, or therapist would be helpful. But it's also a good idea not to wait until things get that serious. Try seeking more guided experiences to enhance what goes on between you.

For any helpful exercise (or therapy) to work, you have to work together. One person "fixing" himself or herself is not enough. You have to sort out your issues together and come to mutual agreements about how to treat each other. Both people have to be committed to improving the relationship.

Self-Help

Self-help refers to ways you can both help yourselves make your relationship better. One simple self-help technique involves asking yourself key questions to uncover issues and get you back on a positive track.

Try this exercise, asking yourself these key questions:

➤ Name three things that initially attracted you to your mate. Perhaps you fell in love with him because he told you wonderful things about yourself. Perhaps he fell in love with you because you were a powerful woman who knew what she wanted. Share your lists and add to them constantly.

➤ List your short and long-term goals for the relationship (what you want in three months and in three years). Use this as a basis for agreements about how you will accomplish these goals.

Ask yourself other questions that help you focus on appreciating and improving your relationship. These include:

➤ "What's good about this relationship?"

➤ "What's not perfect about this relationship?"

➤ "What am I doing to make this relationship go the way I want?"

Keep Dating

Couples start out trying to impress one another, asking questions and listening attentively, wanting to know everything about each other. Then, they stop asking questions, fall into a rut, and take each other for granted. The solution to this: Always treat each other like new lovers, eager to intrigue the other. Don't assume you know everything; there is always something new to learn. Refer to my previous book, The *Complete Idiot's Guide to Dating,* and to Chapter 10 of this book, "Making the Honeymoon Last," for good ideas. My bottom-line, favorite advice: Keep asking each other questions that you would a new date. Any question can have a different answer over time—even your favorite color may change!

The Getting to Know You Quiz

Ask your partner questions you would of someone you just met and want to impress. Use the following questions, or make up your own. Listen to the answer with the same rapt attention as you would if you were falling for your partner for the first time. Write down your own answers and share them, if you like.

Questions about each of you:

What's the funniest thing that ever happened to you?

What's the quality you most like that you inherited from your mother/father?

What did you want to be when you grew up?

What new thing would you most like to learn to do?

What one lesson has served you best in life?

Other:

Questions about your relationship:

What was the best/worst time we ever had together?

What is the best thing you ever received from me?

What gives you the most joy about us?

When did you know it was love?

How have things changed between us?

Other:

Modeling

Remember the old phrase, "Do as I say, not as I do." Instead of complaining about what you want your mate to do, be an example. Do what you would like him to do.

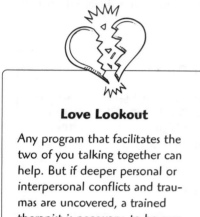

Instead of Elizabeth nagging Kenny that he was not being romantic enough, she nuzzled next to him, to show him what she liked.

Love Lookout

Any program that facilitates the two of you talking together can help. But if deeper personal or interpersonal conflicts and traumas are uncovered, a trained therapist is necessary, to be sure that you can handle and integrate the material revealed.

Self-Disclosure

In a variation of modeling, instead of asking a mate to open up about an issue, talk about yourself. So when Elizabeth wanted Kenny to talk more, instead of insisting he do the talking, she started out saying how she herself felt about being open.

Taking Time Out

I described this technique in Chapter 23, "Time Out on Fighting." Instead of continuing to argue or fight about something in an endless circle, take time out. Consider this a cool-down period to clear your heads so you can talk more rationally.

Healthy or Unhealthy?

Pillow fights and wrestling can be a healthy way to get out your aggression and spark your energy for lovemaking. Raymond called my radio show saying he would like to wrestle with his girlfriend, but she objects. She is likely frightened of aggression, but needs to allow herself to engage in innocent energetic play with him.

"As If"

This is another of my favorite psychological techniques. Instead of complaining about how things are not the way you want, act "as if" they are the way you want. This may sound like pretending, but it can make things better. Acting as if things are a certain way makes it more likely that they will actually become that way.

"Back in Time"

As described earlier about your first dates, go back in time and relive the way things were between you when they were at their best. Like the "as if" technique, this may feel phony at first, but it becomes more natural and more real. Remembering and reliving good times gives you a head start on starting new positive patterns now.

Couples' Journal

Just as you would keep a diary of your own life, keep a diary of the events and feelings that happen to you as a couple. Review these entries monthly to recover your memories, and to make new resolutions about what is both positive in your relationship and what needs more help.

Picturing It Makes It So

Rehearse and review in your mind what you would like to have happen in your relationship. This technique, called "imaging," makes it more likely that it will happen, like making a mold of how you'd like to behave. I know this from extensive work I've done with brain researcher Ned Herrmann and from the work of popular author and motivational speaker Tony Robbins. Such programming has long been an accepted technique to help sports stars achieve peak performance. Likewise in sex, get a picture in your mind of how you want the encounter to go, rehearse it in your head, and then "feel" the sensations in your body as if they were really happening. Now you're ready to tell your partner all those wonderful discoveries to increase both of your pleasure.

Love Bytes

Remember: You choose. You are not stuck in the relationship. Every day you choose to be together. Happiness comes from choice; depression comes from feeling trapped.

Communication Workshops

As you learned in Chapter 10, "Communication—Can We Talk?" communication is key to a healthy relationship. Every therapeutic program includes some processes for improving communication between partners. The specific methods to achieve this and the nature of the program (length, leader's background, setting, type of participants) vary immeasurably.

I-Power

I-Power is a management tool developed by my friend Marty Edelston, a business guru whose company, Boardroom, Inc., runs workshops on business and life improvement. The "I" in I-Power relates to many words that start with "I," including "Ideas," "Imagination," "Improvement," and "Innovation." The principles of "I-Power" apply to every aspect of your career and personal life, including your love relationship.

Ken Glickman is Boardroom's coordinator of educational services. He and his wife Daphne, an attorney for an international law firm, use I-Power in their marriage to show how important they are to each other. Ken and Daphne both work long and late hours, but when each gets home, the other drops whatever he or she is doing for a warm greeting. You know how easy it is in a relationship to continue watching TV, logging on your computer, or putting the kids to bed when your partner comes in.

But if Daphne is on the phone when Ken gets home, she says good-bye and hangs up immediately for a hug.

Ken recommends you do this exercise. Ask yourself, "Am I willing to come up with something right now that I can do, to make my relationship better?" (Hopefully, you said yes.) Now write down one idea that you can use to do that. You can draw in outside sources (for example, "I will read a book about relationships."). Writing it down is important because the conscious and the subconscious unite magically when you write something down. Begin with one small thing that you can do to show appreciation to your lover, be more lovable, or improve your communication. That will lead to another big step, which will lead to something bigger.

I-Power card.

> ### The "I"-Power® of Love
> *(ideas, imagination, involvement, etc., to improve my relationship)*
>
> From _____ To _____
>
> Today's Date _____
>
> **What one, little thing can I do to make this relationship better?** (one idea per card)
>
> _____
> _____
> _____
> _____
> _____
>
> Response From _____ To _____
>
> Today's Date _____
>
> (e.g. "That sounds great!," "Thanks for thinking about me, but not now," "That's not quite what I need," "Wow!," "What I'd prefer is...," etc.)
>
> _____
> _____
>
> ® The Greenwich Institute for American Education

Have an Idea box with a stack of index cards that you can write your idea on. Each of you should submit at least one card a week. Keep coming up with new ideas. One evening a week, review your submissions, taking turns to present your own ideas while the other listens. Reward yourselves for an idea you both agree on. Rewards should be for both of you, such as a dinner out (so neither of you has to cook or clean).

A Love Ritual

In Chapter 4, "Is It True Love?" I described how performing certain rituals—a series of deliberate acts as if in a ceremonial form—is becoming a trend in healing. The goal of these rites is to clear negative patterns and to show each other that you are special to one another.

Love Bytes

Most people look at relationships and think about what the other person can do to make it better. "Our relationship would be better if he listened to me more," or "We wouldn't argue so much if she weren't so demanding." Instead, always think, "what can I do?" If both people do this, the positive results escalate.

Maria and John were experiencing a typical problem for couples: When they first met, it seemed like a dream come true, but once the romantic high wore off, everything seemed negative and not worth the effort. If something positive is not done at this point in the relationship, communication stops and passion fades. The couple starts focusing on all the negatives, and ignores the positives. If this continues uninterrupted, people end up leaving each other to find another love.

Barbara Bizou, a pioneer and expert in rituals for healing, and author of *The Joy of Everyday Rituals* (St. Martin's, 2000) told the couple that they weren't giving their relationship enough of a chance because they were holding negative pictures of each other in their minds. This was clouding their judgment and making it hard for the two of them to communicate their needs.

As Bizou explains, when you hold "negative thought forms" of a partner in your mind, you cast that person in a negative light and close off the whole picture of how he or she is. As a result, even if the person is willing to change certain behaviors, it is impossible for him or her to do so. Think of how you act when those around you expect the best from you, versus when nothing you can do is ever right. Eventually you stop trying and communication shuts down.

Try this exercise, a ritual Bizou created to help Maria and John establish a more positive focus on their relationship. Provide two pictures of each other. Each of you take the first picture of the other and place it in the middle of a clean sheet of paper. Write all the big complaints and small irritations you are experiencing around the picture. For example, "He is not sensitive enough to my feelings," or "She laughs too loudly." When you finish, look at all the negative thought forms you hold about your partner.

Next, take turns reading aloud what you wrote, lighting a match to the paper, and then burning the paper over the metal bowl. As you do so, say aloud: "I affirm that I release this image I have of you." Both of you must agree to be open to hearing what bothers the other, without lashing out defensively at each other. Remember that the intention is to heal, not hurt.

Now take the second picture and surround it with positive qualities. For example, write, "He is a deeply caring person," or "She has a great sense of humor." Look into each other's eyes and take turns reading aloud what you wrote on the paper. After one of you reads, the other (who listened to the positive qualities) takes the paper and reads them, saying, "I hear that you think that I am …" After the reading, hug and hold each other and then do some activity together, such as making dinner or taking a walk.

Put the picture where you can see it (near the bed or on the refrigerator). Every day for a month, write in a notebook more good qualities that you see in your partner. As weeks go on, both of you will begin to create a new positive image of each other. Feeling more appreciative helps your love for the other grow. Feeling appreciated increases your positive self-image and that of your partner.

Bare, Dare to Share

Some communication exercises encourage sharing between the couple not only to deepen the bond between them, but to help them become therapeutic aids to each other. The exercise helps them uncover how their own interactions have roots in the past.

Love Bytes

First, clear the air—express what upsets you lately with your mate. Then review similar interactions from the past. Your mate helps repair the old hurt by acting as a "stand-in" for that person from the past, reliving the experience with an outcome that makes you feel better.

"Daring, Baring, Sharing and Caring" is a unique program developed by Dr. Sasha Lessin, a Hawaii-based voice dialogue facilitator, holotropic breathworker, and relationships counselor. It incorporates some techniques of marriage counseling from famed psychologist Harville Hendrix and the voice dialogue techniques developed by Drs. Hal and Sidra Stone. Couples are guided through specific dialogues with one another, intended to uncover upsets between them and similar painful interactions from the past. Couples ask each other a series of questions, while using active listening (as described in Chapter 8). Through expressing suppressed feelings to each other, they develop more trust and experience acceptance and help from each other.

One woman in Dr. Lessin's workshop used to fly into violent rages when her husband woke up first and hugged her from behind while she slept. In a "Daring, Baring, Sharing and Caring" workshop exercise, she told him how, as a child, she'd been sexually molested at night in this position. She asked him, as a healing service, to make sure that she was awake before he pressed his aroused manhood against her, and to whisper his name (so she wouldn't unconsciously think he was her abuser) and that he loved her. When he did as she asked, her violent impulses no longer triggered, and she could respond sexually to his advances.

When to Go for Therapy

Every couple has upsets, but it's time to get professional help when:

➤ You are arguing more often than keeping the peace.

➤ One of you is unhappy most of the time.

➤ The two of you are not communicating.

➤ You complain a great deal about each other to other people.

➤ The stress between you is affecting other areas of your life.

➤ The problem between both of you has been going on for three months or more.

➤ You feel "stuck" or unable to change by yourselves.

➤ Other people point out to you that your relationship is in trouble.

Dr. Judy's Rx

Even if you're not sure what the problem is, going for a session can help you find out. There is very little to lose and much to gain from reassurance that you are on the right track.

Couples Counseling

Couples are facing increased stress from all aspects of financial, work, and family life. Fortunately, as in the case of individual therapy, couples counseling no longer has a stigma attached.

While there are many types of counseling programs to help couples improve their relationship, they generally fall into two basic categories:

➤ Programs to enhance your relationship, usually centering on communication techniques and focusing on specific behavior and attitude changes, without delving into deep psychological problems or dynamics.

Love Bytes

One study showed counseling reduced separations to 20 percent less than average and decreased physical aggression by half. As a result of such findings, some states are considering laws to help reduce high divorce rates, such as instituting a "covenant marriage" that would require premarital counseling.

➤ Therapy programs that probe into deeper psychological and emotional issues in each individual, and the complicated interpersonal dynamics between the two people. They uncover deep feelings toward each other, unexpressed disappointment or anger, or patterns from childhood.

A plethora of group programs are also available, run by individual therapists or organizations ranging from local YMCAs and churches to specialty schools and health expos. When not in the context of formal therapy, these programs don't involve extensive or long-term commitments. Any number of couples who sign up can meet together with the leader or facilitator, in locations that vary from offices to exotic weekend getaways. The sessions are usually highly structured and include assigned exercises to be done at home.

Ask Dr. Judy

"Our marriage has not been good for the last three years, but my husband insists there is nothing wrong and refuses to go for help. I keep telling him he's wrong and warn him if the marriage falls apart it'll be his fault. I'm at the end of my rope. What do I do?"

Since any problem in your relationship is usually not one person's but both people's fault, create a united rather than an adversarial atmosphere by replacing blame and threats with an emphasis on shared feelings (need for more harmony, respect, agreement) and hopes for the future. Start a conversation at a time when you are both feeling relaxed and close, and emphasize your desire to expand those pleasurable moments.

Reconsider your husband's denial not as defiance against you, but as a defense against his anxiety (fear of change, shame, guilt, even worry over the expense of therapy). Offer reassurances (confidentiality, respect, availability of clinics offering services by your ability to pay). Appeal to his rational mind by explaining that seeking professional help for a relationship problem is equivalent to a medical consultation for a physical disorder. As a last resort, ask him to come with you for help as a favor (to take the pressure off him). Or go alone, for more confidence and support about what to do next.

Couples Therapy

Formal couples therapy involves sessions in the therapist's office, at a hospital, special clinic, or (more likely today) in the therapist's home. Each of you might be seen privately for several sessions, or at the beginning of a session, and then together. For years, I like other therapists, worked in a team, so couples could see a male and female in different combinations; but rising costs have made this option less available.

The first session should include a history of your problems including a diagnosis and treatment plan (as with any doctor), as well as expectations, and explanation of the process. Questions you should be asked include: "What's bothering you both now?" "How bad does it get?" "What do you each want to happen from the therapy?"

Questions you ask should include: "What does this involve?" "What will it cost?" "How long do you estimate we will have to come?" "What is the nature of what will happen?"

Subsequent sessions involve helping you both express feelings, facilitating your communication, diffusing blame, and planning specific solutions (for example, "schedule time for each other into your daily planners").

Counseling can be long-term and occur over years, but more likely these days—partly due to costs and insurance allowances—it is short-term, meaning over a period of three to six months. Intensive weekend retreats or 10-session programs are increasingly popular.

Costs can vary, depending on the setting and the training of the therapist, from $45 to $250 an hour. Some hospitals, clinics, and private practitioners have sliding scales, charging according to what you can afford.

Dr. Judy's Rx

Always check with your insurance company about reimbursement for specific diagnostic categories and couples counseling. Find out what amount is allotted and for how many sessions.

Love Lookout

People of varying credentials call themselves counselors. Don't be afraid to ask about training, degrees, and experience. Contact any national organizations in their particular discipline for information, referrals, and licensure. Feel free to interview more than one source or counselor to find someone you feel good about.

Finding the Right Therapist

There are many titles for people who offer services to help couples with their relationship problems. These include more medical-centered therapists—"psychiatrists" and "clinical psychologists" like myself. Then there are advisors of various backgrounds, from "marriage counselors" to "facilitators," "leaders," and even "healers." As the saying goes, even your next-door neighbor can put up a shingle to do therapy. Across the United States there are about 40,000 clinical psychologists, 40,000 psychiatrists, and over 100,000 social workers (versed in community resources), pastoral counselors (with religious backgrounds), psychiatric nurses, and marriage and family therapists.

As with any medical doctor you choose, you are most assured of professionalism by seeing someone who is a graduate of an accredited training program, and who has a professional license and years of experience. But "lay" practitioners can have much to offer in their field of specialty (communication, anger, sexual enhancement), depending on the match between your needs and their expertise. It's always best to have a recommendation from someone you trust who has worked with the practitioner. You can also ask your doctor, call your local hospital, or contact the various professional organizations (such as the American Psychological Association or the Association for Marital and Family Therapists).

Does Couples Counseling Work?

Over the many years I have been a therapist, I've been impressed by how much couples can be helped in just several sessions. Three top benefits are:

1. Getting an objective opinion about the problem between them

2. Getting some direction on what to do about it

3. Facilitating communication between the two partners

Love Bytes

Couples counseling is not just for people who have made a considerable commitment to each other (getting engaged or married). You can gain a great deal of knowledge about yourself individually and in the relationship by going to counseling sessions with any willing partner, even if you are not married.

Counseling is not a magic cure. It takes work. Often the tensions between you get worse when they are revealed and examined. There are ups and downs. Some couples split up. Therapy couldn't save the marriage of Liz Taylor and Larry Fortensky, or dozens of similar high-profile Hollywood couples, as well as average people. What makes it work is your commitment to make it work, no matter what.

How long does therapy take? You'll know you're finished when you've reached the goals you and the therapist outlined, and when changes in your relationship (from communication to sex) become stable.

Going for therapy is not a sign of weakness in yourself or your relationship, but a sign of strength that you are willing to confront and conquer your own demons, and a sign of respect for your partner's well being. Even though it may be painful along the way, it is an exciting journey to more freedom and happiness for both of you.

Here are three key signs that you are better:

➤ You no longer argue all time.

➤ You don't need to tell your friends your problems.

➤ Your life together is more balanced (between responsibilities and enjoyment).

Couples Sex Therapy

There are so many types of help available for couples that it can be very confusing. As with couples counseling, sex therapy counseling basically falls into two categories:

➤ Programs for enhancement of your sexual relationship, offering techniques and exercises to improve your sexual interaction and increase your pleasure together, without delving into deep psychological problems or dynamics. These usually involve various behavioral sex therapy techniques—specific "what to do" steps to change your behavior. The sessions would cover giving permission (to enjoy sex); making specific suggestions (about positions, timing, activities, books, and sex aids); correcting inaccurate information (for example, that men must have erections to enjoy sex or that vaginal orgasms are superior to clitoral ones), and reviewing "homeplay" exercises.

➤ More formal therapy programs, as described earlier, that probe into psychological issues in each of you as individuals, and complicated interpersonal dynamics. In most cases, these therapies go beyond sex, toward resolving more general interpersonal problems.

Some group programs also exist that focus on improving couples' sex lives. Four or more couples meet together with the leader, facilitator, or therapist, to discuss problems, hear feedback, and get suggestions and support from the others.

Finding a Sex Therapist

There are just as many types of sex therapists as the general therapists I mentioned earlier. Seeing a qualified sex therapist to treat your sexual problem is just as important as seeing a cardiac specialist, rather than a general practitioner, if you have a heart problem. It's usually a good bet to see a "clinician" who is trained in a specific discipline—such as

Love Bytes

Research has shown therapy success depends on three main factors: 1) How much you both really want to improve your relationship, 2) trust in your therapist, and 3) hope that your relationship can improve.

Love Bytes

If one of you has more severe personal problems or personality disorders, it may be necessary to seek individual counseling either before couples counseling or concurrently. Additional therapy is particularly important in cases where addictions, abuse, and lifelong patterns of intimacy problems are present. Since half of sexual problems have associated physical causes, medical assessments should always be made.

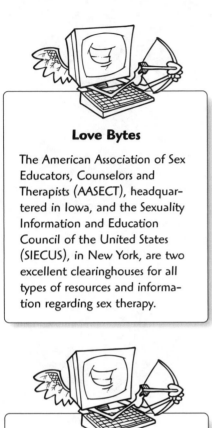

Love Bytes

The American Association of Sex Educators, Counselors and Therapists (AASECT), headquartered in Iowa, and the Sexuality Information and Education Council of the United States (SIECUS), in New York, are two excellent clearinghouses for all types of resources and information regarding sex therapy.

Love Bytes

Sex therapy has spread to other countries in the world. There is even a "World Congress of Sexology" that meets every two years in a different country around the globe, where professionals in all aspects of sexuality (medical, psychological, social) meet to exchange information and research. I have presented some of my work at these gatherings in Brazil and Japan.

psychology or psychiatry—who has studied personality dynamics and then specializes in treating sexual dysfunctions and applying various therapy techniques to help people change sexual attitudes and behavior. There are also various highly qualified sexuality educators, trained to give information about sexuality. In the past few years, a few accredited training programs have been established to train people specifically in sexuality. Many healers with years of experience in various alternative approaches can also be helpful.

As with tips about seeking a couples counselor, seek referrals from friends, family doctors, hospitals, and accrediting organizations. Don't be afraid to ask about the counselor's credentials, or to seek another opinion if you don't feel right in the session.

When to Go for Help With a Sexual Problem

It's time to seek professional help for a sexual problem when:

❏ The sexual problem lasts more than three months.

❏ The problem interferes with other areas of your work or relationships.

❏ You feel "stuck."

❏ You have what you think is a simple question (like "Why am I not as excited in sex as I used to be?") but never get a satisfying answer from any source (books, videos, friends).

Common Sexual Problems

Sexual problems run the gamut from involving one or both partners to being limited to one situation, happening all the time, being a simple straightforward issue, or being complicated by other problems.

Problems can be medical, psychological, interpersonal, or social. They can be related to attitudes or experiences and complicated by social stigmas or personal fears.

But in all my years of experience as a sex therapist, I've found the most common sexual problems include:

❏ **Couples getting bored with their sex life and not feeling turned on to each other after being together for a while.** Losing sexual desire used to commonly happen after seven years of togetherness and was called "the seven-year itch." Now, with the pace of life faster and people's expectations increasing, it can happen as "the two-year itch" or even less!

❏ **Problems with sexual desire.** This happens for women as well as men, especially now that women are working more and the pressures on them are greater. As a result, they too often get tired or stressed for sex.

❏ **Problems with sexual performance.** Ten million men in America have problems with erections. Many complain about not lasting long enough. Women have problems having orgasm: two thirds do not have orgasm in intercourse with their partner, and many women still don't have orgasm at all.

What Does Sex Therapy Cost?

Fees will vary. Top professionals charge from $100 to $175 for an hour-long private session; social workers or hospital clinics can be $35 to $100 a session. Groups may cost from $20 to $50 for a two-hour meeting. Although sexual problems are included in the official diagnostic manual of the psychiatric association, reimbursement allowances vary according to your insurance program.

Prognosis for a Cure

One of the reasons I gravitated toward treating sexual problems, after my extensive training as a clinical psychologist treating serious problems like depression and schizophrenia, was that I saw how quickly people could get better and what joy was restored into their lives. If a couple is really committed to each other and basically has a loving relationship with good communication, as few as 10 sessions once a week may solve the sexual problems between them. This might involve just structuring more time together, stating sexual needs, agreeing on acceptable behaviors, and specific suggestions about spicing up their sex life (as discussed in Chapter 17, "Keeping the Sex Fires Burning"). Improvements can occur in just a few sessions, as couples simply start communicating more with each other, and significant gains can occur with once-a-week sessions over a three-month period.

Sex therapy can work wonders. People get better from talking about their problem, realizing they are "normal" in their feelings, and putting specific suggestions into practice. I see so many couples walk out of my office smiling when they learn that just because they haven't made love together in months, it doesn't mean their relationship or love is over.

Newer Alternative and Nontraditional Sources of Therapy

While traditional couples counseling involves face-to-face sessions with a counselor, advances in technology, cost restraints, and innovation have led to many alternatives. These include innumerable audio and videotape series on making relationships work, seminars and workshops of all kinds run by all varieties of health professionals or healers, and forms of "media therapy" where people seek advice on radio, television shows, or on Web sites.

Love Bytes

It is always crucial to determine whether a problem is due to physical or psychological causes, so you can be referred for certain medical examinations before or during the treatment process.

Love Bytes

Several research studies done on my call-in shows over the years have shown that the majority of callers felt significantly helped by the short interaction on the air, citing reassurance, specific suggestions, and support.

Advice on the Radio

You can get help for relationship problems over the airwaves. All you need is a telephone and patience to get through after dialing the 800 number. Describe your situation, and you get about five minutes of advice. After 20 years of doing this work as a pioneer of such radio call-in advice talk, and doing therapy in hospitals and private practice before that, I've come to consider it the "5-minute" hour as opposed to the "45-minute" hour that is the traditional therapy session. Despite the shortness of the contact, my experience and pioneer research in this work have proven that callers can be greatly helped! Other advantages: Callers can be anonymous, at a safe distance, and in control (on the phone). On top of that, it's free.

Listeners are helped, too. Certainly, listening to people talk about their relationship problems over the air can be entertaining—as a guy speculates about where a woman's G-spot is, or a girl worries about her boyfriend's flirtation with her best friend. But after so many years on the air, I'm convinced that hearing other people's problems on the radio is not just amusing but therapeutic, for the listeners as well as the callers. Time and time again, people tell me how they were helped by hearing other people's problems similar to their own on the air, and how listening to the suggestions on solving the caller's problem helped them solve their own. Many times I have referred people with serious relationship problems who call on the radio to counseling or other sources of help. But consistently listening to the show, every weeknight for two hours, has been shown by research to provide a kind of continuous "vicarious therapy" experience.

Research on my radio show has also revealed people benefited in three major ways: being reassured they were not abnormal for their problems, finding out they were not the only ones in that dilemma, and getting specific help. Sometimes people call for help for one issue, and find themselves taking a turn in another, more constructive, direction. For example, Pam, a 28-year-old mother of two and married two years, called about her affair with a married co-worker. Initially, she wanted to know how she could get this man to leave his wife to be with her. Here's how some of our interaction went:

> **Dr. Judy:** How does that man treat you differently than your husband?
>
> **Pam:** He always says how happy he is to see me, and notices things like a new dress I'm wearing.
>
> **Dr. Judy:** Does your husband do that?
>
> **Pam:** No! He never seems to notice me or say nice things.
>
> **Dr. Judy:** So you need more attention from your husband. This is important for you, Pam. Think about how your lover is treating you. Can your spouse change? Can you work things out with your mate rather than just give up on your marriage?
>
> **Pam:** I always thought if I asked my husband to do things, he wouldn't anyway.
>
> **Dr. Judy:** Pam, you have to give him a chance. And be more assertive yourself. I'd like you to do an exercise. Write down on one side of a piece of paper all the things the perfect man would do for you. Then share these with your husband, and see which ones he will agree to do. Call us back and let us know how it went.

Fortunately, Pam did call back (and got through!). She said things were a little better since she did talk with her husband for the first time in ages. She still wasn't sure she'd stay with him, but it was a start.

Love Bytes

As radio advice shows became more popular, the Association of Media Psychologists was formed as a division of the American Psychological Association (APA), to recognize this form of advice-giving, provide guidelines, and ensure professionalism.

Television Talk Shows

Exposing couples' relationship problems on TV became the popular fare of daytime talk shows in the 1990s. I'm sure you've seen many of these, with hosts Oprah, Sally, Ricki, Geraldo, Montel, Maury, Leeza, Jenny, and Jerry. I've been a guest on all of them, with the distinction of being submitted to the Guinness Book of Records as the psychologist on the most talk shows the most often. I'm sure you also know how

Love Lookout

Beware of going on a TV to get revenge, embarrass, or expose a partner. Some TV producers have become just as concerned about people using such shows for their own purposes.

these shows came under great criticism for exploiting people's problems (especially when a guest on one show was tragically killed). But ratings still soar, proving, as with radio advice, that hearing other people's problems is compelling.

Critics of TV therapy say the shows give a false impression that problems have quick cures, prompt viewers to make drastic changes (like leaving a spouse) mistakenly, and leave the patient-guests on the show with exposed but unresolved problems. Defenders of TV therapy say that by demystifying marriage counseling and other forms of therapy, programs inspire viewers with similar problems to get help. Having been the "expert guest" on many of these shows, I have been touched and impressed with how these shows can actually help the people on them, and the people who watch them, deal with difficult or painful issues they may not otherwise have faced.

When couples make such a public admission, they are more committed to change. On one show I counseled a couple who had not had sex for the past 15 years. To the woman who had put up with her husband's disinterest for so long, my suggestion was that she really wants and deserves more love and attention and is just afraid to ask for it. We traced this to the fact that she had been sexually abused as a teenager, causing her to withdraw. The support of the live audience cheering her and challenging her husband made her tell him she didn't want to put up with such poor treatment anymore and wanted therapy. After the show I helped her get a referral in her town. The experience was very touching for everyone involved and certainly changed her life in a positive way that might not have happened otherwise.

So the "lights, camera, action" of TV therapy may air couples' dirty laundry, but can also lead to cleaning up their act!

Online Advice

I've discussed the impact of technology on a relationship extensively in Chapter 5, "So, You're a Couple—but Are You Friends?"

As the computer becomes a more common part of daily life, there are an increasing number of opportunities to obtain advice via the Internet. As with my radio show, my Web site was one of the first extensive sites to offer chat sessions and various formats for advice. You can surf the Internet for information now about any topic you are interested in. Since surfing the Net can cause division between you if one person indulges more than the other, create occasions to log on together (even with one keyboard). Check out sites, play computer games, and even participate in chat rooms together just as you might watch TV or read together. Playing on the computer can give you a great reason to spend time together and develop mutual interests.

The Least You Need to Know

➤ Anything you do together can be turned into an opportunity to learn about each other.

➤ Talk, write, and experience new things together to increase your closeness.

➤ Keep dating so you keep your interest in each other fresh.

➤ Seek professional help early and readily.

➤ Consider going to a couples workshop or seminar as a vacation. Use it as an opportunity for learning as well as fun, rather than as a burden or trouble.

➤ Use media outlets to ask questions about relationships, or to learn from other's experiences.

➤ Take advantage of any opportunity to improve your relationship.

Answers to the "Is It Healthy?" Quiz in Chapter 1

Now that you've learned about all the aspects of a healthy relationship, check your answers to the quiz you took in Chapter 1. How well did you do? Do you have the aspects of a healthy relationship down pat? Do you know how to achieve that ideal—the ideal that is your right to have: the relationship that is *working* on all five dimensions—physical, mental, emotional, sexual, and spiritual? And do you know how and why an attitude or behavior—that one or both of you may have—could be unhealthy? After reading through all these chapters, hopefully you have a better idea of how to prevent problems from interfering with the happiness you so well deserve.

Here are the answers to the questions about what is healthy or unhealthy in a relationship, and the chapters you can refer to, to read more about the particular issue. There is no reason why you can't have the healthiest relationship possible.

	Healthy	Unhealthy

1. **Q:** You say, "I love her/him to death."

   A: Saying "I love her to death" is unhealthy. Linking love   ✓
   with death has undesirable connotations. In addition,
   research proves that language affects reality. So watch
   your words carefully. It is healthier to say, "I love her
   till death" or even more preferable to use the word
   "life" associated with love. If you mean to imply
   longevity, say, "I will love him all of my life." Or if
   you mean to imply the extent of your love, say, "I
   love her more than anything." (See Chapter 4, "Is It
   True Love?")

	Healthy	Unhealthy

2. Q: You decide to marry because you're fed up with the dating scene.

   A: Of course, being "ready" to settle down may mean that you have sowed enough of your wild oats, but rather than *running from* the problems of being single, it is healthier to think of *moving toward* the value of being a couple. Deciding to marry should not be based just on your being tired of dating, but on the merits of the relationship itself. Otherwise, you will likely wake up months or years from then, wondering what you did. (See Chapter 11, "Commitment— Warming Up Cold Feet," for a full list of the issues, criteria, and factors to consider in determining whether this person is "the one" or whether it's the right time for you.)   ✓

3. Q: You ask for all the details about a past love or affair.

   A: Asking for all the details about an ex is unhealthy. Dwelling on what happened between your mate and another person in the past only prevents you from focusing on what's really important—what's going on between the two of you in the present, and making that the best it can be.   ✓

4. Q: You think that dreaming about an ex-love means you don't love your present mate.

   A: Worrying about your dreams is unhealthy. Dreams about an ex are not unhealthy—unless you obsess about them, or purposefully repeat a conscious fantasy about an ex. Dreams are the unconscious mind's way of working out feelings, and do not automatically mean your mate is cheating, thinking about cheating, or not in love with you. (See Chapter 7, "A Healthy Self First.")   ✓

5. Q: You cannot bear to be separated.

   A: Being unable to bear separations is unhealthy, and a sign of co-dependence and attachment, not of mature love. (See Chapter 1 on what is healthy, and Chapter 25, "Dealing with Crises as a Couple," for information on surviving separations.)   ✓

6. Q: Your mate's ex calls all the time.

   A: Healthy relationships respect each person's past and individual present life, without being threatened by them. Each partner can allow the other to have some independent activities and friendships. These can even fulfill you individually and allow your relationship to be richer. Objections should be curbed if they are motivated by your own insecurity or a need to control.   ✓

	Healthy	Unhealthy

However, it's important to point out that persistent contact with others, or an ex, is unhealthy if it is meant as an escape from intimacy, erodes your relationship (which should be top priority) or tempts infidelity. (See Chapter 26, "It's Not Just the Two of Us," on dealing with exes.)

7. **Q:** You blindly agree with parents or friends about whether your relationship is good.

   A: Parents and friends may have valid observations about your love affairs, since you can be blinded by love, but if *you* know your relationship is a healthy one, going along with others' fears or needs is unhealthy. (See Chapter 26, "It's Not Just the Two of Us," on dealing with family.) ✓

8. **Q:** You disappear from your mate's children's lives if you break up (or you don't let your children see your ex).

   A: Automatically shutting your partner's children out of your life if you break up is unhealthy. Consider the children's attachment to you, and continue the relationship with them. ✓

9. **Q:** Whatever worked to help you get ahead in your career, you should also do in your love life.

   A: Behaving the same way in both work settings and love can be unhealthy. Some behaviors are more appropriate in one or the other situation. (See Chapter 21, "Working Nine to ... with Time Off for Love.") ✓

10. **Q:** The more easy-going person should always be the one to go along with the other's plans if there's a conflict.

    A: It is all too easy for one person to dominate in a relationship and for the other to take a back seat and be more agreeable. Compromise on what each needs in life is healthy in a relationship in order for both people to grow. (See Chapter 8, "Are We Compatible?") ✓

11. **Q:** After you are together for a while, you can finally relax and not worry about impressing one another.

    A: It is unhealthy to "relax" and stop impressing one another after you've known each other a long time. While you can certainly feel more secure and less nervous about whether the person wants to be with you or whether you enjoy each other, you do have to keep coming up with new ideas about how to spend your time together. (See Chapters 28, "Keeping Your Love Exciting with New-Millennium Body and Mind Techniques,: and 29, "Helping Each Other Toward a Healthier Relationship.") ✓

	Healthy	**Unhealthy**

12. **Q:** Pleasuring yourself or having more sex fantasies or dreams when you're with your partner than when you were single means that you aren't having enough sex (or satisfying sex) now.

    A: It is unhealthy to automatically assume that talking or thinking about sex, pleasuring yourself, or having sexual fantasies that don't involve each other is wrong or indicates a problem in your relationship. It *is* possible that such activities can be a substitute for not having sex, but these activities might just as well increase with more activity and satisfaction together, since you become attuned to sexuality and more comfortable with expressing your desires. Everyone deserves private time, and time alone exploring one-self can lead to just the right growth and spice for your love life together. (See Chapter 15, "How Important Is Sex?")   ✓

13. **Q:** Having lots of sex is essential for a good relationship.

    A: You don't have to have a *lot* of sex. You just both have to agree on the role of sex in your love life. The best relationships, however, do include sexual intima-cy. Sex is a beautiful way to express your love and can bond couples closer. (See Chapter 15.)   ✓

Review how well you did. If you answered more than nine correctly, you're doing well. You have a good understanding of the nature of a healthy relationship and you're able to balance your individuality with the joys of being part of a couple. If you answered fewer than nine right, you should carefully reread the chapters indi-cated to see how you can improve those areas, either by changing your attitudes or working on your relationship. And if you answered five or fewer right, it's possible that your relationship is unhealthy as a result of your fears or misguided notions. Relationship counseling is definitely in order to help you figure out what you may be contributing to the problem, what your partner may be contributing, and what is awry between the two of you.

In all cases, remember there is always hope. No matter how badly you think things are going now, if the two of you want to work on making your relationship better, you have a chance.

Answers to the "Is It Healthy?" Sex Quiz in Chapter 16

1. **No.** But you both have to agree on how important sex is to your life together. Otherwise, one person will feel deprived and the other guilty, and both will end up resentful and alienated from one another.

2. **Yes.** Scheduling sex may be necessary. Sexual desire can be natural, but in busy lives, you often have to make time for sex, scheduling it as you would any important appointment. After you get back on track, things can flow more spontaneously and naturally again.

3. **No.** Desire can grow from touch, imaging, positive feelings, and feedback.

4. **Yes.** It is possible to have sex when only one person feels the urge at that moment, as long as the other person agrees to participate, if only on a minimal level. But you should never be obliged or forced to have sex. There's intrinsically nothing wrong with giving in to sex once in a while when your partner wants it, but you don't. It's unreasonable, especially in a long-term relationship, to expect that both people will always want sex at the same time, and with the same degree of interest.

5. **No.** Some men today are threatened by women taking the initiative, but most would appreciate if the woman shows she is interested and makes the first moves. That takes the burden off him to have to take the lead all the time and constantly be the one to risk rejection.

6. **Not necessarily.** Unless they are an escape from intimacy and commitment, they can show you what you would like to have happen with your partner.

7. **Yes.** Partners can't always guess. Sharing what you like doesn't have to take the surprise or pleasure out; the behavior can still be new.

8. **No.** Other forms of sex are just as legitimate. But certainly if you avoid intercourse, you should figure out what fears or inhibitions are causing that.

9. **No.** Some religions impose interruptions in sex (like Judaism that proscribes sex during the woman's menstrual period) to build sexual desire, but not everyone agrees with such moratoriums. In fact, desire can increase with increased satisfaction. But certainly if you are sexual and you are deprived of sex for a while, you can build up your passion and be very "hot" for a long-awaited encounter.

10. **No.** Some people can go for four-hour marathons before they get tired and emotionally satisfied, but bounce back the next day. The number of times you want, or have, sex is based on a lot of factors, from your desire, to mental and physical health, time, and availability of your partner. I don't like to give statistics for people to measure themselves against, because that can set off anxieties. What number is right for you? A number of surveys suggest that the average number of times married couples have sex is 2.2 times a week; less often, obviously, for those without a regular partner.

11. **Yes.** You never have to stop wanting sex. Performance can change somewhat as you age, but desire can stay strong. There is no such thing as a dirty old man or woman. Everyone can enjoy pleasure well into their mature years. Check out the Web site www.matureamerica.com where I've written about sexuality throughout life stages.

12. **No.** On a scale of 0 to 100 (with 0 being not at all and 100 being a lot), how interested are you in sex? You'll surely find somebody at the same level. Once you're serious about someone, ask them to rate themselves so you don't get into a relationship where you're incompatible. Low desire—or "inhibited sexual desire"—is caused by several factors, including physical causes (exhaustion, hormones, drug or alcohol use, medications, physical illnesses); emotional problems (stress, anger, depression, fear of intimacy, lack of confidence, lack of knowledge); relationship problems (distrust, anger, different styles); or situations (partner availability). Figure out which, if any, are applicable for you.

13. **No.** But people do get turned off after marriage. Unfortunately, some women put up with sex when dating, but once they have their man, they feel they don't have to work at it anymore. These women weren't that interested in sex in the first place. If that's the case, it'll be hard to get her going. You'll probably have to accept that you're just not going to have sex as often as before. She may come around a little, if you impress upon her how important sex is to you. And some men become less passionate once they see themselves in the role of husband (or father, after you have children) than they did before marriage, when they were a "lover."

14. **Yes.** Most doctors say it is healthy as long as you check your individual situation. But be aware that hormones during pregnancy can cause changes in sex drive. Certain medical conditions can threaten the woman's reproductive system. In addition, body changes can affect a woman's confidence and comfort in positions. Adjust positions, but always continue affection and always consult your doctor.

15. **Yes.** Understand the reasons for his fears and withdrawal. Some men are terrified when the woman gets pregnant. They have fears about injuring the baby. Psychologically, the man can become insecure about how to behave as a father-to-be, resentful about impending responsibilities, and fearful about both of you assuming new roles in life.

16. **Yes.** There is such a thing as sexual addiction. Some critics disagree, maintaining that you cannot want too much of a positive thing. But people with "compulsive sexual behavior" or "hypersexuality" have sexual thoughts and behaviors that are out of control which interfere with other aspects of their lives.

17. **No.** Unless you're avoiding doing your taxes or something else, indulge yourself. Prolonged lovemaking sessions can be healthy, to boost your self-esteem, deepen intimacy between partners, and achieve desperately needed physical relaxation and emotional refreshment. Set aside time, ensure privacy, draw out seduction with touching and flirting, and confront resistance and fears.

18. **Yes.** A major survey showed, surprisingly, that conservative people use love toys even more often than liberals. They are helpful to add variety, spice, and fun to lovemaking, as long as they are not an escape from intimacy with your partner.

19. **Yes,** unless they are an escape from being with your partner and enjoying his or her real touch and stimulation. But they are an excellent aid for women to have orgasm. Men should not be threatened but embrace using them during lovemaking.

20. **Yes.** As long as they, like sex toys, are not a replacement for or an escape from intimacy, and as long as you both agree on how to play and when to stop. Agree on a code word for "stop" that you respect. Give each other instructions about how to change the game along the way. As long as you both get equal pleasure, play on!

21. **Yes.** Some films that are helpful are erotic entertainment. These are different from films that are denigrating to either sex, or just show crude actions—those are not conducive to a healthy view of love.

22. **No.** Women are especially all too quick to assume it is their fault for not being attractive, skilled, or sexy enough. Sometimes, if he can't get an erection, the man may allow the woman to take responsibility or deliberately make her think it is her fault to protect himself from feeling like a failure.

23. **Yes.** It shows you care more for appearances than the person. Withdrawing only makes the partner feel worse, and possibly retreat more into food. Change attitudes, adjust positions, and start health programs together to reinforce your relationship.

24. **Yes.** In a review of over 200 studies on sexual fantasies over the past 50 years, University of Vermont psychologists found that more sexually active and experienced people had more fantasies. In other words, fantasies were not an attempt by

nonsexually active people to fill in the gap. Rather, sexual fantasies occur most often in people who exhibit the least number of sexual problems and are the least sexually dissatisfied. Besides, thinking about something is not the same as doing it.

25. **No.** The ejaculate can get absorbed, so he will not (as some men fear) explode. Also, Eastern sexologists believe that not ejaculating can conserve a man's energy so he can be a more vital lover. Of course, some men who constantly hold back their ejaculate may not have something physically wrong with them, but have some emotional issues they should deal with.

26. **No.** A woman can experience fulfillment being close and loving without orgasm. I don't want women to feel pressure to perform sexually. But I must admit that although women will not be sick from not reaching orgasm, they have a limitless capacity to orgasm, and reaching peaks increases energy. Letting go gives a woman her emotional confidence that can increase her success in all aspects of life.

27. **Yes.** Although many men cannot tell whether a woman is experiencing her peak because they don't know exactly what a woman's orgasm is or because they are too caught up in their own arousal, tricking a man only prevents him from learning how to really please her, and may perpetuate his practicing behaviors that displease her. Men who find out the truth usually feel foolish, cheated, and insulted.

28. **Yes.** Even if you have a partner, you can still have a personal sexual life! Masturbation helps you learn what turns you on so that you can share it with your partner. It also relaxes you, trains your body to respond, and teaches you self-love that helps you feel loved by your partner. It is only unhealthy when it's a substitute for or an escape from loving your partner.

29. **No,** unless you have religious proscriptions against it. Since women are even more turned on during this time, others are turned off, emotionally or physically. Having orgasm can even ease some of the pelvic congestion.

30. **Yes,** if you are both monogamous and only if you do not have any sexually transmitted diseases (STDs). Certainly you should respect any religions proscriptions against this behavior, but otherwise confront fears of not being appealing. Women who welcome this act may consider it an ultimate show of love and acceptance.

31. **Yes.** Crying during or after sex is not incompatible with being in love, and has several explanations and purposes. Physiologically, crying is a way to release the buildup of tension associated with sexual excitement, especially if you did not orgasm (and even if it reflects sadness or past abuse). Crying can add to the release of emotions and intensify orgasm. Don't be afraid of it.

32. **Yes.** Lovemaking does not always have to be a prolonged experience. A short encounter can be exciting to both of you, as long as you agree to it, and as long as it's not the only sex you have.

33. **No.** While openness is a desirable quality in any intimate relationship, it is not necessary to always express what's on your mind; sometimes it pays to protect the other person's feelings. Always examine why you want to share something.

34. **No.** Contrary to what some people think, there is no reflex reaction that makes men roll over and fall asleep after orgasm, although some men behave as if this was an automatic, biologically determined event. Sleepiness can be caused by relaxation that comes with release of tension at the point of sexual peaking, a psychological sense of satisfaction, habit, or chemicals released by sexual activity. But lingering for afterplay is a healthier response.

35. **No.** I would not recommend that you try to eliminate these urges, since that will make it difficult to revive them when you want them. Decide that sexual desire does not make you "bad" or loose. Beware, however, that certain medications for medical problem can dull sexual desire or ruin performance.

36. **No.** Reaching orgasm at the same time is possible and pleasurable, but not necessary. You certainly shouldn't strive for it, since such performance pressure on either partner would ultimately inhibit rather than expand your enjoyment.

37. **Yes.** Both people don't have to orgasm, and one person can be more active in pleasuring the other during any one lovemaking session (even if the other participates minimally), but both should feel satisfied that they are considered and respected.

Resources

Listed here are some of the programs and organizations referred to in this book. When you call, be sure to mention that you were referred by me, Dr. Judy Kuriansky.

American Association of Sex Educators, Counselors and Therapists (AASECT)
106 E. Cary Street
Richmond, VA 23220
804-644-3288
Web site: www.aasect.org
E-mail: aasect@worldnet.att.net
A national clearinghouse for information, resources and referrals concerning sexuality education, and counseling.

Sexuality Information and Education Council of the United States (SIECUS)
130 West 42nd Street, Suite 350
New York, NY 10036
Phone: 212-819-9770
Fax: 212-819-9776
Web site: http://www.siecus.org
E-mail: SIECUS@siecus.org

American Psychological Association (APA)
750 First Street N.E.
Washington, DC 20002
1-800-374-2721 or 202-336-5500
Web site: www.apa.org
E-mail: apa@apa.org
Referrals for therapists.

New Life
218 West 72nd Street
New York, NY 10023
212-787-1600
Web site: newlife@newlifemagazine.com
For a magazine and information on all kinds of interesting health options and expos around the country.

Tantra Experts

Tantrika International
6611 Edwood Avenue
Cincinnati, OH 45224
1-888-826-8745
Web site: www.tantrikainternational.com
E-mail: tantrikain@aol.com
Offers workshops, retreats, and trainings in tantra at regional centers throughout the United States and the world. Based on the teachings of Bodhi Avinasha in her book, *Jewel in the Lotus.*

Hawaiian Goddess, Inc./Source School of Tantra
PO Box 1451
Wailuku, HI 96793
808-243-9851
Fax: 808-243-9843
Web site: www.sourcetantra.com
E-mail: tantra@mauigateway.com
Relationship enhancement programs, audio and videotapes, books on tantra and conscious loving given by Charles and Caroline Muir.

School of Counseling Psychology and Holistic Health and School of Tantra
1371 Malaihi
Maui, HI 96793
808-244-4103; 877-244-4103
Web site: www.schooloftantra.com
E-mail: tantra@schooloftantra.com
"All Chakra Tantra" and other seminars and workshops by Dr. Sasha Lessin, Ph.D., noted voice dialogue facilitator, holotropic breathworker, and relationship counselor, and by relationship options expert and Web counselor Janet Kira Lessin at planetsexy@aol.com.

Celebrations of Love
45 San Clemente Drive, Suite C-200
Corte Madera, CA 94925
415-924-5483
Web site: www.celebrationsoflove.com
E-mail: tantra@celebrationsoflove.com
For newsletters, events, and workshops with teacher Lori Starr and staff.

Other Experts

Roberta Herzog, D.D.
PO Box 20188
Greenville, NC 27858
1-800-724-4883
Web site: www.robertaherzog.com
E-mail: iamlux@aol.com
Minister, clairvoyant, metaphysical teacher, and one of the few individuals in the world given access to "Akashic" Records (our souls' journey through time) offers readings, audiotapes, and booklets (including *The Blueprint for a Loving Lifetime Mate* and *The Akashic Reading Guidelines*).

Herrmann International
794 Buffalo Creek Road
Lake Lure, NC 28746
1-800-432-HBDI (4234)
Web site: www.hbdi.com
E-mail: thinking@hbdi.com
For information on workshops and extensive profiles on your brain styles.

Laura Norman and Associates, Reflexology
41 Park Avenue, Suite 8A
New York, NY 10016
1-800-FEET FIRST (1-800-333-8347)
Web site: www.lauranormanreflexology.com
E-mail: lauragnorman@aol.com
For information, sessions, books, and other materials on reflexology.

Ohana of Joy
PO Box 1173
Haiku, HI 96708
1-800-841-7457 or 808-249-6434
Web site: www.soundandvoice.com
E-mail: karin@soundandvoice.com
Workshops and sound training and toning led by Karin Schelde, intuitive teacher from Denmark, shamanic sound healer, and bodyworker, who developed "sound initiation."

Ken Glickman and Chris Platt
The Greenwich Institute for American Education
55 Railroad Avenue
Greenwich, CT 06830
1-800-625-2424
E-mail: ideas@i.power.com
For information and workshops on I-Power led by trainers and media experts.

Blue Lotus Productions
PO Box 500
New York, NY 10004
212-741-3358
Web site: www.joyofritual.com
E-mail: britual@aol.com
For information on workshops and books on ritual by spiritual facilitator Barkam Bizou.

Alex Stark
1220 Broadway
New York, NY 10001
212-564-4178
E-mail: AlexStark@earthlink.net
For information and sessions on feng shui.

Index

A

abuse, dealing with, 303
acceptance, 9
accidents, dealing with, 300
accommodation, 9
acting in relationships, 360
active listening, communication techniques, 135
activities for dating, 171
  business-related, 176
  classes, 176
  exercise and sports, 174
  musical performances, 172
  self-improvement courses, 177
  shopping, 173
  volunteer activities, 173
activities with your partner
  acupressure, 346
  aromatherapy, 349
  exercise, 337
    choosing a routine, 338
    improving lovemaking, 340
    stretching exercises, 338
  feng shui, 351
  love molding, 351
  making music together, 350
  massage, 344
  meditation, 343
  past lives, 354
  reflexology, 347
  toning, 350
acupressure, activities with partner, 346
adaptability, 9
ADD (Attention Deficit Disorder), dealing with, 302
addictions, dealing with, 303
adversarial attitudes, avoiding (communication), 137
affairs. See also marital affairs
  dealing with, 53

affection, expressing, compatibility problems, 106
affirmations, overcoming sexual inhibitions, 220
age gaps, compatibility problems, 105
aggressiveness, avoiding (communication), 137
aging, growing old gracefully, 306
agreements/disagreements. See also fighting
  agreeing to disagree, 11
  importance of agreements, 9-11
  importance of disagreements, 12
  money, spending, 244
AIDS/HIV. See safe sex
alcohol, effects on seduction, 191
alternative medicine, 20-21
andropause, 306
anxiety, dealing with, 302
appreciating each other's work, 255
appreciation, 9
  showing for gifts, 180
arguments. See also fighting
  for the sake of arguments, avoiding (communication), 137
  sex after, 194
aromatherapy, activities with partner, 349
arthritis, dealing with, 299
assertiveness, communicating about sex, 143
Attention Deficit Disorder. See ADD
attitude adjustments, 84
attraction
  opposites, 7
  to people outside relationship, dealing with, 53

B

bad habits, compatibility problems, 109
birth control, 211
boredom. See Love Burnout
breaking up before weddings, 333
breathing
  exercises, 23-25
  tips, spirituality, 23-25
BSH (benign sexual headaches), 104
burnout. See Love Burnout
business-related activities with partner, 176

C

calendars of romance surprises, 182
cancer, dealing with, 299
chakras, 13
chemistry between couples, 201. See also hormones
  attraction of opposites, 7
  increasing self-confidence, 202
  pheromones, 201
  tension-causing factors, 201
children
  compatibility problems, 105
  crises with, 305
  death of, 305
  effects on romance, 185
  fighting in front of, 279
  interference in relationships, 316
  starting a family, 335
chlamydia. See STDs

Chore Wars, gender-based stereotypes, 121
  combating, 123
chores, cooperation, 117
clamming up in relationships, 139
classes, taking with partner, 176
cold feet, 154
  timing and commitments, 158
  turning around phobics, 156
commitment
  expectations, 153
  Fidelity Quotient Quiz, 151
  hypothetical test of devotion, 307
  inequality of in relationships, 154
    cold feet, 154
    timing and commitments, 158
    turning around phobics, 156
  long-distance separations, 162
  long-term
    adjustments when living together, 327
    engagements, 327
    honeymoons, 335
    jitters before marriage, 332
    marriages, 330-331
    moving in together, 326
    proposals, 327
    remarrying an ex-spouse, 336
    setting up house, 326
    starting a family, 335
    wedding day, 333
    wedding vows, 334
  meaning of to individuals, 147
  monogamy, discussing with partner, 152
  nature of, 146
  stages of life, 160
  timelines, 158
  ultimatums, 160
Commitment Readiness Quiz, 147

communication, 132. *See also* talking
  about sex, 141
    asking for what you want, 143
    clarifying and explaining, 141
    likes and dislikes, 143
    saying "no," 143
  Communication Skills quiz, 132
  compatibility areas, 94
  criticism, 265
    constructive vs. destructive, 266
    giving, 267
    receiving, 266-268
    self-criticism, 272
    sexual, 270
    toxic, 272
  fighting. *See* fighting
  partners who won't talk, 139
    handling different styles, 139
    reassuring partner and improving skills, 140
  pillow talk, 193
    styles of, 193
    what to say, 194
  sexual negotiations, 220
  techniques, 134
    active listening, 135
    direct, 134
    giving feedback, 136
    showing appreciation, 137
  things to avoid, 137
    adversarial attitudes, 137
    aggressiveness, 137
    argument for the sake of argument, 137
    defensiveness, 137
    jumping to conclusions, 137
    playing games, 137
    prophesying doom and gloom, 137
    raining on each other's parade, 137
  what to tell and when to tell it, 138

communication workshops
  "Daring, Baring, Sharing, and Caring," 364
  I-Power, 361
  love rituals, 363
compatibility, 92-94
  roadblocks, 101
    age gaps, 105
    bad habits, 109
    cultural differences, 104
    expressing affection, 106
    family matters, 105
    handling, 108
    politics, 109
    religious differences, 104
    sex drive, 101
    sharing chores, 108
    twelve major areas, 92
  vs. cooperation, 116
competition, avoiding, 125
  team-building, 127
condoms, 211
connecting chakras, 13
confidence, 83
  attitude adjustments, 84
  dieting, 84
  fears, 86
    of intimacy, 87
    of missing out, 87
    of success, 88
  love scripts, 85
  positive self-talk, 84
conflicts, resolving
  givers/takers, 78
  love style conflicts, 77
confronting, spouses (marital affairs), 290
connecting with your partner
  acupressure, 346
  aromatherapy, 349
  exercise, 337
    choosing a routine, 338
    improving lovemaking, 340
    stretching exercises, 338
  feng shui, 351
  love molding, 351
  making music together, 350
  massage, 344
  meditation, 343

past lives, 354
reflexology, 347
toning, 350
Conservative Lovers, 76-77.
See also love styles
sex, 211
contraception (birth control),
211
family planning, coopera-
tion, 118
control issues, smokescreens
(fights), 279
cooperation, 116-117
avoiding competition, 125
team-building, 127
determining the problem,
120
domestic chores, 117
entertainment leisure, 118
family planning, 118
finances, 117
friend/roommate test, 124
gender-based stereotypes,
121
being old-fashioned,
122
Chore Wars, 121, 123
private space/individuality,
118
quiz, 118
romance and sex, 118
spending time with family
and friends, 118
Teflon test, 125
vs. compatibility, 116
couples counseling, 365
dealing with crises, 298
couples therapy, 366
benefits of, 368
finding a therapist, 367
sex therapy, 369
common problems, 370
costs, 371
finding a therapist, 369
prognosis for cure, 371
when to seek help, 370
Creative Lovers, 75-76. *See
also* love styles
sex, 210
credit/debt problems. *See*
money

crises, 297
counseling, 298
emotional problems, 302
family illness, 304
illness, 298
mid-life crises, 305
reactions to, 297
sexual problems, 302
with children, 305
criticism, 265
constructive vs. destruc-
tive, 266
giving, 267
receiving, 266-268
self-criticism, 272
sexual, 270
toxic, 272
cultural differences, compatibility problems, 104
cybercheating, relationships,
41-43
cybersex, relationships, 40-41

D

Daddy–Don Juan syndrome,
67
"Daring, Baring, Sharing, and
Caring" workshops, 364
dating
continuing during relationships, 166
business-related activi-
ties, 176
considering partner's
interests, 167
local activities, 171
making the time, 168
mutual interests, 166
self-improvement
courses, 177
staying at home, 170
taking classes together,
176
traveling, 175
continuing to improve
relationships, 358
death of child, 305
debt/credit problems. *See*
money
deciding to have sex, 197

defensiveness, avoiding (communication), 137
dependent parents, dealing
with, 314
avoiding parental interference, 315
depression, dealing with, 302
diabetes, dealing with, 299
dieting, 84
digital love, relationship tips,
37-38
direct communication, 134
disability, dealing with, 299
disagreements
agreeing to disagree, 11
importance of disagree-
ments, 12
money, spending, 244
distance/time, effect on
romance, 183
domestic chores, cooperation,
117
Dozen Dollar Decisions, 248
dysfunctional relationships, 4.
See also unhealthy relationships
love/sex/intimacy junkies,
56

E

eating disorders, dealing with,
303
eating. *See* food
emotional benefits of sex, 200
emotional commitment to a
relationship, 146
Emotional Lovers, 76. *See also*
love styles
sex, 211
emotional problems, dealing
with, 302
emotions, compatibility areas,
93
empathy, 8
employment. *See* work
empowerment, 9
energetics, 8
meditation, relationships,
26
engagements, 327
proposals, 327

enmeshed families, 312
  intrusive parents, dealing
    with, 314
entertainment leisure, cooperation, 118
enthusiasm, 9
equality, 8
ex-partners, interactions with,
  319
ex-spouses, remarrying, 336
exercise
  activities for dating, 174
  activities with partner, 337
    choosing a routine, 338
    improving lovemaking,
      340
    stretching exercises, 338
  seductiveness of, 194
exercises
  friendship, 64
  healthy relationship traits,
    10
  love ghosts
    decision-making influ-
      ences, 236
    family love scripts, 235
    uncovering love ghosts,
      234
  money
    Is It Healthy? Quiz, 242
    Principal Priorities Quiz,
      240
exertional headaches, 104
expectations about commitment, sharing with partner,
  153
eye locks, flirting, 191

F

failure, setting yourself up for,
  88
false intimacy, 54
family
  compatibility areas, 94,
    105
  contraceptional planning,
    118
  interactions with, 310
    avoiding parental inter-
      ference, 315
    children and relation-
      ships, 316

dependent parents, 314
disapproving parents,
  311
enmeshed families, 312
intrusive parents, 314
priorities, 310
siblings, enmeshment
  with, 317
spending time with, 118
family illness, dealing with,
  304
family love scripts, 235. *See
  also* love ghosts
  exercise, 235
fantasies (sexual), 182, 203,
  217
  meanings of, 218
  sharing/acting out, 219
fears, 86
  of intimacy, 87
  of missing out, 87
  of success, 88
feedback
  giving (communication
    techniques), 136
  to partners about sex, 141
feng shui, activities with partner, 351
Fidelity Quotient Quiz, 151
fighting, 275
  fair fighting, 277
  holding in anger, 276
  in bed, 282
  in front of children, 279
  interrupt technique (time-
    outs), 278-281
  making mountains out of
    molehills, 280
  preventing blow-ups, 276
  preventing fights, 283
  sex after fights, 282
  smokescreens, 279
  stopping escalating fights,
    278
  truth as a weapon, 281
finances. *See also* money
  compatibility areas, 93
  cooperation, 117
fitness. *See* physical fitness
flirting, 190
  by mate, stopping, 288
  effects on mate, 286
  eye locks, 191
  harmful or harmless, 286

food
  eating after sex, 192
  sensuous meals, 191
four F's of romance, 182
friend/roommate test, 124
friendship, 61, 118
  between lovers, 61
    exercise, 64
    maintaining
      passion/romance, 65
    test, 64
  effects on relationships,
    318
  friends becoming lovers, 62
    When Harry Met Sally,
      62, 68
  platonic relationships, 64
  vs. love, 67
    Daddy–Don Juan syn-
      drome, 67
    Madonna-Prostitute syn-
      drome, 67
frustration (sexual), 203

G

gender-based stereotypes,
  cooperation, 121
  being old-fashioned, 122
  Chore Wars, 121, 123
ghosts. *See* love ghosts
gifts, showing appreciation,
  180
givers/takers, 78
going back in time in relationships, 360
growing old gracefully, 306

H

headaches, 104
  BSH (benign sexual
    headaches), 104
  exertional, 104
  tension-type sexual
    headaches, 104
health benefits of sex, 199
health problems, dealing
  with, 298-304

healthy relationships, 4-6
   agreements/disagreements, 11
   Is It Healthy? Quiz, 13
   Is It Healthy? Sex Quiz, 208
   qualities of, 309
   relationship traits exercise, 10
   team players, 12
   "yes" affirmation, 10
heart problems, dealing with, 299
help
   couples counseling, 365
   couples therapy, 366
      benefits of, 368
   finding a therapist, 367
   online advice, 374
   radio talk shows, 372
   sex therapy, 369
      common problems, 370
      costs, 371
      finding a therapist, 369
      prognosis for cure, 371
      when to seek help, 370
   TV talk shows, 373
   when to seek from professionals, 365
herpes. *See* STDs
HIV/AIDS. *See* safe sex
honeymoons, 335
hormones
   effects of sex on female hormones, 200
   oxytocin (love chemical), 205
   phenylethylamine (PEA), 181
   pheromones, 201
hypothetical test of devotion, 307

I

I-Power workshops, 361
illness, dealing with, 298, 304
imaging in relationships, 361
improving relationships
   acting, 360
      "Daring, Baring, Sharing, and Caring" workshops, 364

dating, continuing in relationship, 358
   diary or journal, 361
   going back in time, 360
   I-Power, 361
   imaging, 361
   love rituals, 363
   modeling, 360
   self-disclosure, 360
   self-help, 358
   taking time out, 360
incompatibility, 101
   age gaps, 105
   bad habits, 109
   cultural differences, 104
   expressing affection, 106
   family matters, 105
   handling, 108
   politics, 109
   religious differences, 104
   sex drive, 101
      frequency, 102
      headaches, 104
      when to have sex, 102
   sharing chores, 108
independence, compatibility areas, 93
individuality
   compatibility areas, 93
   cooperation, 118
inequality of commitments in relationships, 154
   cold feet, 154
   timing and commitments, 158
   turning around phobics, 156
infertility, dealing with, 300
infidelity in friend's relationship, 320. *See also* marital affairs
inhibitions (sexual), overcoming, 220
intellect, compatibility areas, 92
Intellectual Lovers, 76-77. *See also* love styles
   sex, 211
interactions with family, 310
   children and relationships, 316
   dependent parents, 314
      avoiding parental interference, 315

disapproving parents, 311
      dealing with, 311
   enmeshed families, 312
   intrusive parents, dealing with, 314
   priorities, 310
   siblings, enmeshment with, 317
interfaith relationships, 104
interrupt technique (fighting), 278-281
intimacy, 54
   emotional benefits of sex, 200
   false intimacy, 54
   fear of, 87
   intimacy junkies, 56
intrusive parents, dealing with, 314
inventories
   love inventory, 53
   mate traits, 54
Is It Healthy? Quiz, 13
   money quiz, 242
   sex quiz, 208

J–K

Jewel in the Lotus, 28
jitters before marriage, 332
jobs. *See* work
journals in relationships, 361
jumping to conclusions, avoiding (communication), 137

L

learning to love, 57
letting go of the past with ex-partner, 333
life habits, compatibility areas, 94
listening, 9
   active listening, communication techniques, 135
long-distance
   romance, 183
   separations and commitments, 162
long-term commitments, 150

engagements, 327
  proposals, 327
marriages, 328
  honeymoons, 335
  jitters before wedding, 332
  remarrying an ex-spouse, 336
  seasonal trends, 331
  starting a family, 335
  statistics, 330
  timing of, 331
  wedding day, 333
  wedding vows, 334
moving in together, 326
  adjustments to make, 327
  setting up house, 326
love, 9, 46
  at first site, 51-52
  hypothetical test of devotion, 307
  inventories
    love inventory, 53
    mate traits, 54
  learning to love, 57
  love junkies, 56
  making. *See* sex
  myths, 47
  qualities of, 309
  soulmates, 58
  talk. *See* pillow talk
  true love, determining, 49
    five requirements of real love, 49
    love at first site, 51
    love but not in love, 52
    tests, 50
  vs. friendship, 67
  vs. lust, 46
Love Burnout, 225
  causes, 226
  making time for each other, 229
  overcoming boredom, 228
  quiz, 228
love ghosts, 233
  completing unfinished business, 237
  exercises, 234-236
  family love scripts, 235
  letting go of old loves, 237
  uncovering, 234

love molding, activities with partner, 351
love rituals, 363
  spirituality, 27
love scripts, 85
love styles, 72
  Conservative Lovers, 76-77
    sex, 211
  Creative Lovers, 75-76
    sex, 210
  Emotional Lovers, 76
    sex, 211
  givers/takers, 78
  Intellectual Lovers, 76-77
    sex, 211
  quiz, 72
  resolving conflicts, 77
lovemaking, exercising with partner to improve, 340
lovers. *See also* love styles
  friends becoming lovers, 62
    When Harry Met Sally, 62, 68
  friendship between lovers, 61
    exercise, 64
    maintaining passion/romance, 65
    test, 64
  seduction, 187
    flirting, 190
    increasing sensuality, 189
    physical fitness, 194
    pillow talk, 193
    sensuous meals, 191
    suggestions for, 188
  vs. friends, 67
loyalty, 9
lust
  benefits of, 9
  vs. love, 46

M–N

Madonna-Prostitute syndrome, 67
maintaining relationships, continuing to date, 166
  business-related activities, 176
  considering partner's interests, 167

local activities, 171
making the time, 168
mutual interests, 166
self-improvement courses, 177
staying at home, 170
taking classes together, 176
traveling, 175
making up after arguments with sex, 194
male menopause, 306
marital affairs
  celebrities
    Bill Cosby, 285
    Frank Gifford, 285
  flirting
    effect on mate, 286
    harmful or harmless, 286
  infidelity quiz, 286
  marriage, rebuilding, 292
  mate's attitudes, identifying, 287
  prognosis for recovery, 292
  reasons for
    increased opportunities, 291
    life crises, 291
    monotony, 291
    sexual boredom, 291
    unexpressed anger, 291
    unrealistic expectations, 291
  recovering from, forgiving and forgetting, 293
  signs of infidelity, 288
  spouses
    confronting, 290
    leaving, 294
    repeat performances, 294
  statistics
    men, 285
    women, 285
  survival checklist, 294
  trust, rebuilding, 293
  visual images, 293
  warning signs, 286
marriage, 328
  commitment and, 146
  honeymoons, 335
  jitters before wedding, 332
  marital affairs, forgiving and forgetting, 293

rebuilding after marital affairs, 292
remarrying an ex-spouse, 336
seasonal trends, 331
starting a family, 335
statistics, 330
timing of, 331
wedding day, 333
wedding vows, 334
massage, activities with partner, 344
meals. *See* food
meaning of commitment to individuals, 147
medicine, alternative, 20-21
meditation
  activities with partner, 343
  energetics, relationships, 26
  spirituality, 25-26
men
  love styles, 75
  preferences
    seduction, 188
    sex, 203
menopause
  male menopause, 306
  sexual desire during, 305
mental commitment to a relationship, 146
mid-life crises, dealing with, 305
mistakes in commitments, 161
modeling behaviors in relationships, 360
money, 239
  cooperation, 117
  debt/credit problems, 247
  effect on sex, 248
  exercises/quizzes
    Is It Healthy? Quiz, 242
    Principal Priorities Quiz, 240
  spending agreements/disagreements, 244
  talking about money, 247
    Dozen Dollar Decisions, 248
    rules, 249
  tracing attitudes, 242
  twelve key switching points, 245

monogamy. *See also* fidelity
  and commitment, discussing with partner, 152
  marital affairs, infidelity quiz, 286
  safe sex/contraception, 211
moving in together, 326
  adjustments, 327
music, making, activities with partner, 350
musical performances for dating, 172
myths, love, 47

O

old-fashioned couples, gender-based stereotypes, 122
online advice, 374
opposites, attraction of, 7
orgasms, 203
  health benefits of, 199
oxytocin (love chemical), 205

P

pain relief, benefits of sex, 199
parents
  avoiding interference in relationships, 315
  dependent, 314
  disapproval of partners, 311
    dealing with, 311
  enmeshed families, 312
  intrusive, dealing with, 314
partners who won't talk, 139
  communication styles, how to handle, 139
  reassuring partner and improving skills, 140
passion. *See also* Love Burnout; sex maintaining, strong friendships, 66
  seduction, 189
past lives, activities with partner, 354
past loves. *See* love ghosts
PEA (phenylethylamine) hormone, 181

people-pleasing, 6
pets, interactions with partners, 321
phenylethylamine hormone. *See* PEA
pheromones, 201
physical commitment to a relationship, 146
physical fitness, seductive power, 194
physical separation, dealing with, 304
physicality, compatibility areas, 92
pillow talk, 193
  styles of, 193
  what to say, 194
platonic relationships, 64
playing games, avoiding (communication), 137
politics, compatibility problems, 109
Post-Traumatic Stress Disorder. *See* PTSD
pregnancy, contraception (birth control), 211
previous relationships influencing new, 319
Principal Priorities Quiz, 240
priorities in relationships
  ex-partners, 319
  friends, 318
  pets, 321
private space, 118
prophesying doom and gloom, avoiding (communication), 137
prostate problems, dealing with, 299
PTSD (Post-Traumatic Stress Disorder), dealing with, 304

Q

qualities of healthy relationships, 309
quizzes. *See also* tests
  Cooperation, 118
  Is It Healthy? 13
    money quiz, 242
  Is It Healthy? Sex Quiz, 208
  Love Burnout, 228
  love styles, 72

money
Is It Healthy? 242
Principal Priorities, 240
spirituality, 21-22
work
job satisfaction, 254
workaholism, 255

R

radio talk shows for advice, 372
raining on each other's parade, avoiding (communication), 137
reactions to crises, 297
readiness for commitment (quiz), 147
rebuilding
marriage after marital affairs, 292
trust after marital affairs, 293
reflexology, activities with partner, 347
relationship problems, friends' influence on, 318
relationships
cybercheating, 41-43
cybersex, 40-41
digital love, tips, 37-38
loveonline netiquette, examples of, 36-37
meditation, energetics, 26
spirituality, 20
breathing exercises, 23-25
techies, 38-40
technological communication, 32
advantages of, 32-33
cyberworld love, 34-36
traits exercise, 10
religion
differences, compatibility problems, 104
spirituality, 21
remarrying an ex-spouse, 336
resolving conflicts, love styles, 77
givers/takers, 78

roadblocks to compatibility, 101
age gaps, 105
bad habits, 109
cultural differences, 104
expressing affection, 106
family matters, 105
handling, 108
politics, 109
religious differences, 104
sex drive, 101
sharing chores, 108
romance, 179
four F's, 182
importance of, 179
meaning of, 180
overcoming obstacles
children, 185
time/distance, 183
romantic fantasies, 219
sex, 118
surprise calendar, 182
ways to express, 181

S

safe sex, 211
scheduling time and activities together, 169
seduction, 187
flirting, 190
increasing sensuality, 189
physical fitness, 194
pillow talk, 193
styles of, 193
what to say, 194
sensuous meals, 191
suggestions for, 188
ten tips, 189
self-confidence, increasing, 202
self-criticism, 272. *See also* criticism
self-disclosure in relationships, 360
self-help in relationships, 358
self-improvement courses, 177
sensuality
awakening senses, 189
increasing, 189
sensuous meals, 191
separation, dealing with, 304
setting up house together, 326

seven love truths, 47
sex
after arguments, 194
after fighting, 282
benefits of
effect on pain, 199
emotional, 200
physical/emotional/mental, 199
chemistry, 201. *See also* hormones
increasing self-confidence, 202
pheromones, 201
tension-causing factors, 201
communication about, 141
asking for what you want, 143
clarifying and explaining, 141
likes and dislikes, 143
saying "no," 143
compatibility areas, 94
compatibility problems, 101
frequency, 102
headaches, 104
when to have sex, 102
contraception, 211
family planning, 118
criticism, 270
deciding to have, 197
eating after, 192
exercising with partner to improve, 340
fantasies, 217
meanings of, 218
sharing/acting out, 219
frequency, 213
inhibitions, overcoming, 220
Is It Healthy? Sex Quiz, 208
lust, 9
money, effects on sex, 248
negotiations, 220
oral sex, 216
positions, 217
safe sex, 211
seduction, 187
flirting, 190
increasing sensuality, 189

physical fitness, 194
pillow talk, 193
sensuous meals, 191
suggestions for, 188
sex junkies, 56
STDs (sexually transmitted diseases), 211
stopping, 198
toys, 217
variety, 215
virginity, 198
work
  effects of work successes/failures, 261
  five steps to better business *and* better sex, 263
wrong reasons, 210
sex therapy, 369
  common problems, 370
  costs, 371
  finding a therapist, 369
  prognosis for cure, 371
  when to seek help, 370
sexual fantasies, 203
  frustration, 203
  preferences, differences between men and women, 203
  role in romance, 182
sexual desire during menopause, 305
sexual problems, dealing with, 302
sexually transmitted diseases. *See* STDs
sharing, work, 108
shopping activities for dating, 173
showing appreciation, communication techniques, 137
siblings, interference in relationships, 317
sickness, dealing with, 298, 304
six H's to healthy relationships, 7
smokescreens (fighting), 279. *See also* fighting
sociability, compatibility areas, 93
soulmates, 58
spiritual growth, 20

spiritual leaders, 20
spirituality
  breathing
    secrets, 23-25
    tips, 23-25
  compatibility areas, 93
  fundamental steps, 21
  growth, 20
  leaders, 20
  levels of, 27
  love rituals, 27
  meditation, 25-26
  putting it together, 27-28
  quizzes, 21-22
  relationships, 20
    breathing exercises, 23-25
  religious aspects, 21
  self-test, 21-22
  teachers, 27
  third eye, 25-26
spouses
  attitudes toward after affairs, 287
  confronting after affairs, 290
  flirting, ending, 288
  marital affairs
    signs of infidelity, 288
    survival checklist, 294
  repeat performances of marital affairs, 294
  trusting after marital affairs, 293
staying in (at home) with partners, 170
  relaxing, 171
  working together, 171
STDs (sexually transmitted diseases), 211
  dealing with, 300
stereotypes, gender-based, 121
stopping flirting by mate, 288
stopping sex before marriage, 198
stress. *See also* crises
stretching exercises, 338
surprises, romance surprise calendars, 182
survivor guilt, 301

T

takers/givers, 78
talking, 9. *See also* communication
  after work, 255
  communicating sexual preferences, 204
  healing, 8
  in bed
    pillow talk, 193
    troubling conversations, 194
  money talks, 247
    Dozen Dollar Decisions, 248
    rules, 249
teachers, spirituality, 27
team-building, avoiding competition, 127
team players, 12
techies, relationships with, 38-40
technological communication
  advantages, 32-33
  cyberlove, 34-36
Teflon test, cooperation, 125
television talk shows, 373
tempers. *See* fighting
tenderness, 10
tension between couples, sexual chemistry, 201
tension-type sexual headaches, 104
tests. *See also* quizzes
  of friendship, 64
  love inventory, 53
  true-love tests, 50
therapy
  benefits of, 368
  couples counseling, 365
  couples therapy, 366
  dealing with crises, 298
  finding a therapist, 367
  sex therapy, 369
    common problems, 370
    costs, 371
    finding a therapist, 369
    prognosis for cure, 371
    when to seek help, 370
  when to seek, 365

third eye, spirituality, 25-26
thoughtfulness, 10
time
    making for the relation-
        ship, 168
        scheduling time and
            activities, 169
    time together, 10
    time/distance, effect on
        romance, 183
time out in relationships, 360
time/distance, making time
    for each other, 229
timing and commitments,
    158
    factors, 158
    stages of life, 160
toning, activities with partner,
    350
toxic criticism, 272
traveling with partner, 175
true love, determining, 49
    five requirements of real
        love, 49
    love at first site, 51
    love but not in love, 52
    tests, 50
trust, 9
    communicating about sex,
        143
        likes and dislikes, 143
    rebuilding after marital
        affairs, 293
twelve compatibility areas, 92
twelve key money switching
    points, 245

U

ultimatums and commitment,
    160
unemployment, 257. *See also*
    work
unhealthy relationships, 4
    fighting. *See* fighting
    love myths, 47
    people-pleasing, 6
unhealthy relationships,
    wrong reasons for sex, 210

V

virginity, 198
viropause, 306
volunteer activities for dating,
    173

W–X–Y–Z

waiting to have sex, 197
weddings. *See* marriages
When Harry Met Sally, 62, 68
withholding information
    from partner, 138
women
    love styles, 75. *See also* love
        styles
    preferences, seduction, 188
    sexual preferences, 203
work, 253
    appreciating each other's
        work, 255
    balancing work and love,
        258
        workplace romance, 260
    Chore Wars, 121, 123
    compatibility areas, 93
    competition between
        lovers, 260
    effects of successes/failures
        on love/sex, 261
    job satisfaction, 253
    quizzes
        job satisfaction, 254
        workaholism, 255
    sharing, 108
    talking after work, 255
    unemployment, 257
    workaholism, 255

"yes" affirmation, 10

I have had many requests over the years to give a speech to various groups (college, corporation, or organization), for information on products that help couple's relationship and sexual responsiveness, and for copies of articles and tapes of my work or for items related to my popular *LovePhones* radio show.

We are pleased to make some of these available. To make this request or to be part of the mailing list, offer suggestions, or order items, please e-mail apoll143@aol.com or call 718-761-6910, or fill in the following form, tear it out, and send it to the address indicated.

Thank you and I look forward to hearing from you and fulfilling your requests and interests.

Speaking to Your Group

Have your best meeting by having Dr. Judy address your organization. Topics can be tailor-made to suit your needs. Check any topic in the pages of this book regarding making relationships work in this new century or discuss what you need and it will be accommodated.

Contests

Have Dr. Judy plan or judge your contest, as she has done for Close-Up's, Rap 'n Roll, Revlon's Most Unforgettable Woman, and *Cosmo*'s Bachelor of the Month.

Spokesperson

Have Dr. Judy be a spokesperson for you and develop a unique concept for you, as she has done for Universal Studios' "Theme Park Therapy," or host your events like "The Dating Game" for Calvin Klein and Bloomingdales, or develop tips for "Making a Good First Impression" for Church & Dwight.

Phone Consultations

For private sessions on your relation questions, e-mail apoll143@aol.com.

Consulting for Your Company

Have Dr. Judy consult for your group as she has done for Clairol, Revlon, Riders, H. Stern, SmithKline Beecham, Organon, Church & Dwight, Bloomingdales, New York Cares, and JCPenney.

Name: _____

Address: _____

City: _____ State: _____ ZIP: _____

Country: _____

Phone (Daytime): _____ (Evening): _____

Fax: _____ E-mail: _____

Please:

_____ Contact me about Dr. Judy coming to speak to my organization.

_____ Call or e-mail me at _____.

_____ Put me on the mailing list.

_____ Send information. Specify: _____

_____ Order the items checked.

_____ Note these suggestions: _____

_____ Other. Specify: _____

For Fans of *LovePhones* and Others

Please check the following items that you are interested in:

Item Description	Number of Copies	Price Each	Total Price
C1 New, exciting cream that increases women's sexual response ($20 a packet)			
Videotapes ($14.95 each)			
V11 Video of lecture on Creativity in Love			
V12 Video of college lecture on sex			
V20 Video of Dr. Judy and Jagger at rock festivals			
Booklet ($9.95 each):			
Booklet I of *The Best of LovePhones* (including calls, tab lists, *LovePhones* facts, jokes, e-mails, and *LovePhones* dictionary)			
Articles by Dr. Judy (packet containing many articles; $4.95):			
Includes: "Pillow Talk: What Loving Couples Say in Bed," "Panic Attacks," "Sexual Compatibility," and "Too Tired for Sex."			

Order the popular here:

Item Description	Number of Copies	Price Each	Total Price
Color photos (5×7 for $5.95, 8×10 for $9.95):			
P10 Autographed photo of Dr. Judy in radio station			
P11 Autographed photo of Dr. Judy and Jagger in radio station			
P12 Autographed photo of Dr. Judy with rock star at music festival			
Audiotapes ($9.95 each):			
A11 Best of *LovePhones*			
A12 Best of *LovePhones*			
A13 Advice from Dr. Judy on dating			
CDs ($19.95 each):			
C11 Best of *LovePhones*			
C12 Best of *LovePhones*			
C13 Advice from Dr. Judy on dating			
T-shirts ($15.00 each):			
T1 Generation Sex T-shirt			
T2 T-shirt with photo of Dr. Judy and Jagger			

Merchandise Total		
Sales tax (New York state residents pay 8.25%)		
Shipping and handling (use table at left)		
Total		

Shipping and Handling Charges

Up to $20 ....$4.75
$20.01 to $30.................$5.75
$30.01 to $40.................$6.98
$40.01 to $50.................$7.98
$50.01 to $75...............$10.75
$75.01 to $100.............$12.75
$100.01 to $150...........$14.98
Over $150...................$15.98

Send this form, along with a check or money order, to:

Planet Love
c/o Alissa
59 Commerce Street
Staten Island, NY 10514

Please allow four to six weeks for delivery. Payment to be made in U.S. funds. Price(s) and availability subject to change without notice.

70082

THE COMPLETE IDIOT'S GUIDE® TO

Arts & Sciences | Business & Personal Finance | Computers & the Internet | Family & Home | Hobbies & Crafts | Language Reference | Health & Fitness | Personal Enrichment | Sports & Recreation | Teens

IDIOTSGUIDES.COM
Introducing a new
and different Web site

Millions of people love to learn through *The Complete Idiot's Guide®* books. Discover the same pleasure online in **idiotsguides.com**–part of The Learning Network.

Idiotsguides.com is a new and different Web site, where you can:

⚛ Explore and download more than 150 fascinating and useful mini-guides–FREE! Print out or send to a friend.

🌐 Share your own knowledge and experience as a mini-guide contributor.

💬 Join discussions with authors and exchange ideas with other lifelong learners.

🏛 Read sample chapters from a vast library of *Complete Idiot's Guide®* books.

✗ Find out how to become an author.

✂ Check out upcoming book promotions and author signings.

🏠 Purchase books through your favorite online retailer.

Learning for Fun. Learning for Life.

IDIOTSGUIDES.COM • THE LEARNINGNETWORK.COM

Robinson, Darren W.
Complete idiot's guide to a healthy relations
306.7 K96c
70082

Kuriansky, Judith